PRINCIPLES OF MANAGEMENT AND LEADERSHIP

Second Edition

By Stephen F. Hallam
The University of Akron

First published in the United States of America in 2014 by Cognella, Inc.

15 14 13 12 11 1 2 3 4 5

Printed in the United States of America

ISBN: 978-1-62661-296-9 (pbk) / 978-1-62661-297-6 (br)

www.cognella.com 800.200.3908

Table of Contents

Dedication

This book is dedicated to my past, present and future students, many of whom are already making a positive difference in organizations of all types all around the world. To my students from the past, thank you for sharing so many experiences from your jobs and your questions about becoming successful managers and leaders. To my current and future students, I hope this book provides sound principles that will help you fulfill your hopes and aspirations for a successful career and productive life. Put these concepts to work by going out and becoming great managers and leaders and making a positive difference in the world.

Acknowledgments

I wish to acknowledge my wife, Dr. Teresa A. Hallam, without whom nothing of any importance within the Hallam Family would ever happen. Thank you for your wisdom, love and encouragement on this project and throughout the years.

Another acknowledgment is owed to everyone at University Readers/Cognella who kept this project on track and on schedule. A special thank you goes to Sarah Wheeler, Project Editor, Jamie Giganti, Managing Editor, Melissa Barcomb, Acquisitions Editor, Natalie Piccotti, Cognella Marketing Program Manager, Jess Busch, Creative Director, Patty Duetmeyer, Cognella Digital Resource Coordinator, and Stephen E. Kaufman, Senior Instructional Designer, The University of Akron. Everyone at University Readers/Cognella has been great to work with from start to finish. Thank you all.

Part I

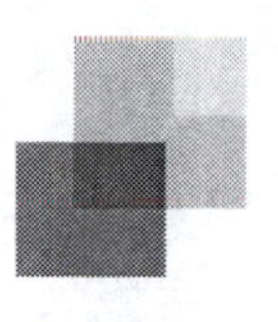

Foundations of Great Management

Chapter 1

Motivation

Imagine you have just been given your first opportunity to manage people. You have been told that the people you are about to manage lack motivation. When you asked the previous manager about them, he said, "They're just plain lazy. They don't care about what we do here. They just want to come to work, do the absolute minimum, get their paycheck, and go home. Good luck motivating this bunch."

You are now standing in front of your employees. What will you say? What will you do? You realize you will need to replace the negative attitude of your predecessor with a more positive one, but how will you do it? This chapter will help. It will explain some of the basic principles of motivating yourself and others. It can also help you motivate yourself now as you begin this course and later as you begin your professional career.

"You cannot lead others, if you cannot lead yourself."

—Med Jones, president of the International Institute of Management

Why Will You Have to Motivate Your Employees?

Perhaps you are thinking, "Why should I have to motivate my employees? Shouldn't they be motivated enough by their paycheck?" As this chapter teaches, money has its limitations. Of course, employees want to keep their jobs and their paychecks. However, great managers and leaders inspire their followers to go far beyond just showing up for work and going through the motions. Your aim in studying this chapter about motivation should be to learn how to go beyond motivating, and discover how to inspire yourself and others to do their absolute best. The word *inspire* comes from the Latin *inspirare*, which means to breathe life or spirit into.

Assuming part of your job as a manager will be to hire new employees, you will need to convince potential employees that this is a GREAT place to work. Notice I put the word "great" in all capital letters. What would it take to have your employees, when asked about working conditions at your organization, respond with, "This is a GREAT place to work."? You do not want them to simply say, "This is an okay place to work." Or even, "This is a good place to work." To become a great leader, you should aim for GREAT.

So, when your job as a manager includes hiring the best employees you possibly can, you will need to motivate applicants to consider your organization as a GREAT place to work. When people work 40 hours per week, they spend approximately 2,000 hours per year at their job. You have probably heard more people refer to their place of work as the "salt mine" rather than as a "GREAT" place to work. No doubt you have also heard workers say, "I can't wait for the weekend." What makes a workplace a GREAT place to work instead of a "salt mine" or a place to escape from?

To begin our study of motivation, we need to start with how you perceive the motivation of others and yourself. Do you believe others are self-motivated? Are you?

How You Perceive Others: Theory X versus Theory Y

Douglas McGregor, a professor at MIT, published a book in 1960 entitled *The Human Side of Enterprise*, which had a profound impact upon the field of management. He coined the terms Theory X and Theory Y to describe two opposite approaches to management. According to McGregor, it all starts on the inside of you. How do you perceive others?

A *Theory X* manager perceives employees as lazy and unmotivated to do good work. On the other hand, a *Theory Y* manager sees employees as naturally motivated to do a good job. Theory X managers see their role as forcing these lazy employees to show up on time, work hard, and avoid errors. Theory Y managers see their role as providing their self-motivated employees with the resources enabling them to produce high-quality results efficiently.

Of course, most human beings are somewhere between the two extremes. However, can you see that if you look at all your employees as lazy and unmotivated and perceive your role as a manager as forcing them to do even the minimum, you will come across as a negative person. Instead of being perceived as a LEADER, you will likely be viewed as the BOSS.

Basic Principles of Motivation

Thorndike's Law of Effect. Beyond the basic concept of how you consider others—people are naturally lazy (Theory X) versus people are naturally ambitious (Theory Y)—the next most basic idea is called the Law of Effect. This basic idea was formulated by Edward Thorndike in 1911. It simply says that a behavior that is followed by positive consequences (a reward) will likely be repeated. This is where most of my students respond with "duh." It sounds so obvious. Yet think about your work experiences to date. Does your place of employment have a policy of only approving raises once per year—if at all? Perhaps you work at a place where raises are not even related to your behavior. Maybe a union contract establishes a reward structure based more upon seniority or the rising cost of living than worker behavior.

If you have ever attempted to train a puppy, you know about Thorndike's Law of Effect—you just didn't know the proper name for it. You have called for your puppy to come to you and then you gave the puppy a treat. In general, you train a dog by catching him or her doing something good and rewarding that behavior as quickly as you can. Of course, people are more sophisticated than puppies, but there are basic concepts of motivation than can be learned by studying how people train puppies.

Some new dog owners make the mistake of punishing a puppy for behavior that, from the puppy's point of view, is long past. For example, you let your puppy outside for it to go to the restroom and the puppy completes the task but is more interested in smelling all the exciting smells in the yard than in coming back in the house. You call and call and get upset with your puppy. Eventually, the puppy gets hungry or thirsty and decides to go back inside, whereupon you scold or even hit the dog. What have you just taught the dog? From the puppy's point of view the lesson learned was, "I came into the house and got punished." The delay between the behavior and either a positive or a negative consequence can reverse the effect of Thorndike's Law of Effect. This simple example is, unfortunately, repeated by poor managers every day. Instead of instantly recognizing the good behavior of an employee immediately following that behavior, perhaps just by saying "Thank you" or "Good job," the opportunity to apply Thorndike's Law of Effect has been missed. Great leaders apply Thorndike's Law of Effect by recognizing the good behavior of their followers as soon as possible after the behavior. Also, instead of scolding or punishing bad behavior, great leaders use the opportunity to teach the correct behavior. As a manager, scolding your employees may give you a feeling of power over them, but it seldom works to motivate them; in fact it often does the opposite.

A way to apply Thorndike's Law of Effect to yourself is to reward yourself shortly after you have performed some good behavior. For example, as you read this chapter, reward yourself every few pages by simply standing up and stretching or by taking a sip of your favorite drink. Break a long task into several smaller tasks and give yourself something you enjoy as each small task is completed.

Goal-setting Theory. Goal-setting Theory states that people have conscious goals that energize them and direct their behavior toward a particular end. Right now, for example, some of you are motivated to learn as much as possible about this topic while some of you could not care less. Why is that?

Goal-setting Theory teaches us that goals can be motivating or de-motivating. Stretch goals that are set too high can be discouraging when we shoot for them and miss. Imagine you are teaching a child to play basketball. The child is likely to want to start shooting baskets by standing far away from the hoop. The wiser approach is to stand close to the hoop. If the child is short, lower the hoop. As the child gets the feel for shooting the basketball so it goes through the hoop time after time, then have the child move a few steps away from the basket. Eventually, you may even increase the height of the hoop. Do not rush this. You want the child to experience success. There is a "feel" for shooting a basketball with exactly the right arc and spin so that it goes through the hoop hitting nothing but net and making that cool "swoosh" sound. In contrast, the child who began shooting baskets from a distance of 20 feet and missed time after time soon gets discouraged and quits. That child has learned what it feels like to fail. Basic Goal-setting Theory suggests goals that motivate must be challenging—but attainable.

As a manager, it will also be important for you to involve your employees with defining the goals whenever possible. People respond better to goals that they have helped establish and that are meaningful to them. As their manager, you may have organizational goals related to a certain profit level, return on investment, or earnings per share. However, for your employees who are not shareholders, such goals have little meaning. Often, you will need to translate those goals into something similar to what you see in sports. Instead of saying that our goal is to increase earnings per share by ten percent, consider framing it as, "We've got to beat our rival, ABC Company, in sales this month. We're shooting to be Number 1."

How can you use Goal-setting Theory to motivate yourself? What is your goal for this course? Are you shooting for a grade of A+? Is your goal to have the highest point total in the class? Perhaps you want to get more points than your brother or sister or friend who also took this course. It is better to make your goals specific and quantifiable. Break the semester-long goal down into goals for each assignment and each test. If you, like so many students today, are working many hours per week to pay tuition and other expenses, then it may be more realistic to set your goal a little lower. Adults have competing goals and have to set priorities. Some of you may have already begun your families and have to consider balancing your college work with your family responsibilities. As you become managers, your employees will also be adults who will have to find the right balance in their lives. Do not expect all your employees to care as much about the organization as you do. Do consider how you can align the goals of the organization with the individual goals of your employees. Whenever possible, organizational successes should result in meaningful consequences for the employees.

> *Goals are the fuel in the furnace of achievement.*
>
> *—Brian Tracy, life coach*

Expectancy Theory. As the name implies, Expectancy Theory is concerned with the expectations of employees. Does the employee have an expectation that his or her extra effort will help attain their goal? Most of us have experienced the situation where we felt our extra effort has gone unnoticed. How does that make you feel? At some point, most of us will stop putting in the extra effort. So, as managers, it is vital that you show you have noticed each employee's extra effort.

Within Expectancy Theory, it is important to distinguish among the concepts of instrumentality, valence, and expectancy.

> *Who aims at excellence will be above mediocrity;*
>
> *who aims at mediocrity will be far short of it.*
>
> *—Burmese saying*

Instrumentality is the term used to describe the perceived likelihood that performance will be followed by a particular outcome. For example, if you work extra hard at your job, will your organization make more profit? Some jobs, such as sales, have a high level of instrumentality. If you have experience in sales, you have seen firsthand how your extra effort at calling on more potential customers, putting more effort into your sales pitch, and doing more to meet the needs and wants of your customers has resulted in more sales. However, if your work is in accounting, then it is much more difficult to build such a tight relationship between your extra efforts and more profit for the organization. As a manager, some situations will be more difficult than others to build the expectancy of your employees.

Valence is the term used to describe the value a particular outcome holds for the employee. If you really need a raise, then you will put a high valence on getting that raise. If a promotion is really important for you, then it has a high valence. As you go through your career, your valence will likely change. As you are raising your children, you may put a high valence on getting time off to spend with your children. Some people highly value a flexible schedule that allows them to pick up their children after school or to do some of their work at home. Some people highly value overseas travel. If you have a child who is ill, having good health insurance will have a high valence for you. As managers, it is important to get to know your employees so that you have a better idea of what they value. People are like snowflakes: Each one is different. Some managers make the mistake of assuming all their employees want the same thing.

> *If your actions inspire others to dream more, learn more, do more and become more, you are a leader.*
>
> *—John Quincy Adams, sixth president of the United States*

Expectancy is the term researchers apply to the employees' perception of the likelihood that their efforts will result in their goal attainment. For example, if you work hard at your current job and your organization makes more money, will this help you reach your personal goals? At some jobs, the expectancy is high. However, at others it is difficult, if not impossible, to see the connection between your efforts and the achievement of your goals. Consider the teacher you have for this course. Will his or her extra effort in teaching this course result in an increase in tuition income for the college, and will that result in more money in your teacher's paycheck? Probably not; at most colleges, when there is an increase in enrollment, the teachers find they have more tests and assignments to grade and parking on campus is harder to find. As a manager, it will be important that you make a connection between the attainment of organizational goals such as increased profits and the attainment of the personal goals of your employees.

Maslow's Hierarchy of Needs Theory

Most students have heard of Abraham Maslow's Hierarchy of Needs Theory from your Introduction to Psychology class. The general idea is that our lower-level needs must first be satisfied before we can care much about those higher on Maslow's hierarchy. Maslow's hierarchy has five levels, beginning with physiological needs such as the need for food and water at the lowest level. If you are on a desert and dying of thirst, then your attention will be focused on finding water. If you are about to die of hunger, then finding food is your highest priority. After you have satisfied your basic physiological needs for food and water, then you may begin to consider higher-level needs such as safety and social needs. Maslow contended that people have ego and self-actualization needs that come into focus only after our lower-level needs are met. For example, teachers have long known that it is nearly impossible to teach higher-level mathematics to children who are hungry. That is why many elementary schools provide food as well as mathematics.

Managers need to consider Maslow's Hierarchy of Needs so they do not make the mistake of assuming all their employees are at the same level as they are. Managers may be focused on self-actualization for themselves, but some of their employees may be focused on physiological needs, some on safety needs, and others on social or ego needs.

As a student today, where is your focus? Do you see how your focus will likely change as you grow older, and hopefully, some of your lower-level needs are met?

Every ceiling, when reached, becomes a floor, upon which one walks as a matter of course and prescriptive right.

—*Aldous Huxley, English writer*

Need for Achievement, Affiliation, and Power

David McClelland said people have basic, yet varying, needs for achievement, affiliation, and power. Some people have a high need for achievement and just can't wait to get that job as a Chief Executive Officer, while others just work to make a living and prefer to spend more time with their family or with hobbies or whatever. Some people have a strong affiliation need and want to be loved by everyone. Most of the research suggests that if you have such a strong need for affiliation, you should not pursue a career in management. You may find it too hard to risk a friendship and fail to provide an employee with an objective assessment of their work. As a manager, your responsibility to your organization should take precedence over your need to make each of your employees your friend. Finally, some people have a strong need for power, while others shy away.

Where do you stand with regard to McClelland's three basic needs? Successful managers and leaders have been found to have high achievement and power needs and a somewhat lower need for affiliation. The need for power can be a good motivator, up to a point. However, it can often lead to power-hungry behavior others resent. Extremes in any of these areas can throw you off balance. The key is to maintain your balance. Also, it is important you recognize and accept differences in these needs among your employees. You need to understand and appreciate your own needs and the needs of others.

Herzberg's Two-Factor Theory (Satisfiers and Dissatisfiers)

Frederick Herzberg is famous for saying some factors of a job, if lacking, have a high potential for making employees dissatisfied, but little potential for making them satisfied or motivated, regardless of their level. The most surprising and controversial of Herzberg's research findings is that PAY is a dissatisfier. Low levels of pay can make an employee dissatisfied, but high levels are not likely to produce a satisfied employee. Do you believe that?

Herzberg called his dissatisfiers (company policies, working conditions, pay, coworkers, supervision) *hygiene factors*, and his satisfiers (the nature of the work itself, actual job responsibilities, opportunity for personal growth and recognition, and the feelings of achievement that the job provides) *motivators*. In general, managers following Herzberg's two-factor theory should not place too much emphasis on dissatisfiers, but instead focus on satisfiers. You cannot ignore dissatisfiers, because they can cause your employees to be upset. However, excessive efforts by management to enhance pay, working conditions, and other hygiene factors will only go so far. To truly motivate your employees, you should look more toward Herzberg's satisfiers. Most of them are concerned more with the work itself than the pay and working conditions.

Many people think Herzberg was right up to a point. For example, if you are already making $500,000 per year and your boss offers to give you a raise of $10,000 for reaching a goal, you will probably not get as motivated as someone who is earning only $20,000 and receives a promise of $10,000 for reaching the same goal. Still others think Herzberg's main contribution to the topic of motivation was to get managers thinking more about <u>intrinsic rewards</u> rather than just <u>extrinsic rewards</u>. An *extrinsic reward*, such a raise or a promotion, is one given to a person by the manager, company, or some other person. An *intrinsic reward* is a reward a worker derives directly from performing the job itself. "Good work is its own reward" is an old, but powerful, expression that summarizes much of Herzberg's work.

Equity Theory. Equity Theory is based on the idea of an equation. On one side of the equation, you put the ratio of your own outcomes divided by your own inputs. On the other side, you put the other person's outcomes divided by their inputs. You consider it fair or equitable if the two sides of the equation are equal. For example, if you get $10,000 in pay for doing a task that takes 100 hours of your time and talent, but another person of equal education, experience, and talent gets paid $12,000 for 100 hours doing essentially the same work, then you will consider your pay as unfairly low. If the person getting the lower pay for equal work asks for more pay and gets turned down, he or she is likely to attempt to make the equation balance by reducing the variable they can control—how hard they work. As a manager, you are likely to interpret this action as laziness, but your employee may view it as merely making the situation equitable or fair. Your employee cannot control what pay you provide, but he or she can control the amount of effort put into the job.

Managers must also be aware of how employees select the "other" person on the one side of the Equity Theory equation. The worker is likely to select someone with a similar level of education, training, ability, experience, and responsibility. The manager may be tempted to think only of that individual employee now versus when that employee first came to work for this organization. The manager may remember how he or she selected that employee from a long list of applicants, trained that employee, promoted him or her, and raised that employee's pay over the years. This approach is similar to when you want to have an adult-to-adult conversation with your parents but instead you hear, "I remember when you were in diapers." You will likely find that comment demeaning. You do not want to be compared to when you were a baby in diapers. Your employees too will not appreciate being compared to when they were a beginner in the organization. Instead they will use a referent group of their peers to assess whether their pay is equitable and you, as their manager, should do likewise. This means that it is part of your responsibility as a manager to be aware of what the market pay rates are for your employees. If your organization is paying far below those market rates, then it will be difficult to convince your employees that your organization is fair. So, managers, when they observe an employee slacking off on the job, should not automatically conclude that employee is lazy. Instead, that employee may be attempting, in their own way, to achieve equity and fairness.

What Managers Should Reward

As a manager, you will need to look for all possible reasons to reward your employees. First, look for employees doing smart work instead of just busywork. You have probably heard someone say, "Look busy. The boss is coming." Such behavior should not be rewarded. Instead, look for employees who do things that actually help the organization achieve its goals, even when no one is watching. Be careful not to simply grease the squeaky wheel. Instead, look for employees who quietly perform their jobs in an effective and efficient manner. It is especially important, during times when an organization is trying to cut costs, to reward those workers who find ways to simplify procedures and save time and other organizational resources. If you want your employees to be creative, encourage open thinking and reward their efforts. Instead of just rewarding "yes men" and "yes women," look for ways to recognize those workers who will take a risk and question existing procedures. Finally, if teamwork is important in your organization, be sure to reward collaborative efforts and not just individual efforts.

Nonmonetary Rewards

When students graduate from college and get their first opportunity at management, they often complain that they are not given the necessary authority to go along with their responsibilities. They say they are not allowed to select which employees to put on their team, how much each employee is paid, who gets a raise or promotion, and which employees are terminated. A common whine is, "With such little power, how do they expect me to manage?"

The simple answer is, "You will just have to play the hand you are dealt." Large organizations seldom give new managers much authority. In a later chapter, we will discuss how organizations often get sued over wrongful termination of employees and lose millions in damages. In our litigious society, it is not wise for organizations to trust new, inexperienced managers with decisions that might cost millions in a wrongful termination. So, you will simply have to motivate employees with other tools.

A simple way to reward an employee for a job well done is to say, "thank you." Many managers fail to say "thank you" enough. Most employees appreciate sincere and prompt thanks. It does not cost the organization anything, and there is no rule that says you have to delay saying "Thank you" until the annual employee performance review. Of course, nonmonetary rewards should not be used to cheat employees out of well-deserved monetary rewards. However, as a new manager, nonmonetary rewards may be all the rewards you have the authority to give. But, even if you have practically unlimited rewards to distribute, frequently saying "thank you" is still a good idea.

Another low-cost—but highly effective—reward is to write a letter of praise and have that letter put in the employee's personnel file. Most organizations keep a personnel file on each employee, and managers should not think of such files as holding only negative things. While you may not now think of a letter of praise in a personnel file as any big deal, it may be what eventually helps that employee get a promotion or pay raise. The letter can remain in the employee's personnel file until that employee is being considered for a raise or promotion or even for a layoff, and it may be what separates that employee from all the others being considered at that time. Now, as a student, you should consider what your teacher will be able to say about your performance in this course in a letter of recommendation as you apply for a job or for graduate school. One way to have an application that stands out is to have it accompanied by a highly complimentary letter of recommendation.

Since much of the research points to the importance of the job itself as a motivating factor, another thing a new manager can do is look for ways to enrich the jobs of their employees. A simple solution is *job rotation*, defined as allowing employees to rotate through a series of jobs so they do not get so bored doing the same thing over and over. *Job enlargement* is giving people additional tasks to do to relieve boredom and increase their chances for a promotion at a later time. In general, *job enrichment* is about changing a task to make it inherently more rewarding, satisfying, and motivating. As a student, no doubt you have already used this technique to avoid boredom as you study—instead of studying for many hours, you likely take breaks and do something else for a few minutes so you can return to your studies less bored. Of course, you are never bored studying this exciting textbook; this concept only applies to other subjects.

Producing a High Quality of Work Life Environment

For your existing employees, you will need to motivate them to not only come to work and do their jobs properly, but also to be good citizens of the organization. Good citizens go beyond the minimum. For them, work is more than just a way to get a paycheck. Assuming you work 40 hours a week for 50 weeks (you have a two-week vacation), you will spend 2,000 hours at work during a year. Think about what you can do as a manager to make this a GREAT place to work. What would it take to have your employees, when asked about working conditions at your organization, answer with, "This is a GREAT place to work."?

When employees have a choice, they prefer to work at a place where they will be respected as human beings. An employee is, first and foremost, a person. They do not deserve to be treated like some easily replaceable cog in the vast machinery of an organization. So, your first order of business as a new manager is to show your employees that you respect them as people. They may lack education, training, experience, and motivation, but remember the phrase, "All roads lead to management."

If the employees are lacking, whose fault is that? Was it not management who hired these employees? Was it not management's responsibility to train them? Whose job is it to properly supervise them and correct them when they make mistakes? Do not blame the employees if management has failed to properly recruit, hire, train, supervise, and reward employees. Good management begins with you having the proper attitude toward your employees. Treat them as you would want to be treated if the situation were reversed. It is as simple as applying the Golden Rule: "Do unto others as you would have them do unto you."

Once an employee is hired, management's attention must turn to training that employee. Most large organizations have a new employee orientation program that explains some of the basic procedures all new employees need to follow. The organization needs to collect information from the new employee so they can properly print payroll checks and enroll the employee in whatever benefit programs the organization offers. Beyond such basics, the orientation program should impart a sense of the organization's history and culture. A key factor is to impart a sense of pride in being a part of this organization. What is it about this organization that makes it a great place to work?

Management needs to impart a sense of what it means to be a part of this organization. It is somewhat like joining a new family. What will be expected of the employee? What should the employee expect of the organization? In management-talk, this is called the *Psychological Contract*. This contract is often unwritten, but it is powerful. It is the basis for an understanding between workers and management. It is the glue that holds the organization together. Among the things an employer generally expects of employees are the following:

1. Do your job to the level that it increases the company's ability to gain a sustainable competitive advantage over the competition.
2. Continue to learn and develop new skills of value to the company.
3. Listen to constructive feedback and act upon it.
4. Demonstrate a commitment to the company's goals.
5. Exhibit no prejudice or bias in dealing with colleagues, suppliers, and customers.
6. Behave consistently with the company's ethical standards.
7. Treat all customers with the utmost respect and courtesy.

And the things an employee generally expects of his or her employer are the following:

1. Provide competitive pay and rewards based on employee performance.
2. Work that is meaningful and challenging.
3. Recognize each employee for their accomplishments.
4. Create learning opportunities through education, training, and job assignments.
5. Support in defining and achieving employee career goals.
6. Feedback on employee job performance that is objective and free from bias.
7. Foster an environment of respect and dignity toward all employees.
8. A balance between work and personal life.

Today, you may hear that the psychological contract between employee and employer is broken. What they likely mean is that there is no longer any assurance of lifetime employment with a particular organization. Business organizations such as IBM used to brag about never laying off any of their employees. However, that is no longer the case. Wall Street investors watch the relationship between earnings and the number of employees, and when the earnings per employee for a particular company drop far below that of their chief rivals, those Wall Street investors put pressure on the company to reduce the size of their workforce. Also, one of the main consequences of the recent advances in technology has been the ability of organizations to produce much more with fewer employees. However, the fact that lifetime employment is no longer guaranteed does not mean that all aspects of the psychological contract between employer and employee are forgotten.

As a new manager, you would like your employees to show up for work each morning on time and ready to put forth their best effort. If you are the owner of the business, you will experience directly the consequences of the business making a large profit or experiencing a sizeable loss. However, for the ordinary employee, management must translate that feeling of ownership throughout the organization. In the ideal situation, from the Chief Executive Officer to the janitor, everyone has a sense of ownership about the organization: "This is my company. I care deeply about what happens here."

These days, most businesses have to produce services and/or products of high quality efficiently. Products made in Akron, Ohio, USA, must compete with similar products made in China, India, Brazil, or anywhere in the world. In this globally competitive economy, the pressure is enormous. In many parts of the world, employees are paid only a tiny fraction of what American workers expect, so it is practically impossible to compete globally on the basis of the cost of labor that goes into a product. That means we must compete on other factors, such as quality, innovation, style, and brand image. If you can't make the product cheaper, then you've got to make it better. As a manager, you will need to motivate your employees to build that higher quality into everything they do. It will be a great challenge. In summary, as a manager you will need to motivate your employees to join the organization, to come to work regularly and on time, to work to constantly improve whatever goods or services the organization produces for sale, and to take an attitude of ownership regarding the organization.

Motivating Yourself?

A few years ago, Robert Fulghum wrote a bestselling book, *All I Really Need to Know I Learned in Kindergarten*. When asked by a group of parents what he suggested they do when their children failed to listen, he responded, "Do not be concerned that your children do not listen to everything you say. Be concerned that they watch everything that you do." The same holds true for managers. Your workers will often ignore what you say, but they will carefully watch what you do. The worst thing you can do is to say one thing and do the opposite. For example, as a manager you may tell your employees that you expect them all to be at work promptly at 8 A.M. What lesson does it give to your employees when you show up at 10:30? You may say to your employees that you expect them to be loyal to the organization, but then you say derogatory things about top management. As a manager, you may be able to get by with such behavior, but should you? What is the likely consequence of such behavior? You will become known as the manager who talks the talk, but doesn't walk the walk. You are a hypocrite, and your employees will not respect you.

If once you forfeit the confidence of your fellow citizens, you can never regain their respect and esteem.

—Abraham Lincoln (1809–1865), 16th president of the United States

You can begin today to motivate yourself to become a great manager and eventually a great leader. People do not instantly become great motivators when they become managers. It is something you must develop over time. Start by thinking about your motivation for this course. Have you decided what you goal is for this course? Are you shooting for an A+ or a D-? Why? What is behind your choice? If you have gotten this far in your college curriculum, it is likely you have sufficient intelligence to succeed in a course such as this. The theoretical concepts underlying management are not overly complex. Putting them into effective practice will be a challenge, but the concepts are not difficult. So, you should be able to decide on the very first day of this course that you are going for an A+. Some of you may have other major commitments of your time with your job and your family responsibilities, so it may make more sense for some of you to go for a B. At any rate, the first step is to establish a goal.

Good goals are stretch goals. They should require you to do your best, but not be set so high they are impossible. Good goals are at the heart of motivation. As a manager, it will be a major part of your responsibilities to establish all sorts of goals. Instead of the letter grade for a course, your professional goals will involve time deadlines, cost budgets, revenue targets, quality standards, etc.

Today you may be majoring in accounting, finance, marketing, information systems, human resource management, entrepreneurship, or other areas in business administration, engineering, etc. Your grades depend primarily on your individual effort. Soon after graduation, you will likely be called upon to accept the responsibility of management. Managers accomplish results through the efforts of others. Your attention will turn from specific tasks you need to perform on the job, to motivating others to perform up to their highest potential. For many of you, this may be your one and only course in management and leadership. Yet most of you will eventually be managers. Why? Most people go into management because they want to make a difference, not to mention the pay is much better.

Those who manage and lead others make a major difference. You will decide who gets hired. You will decide how much people get paid, what their working conditions are, and who gets a raise or a promotion. As your level of management responsibility goes higher up the organizational ladder, your opportunity to make a difference expands. More people will rely on you to make wise decisions. Should the organization move into different products or services? Should it expand overseas? Should it purchase other businesses? In difficult times, managers must decide which employees stay on the job and which ones are laid off. Some of you will work within huge corporations with thousands of employees, annual revenues in the billions, and thousands of shareholders. Your decisions will make a difference in the lives of all of those people. Others will work for smaller organizations. No matter what the size of the organization, managers and leaders matter. Now is the time to prepare. As Abraham Lincoln said, "I will study and prepare and perhaps someday my chance will come."

> *Choosing goals that are important to you is one of the most essential things you can do in order to live your dreams.*
>
> *—Les Brown, motivational speaker and author*

Managers of large organizations also earn huge compensation, sometimes measured in millions of dollars per year. Of course, such salaries are the exception, but in general, managers are well compensated for their work. Many students say they are not all that interested in making a huge amount of money. However, as you graduate, many of you will already have a burden of several thousand dollars of debt due to your education loans. Many of you will want to start families, buy a car, purchase a house, and start saving for your own children's college education and your eventual retirement. The amount of salary you earn at your job does matter. Few careers are more lucrative than management. According to a recent study by the AFL-CIO, the average annual pay for the top executive at over 300 of America's biggest corporations exceeded $12 million, or 350 times the

> *I think management is the highest calling there is. Management and leaders affect a great many lives. They are responsible for creating the kind of environment in which people can flourish or shrink. They have enormous power.*
>
> —*M. Scott Peck, author of* The Road Less Traveled

average pay of America's workers. In 2013 the highest paid Chief Executive Officer (CEO) was Eric Schmidt of Google at $101 million, which breaks down to over $48,000 per hour. The average U.S. worker's annual pay is approximately $35,000 per year, so Eric Schmidt makes more in an hour than the average American makes in a year. Of course, these are the superstars of the management profession, but managers in general earn far more than non-managers.

Learning how to motivate, manage, and lead others is, by itself, fascinating. Imagine you have just been given your first management job. You are standing facing your employees. Perhaps the number of employees is two or three, or perhaps it is over a hundred. No matter how large or small your number of employees, as their manager they are looking to you for leadership. What will you say? What will you do? How will you gain their respect? Some may be much older and more experienced than you; how will you handle the age difference? This course shows you how. It could well be the most interesting and valuable course you will take in your entire college curriculum.

So take some time right now, as you begin this course, to set some goals for yourself. Set a goal for this course to earn an A. Set a lifetime goal of becoming a great manager and leader. Begin today by completing your studies and by doing things with your family, friends, fellow students, and others that will further your reputation as a trustworthy person. Most of all, make goals that are yours.

Questions for Discussion

1. Discuss your own work experience and which manager you would consider *great*. What makes them *great*?
2. If your work experience has, unfortunately, put you in contact with a terrible manager, what made that person a terrible manager? What would you do differently if you had that managerial position?
3. Which theory of motivation presented in this chapter appeals to you the most? What is it about that particular theory of motivation that most interests you?
4. Some argue that American CEOs are grossly overpaid. While top lead executives in America's largest corporations are paid 350 times the average pay of America's workers, similar executives in Canada are paid around 200 times the average Canadian worker; in the United Kingdom, 84; and in Japan, 67. What level do you think is fair? Why?

Chapter 2

The History of Management and Leadership

For as long as people have gathered together in groups to accomplish common goals, there has been a need for some principles of management. Early cave drawings provide scientists with evidence that there were leaders and followers thousands of years ago. Picture the current management theory as a giant jigsaw puzzle. Over the past few thousand years, each of the following people contributed a small piece to that puzzle.

Sun Tzu and *The Art of War*

One of the earliest books describing some of the basic principles was Sun Tzu's *The Art of War*, written over 2,500 years ago. Although the title implies the book was intended as a guide for leading an army (and it was), the principles apply today to practically all forms of management and leadership. Tzu taught that an army leader who actually had to put his soldiers into battle was not properly managing the situation. Instead, the wise general outsmarted his opponent. He used what today would be called military intelligence to find out all about the enemy's strengths and weaknesses, and would then outmaneuver his opponent by capturing the high ground or by surrounding the enemy and convincing the opposing general to surrender without a fight. Sun Tzu's contribution to modern-day management theory is the idea that good managers, like good generals, use their intelligence more than their muscle to obtain a sustainable competitive advantage.

Know thy self, know thy enemy. A thousand battles, a thousand victories.

—*Sun Tzu, author of* The Art of War, *ca. 500 B.C.*

MACHIAVELLI, *THE PRINCE*

Niccolo Machiavelli wrote *The Prince* about 500 years ago to encourage the leaders of Florence, Italy, to be more forceful. Florence had a long history of being conquered by invading armies, and Machiavelli wanted the royal family of Florence to better defend the territory. Today, Machiavelli is best known for some of the stern advice he provided such as, "It is better to be feared than loved." Some people misinterpret Machiavelli's message and think he is suggesting that it is okay to be a tyrant. Instead, he was trying to persuade the leaders of Florence to take their leadership responsibility more seriously. Having the city overrun by every army that came along was not good for the citizens of Florence. Someone had to stand up and be brave. Machiavelli's contribution to modern management theory is the concept that leaders have a responsibility to protect and defend their followers. Managers need to be strong to defend their people from rivals. Finally, it is important for managers to gain the respect of their employees.

He who wishes to be obeyed must know how to command.

—Niccolo Machiavelli, Renaissance writer and philosopher

ADAM SMITH, *THE WEALTH OF NATIONS* AND *THE THEORY OF MORAL SENTIMENTS*

Most students know that Adam Smith wrote *The Wealth of Nations* in 1776, but not so many know he also wrote *The Theory of Moral Sentiments* in 1759. To best understand Adam Smith's contribution to modern management theory, it is important to consider both books.

In *The Wealth of Nations*, Smith describes how the free market system can establish a fair price for a product at the point where supply meets demand. As the demand for a product goes up, but the supply stays the same, it is only natural for the price to go up. As the demand goes down, of course the price goes down. This phenomenon is widely known as "The Law of Supply and Demand," or as "the Invisible Hand of the Market." Efforts by the government or other forces to change the natural workings of the law of supply and demand typically result in either a shortage of supply, as when prices are artificially held to a level below the place where supply and demand are equal, or a surplus when prices are artificially held too high. The Law of Supply and Demand works almost like a natural law such as gravity. The theory implies that the free market naturally works to set the fairest price for any good or service, as long as the market is left to operate freely.

It is not from the benevolence of the butcher, the brewer, or the baker that we expect our dinner, but from their regard to their own interests.

—Adam Smith, Scottish political economist and philosopher

In *The Theory of Moral Sentiments*, Smith told his readers that real capitalists should operate out of sympathy, courage, duty, benevolence, and self-respect, not greed. Smith was also an early advocate of the division of labor and scientific management, topics we will discuss later. To get the full view of Adam Smith's contribution to management theory, it is important to consider more than just "the Invisible Hand." It is necessary to understand that Smith did not advocate for an unregulated capitalistic system. To put his thoughts in modern-day terms, an unregulated capitalistic system is similar to playing a game of football without referees—a fair game can easily turn into a brawl where many people get hurt. Today, politicians wrongly use Adam Smith's writings as the basis for a philosophy of totally unregulated markets. They argue that *any* interference with "the Invisible Hand" is wrong. However, Adam Smith realized that not all capitalists have high morals. Capitalists with the most money can use that money to buy up all of some product and create a monopoly. Monopolies thwart the natural operation of a free market and unfair prices result. Some even imply that Adam Smith supported the concept that greed is good. Instead, Smith argued for a reasonable amount of regulation of the free market system. Adam Smith's contribution to the history of management thought is huge. The free market system has created immense productivity and wealth, but some regulation is needed to make certain a few greedy and immoral capitalists do not circumvent the free market system. Also, as Adam Smith wrote, a good manager is someone with sympathy toward others, rather than someone consumed with his or her personal greed. Unfortunately, this balance is often forgotten.

> *To feel much for others and little for ourselves; to restrain our selfishness and exercise our benevolent affections, constitute the perfection of human nature.*
>
> *—Adam Smith*

Frederick W. Taylor

Frederick W. Taylor lived from 1856 to 1915 and is considered the father of scientific management. He scientifically studied each movement a worker would make in completing a task, and then redesigned the task to minimize the worker's movements and speed up the process. Many have an image of Taylor walking around a factory floor with a stopwatch and clipboard in his hand and forcing workers to work faster and harder. While it is true that Taylor did use a stopwatch to time workers' motions and a clipboard to take notes and draw diagrams, it is also true that he advocated for workers to get a fair share of the profits of their increased productivity. He was not suggesting that factory owners exploit their employees. Taylor's main contribution to management theory is the idea that a complex task can be broken down into a series of steps and each step analyzed scientifically

> *In the past the man has been first; in the future the system must be first ... The first object of any good system must be that of developing first class men.*
>
> *—Frederick W. Taylor, father of scientific management*

to determine how best to complete it, and that, when applied to an entire factory operation, saves time and money, a concept known as *Scientific Management*.

Ford W. Harris

Ford W. Harris is considered the father of quantitative management. In 1913 he published an article where he applied mathematics to such business problems as determining the best amount of stock to order to keep a company's inventory from running low, but also not ordering too much and thereby increase the costs of storing and maintaining that excessive inventory. Before Harris's application of mathematics to inventory management, most managers simply used a rule of thumb such as, "When the number of items on the shelf gets below this line, order more." Harris demonstrated mathematically that there was an exact inventory level where it was best to order a precise number of items; he called it the economic order quantity, thereby balancing the cost of ordering with the cost of holding items in storage. Thanks to the pioneering work of Ford W. Harris, today's management theory borrows heavily from the field of mathematics in measuring both the quantity and the quality of goods and services.

Walter A. Shewhart

Another person to bring higher mathematics into the field of management theory was Walter A. Shewhart, a statistician at Bell Labs. In 1931 Shewhart published *Economic Control of Quality*, a book now considered a classic in the field of quality control. Today, it is common for business managers to describe their quality control program in terms such as Six Sigma, a phrase borrowed from mathematical statistics referring to less than 3.4 defective parts per million. Shewhart's contribution to management theory is the application of mathematics from the field of statistics and research methodology to the field of quality control of manufactured parts. These days, for any American business to compete successfully on the global market, the use of strict statistical control methods is absolutely essential.

Max Weber

Max Weber lived in Germany from 1864 to 1920 and wrote about the benefits of bureaucratic management. Before you decide to hate Max Weber for promoting bureaucracy, understand that he was trying to convince businesses in Germany, most of which were privately owned by wealthy families, to move away from a family-based business model to a merit-based model. In the old family-based model, the only people eligible to move up the ladder of power were family members. The ordinary worker, no matter how intelligent he was or how hard he worked, did not have a chance to ever be anything other than a common laborer. Weber suggested career advancement should be based on merit, not family relationships. So, while we often criticize bureaucracies, Weber was fighting against something even worse. However, we do have Weber to blame for the idea that formal rules and procedures and a well-defined hierarchy are necessary and that managers need to act with impersonality, often expressed as, "It is nothing personal, just business." Despite all the disadvantages of a stodgy bureaucracy, the application of formal rules and procedures to the field of business did result in considerable advances in efficiency and effectiveness, two key components of good management still in use today.

Henri Fayol

Henri Fayol (1841–1925) is known as the father of administrative management. He wrote that there are principles of management that apply to practically all types of businesses. Fayol's 14 Principles of Management were:

1. There should be specialization of labor for higher skills development.
2. Management has the authority to give orders.
3. Management is responsible for strict discipline—no bending of the rules.
4. There should be unity of command—each worker should have just one boss.
5. There should be unity of direction—everyone should be working toward the same goal.
6. In a business, there needs to be subordination of individual interests to the greater interest of the whole organization.
7. There should be a fair remuneration to workers—not just paying the lowest wages the company can get away with.
8. There should be a centralization of decision making—decisions are made at the top of the organization.
9. There should be a scalar chain of authority similar to the military chain of command structure.
10. Everything should be in its place—orderliness is required.
11. There should be equality of treatment of all.
12. There should be stability and long-term tenure of workers—work toward lifetime employment of good workers.
13. Management should carefully think out a plan and implement it—take the initiative.
14. Management should work toward an esprit de corps—work toward harmony and cohesion among all the personnel.

Today the thousands of business schools all, to some extent, owe their existence to Henri Fayol, because he was the one who first suggested that there are common principles of management that apply to all types of businesses. Most of the thinking, until Fayol's time, advocated having the one in charge be the one most skilled at the task. If we were still thinking that way today, instead of a business school having a curriculum composed of courses in accounting, finance, production, management information systems, etc., your preparation to become a manager would be training you to become the most skilled at a particular trade. For example, the person that would be put in charge of all the builders at a construction site would be the most skilled carpenter instead of the business school graduate. So, when you get that first high-paying management position, don't forget to thank Henri.

Elton Mayo

Elton Mayo is considered the father of the behavioral approach to management, which acknowledges the psychological and sociological aspects of human behavior as being important to worker productivity and job satisfaction. Psychology, the study of individual behavior, and sociology, the study of group behavior, are both important in today's management theory.

Perhaps Mayo's most famous experiment, the Hawthorne studies, are best known for suggesting that paying special attention to employees motivates them to work harder and be more productive. These studies, conducted at the Hawthorne Electric Company near Chicago, began as a study of the effect of proper lighting on the productivity of workers. As the lights inside the factory were turned brighter and brighter, the workers' productivity went up. The initial thought was that the workers could see better to put together the small electrical components, and that is why their productivity went up. However, as the story goes, one of the researchers eventually suggested they turn the lights down to test to see if productivity would decrease as it got more difficult to see and, to everyone's surprise, the workers' productivity continued to rise. This led to "the Hawthorne Effect," the concept that workers appreciated the attention they were getting and suggested to management that they could get better productivity out of their employees simply by showing an increased interest in what the workers are doing. Later, it was suggested that the test results were falsified, but the Hawthorne Effect is still remembered as the start of a series of research studies aimed at relating psychological and sociological elements to management theory.

> *One friend, one person who is truly understanding, who takes the trouble to listen to us as we consider our problems, can change our whole outlook on the work.*
>
> *—Elton Mayo, Australian psychologist and organization theorist*

Abraham Maslow

Abraham Maslow lived from 1908 to 1970 and is best known for developing the concept of a hierarchy of needs. According to Maslow, human beings have needs that range from the most basic needs for food and water (physical needs), to security, social relationships, self-esteem, and finally, self-actualization. He further suggested that a person needs to fulfill his or her lower-level needs before a higher-level need can be a motivator. For example, if you are dying of thirst, then you will be highly motivated by the offer of a drink of water, but you will not be motivated by something that will improve your self-esteem.

Likewise, if you are extremely worried about your personal security, as when you are in a war zone and bullets are flying over your head, you will be highly motivated to seek a safer and more secure location, but not motivated to seek social relationships.

> *Classic economic theory, based as it is on an inadequate theory of human motivation, could be revolutionized by accepting the reality of higher human needs, including the impulse to self-actualization and the love for the highest values.*
>
> —*Abraham Maslow, psychologist*

Maslow's major contribution to management theory is the concept that managers must get to know their employees and understand that each employee is different and that what motivates one person may not motivate another. Someone who already has their lower-level needs met may be highly motivated by a job that improves that person's self-actualization, but other employees may still be attempting to earn just enough money to feed themselves and their families. A benefit such as health insurance may be highly motivating for one employee, but taken for granted by another. Today, many management theorists argue against Maslow's position that a person basically just works on one level of the hierarchy of needs at a time. Instead, they suggest most of us work on several levels of needs simultaneously. At any rate, managers need to know their employees individually and not assume that everyone is motivated by the same things.

Douglas McGregor

Douglas McGregor (1906–1964), a professor at MIT's Sloan School of Management, suggested managers have two basic viewpoints regarding their employees; he called them Theory X and Theory Y. If a manager views his workers as basically lazy and lacking in ambition, intelligence, and concern for doing good work, then McGregor labeled that manager as following Theory X. On the other hand, a Theory Y manager views his or her workers as people who are intelligent, self-motivated to work hard, and want to do a good job. If a manager views workers through the Theory X looking glass, then that manager will believe it is necessary to be harsh toward workers to get them to overcome their natural lazy tendencies. The Theory Y manager will assume workers naturally want to do good work and will see his or her major task as providing those self-motivated workers with the tools and resources to be highly productive.

As you think about McGregor's theories, which camp are you in? Do you view people you know as lacking in intelligence and motivation? How do you view yourself? Do you have to sort of beat yourself up to force yourself to study hard for a test or to put in that extra effort at work? McGregor's major contribution to modern management thought is that how we feel about ourselves and about others greatly influences our perception of what motivates us and others.

Coercive power is the curse of the universe; coactive power, the enrichment and advancement of every human soul.

—Mary P. Follett, pioneer theorist on management theory

Mary P. Follett

Mary Parker Follett lived from 1868 to 1933 and is called the mother of conflict resolution and was one of the first to look at management and leadership holistically. Follett wrote about the difference between "power-with" and "power-over" and argued that, in the long run, power-with was stronger than power-over. People can gain power over others through a variety of means, such as brute force, but genuine power comes more from working with people in a cooperative mode than ruling over people in a command mode.

Some suggest Follett was denied a doctorate from Harvard because she was a woman, but later she became the first woman to be invited to lecture at the London School of Economics. She advocated managers put an emphasis on human relations equal to the scientific approach Frederick W. Taylor was advocating. Follett stressed the interactions of management and workers, a concept that became known as the Human Relations Approach to Management. Peter Drucker, whom we will consider shortly, called her the "prophet of management" and his "guru." Many of Mary Parker Follett's best papers were published after her death in 1933. Modern management theory owes a lot to this early advocate of more civil human relations between managers and their employees.

Lillian Gilbreth

Lillian Gilbreth and her husband, Frank, were engineers who picked up where Frederick W. Taylor left off. Instead of merely employing a stopwatch and clipboard, Lillian and Frank used motion picture cameras to better analyze workers' movements and scientifically improve various production processes. Lillian lived from 1876 to 1972, but her husband died in 1924, leaving her to raise their 12 children by herself. She started the Motion Study Institute in her home, applying her industrial engineering approach both to business and to running her home. Two of her children later collaborated on the story of their family, which resulted in a 1950 movie entitled *Cheaper by the Dozen*. In 2003 another

The best leader knows how to make his followers actually feel power themselves, not merely acknowledge his power.

—Mary P. Follett

movie used the same title for a comedy starring Steve Martin, but this 20th Century Fox comedy bears no resemblance to the original book or movie, except that Steve Martin plays the part of a coach who is also the father of 12 children.

W. Edwards Deming

It's not good to be envied. But if you have to be envied, it's better to be envied for what you are than for what you own.

—Lillian Gilbreth, mother of industrial psychology

William Edwards Deming (1900–1993) was an American statistician who first attempted to convince American business leaders in the late 1940s to apply his statistical methods. In the United States, Deming was largely ignored, because the American business sector was too busy trying to fill the backlog of demand for consumer goods following the end of World War II. During the war, American industry was converted from making consumer goods such as cars and appliances to making tanks, ships, planes, and other items needed to fight World War II. Immediately following the war, American business managers were only concerned with producing the consumer goods Americans had been denied during the war. However, Deming's ideas struck a responsive chord in Japan, where he worked under General Douglas MacArthur teaching statistical process control methods to Japanese business leaders. The Japanese factories were almost totally destroyed by bombs, and their business leaders were more willing to accept a new approach. While Deming soon became a hero in Japan, it was not until near his death in 1993 that his philosophy became well known, and to some extent, accepted by American business leaders.

Deming taught that all managers need to have what he called a "System of Profound Knowledge," consisting of four parts:

1. Appreciation of their business as a system with feedback that seeks a steady state.
2. Knowledge of how to apply statistical methods to measure and control variation.
3. An understanding of what is normal variation (which cannot be corrected) and variation that is caused by some defect and can therefore be corrected.
4. Knowledge of human nature.

Deming then proposed 14 key principles managers should follow to make their businesses more effective:

1. Create constancy of purpose.
2. Adopt the new philosophy.

3. Build quality into the product as it is being built rather than inspecting only the final product.
4. Drop the idea of buying from the lowest bidder and instead move toward a single supplier you can trust.
5. Improve the system of production and service to both improve quality and reduce cost.
6. Do on-the-job training.
7. Institute leadership aimed at helping people do a better job.
8. Drive out fear in the workplace.
9. Break down barriers between departments.
10. Eliminate slogans.
11. Eliminate work quotas.
12. Restore pride in workmanship.
13. Institute a vigorous program of education and self-improvement.
14. Transformation is everybody's job.

All anyone asks for is a chance to work with pride.

—W. Edwards Deming, statistician and author

Finally, Deming identified seven deadly diseases of management:

1. Lack of constancy of purpose.
2. Emphasis on short-term profits.
3. Evaluation by performance, merit rating, or annual review of performance.
4. Mobility of management.
5. Running a company on visible figures alone.
6. Excessive medical costs.
7. Excessive costs of warranty, fueled by lawyers who work for contingency fees.

Deming challenged management to accept more of the responsibility for problems in production. Instead of blaming the workers, Deming pointed out that many aspects of the production process are beyond the control of the individual workers, and it is management who should take the blame when there are flaws in the raw materials, tools, or processes that workers must use. Workers simply have to use the raw materials and tools supplied by management, and should not be blamed for errors that are really the responsibility of management.

Quality is everyone's responsibility.

—W. Edwards Deming

Peter Drucker

Peter Ferdinand Drucker was born in Vienna, Austria, in 1909 and died in Claremont, California, on November 11, 2005, at the age of 95. He was one of the best-known writers in management theory and practice. As a young writer living in Germany, he wrote *The Jewish Question in Germany*, which was burned and banned by the Nazis. Fortunately, in 1933 he left Germany for England, where he married and then moved to the United States. Here, he became a university professor, writer, and consultant. He became a U.S. citizen in 1943 and taught at Bennington College and later New York University. From 1971 until his death, he was a professor at the Peter F. Drucker Graduate School of Management at Claremont Graduate University in Claremont, California. His basic principles and concepts of management could fill many books; in fact, Drucker authored 39 books. Many of today's management professors, including this author, first studied management from Drucker's textbook, *The Practice of Management*.

Effective leadership is not about making speeches or being liked; leadership is defined by results not attributes.

—Peter Drucker, management consultant and writer

In his later life, Drucker scolded CEOs for their excessive pay. In a 1984 essay, Drucker suggested that the CEO should receive no more than 20 times what the rank-and-file worker makes—especially at companies where thousands of employees are being laid off. (According to MarketWatch, in 2011 the average total compensation paid top-level executives is now over 1,100 times the average worker's wage.) Drucker warned, "This is morally and socially unforgivable and we will pay a heavy price for it." Drucker also told executives they should volunteer to help out in the not-for-profit sector. In his final years, he wrote about how some of the good practices of management in the for-profit sector could be used to improve the efficiency and effectiveness of not-for-profit organizations.

We now accept the fact that learning is a lifelong process of keeping abreast of change. And the most pressing task is to teach people how to learn.

—Peter Drucker

Drucker is especially well known for suggesting that the main goal of a business is not to make a maximum profit, but rather to meet the needs of customers, thereby making a profit as a by-product of satisfying those customers. In the not-for-profit sector, he suggested thinking of your primary customer as the person whose life is most changed by what the organization does. For example, an organization of choral singers may occasionally put on concerts where tickets are sold, but the primary customers may not be the ticket buyers, but rather the singers whose lives are most improved by the satisfaction and joy they get from singing in a group.

William Ouchi, Theory Z: How American Business Can Meet the Japanese Challenge

Professor Ouchi studied the Japanese style of management that, by the 1980s, was known for the highest productivity in the world. Japan's accomplishment was especially striking, given that most of their industrial sector was totally destroyed by the end of World War II in 1945. Ouchi's book, published in 1981, suggested the secret to Japan's success was not technology, but rather a special way of managing employees that builds on McGregor's Theory Y and focuses on a strong company philosophy, a distinct corporate culture, long-range employee development, and decision making by consensus. Some have suggested the "Z" in Ouchi's Theory Z could stand for "Zeal". Japanese managers are known for building long-lasting relationships with their workers and trusting their workers to work together for the greater good of the organization. In return, the organization provides an almost certain lifetime employment, and promotions are almost always from within.

Summary

Today's management thought is a collection of all the thoughts of these major leaders and more. Any list of key contributors to the history of management thought is bound to leave out someone who others consider important. However, in general, you should be able to see that our current thinking has progressed from some military leadership concepts from thousands of years ago where managers barked out commands to their employees somewhat like army sergeants yelling at new recruits in basic training to a set of modern management principles and concepts built upon the fields of psychology and sociology.

Questions for Discussion

1. In your study of the history of management and leadership from Sun Tzu's book, *The Art of War*, to modern thinking, what general trends do you see? Describe one or more such trends.
2. Adam Smith, author of *The Wealth of Nations*, described a concept known today as the Invisible Hand, suggesting a free market will set a price fair to both buyer and seller. However, he also wrote a book entitled, *The Theory of Moral Sentiments*, which has been largely forgotten. What appraisal is advocated in Adam Smith's lesser known book, and how do you think it should be applied today?

3. Many of the famous people in the history of management thought were men. However, Mary P. Follett and Lillian Gilbreth were women who also influenced the development of management principles and concepts. Discuss what these two women contributed to management thought and how the small, but growing, number of women entering the field of management may eventually change management.

Chapter 3

Business Ethics: How We Ought to Lead Others

Ethics is nothing else than reverence for life.

—Albert Schweitzer, winner of the Nobel Peace Prize in 1952

A man without ethics is a wild beast loosed upon this world.

—Albert Camus, French existential philosopher

In civilized life, law floats in a sea of ethics.

—Earl Warren, U.S. Supreme Court justice

Ethics is the study of what people in a culture consider right and wrong. Each of the quoted thinkers looked at ethics from their own perspective as each of the readers of this book will do. What is clear is that most great thinkers think ethics is important.

A Tragic Story

What would you think of a man who was the son of Polish immigrants, whose father was a plumber, who earned his bachelor's degree in political science from Hofstra University and then entered law school, but later quit to begin his own investment firm using the $5,000 he had saved from his summer lifeguarding job? Over the years he regularly earned his investors over 10% per year, and by the 1980s his firm handled up to 5 percent of the trading on the New York Stock Exchange. His securities firm began using computer technology to develop stock quotes and the program that his firm tested and helped to develop became the National Association of Securities Dealers Automated Quotations, or NASDAQ. He later served as president of the board of directors for the NASDAQ stock exchange. He was the father of two sons, Mark and Andrew, a generous contributor to numerous charities and to several prominent Democratic political officeholders, and a person highly trusted by thousands of investors, including many celebrities and charitable foundations. Does this sound to you like a highly ethical businessman?

Would it change your mind if you were also to learn that on December 11 of 2008, Bernie Madoff's sons reported their father to federal authorities and in March 2009 he pleaded guilty to 11 federal felonies and admitted to turning his wealth management business into a massive fraud that is considered the largest such fraud in history and is now serving 150 years in prison? Would it also make you sad to learn that on December 11, 2010, exactly two years after turning his father in, his son Mark was found dead in his New York City apartment, an apparent suicide by hanging? Have you ever wondered how someone who seemed to have it all turns out to be such a fraud? Do you ever question how you would handle the temptation to have untold riches simply by dropping your ethical guard?

Today, managers in large corporations often handle more money than others dream exists. It is estimated that the amount missing from Bernie Madoff's client accounts is $65 *billion*. If you have a job paying you $50,000 annually, it would take you 1,300,000 years to earn that much money. How could a man practically everyone thought was a nice guy steal that much money—some of it from charities?

Another Tragic Story

According to McLean and Elkind, authors of *The Smartest Guys in the Room: The Amazing Rise and Scandalous Fall of Enron* (2003), during the night of January 25, 2002, Cliff Baxter, the 43-year-old vice chairman of Enron, slipped carefully out of bed so as not to disturb his sleeping wife. He climbed into his new black Mercedes-Benz S500 and drove to Palm Royale Boulevard, about a mile from his home. With the motor still running and the headlights burning, he lifted a silver .38 caliber revolver to his right temple and blew away most of his head. At the services were photos of Cliff with his loving family, sailing, playing the guitar. His wife Carol, his 16-year-old son, and his 11-year-old daughter were heartbroken.

According to the *Houston Chronicle*, Cliff's suicide note to his wife Carol read:

> *Carol,*
> *I am sorry for this. I feel I just can't go on. I have always tried to do the right thing but where there was once great pride now it's gone. I love you and the children so much. I just can't be any good to you or myself. The pain is overwhelming.*
> *Please try to forgive me.*
> *Cliff*

As tragic as Baxter's suicide was, it was only the beginning. Thousands of Enron employees lost not only their jobs, but also their retirement funds and their self-respect. Many of them had been among the top one percent academically, were former captains of athletic teams, and generally considered among the most likely to succeed. Perhaps most, like Cliff Baxter, had "always tried to do the right thing." The collapse of Enron in 2001 was, up to that point, the largest bankruptcy in U.S. history. Their reported earnings in 2000 were $101 billion, and their employees numbered 21,000. On January 25, 2001, Enron's stock reached a peak price of $81.39 per share, and on December 2, 2001, Enron filed for bankruptcy.

Throughout the 1990s, Enron's stock continued to climb, and "leaders" such as Ken Lay and Jeff Skilling appeared to be business wizards. When the bubble burst in 2001, the calamity resulted in the demise not only of Enron, but also accounting giant Arthur Andersen. Thousands lost their jobs, and even more lost their life's savings as Enron stock dropped from $81.39 on January 25, 2001, to $0.00 on December 2, 2001, when Enron filed for bankruptcy.

Books, articles, and even a movie about Enron claim various reasons for one of the biggest and most sudden business failures in history. Kurt Eichenwald claims it was a *Conspiracy of Fools*. In contrast, Bethany McLean and Peter Elkind claim it was because Enron executives considered themselves *The Smartest Guys in the Room*. Mimi Swartz and Sherron Watkins, a high-ranking Enron executive famous for writing a memo to CEO Ken Lay in 2001, essentially blowing the whistle on Enron's fraudulent accounting practices, claim it was a *Power Failure*.

It is essential students of leadership not assume the problem at Enron was merely the result of a few rotten apples and that all would be saved if only those few rotten apples were thrown out of the barrel.

Ethics is about how we ought to live.

—Socrates, philosopher of ancient Greece

It is not fair or accurate to put all the blame on CEO Ken Lay or COO/CEO Jeff Skilling, or on CFO Andy Fastow. Various judges and juries eventually did determine these guys were rotten apples, indeed. However, the problem might not be solved at Enron or in any large organization merely by tossing out a few rotten apples; especially if the barrel holding those apples is itself rotten. That is, examine the reward structure used at Enron, and unfortunately, at many other American corporations today. Consider whether the merit-based pay system got out of hand. Instead of motivating employees to do their best in the interest of the entire organization, did it motivate some to do what was clearly unethical, fraudulent, and ultimately illegal in order to artificially push up stock prices and earn huge cash bonuses and cash in highly inflated stock options?

Also ask why others at Enron who were not rotten apples failed to speak up. Imagine you are working for a company that, with bonuses and stock options, you are receiving a total annual compensation hundreds, or perhaps thousands, of times more than what you could earn doing exactly the same job at most other companies. Being a whistle blower would likely cost you your job at Enron or worse. If you knew you could get another job paying approximately the same amount, you might have more of the courage needed to speak up.

Enron fell from what was thought to be the seventh largest corporation in the nation to nothing in less than a year. How could this happen? This chapter looks at the ethical issues you, as a manager, will likely face. First we need to briefly consider the beginnings of ethical thought.

Socrates, Father of Ethics in the Western World

Socrates, who lived in Greece around 470 B.C., is supposed to have replied to the question of what is ethics with, "Ethics is about how we *ought* to live." He suggested the best way to live is to focus on self-development rather than to pursue material wealth. We should concentrate more on developing friendships and a sense of community. In his view, the most valuable of all possessions was virtue. He got in trouble with the Greek authorities by questioning the notion of "might makes right" that he thought was common in Greece in his day. Eventually, he was sentenced to death by drinking hemlock, a poison. Today's students of management often forget that it has never been easy to be ethical. When you become a manager, it will become your greatest challenge.

Confucius, Father of Ethics in the Eastern World

Confucius lived in China around 550 B.C., and is considered by many to be the father of ethics in the Eastern world. He defined ethics as the behavior that conforms to a society's accepted principles of right and wrong. One of his many famous quotations is, "To see what is right and not to do it is want of courage." Moral courage consists of the courage to be honest, fair, respectful, responsible, and compassionate. He encouraged others to "Do not do to others what you do not want done to yourself," one of the earliest versions of the Golden Rule. Confucius championed strong family loyalty, ancestor worship, respect of children for their elders, and respect of husbands for their wives and the family as the basis for an ideal government. Today's governmental and business leaders would do well to follow the over 2,500-year-old teachings of Confucius.

Ethics in the Academic World

At universities, the subject of ethics is typically found in the Philosophy Department, where it is sometimes called moral philosophy. *Philosophy* is a word with Greek roots defined as "the love of wisdom." Ethics is a category of wisdom that focuses on the study of what a society considers right or wrong, virtue and vice, good and evil, etc. Because ethics has long been considered a subset of the study of philosophy, the Philosophy Department is where you will likely find university courses on ethics. After students in such courses are presented with some basic terminology about the field of ethics and the major branches of ethics, the issues typically presented include the application of ethics in public policy such as, "Is getting an abortion immoral?" "Is euthanasia immoral?" "Do animals have rights?" "Is lying always wrong, and if not, when is it permissible?"

Ethics is sometimes confused with legality. Some have compared the world of ethics to be like the sea—broad and deep. Law, on the other hand, is like an iceberg on that sea. A society may decide that some action is so unethical that they write a law forbidding it and provide specific punishment to those who disobey that law. So the law is like a frozen or hardened piece of the sea. It is much smaller than the sea, but it is specific and the consequences are defined. Ethical issues are often open to some debate. For example, most societies typically say it is unethical to tell a lie. However, lying is something ethical people sometimes do to protect others. For example, if someone rushed into a building with a gun saying he was going to kill someone and asked you if you know where that person is, it would be considered ethical to lie and say you have no idea where the person can be found. To tell the truth, in this instance, would be to cause someone to be killed. Another common example is the generally accepted ethical principle that it is wrong to kill someone. However, if that person is threatening to kill your family, you may be justified to kill that person to protect yourself and your family.

It is curious—curious that physical courage should be so common in the world, and moral courage so rare.

—Mark Twain, pen name of Samuel Langhorne Clemens, American humorist and author

Ethics versus Morality

Ethics is a branch of philosophy involving the study of what people consider right and wrong behavior. *Morality* is concerned with the performance of good ethics. Ethics is thinking about it; morality is doing it. Leaders must engage in ethical thought and then do what is morally right.

Some say ethics education should be about teaching people how to think, not merely thinking as in 2 + 2 = 4 or in reading a paragraph and understanding what it says. While such numerical reasoning and language skills are important, we also need to learn how to think about what is right and wrong, good and bad, ethical and unethical. Leaders especially need to be good thinkers about taking the proper path, making the right choice, doing the right thing. The study of ethics helps us think about how to think.

Business Ethics

Business leaders are on the firing line. They are not just thinkers; they are doers, risk takers, and choice makers. They have to put good ethics into practice and they must do it themselves. No ethical expert is going to do it for them. Business leaders have to think for themselves; they are the ones with the responsibility to decide.

If ethics are poor at the top, that behavior is copied down through the organization.

—Robert Noyce, inventor of the silicon chip

Business Ethics is a subset of the field of ethics that focuses on the ethical issues you will likely face as a business leader. The business ethics course may start out much like the one about ethics in general, but the questions addressed are typically more along the line of "How can a business manager balance the often-conflicting goals of investors (such as maximizing return on investment) with the goals of their employees (good wages and benefits) and concerns for the environment (keeping the water, air, and soil clean)?" As you enter the profession of business management, it is important to not adopt the attitude that you can do anything so long as there is no specific law prohibiting that action. Remember, the law only addresses a tiny iceberg portion of the sea of ethics.

A common issue facing business managers is that of laying off employees during an economic downturn. You may someday be faced with the thankless task of telling employees they are no longer employed with your organization. To those individuals, you may appear ruthless and unethical. However, as a manager, you must consider the greater good of the entire organization. It may be better to lay off 1,000 of your 11,000 employees so that the remaining 10,000 employees still have a job. To keep everyone employed may result in bankruptcy and the loss of all 11,000 jobs plus the investment of thousands of investors, the jobs of your suppliers, and the economic destruction of an entire community. Potential business managers need to learn all they can about ethics, because your responsibilities will be great and the right thing to do may not always be clear. Great managers and great leaders have a highly developed sense of what is ethical. An ethical manager conducts business the way we ought to conduct business. It is not okay to treat everyone at work poorly all week long and then do some charitable act on the weekend to compensate. Having good business ethics means conducting business, day in and day out, with a good sense of what is right and wrong and with the courage to carry out those ethical business practices, even if those actions come at a high price to you personally and to your organization. It has never been easy being ethical.

Characteristics of an Ethical Manager

Even before you become a manager, you will need to decide where to accept an offer of employment. In times of high unemployment (such as during the writing of this book), graduating students may be forced to take just about any job they are offered. However, periods of high unemployment have always been eventually followed by periods of low unemployment. At some point in your career, you will likely have several choices to make. An important one is to choose to work for an ethical manager. How do you tell if your prospective employer is ethical?

The first test of whether a prospective employer is ethical is *benevolence*. Does the employer care about others? Someone or some organization that lacks compassion for others is likely to be unethical. The ethical employer has learned to balance concern for personal wealth and the profitability of the business with the multitude of other stakeholder interests. Ethical managers have a genuine concern for the well-being of their employees, customers, stockholders, suppliers, and their entire community. They are focused on making a profit, but not blind to all their responsibilities to the entire set of stakeholders. They make money within the bounds of ethical behavior for themselves and their organization.

The second test is a *long-term focus*. Businesses, especially those on the stock exchanges, are pressured by Wall Street analysts and others to produce ever more profits each quarter. A quarter is only three months. The U.S. Securities and Exchange Commission requires each publicly held corporation to report their financial condition every quarter. Investment analysts carefully watch each quarterly report to see whether the corporation met their estimates for that three-month period. Other things being equal, the price of a corporation's stock usually falls when they fail to meet the estimated earnings per share for a quarter, and rise when those estimated profits are exceeded. This puts enormous pressure on some key executives to meet or exceed the analyst's estimates every three months. However, some decisions may be beneficial in the short term, but disastrous in the long term. The more ethical manager will face up to the pressure of these short-term demands and make decisions that will result in sustainable competitive

> *Ethics and religion must not stay at home when we go to work.*
>
> —*Achille Silvestrini, cardinal and Vatican diplomat*

advantages for the overall organization in the long run. If instead your employer tells you, "You must make the numbers by the end of this quarter and I don't care how you do it," start looking for a new job because you have likely fallen into a den of unethical people and they may well drag you down with them. "How you make the numbers" is important. The challenge is to "make the numbers" while conducting business with high ethical standards. Ethical managers accept this challenge. They have a good sense of their values and the courage to stick with them.

The third test of an ethical employer is whether they view boundaries of their behavior as what is ethical or as set by whatever the law does not expressly forbid. Remember, ethics is like the sea and the law is like a frozen iceberg on that huge sea. Ethical employers seek to do better than simply avoid the icebergs: they take the high road. Do not set your standards as simply staying out of prison. You can do better than that. However, if you find yourself employed in an organization with no higher standards than to stay out of jail, then you are on a slippery slope where the likely outcome is unethical behavior that good people find shameful, if not illegal.

Of course an unethical manager does the opposite. He or she looks out for Number One. The job of the company's legal staff is to keep the managers out of jail. The unethical manager looks for ways to avoid getting caught, rather than avoiding unethical actions. Such managers put pressure on their employees to join them in their unethical behavior, because this provides a measure of protection against those employees blowing the whistle. If you incriminate such a manger, you incriminate yourself. It is similar to the initiation into a lawless gang where the initiate is required to commit a crime as a way of joining the gang. Once the new gang member has committed a crime, he or she knows that the gang leaders can always turn him in. It is a way of keeping gang members in line.

Unethical managers and leaders do not wear a badge or other identifying items allowing the job seeker to quickly identify them as unethical. In fact, they often "talk the talk" of a highly ethical person. It makes a good cover. Therefore, it is important to actually view the person's actions. Does the person "walk the walk?" What do the employees say about their manager when their guard is down? What do customers say about the way this organization treats them? Are the various stakeholders treated according to the Golden Rule: DO UNTO OTHERS AS YOU WOULD HAVE THEM DO UNTO YOU?

Ethical Leadership

Ethical leadership begins with being ethical, but it requires much more. An ethical leader teaches others what is right and wrong behavior within this organization. Such a leader demonstrates how employees, customers, suppliers, investors, and others *ought* to be treated by anyone within this organization. Further, the ethical leader rewards ethical behavior and corrects and punishes those who perform unethically. The acid test is how the ethical leader treats someone who contributes greatly to the organization's profits, but does it unethically. It is easy to punish an employee who is both a low producer and unethical. The challenge is to punish the high producer who is unethical. The ethical leader understands that it is his or her duty to do the right thing. Also, he or she knows that the other followers will be

The price of greatness is responsibility.

—Winston Churchill, British politician and statesman

watching to see how difficult decisions are handled. When a manager turns a blind eye to unethical behavior performed by the high producer, the other followers know that manager is a hypocrite. To be an ethical leader you must do three things: (1) Be ethical; (2) teach your followers what is right and wrong in this setting; and (3) reward ethical behavior and punish unethical action.

Can Ethics Be Taught?

Critics often charge that ethics cannot be taught—that some people are simply bad people, and no amount of lecturing about ethics will turn a bad person into a good one. Ethics teachers do not claim to be able to convert a bad person into a good one. Instead, they aim to help good people know how to recognize an ethical issue and how to take ethical actions. For example, at Enron there must have been hundreds, if not thousands, of good people who knew something was wrong about the way Enron was recording inflated revenues and hiding debts. However, for years nobody said a word. Teaching ethics can make people more aware of ethical issues and can provide suggestions for those who do want to take action.

To educate a person in mind and not in morals is to educate a menace to society.

— Theodore Roosevelt, 26th president of the United States

Often an ethical issue is hidden within another business problem. The classic example is the 1972 case involving a small car called the Pinto, manufactured by Ford Motor Company. Because of a manufacturing flaw, the car was prone to catch fire after being struck from the rear, even at low speeds. Employees at Ford calculated the cost of recalling the 11 million Pintos and fixing the flaw and compared those costs to the estimated costs of losing a forecasted number of wrongful death or injury lawsuits that Pinto owners would bring against Ford. Because the costs of the recall were higher than the costs of the wrongful death lawsuits, Ford executives decided not to recall the cars, thus resulting in the fiery deaths of many more innocent people. When the public learned of Ford's decision, Ford's reputation sank to a new low. Instead of applying cost-benefit analysis, Ford executives should have recognized this as an ethical problem involving human lives, not just dollars.

In contrast, consider the 1982 case where seven people died in the Chicago area from taking cyanide-laced capsules of Extra-Strength Tylenol. Johnson & Johnson recalled 31 million bottles of Tylenol capsules from stores and offered customers replacement products in the safer tablet form free of charge, costing Johnson & Johnson over $100 million. Johnson & Johnson emerged from this tragic event a hero, Ford a villain. Perhaps with the proper training in ethics, at least one Ford executive would have displayed the moral courage to object to the heartless approach.

The Social Responsibilities of a Business Leader

President John F. Kennedy declared, "For those to whom much is given, much is required." In Luke 12:48 it is expressed, "To whom much is given is much required." These quotes, and many similar ones, express the concept that those people with much wealth should give generously to others. Also, corporations are an entity of the state created to encourage investment in businesses by limiting each investor's potential loss to just the amount invested. In return for this special privileged status, corporations are expected to be "good citizens" of the state. This "good citizen" status is generally thought to mean that corporations should do their fair share in supporting local charities and the arts. For all these reasons, most corporations take seriously their social responsibilities and donate millions to various causes.

Another famous, but opposite, viewpoint is aptly expressed by Nobel Prize–winning economist Milton Friedman: "There is one and only one social responsibility of business—to use its resources and engage in activities designed to increase its profits so long as it stays within the rules of the game, which is to say, engages in open and free competition without deception or fraud."

So which way is it? Do corporations have a responsibility to support charities and the arts, or does such support subtract from the profits mentioned in Friedman's famous quote? Most corporations strive for a middle ground. They should not give away so much money that it seriously decreases profits, but they also want to cultivate an image of being good citizens who care about the needs of the less fortunate and about supporting the arts, thereby making their communities more enjoyable places to live.

What must be avoided is the approach where the executives conduct their everyday business activities in a ruthless and unethical—or even a borderline illegal—manner, and then attempt to cover up by donating to charity. Being ethical is not about occasionally doing a good deed to compensate for the bad. It is about doing your main activity as it *ought* to be done. If you are a business manager, then having good ethics means being ethical in your role as manager. Doing socially responsible things should not be viewed as an occasional activity or as a way of making up for unethical business practices.

> *For what will it profit a man if he gains the whole world but forfeits his soul?*
>
> *—Matthew 16:26*

Maximizing profits by behaving unethically is not acceptable. A business manager must be ethical and socially responsible while managing for profitability. Maintaining the correct balance is not easy. Sometimes doing the right thing causes managers to sacrifice short-term profits, or even their jobs. They are held accountable for making a profit, but they must also build an honorable reputation, both for themselves and for their organization. Each of us, whether CEO or janitor, must think deeply about our value system and where we will draw the line when under great pressure. In the end, you must decide and then live with yourself.

How Ethical Are We?

Being an ethical business leader does not begin at age 40 or 50 when you become an executive. It is something that we must practice from a young age and work to strengthen throughout our lives. As we grow into positions of greater responsibility and power, our temptations will also grow.

A popular prayer in the Christian tradition includes the line, "lead us not into temptation ..." However, there will be plenty of temptation in your role as a business manager and leader. You need to begin today identifying your system of values and building your moral courage so that when temptation strikes, you will be morally strong. Begin today by conducting yourself as a student *ought* to behave. Do not try to get by doing the minimum amount of work in your classes. Instead, think of the responsibility you are likely to have some day. Think of how you would feel if, as a manager, you make the wrong decision because you really did not understand some principle of business that you would be expected to know. Perhaps that concept was taught the day you decided to skip class. Perhaps it was explained in the textbook you decided was too boring to read. However, as a graduate of a good business school, your employer and others who must rely on your good judgment will expect you to know that accounting principle or that financial concept or that marketing theory. The most ethical thing you could be doing right now is to study your business courses with the attitude that you really need to learn as much as possible about this material so you can become a business manager others can trust to make good business decisions.

Unfortunately, research indicates that many of today's students could stand to improve their ethics. A recent survey of 43,000 high school students by the Josephson Institute reveals that one in three boys and one in four girls admitted to stealing within the past year. A majority of students (59 percent) admitted to cheating on a test during the past year. One in three admitted to using the Internet to plagiarize an assignment. Since 1992 the Josephson Institute has conducted a national survey of the ethics of American youth every two years. This institute also administers the national CHARACTER COUNTS program that aims to help students build character while encouraging academic performance. For more details, see http://charactercounts.org.

Character Counts is an ethics education program based on Six Pillars: Trustworthiness, Respect, Responsibility, Fairness, Caring, and Citizenship. Participants are encouraged to be honest; do what you say you will do; develop the courage to do the right thing; and begin today to build a good reputation. While this program is focused on high school students, other research has confirmed that many adults also seem to lack a sound knowledge of ethics, values, and the moral courage to stand up for what is right.

Kohlberg's Levels of Moral Reasoning

Lawrence Kohlberg (1927–1987) was famous for developing three levels of moral reasoning. Each level contains two stages, for a total of six stages:

Level 1 (Pre-Conventional)

1. Obedience and punishment orientation
    a. How can I avoid punishment?
2. Self-interest orientation
    a. What's in it for me?

Level 2 (Conventional)

3. Interpersonal accord and conformity
    a. What do the social norms expect?
4. Authority and social order–maintaining orientation
    a. What does law and order require?

Level 3 (Post-Conventional)

5. Social contract orientation
6. Universal ethical principles
    a. What is the right thing to do?

A small child is likely to decide which actions to take based on avoiding punishment. Your mother probably told you to stop hitting your little sister or you would be put in "time out," so you stopped hitting your little sister—not out of any complicated understanding of ethics, but rather to just avoid your mother's wrath. On the positive side, a small child is motivated to do those actions that are likely to result in a treat or praise from Mom or Dad. At the pre-convention stage, we consciously or subconsciously ask, "What's in it for me?"

As we mature, most of us become concerned about what others think of us, and with the proper education and encouragement, we grow into what Kohlberg calls the Conventional Level of moral development. We try to determine what society expects us to do. We also become more aware of what the law requires us to do. We ask, "What do others expect me to do?"

Kohlberg's third level of moral development (Post-Conventional) involves living by our own principles of what we firmly believe is right or wrong. Basic principles such as life, liberty, and justice are followed. Great managers and leaders should have a high level of moral development such as described in Kohlberg's Level 3 Post-Conventional Morality. We ask, "What is the right thing to do?" We take the high road. We do what we *ought* to do, whether someone is watching or not.

Why Workers Say They Behave Unethically at Work

Numerous studies have shown that a large percentage of American workers seem to think it is okay to take small items from their employer, call in sick when they really are not ill, and pad expense accounts. While these actions are not major crimes, they can start us down the *slippery slope*, where getting by with small infractions leads to bolder and more serious unethical behaviors. Do these studies prove that American workers are unethical, or is something else at work here?

When such workers are asked to explain their unethical behavior, they say they don't view their own behavior as unethical. Instead, they view it as seeking justice and fairness. They explain that their employer takes away from them far more than they think is fair in terms of time away from the families and friends. Others say the amount of work expected for the wages and benefits they receive is unfair. So, instead of stealing, these employees say they are simply, "evening the score." They are creating their own form of justice.

Each of us has to guard against carrying this concept of justice too far. We realize we cannot take justice into our own hands when it comes to punishing someone for a major crime. Instead, civilized society provides a system of police, courts, and laws to enforce such justice. We can't legally shoot someone we think might be guilty of a crime. People must be considered innocent until proven guilty. We must not assume the roles of judge, jury, and executioner. We must be careful not to excuse unethical, and perhaps illegal, action at work in the name of justice or evening the score. However, as future managers, it is important to realize that an increase in pilfering at work is often a result of employees feeling they have been unfairly treated by management.

Some Basic Approaches to Building an Ethical Framework for Your Life and Work

Most of us especially want to know we are following a leader who is ethical. We want to be led in the right direction. We want to be able to trust our leaders. As you prepare to assume higher levels of leadership, how can you develop your morality? How do we form our ethical positions?

Divine Command

Many argue that we should take our ethics from religion. For Jews, Christians, and Muslims, there are scriptures that many believe contain all the rules for proper living. For many, decisions about what is right or wrong depend on a combination of scriptures, religious traditions, and what certain religious leaders say. The ethical principle of Divine Command says we should obey God's commandments.

Those who believe strongly in Divine Command as the source of ethics might argue that ethics should be taught in the home and in places of worship, not in school, especially public schools. Under this approach, leaders should rely on what the prevailing religion teaches regarding ethical choices.

In America the constitutionally protected freedom of religion has made this an inviting place for immigrants of all faith traditions, including those who disavow all religions. As leaders operating in America, we need to respect the diversity of beliefs.

As we go global with our responsibilities, we have to be even more mindful of the diversity of religious beliefs and customs around the world. What may be considered ethical regarding the treatment of female employees, for example, may differ greatly from region to region. What is considered appropriate to eat, drink, wear, and say varies greatly among the various religions. Observance of religious holidays, holy seasons, and when and where to worship also vary.

Men never do evil so completely and cheerfully as when they do it from a religious conviction.

—Blaise Pascal, French mathematician

Furthermore, we have all witnessed many so-called religious people who are unethical. Some have even used the appearance of being religious to gain peoples' confidence and take advantage of others' faith.

Being religious is, unfortunately, not the same as being good. Some even use their religious beliefs as justification for mistreating others. They insist there are "words of God" that justify their actions. Unfortunately, the moral teaching behind the words and stories is often overlooked. Instead of engaging in debates with religious scholars about the exact meaning of specific words found in scriptures, business leaders need to be respectful of all sincere religious beliefs and look for common ground among all religions. For example, most of the world's major religions agree on some form of the Golden Rule, "Do unto others as you would have them do unto you." In many cases, the business leader merely needs to consider that universal principle to make the correct choice.

The ethical philosophy of Divine Command can be helpful if the leader can avoid arguments over religious differences and instead stick to universally accepted broad principles.

Tzu-kung asked, "Is there a single word which can be a guide in conduct throughout one's life?" The Master said, "It is perhaps the word 'shu.'" Do not impose on others what you yourself do not desire.

—Confucius

Utilitarianism

No academic discussion of ethics would be complete without some reference to the concept of utilitarianism, i.e., doing what will result in *the greatest good for the greatest number*. A corollary is to do what will cause the least harm in situations where all alternatives are bad. For example, when business leaders have to lay off hundreds of workers in order to save a business from total failure, they often use utilitarianism as their justification for the painful layoffs. They had to trim the labor force to save the firm from bankruptcy and the greater harm that would do to even more people.

Running a business so that it prospers, investors are happy, customers are satisfied, and employees are fairly compensated results in much good for many people. Business leaders need to make business decisions that result in minimizing harm and maximizing the good to great numbers of people. At other times, the ultimate results of the leader's choice cannot be fully measured at the time when the choice must be made. We try to predict the future, but no one can see perfectly into the distant future. Big decisions often have consequences not revealed until several years later.

Other decisions appear sound and logical one moment and foolish the next. The tragedy of 9/11 is an example. In addition to the thousands of deaths and injuries of that fateful day, there were unexpected consequences to industries such as the airlines, tourism, hotels, and many others. Decisions that may have seemed so reasonable on 9/10 were totally unreasonable on 9/12.

Historical events such as wars, assassinations of leaders, epidemics, major storms, nuclear accidents, etc., are unpredictable. Utilitarianism is a helpful concept. It assumes, however, we can reasonably estimate how many people will be affected by our choice and that we can put some value on the long-term effects of our choice. When it is possible to estimate results, then leaders should do what will bring the greatest good to the greatest number. However, there are other times when leaders simply have to make decisions with precious little information, yet they are still expected to do the right thing.

Ethics of Duty

There are times when leaders simply have to do their duty. Usually a duty implies an obligation—something owed to others. When American military officers take their oath of office they pledge to do their duty to "*protect the Constitution of the United States against all enemies, both foreign and domestic.*" Any study of military history should bestow a sense of obligation to those millions who have given their lives in service to this country. We would not be doing our duty to their memory to slack off in our obligation to be strong, courageous, and resolute in protecting the rights of citizens as set forth in the Constitution.

As citizens, we have a duty to be informed voters. Having the privilege of living in a democracy carries with it the duty to maintain that democracy. People who fail to learn about the candidates for public office and their stands on important issues are shirking their duty. People who decide to become parents have a duty to feed, clothe, house, and protect their children. Business leaders who use corporate dollars to buy the favor of elected officials should be ashamed of their actions. A democracy is a precious thing, but it must not be for sale.

When a person assumes the position of manager or executive, there is an implied duty to protect that organization and the people within it from harm and to steer a course that is in the best interests of the entire organization. There are times when the Ethics of Duty provides a clear-cut direction for our choices. Unfortunately, there are other times when it is not at all clear which path is the dutiful choice.

This dilemma was especially painful in America during the Vietnam War. Many young citizens were torn between the duty to serve in the armed forces versus their duty to oppose what many thought was an unjust war. Many thoughtful people at one time felt strongly their duty was to join the armed services and later changed their mind and joined the peace movement.

Business leaders have a duty to serve the shareholders. After all, they were the ones who invested their savings into this business. For taking this risk, they have a right to expect a fair return on their money. Maximizing return on investment is a common consideration in business decision making.

But duties often conflict. To keep a business strong, it must serve its customers and reward its employees. However, providing excellent products and paying good wages cut into profits for shareholders. Most leaders, when faced with this type of situation, talk about balance, providing what they hope will be choices satisfactory to all parties concerned. Sometimes this is called satisficing, as opposed to maximizing. In general, business leaders must be mindful of their duty to many others.

Ethics of Respect

Most people will agree we should show proper respect for other human beings. A common colloquialism today is, *"Don't dis me!"*—Do not show disrespect toward me. In most cultures, it is considered improper to disrespect people who are our elders. Men open doors for women as a sign of respect. We behave with respect toward clergy. We respect those who are medical professionals, firefighters, police officers, and sometimes even teachers. Often we demonstrate our respect by the way we dress, talk, and behave. For example, talking loudly in a place of worship is typically considered disrespectful. We show respect for those who have died by going to their funeral and expressing our sympathies to their families.

Every human being, of whatever station, deserves respect. We must each respect others even as we respect ourselves.

—U Thant (1909–1974), Burmese diplomat and secretary general of the United Nations

Simple things like returning phone calls, taking time to explain a product, and acknowledging a customer's needs as important are all ways business leaders can show respect. It might be difficult to show how respect increases profits, but it is clear that a lack of respect can turn away valued customers.

Business leaders who fail to show respect for others, especially their employees, seldom maintain their leadership over the long term. Others can sense the lack of respect and eventually reflect back the same feelings. We find it nearly impossible to trust those who disrespect us. Leaders must understand and acknowledge the Ethics of Respect.

Ethics of Conscience

Our conscience is our moral sense. It is our knowledge or sense of what is right and wrong, together with an urge to do what is right. When we violate our conscience, we feel guilty. We just "know" we have done something wrong. It doesn't "feel" right. Our inner voice tells us this is evil.

A man's conscience, like a warning line on the highway, tells him what he shouldn't do—but it does not keep him from doing it.

—Frank A. Clark, cartoonist

People argue over the source of our conscience, but most agree it is present. Our "gut" tells us when we are about to do something that violates our conscience. We may not be able to put this "sense" into words, but we might experience it as a tight feeling in our throat or stomach. Maybe our hands sweat or shake. We may find it difficult to look the other person in the eye. Our sense of conscience or our instinct for what is right seems to develop in many people as they age and gain wisdom and maturity. Letting your conscience be your guide requires some care, because you might be making a decision based on less than a thorough examination of the issues or with less-than-adequate experience. Beware of how you might confuse expedience for conscience.

Most of us can think of someone we want to consult when we have to sort out a moral dilemma. It is usually someone who is older, wiser, more experienced, and widely respected as a person of good character. It should be the goal of all leaders to become that sort of person.

Ethics of Rights

Most of us believe people are born with certain rights. Our Declaration of Independence asserts:

> *We hold these truths to be self-evident, that all men are created equal, that they are endowed by their Creator with certain unalienable rights, that among these are Life, Liberty, and the Pursuit of Happiness …*

In business, rights are often recorded onto legal documents such as labor contracts, contracts to sell or purchase, and other binding agreements. Whether documented or not, leaders must respect the rights of others.

Television and the movies often depict business leaders as having the power, and often the inclination, to fire people and make other serious choices in haste and without consulting others. In reality, most important business decisions are made after consultation with legal, financial, and other experts. In our litigious society, trampling on the rights of others will almost certainly land the leader in court, often at great expense to the leader personally and to the organization.

When a leader does decide it is the right thing to do to terminate someone, it is important the person is terminated in a way that he or she stays terminated. Imagine the blow to someone's leadership to have everyone know you have fired someone, only to have someone of higher rank or a court decide this was a wrongful termination and the person must be reinstated into their former position and be awarded damages. The key to many successful decisions is to first consider the rights of all others involved.

There are many rights that are not expressed in the law but still influence society. A consumer might claim the right to fair treatment, even if the situation is not clearly spelled out by the law. In much of the United States, consumers believe they have the right to return products for any reason. That is not necessarily true in a legal sense. Laws about return policy vary from state to state. But companies establish returns out of a sense of fairness and accept the practice as a cost of doing business. Customers have an implied right to expect a product to work as advertised. Also understood is that return policies of this kind should not be abused by the consumer. Companies have chosen to stop doing business with some consumers who abuse the return policy.

Some issues are expressed as rights when they are not expressed as law. For example, advocates for gay people contend domestic partners have a right to the same benefits as a legally married spouse. In some areas this is the law, and in other areas the law specifically prohibits it. Issues like these give leaders gray hair and believe they truly earn the big bucks.

> *Justice is justly represented blind, because she sees no difference in the parties concerned. She has but one scale and weight, for rich or poor, great and small. Her sentence is not guided by the person, but the cause … Impartiality is the life of justice, as that is of government.*
>
> *—William Penn, English entrepreneur and philosopher*

Ethics of Justice

The symbol of justice is the blindfolded lady holding a scale in one hand and a sword in the other. She is blindfolded because she is to be blind to everything but the factual evidence and the law. Lady Justice is not to be influenced by anything but the facts and the law.

Leaders must always be mindful of the facts and what is fair. Usually that means people are to be treated equally. For example, we have concepts such as equal pay for equal work. Today, many are questioning the pay of corporate executives, especially during times when many corporations are losing money. In many American corporations, the pay of top executives is measured in millions, while the salary of many workers actually doing the labor that is creating the organization's wealth is below the poverty level. Especially troubling, from an ethical standpoint, is the practice of top executives receiving millions in salary and bonuses during times when their organization is losing business, laying off thousands of employees, and the stock is plummeting. We have to question such leaders' sense of justice and fair play.

Virtue Ethics

Virtue ethics is centered on who you *are*, as opposed to what you *do*. You are to become a good person and good actions will naturally follow.

Instead of rules to specify what to do and not to do, virtue ethics suggests leaders first develop their personal character.

How does one become a person of virtue, a good person? It starts with good intentions, but it takes more than that. A place to start is with consideration of the cardinal virtues or basic virtues of ancient Greek philosophy: justice, prudence, fortitude, and temperance. Yet more to consider are the theological virtues of faith, hope, and charity.

A virtuous leader practices such virtues in everyday life and throughout life. At times business leaders have attempted to appear virtuous by making large gifts to charity. While being charitable with one's own money is virtuous, being charitable with corporate money does not make up for daily greed, pollution, and corruption.

Prevailing Attitudes

Much about ethics is culturally dependent. What seems to be right for one group of people might be very wrong for another. While ethics might be expressed in simple declarative sentences, it is really a more complex body of thought held by a population. It is a way of thinking, a way of doing things that has been learned over time. Any given culture has many people who contribute to the ethical dialog.

How well you are in tune with the prevailing ethics of your culture will have a lot to do with how your ideas and actions are accepted. Many people solve ethical dilemmas simply by going with the prevailing thought of their culture. That can be effective in the short term, but eventually a problem will present itself that has not been thoroughly examined by a culture. That is when character, personal strength, and a disciplined examination of what is fair are required of a leader. The way these issues are resolved goes a long way toward distinguishing the bad from the good leader.

The prevailing attitude of a culture is an important consideration, but the way to determine if a potential action is ethical or unethical is not to conduct a poll. What is popular is not necessarily what is right.

Might versus Right

Through the centuries, the predominant ethical system often has belonged to the culture that has the strongest army. The problems with such a condition were always clear to the cultures with the weaker army. This point was often lost on the victorious armies who believed, "To the victor belong the spoils."

The strength of a man's virtue must not be measured by his occasional efforts, but by his ordinary life.

—Blaise Pascal

The winners of wars write the history and get the loudest voices regarding what is right or wrong. Even our culture, which makes a point of studying issues like justice and fairness, has been accused by much of the rest of the world of being a bully. We sometimes appear to be forcing our will upon others by armed force or by threat of economic sanctions.

As a nation, the United States amounts to only about four percent of the world's population, yet we produce nearly 24 percent of the world's total carbon emissions. Such an imbalance seems unfair to much of the rest of the world. This is another example of how expedience can overwhelm a careful examination of what is fair. Even though the United States has been aware of pollution problems for decades, it has been a difficult task to reduce pollution that we know is hurting our health. Reversing this tide costs more than many people seem willing to pay.

Summary

The ethical dilemmas facing business leaders present great challenges. Business leaders must make the best possible decisions and make them quickly. They do not have the luxury of casual study; they need practical guidelines, not philosophical platitudes.

The highest proof of virtue is to possess boundless power without abusing it.

—Thomas B. Macaulay, British politician

As with any ethical discussion, this chapter has not provided a clear-cut answer to every moral dilemma, only a way to confront the issues. Dealing with ethics can be agonizing, because you are dealing with so many conflicting interests. You know you are doing a good job of being sensitive to all positions when you feel some of the pain of responsibility.

Ethical Decision Tree for Manager's Choice

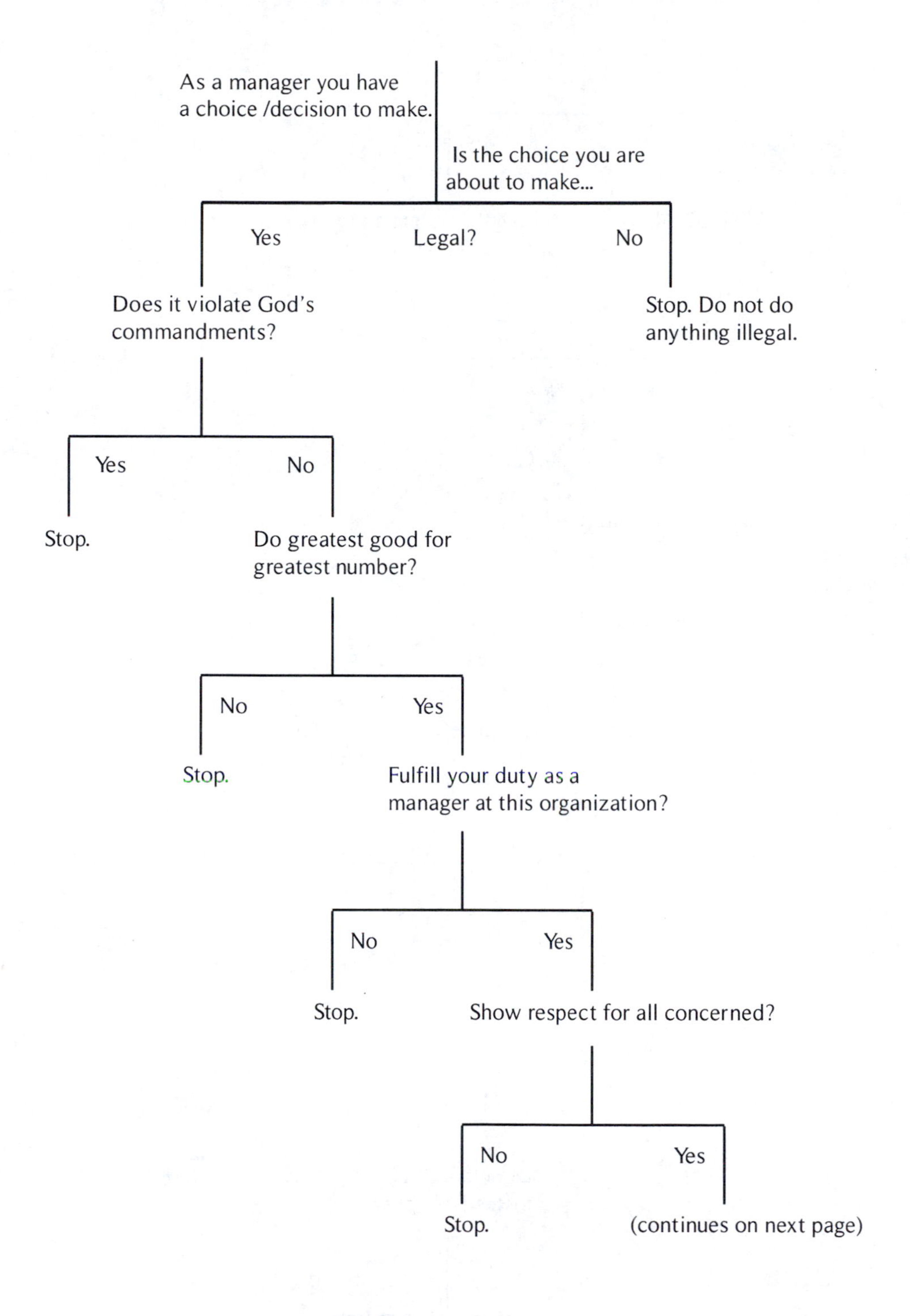

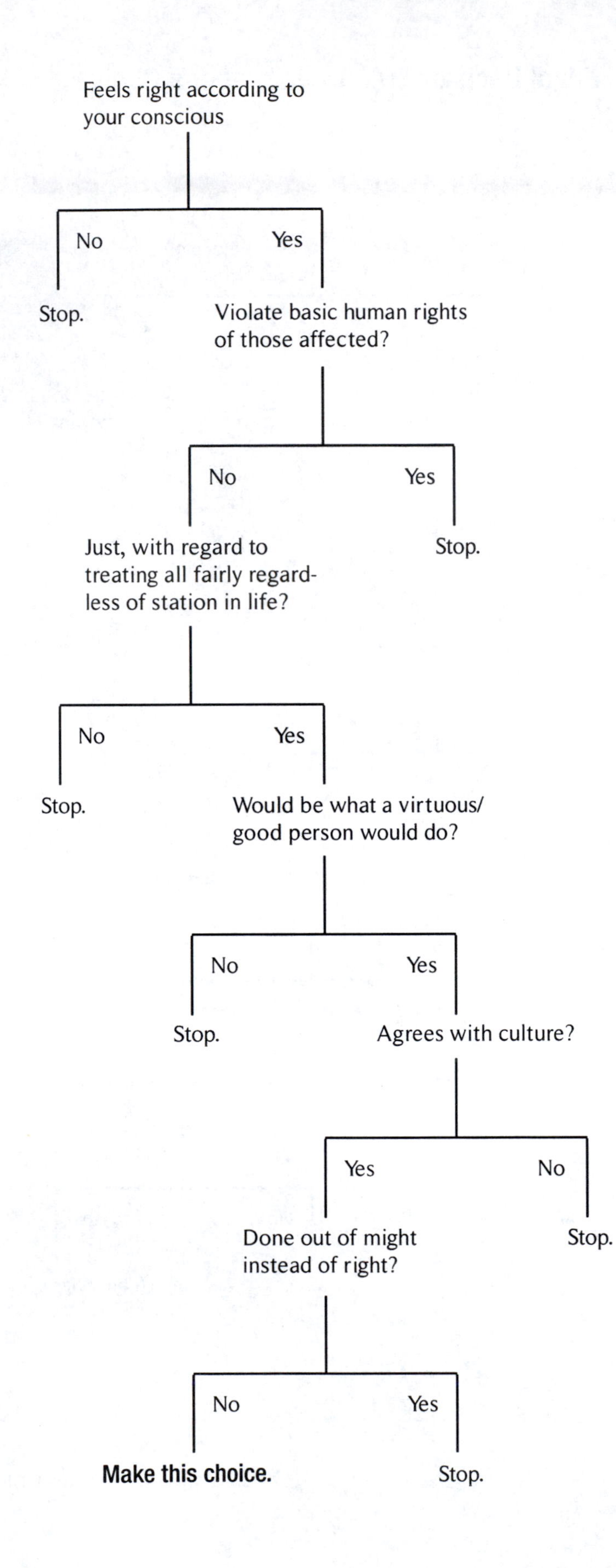
Feels right according to your conscious
No
Yes
Stop.
Violate basic human rights of those affected?
No
Yes
Just, with regard to treating all fairly regardless of station in life?
Stop.
No
Yes
Stop.
Would be what a virtuous/ good person would do?
No
Yes
Stop.
Agrees with culture?
Yes
No
Done out of might instead of right?
Stop.
No
Yes
Make this choice.
Stop.

Questions for Discussion

1. Discuss how you think someone like Bernie Madoff, in prison for embezzling $65 billion, might have felt upon learning that his son committed suicide.
2. Discuss what you think drove Cliff Baxter, vice chairman of Enron in 2002, to kill himself. What do you think could/should have been done to avoid the Enron tragedy?
3. This chapter contains numerous quotes regarding ethics. Discuss which quote stands out for you, and why.
4. Discuss the pros and cons of Milton Friedman's quote regarding profit being the one and only social responsibility of business.

Chapter 4

PLANNING

Planning involves determining where an organization is today, where it could be within a few years, what it would take to go from Point A to Point B, and what would it take to make it happen. This chapter will describe how this process has been used at many large businesses. However, the process applies to all sorts of organizations—even to you as an individual. Where are you today? Where do you want to be in five to seven years? What steps will it take to get you there? What combination of money, hard work, study, etc., will it take for you to get from where you are now to where you want to be? This chapter will help you decide.

When planning for a year, plant rice. When planning for a decade, plant trees. When planning for life, train and educate people.

—Chinese proverb

BASIC STEPS IN PLANNING

Regardless of the size and type of the organization, there are six basic steps in planning:

1. Analyze the situation (What is the problem and what is its cause?).
2. Generate alternatives (What are the possible approaches, goals, and processes regarding this problem or issue?).
3. Evaluate goals and plans (Which ones are feasible?).

The beginning is the most important part of the work.

—Plato, Greek philosopher and student of Socrates

4. Select goals and plans (Which one is best?).
5. Implement goals and plans (How do we get from Point A to Point B?).
6. Monitor and control performance (How do we stay on track until all goals are met?).

These basic six steps are how planning is typically done in all sorts of organizations. It is essentially the same whether the business is for profit or not for profit, whether large or small, and even if you are doing planning for yourself. Planning is planning.

Analyzing

Many planning projects begin with a problem. Perhaps the company is not growing as fast as key individuals would like. Perhaps changes in technology, customer preferences, economic conditions, the appointment of a new Chief Executive Officer, or something else causes the organization to decide it is time to create a new plan for the organization's future. The first step is to clearly establish Point A, the starting point or set of current conditions. For a business, this is usually done by describing the business size in terms of its annual gross revenue, market capitalization and number of employees. For example, Goodyear Tire & Rubber Co. recently had annual gross revenue of $16.3 billion, a market capitalization (price per share times the number of shares outstanding) of $2.83 billion, and 69,000 employees.

These and many other financial figures are typically analyzed to determine the organization's current conditions. A common concern is the company's market share, usually expressed as a percentage of the total sales of some item. For example, ABC, Inc. has 10 percent of the market for widgets. This means that when we consider all of the sales of widgets (the universal name given to a generic product), our company has sold 10 percent of them. The problem may be that this percentage is shrinking for our company and we need to analyze the situation to determine the cause and what to do about it.

Strengths, Weaknesses, Opportunities, and Threats

A common tool used at this initial planning stage is SWOT. *Strength* is something the organization does exceptionally well, or something it has that gives it a sustainable competitive advantage over the competition. For example, an organization may hold a valuable patent or own property in an especially good location. It may employ people with exceptional talents.

A *weakness* is, of course, the opposite of a strength. It is something your organization is missing or does not do well. Because of this weakness, our competition gains a competitive advantage over us. Examples include a lack of brand awareness for our products, the lack of a unique product to offer our customers, or a location that makes it hard for our customers to reach us.

An *opportunity* is something we could buy or build that could give us a future competitive advantage. It may include expanding into a new market area, hiring an especially talented employee, or marketing a new product or service our customers really need or want.

A *threat* would be anything that could reduce our revenues or substantially increase our expenses. The change in a government regulation could make it more difficult to manufacture one or more of our products. Changes in consumer preferences could threaten our market share.

Doing a proper SWOT analysis takes time and research skills. It looks easy but it is not. People with a long history of being employed within an organization are often blind to threats and overly optimistic about opportunities. Identifying strengths and weaknesses requires a thorough, objective internal search. Finding the opportunities and threats requires an external search. You first examine the close-in or micro environment of your industry and close rivals. Then you expand to consider the macro or broader environment of the economy, government regulations, and general business climate.

SWOT analysis can also be applied to you. What are your personal strengths, weaknesses, opportunities, and threats? Since you are taking this course, one of your strengths could soon be your knowledge of management and leadership principles and concepts. Another could be your grade point average. Your ability to work in teams, your public speaking skill, and your ability to write correctly and concisely could all be strengths. Identifying your weaknesses could help you address them. If, for example, you are afraid of public speaking, joining an organization such as Toastmasters could help you overcome that fear. An opportunity for you could be the jobs that will soon be opening up as the country switches from fossil fuels to the various alternative energy sources such as solar and wind. Another could be the ever growing health care needs of an aging population. Threats include the globalization of the economy and the competition from highly educated workers from many other nations, economic recessions, and the ever changing technology.

Goals

Whether you are planning for a billion-dollar business or yourself, most experts agree, you need to use *SMART* goals that are *Specific*, *Measurable*, *Attainable*, *Relevant*, and *Timely*. For example, right now most students should be thinking in terms of when you plan to graduate, what kinds of profession you want to be in, whether you want to be in a big-, medium-, or small-sized firm, whether you want to live in Akron, Ohio, or New York, New York, or Paris, France, or someplace else. What salary do you hope to have five years after you graduate? What level of responsibility do you hope to obtain within ten years of your graduation? All of these goals are likely to change, but that does not mean they are not important.

For the typical business, specific goals would include annual gross revenue or sales figures, target earnings per share, a particular return on investment, etc. They would be measurable in dollars or percentages and would be tied to specific dates. If a large business is currently experiencing earnings per share of $1.10, it would not be reasonable to target EPS of $20 next year; it would not be considered attainable in such a short time. Making such financial targets relevant to all employees is a challenge.

If you don't care where you are going, then any road will get you there.

—*Lewis Carroll, author of* Alice's Adventures in Wonderland

Most employees will not be stockholders in the firm, so getting them excited about increasing the EPS is unlikely. Typically, business leaders convert such financial targets into a competitive comparison such as beating our main rival, XYZ, Inc. in terms of market share. Finally, goals are more effective if a time deadline is set. Otherwise, it is just too easy to keep putting important things off. This is true for students assigned a term paper and it is also true for business executives striving for that elusive target that always seems to be just around the corner.

Evaluate Goals and Plans

Most individuals and organizations have multiple goals, but not all are of the same value. Having too many goals, especially goals of equal value to you, is counterproductive. For individuals, experts agree that it is best to have just a few, typically less than ten. However, a useful exercise for your personal planning is to list 50 or 60 and then put them into categories such as Professional, Family, Health, Wealth, Spiritual, Travel, etc. A priority can be given to each category and within each category to each specific goal. For a large corporation, the categories might include goals for Sales, Growth, Financial Strength, Profitability, Efficiency, and Management Effectiveness.

By failing to prepare, you are preparing to fail.

—*Benjamin Franklin, one of the Founding Fathers of the United States*

After a clear picture has been drawn of the target, the next step is to plot a clear path to that target. That path is called the plan. A key element in evaluating alternative plans is to attach a cost to each alternative. Of course, these costs will only be estimates, but the process of assigning some reasonable cost estimates to each alternative will typically reveal that some alternatives would simply be beyond the reach of the organization. A key question to ask of any organization considering various plans is, "Where will the money come from?" The annual budgeting process typically allocates every dollar of expected revenue into some budget category. It is not possible to greatly increase some category without pulling money away from some other category. Perhaps production costs can be reduced by using more efficient technology, and those savings can be used to expand the business into a new market territory. The plan is not complete until the costs and sources of funds have been clearly identified. Once the costs and benefits of each alternative have been determined, then some alternatives can usually be eliminated from further consideration.

We can't forget about Chapter 3 and the topic of ethics. Some goals simply aren't worth it. A short-term increase in profits that comes at the expense of the organization's reputation is a poor bargain.

If ethics were of no concern to the executives of an organization, the most profitable alternative might be to get into the prostitution or illegal drug business. On the other hand, it is important not to get so restrictive that great opportunities are summarily dismissed based on one person's extra-lofty values. A business is not a charitable organization. It must make money for the shareholders if it expects to stay in business for long. So, the challenge is to select alternative plans that are in line with the organization's values, yet profitable to shareholders. This balancing act is never easy.

The old adage "If it's not broken, don't fix it" should not apply to business. As John F. Kennedy said, "The time to fix the roof is when the sun is shining." Do not wait until there is an emergency. Do not assume that because your business is currently profitable that you should just stay the course. Any corporation on the stock market needs to keep growing to satisfy investors. Competitors are constantly trying to steal away your market share. Just because things are going well right now is no excuse for ignoring the challenges of the future. When things are going well is likely when the business has sufficient financial resources to invest in the future.

In summary, this step in the planning process involves evaluating a set of plans to determine which plan gets you to your goals effectively, efficiently, and ethically. Remember the 3 E's: Effective, Efficient, and Ethical. All three are critical. None can be ignored.

Select Goals and Plans

Planners have to accept the fact that a decision has to be made, even though the future is uncertain. Most planners consider three scenarios: Optimistic, Pessimistic, and Most Likely. Typically, the optimistic scenario assumes the general economy will be robust and sales will be at the highest estimated levels and expenses will be at the lowest. Naturally, the pessimistic scenario is the opposite. What should we do if the economy fails and sales fall off to our lowest forecast? What will we do if expenses escalate? What if everything that can go wrong does go wrong, and at the worst possible moment? Will the organization survive? Somewhere between these extremes lies the most likely scenario. After every effort has been made to consider all the alternatives, a decision has to be made. Writers, academics, and think-tank experts have the luxury of just analyzing situations. Business managers have to decide. Do not fall victim to analysis paralysis, and fail to make a timely decision. Keep in mind that business organizations operate in a highly competitive environment. While you are analyzing and analyzing some more, your competition is moving forward. They may grab that great opportunity while you are continuing to analyze. Again, balance is the key. Business leaders have to objectively and thoroughly analyze, but they also must make timely decisions with imperfect information about what the future holds.

Implement Goals and Plans

Business leaders also have to be implementers. Having a good idea is not good enough. Making the proper decision is not good enough. You have to put ideas into action. In most situations, the key element to a successful implementation of a plan is to properly allocate money and people. The key document is the annual budget. A wise business manager once claimed, "If your budget for next year is the same as it was for last year, then your plan for next year is to do what you did last year."

The other key element is people. Most major changes involve having people perform different tasks. Workers are typically moved from one department to another as plans dictate. Job descriptions may need to be rewritten. People may have to report to a new boss. Expectations for raises and promotions may have to change to reflect the new corporate goals. If the necessary talents are not to be found or developed within the organization, then they must be recruited from the outside. The key concept to remember is that if you don't move money and/or people, then nothing changes.

Monitor and Control Performance

Managers must keep the ship on course. As the organization leaves Point A to go toward Point B, management must keep track of progress and make any necessary mid-course corrections. One wise business leader compared this challenge to "Changing tires on your car while it is speeding down the freeway at 70 miles per hour." Most businesses cannot afford to stop everything they are doing to go in a new direction. The flow of cash into the business must be maintained in much the same manner that you must keep blood flowing in your body at all times. Business leaders need to keep selling the old product while the new product is being marketed. It is similar to watching relay runners passing the baton while running at full speed. The competition is not going to stop to give you time to change.

If it takes several months or even years to fully implement a corporation's new plan, then expect many changes within that time. The competition is likely to see what changes you are making and do the same. The economy is seldom stable for long; we are almost always in a period of either recession or growth. Any plot of our nation's economic condition over time looks like the mathematical sine wave with lots of ups and downs. The only questions are, how long and deep will the recession be, or how high will the recovery go and how long will it last until another recession sets in. Most companies are similar to a surfer riding the ocean waves up and down. The ocean is seldom calm; neither is the economy. It takes skill and courage to ride either.

> *Trust, but verify.*
>
> *—Ronald Reagan, 40th president of the United States*

Customer preferences also change rapidly. Some industries, such as the electronic gaming industry, experience more rapid customer preference changes than more stable industries such as the food and beverage industry. People are still eating foods high in fat and salt, even though studies prove they are harmful to our health. In contrast, once a new electronic game hits the market, sales for the outdated game practically halt overnight.

Changes in technology have been the factor that has made or broken many companies. According to Moore's Law, the number of transistors that can be fitted on an integrated circuit doubles every two years. As a consequence, processing speed and memory capacity also increases rapidly. The law is named after the cofounder of Intel, Gordon E. Moore. To some extent the forecast is almost bound to come true, because the semiconductor industry uses Moore's Law as a forecasting device in their internal planning. Such a rapid pace of new technology, especially in computers, makes it nearly impossible to predict how new technologies will require us to alter our long-term plans.

Available resources (especially money and people-power) are also likely to change during the implementation of a long-term plan. Anticipated revenue may fall short. Expenses may grow. Talented people may move on to better positions or to rival firms. Sometimes, adding resources to a new project can speed up implementation. However, some simply need time to develop. It is similar to the process of having a baby. No matter how many women you put on the task, it still takes nine months. Creative processes often require gestation time. Telling the songwriter to hurry up is not likely to result in a better song.

Basic Company Strategies

Today, major corporations use a wide variety of corporate-wide, long-term strategies. We will consider the most widely used. A fundamental decision practically all businesses have to make is whether to use a strategy of low cost so they can sell their products or services in large quantities to cost-conscious buyers or to aim for the customer who demands high quality and is willing to pay a higher price.

Low-Cost Provider Strategy (Wal-Mart)

Wal-Mart is one of the most successful *low-cost providers* of all time. Do not confuse the strategy of being a low-cost provider with being the business that sells for the lowest price. Any business can simply lower the price they charge for their goods or services and operate on a lower gross margin. The *margin* is the term, expressed as a percentage, applied to the difference between the cost of the good being sold and the selling price divided by the selling price (Gross margin = (Revenue – Cost of Goods Sold)/Revenue). If a business manufactures a product for $9 and sells it for $10, the margin is $1, or 10%. If this business lowers the price of the item to $9.50 while the cost of goods sold stays the same, the gross margin drops to 5%—not a wise move.

I believe in the Wal-Mart school of business. The less people pay, the more they enjoy it.

—Garth Brooks, country music singer

The wise move is to lower the cost of goods sold. Using the above example, if the company can reduce the cost of the good they sell from $9 to $8.50 while keeping the price to the consumer the same ($10), then the gross margin becomes 15%. Wal-Mart works with the companies that manufacture the products they sell to get their costs as low as possible. It is not nearly as simple as just reducing the price to the ultimate customer, but it is much more effective.

Differentiate Your Product or Service and Charge a Higher Price (Cadillac)

The key to competing and surviving against Wal-Mart is to focus your business into a niche or pocket where you can leverage your strengths in the local marketplace.

—Michael Bergdahl, former executive at Wal-Mart

How do many smaller businesses compete successfully with Wal-Mart? The secret is to differentiate your product so it is different from and better than what customers can purchase from Wal-Mart. Differentiation can be in terms of the quality of the product or in the customer service your business provides. For example, a business that specializes in specialty food products such as high-quality wines, cheeses, and snack items may successfully exist right next to a Wal-Mart store as long as the customers know of the difference in quality you offer and have a reason to care about that higher quality. A tiny bed and breakfast can compete with a major motel chain as long as customers know about and care about and are willing to pay extra for the added charm and personal attention provided by the people running the bed and breakfast retreat. This approach is not limited to small businesses. Lord & Taylor uses a differentiation strategy to attract customers looking for high fashion. Cadillac buyers expect a differentiated product in terms of luxury. When thinking about increasing the quality of a product or service, think first about what the customer would value.

Concentrate on Doing One Thing Exceptionally (Starbucks)

Some businesses have been successful focusing on doing one thing exceptionally well. Starbucks has a focus on coffee. Of course, you can buy a few other items at Starbucks, but the focus is on the flavor and aroma of their particular brand of coffee. In fact, the allure of the aroma is such a major factor in drawing in customers that Starbucks has a rule preventing individual Starbucks stores from cooking other items that might change the smell of the store. Starbucks today employs over 137,000 people in more than 17,000 stores in over 50 countries. Total annual revenues are over $10 billion—not bad for a little coffee shop.

Expand through Acquisition (Smuckers)

Quality in a product or service is not what the supplier puts in. It is what the customer gets out and is willing to pay for.

—Peter Drucker

Some companies use their financial strength to buy other companies, using an expansion through acquisition strategy. In 1897 Jerome Smucker started pressing apples into cider and apple butter at his farm in Orville, Ohio. Within the past few years this company, known primarily for making jams and jellies, has expanded through acquisition of Jif, Crisco, and Folgers, to name just a few. Annual total revenue for J. M. Smucker Company is nearly $5 billion. This little jam-and-jelly company today employs 4,850 people and is often ranked by *Fortune* among the top ten places to work in the United States.

Expand through Globalization (Avon)

Over the past several years, many American businesses have looked toward China's population of over 1.3 billion people and their growing economy as the ideal place to expand through globalization. Of course, China is not the only target for expansion through globalization, but it does represent the greatest potential simply because of the size of their population and because China's government used to severely restrict foreign investment. Now that China is more open to globalization, many businesses find the temptation hard to resist. Andrea Jung, former CEO of Avon Products, Inc., maker and marketer of cosmetics such as lipstick and makeup, decided to expand into China a few years ago. Avon currently employs over 200,000 sales representatives in China and operates 5,500 beauty boutiques (small stores mostly within malls). Many business executives, including Jung, who speaks Mandarin and has a Chinese father, have found the going rough in China. The Chinese government, while not as anti-American as previous regimes, is still capable of suddenly changing the rules and making life difficult for non-Chinese businesses. However, for those who are successful at overseas expansion, the growth can be dramatic.

Conglomerate Diversification (GE)

A conglomerate is a company composed of many businesses, often in unrelated industries. For example, in some years, especially during the tenure of former CEO Jack Welch, General Electric purchased over 100 companies. Today, GE is involved in products and services ranging from aircraft engines, power generation, water processing, household appliances, medical imaging, and many more. It operates in more than 100 countries and employs over 300,000 people. What is so unusual about GE's corporate strategy is how it has been so successful in so many different industries. Welch put a lot of emphasis on training his key managers in the areas of management and leadership and believed he had the best managers in the world. If he found a business that he could purchase at a rock-bottom price and install his managers to run the company more effectively and efficiently, then he could increase stockholder wealth regardless of the industry. While this corporate strategy worked remarkably well for Jack Welch during his 20 years at the helm of GE, it is a high-risk strategy that only a few organizations have found successful.

Boston Consulting Group (Cash Cows, Dogs, Question Marks, and Stars)

The Boston Consulting Group (BCG) is famous for putting businesses into the four categories of cash cows, dogs, question marks, and stars. BCG uses a graph where relative market share is plotted against the market growth rate. A cash cow is a business that has a relatively high market share, but the market growth rate is low. Cash cows generate cash that can be used in other business units. Dogs are business units where the company has a small market share in a business where the market growth is low. Dogs should be sold to generate cash to be used more productively elsewhere. A question mark is a business unit with a small market share in a market with high growth potential. Cash from cash cows and from the sale of dogs should be invested in selected question marks in the hopes of growing them into stars. A star is a business unit with a large market share in a fast growing market. The BCG matrix provides a framework for allocating resources among the different business units within a conglomerate. A key point is to properly support (feed and care for) cash cows so they can generate cash to be invested in selected question marks so they can grow into stars. The second key point is to sell off all dogs. The use of the "dog" symbol is important, because people who own and love dogs often are extremely reluctant to part with their beloved dogs, even when the dog is sick and old. BCG urges business leaders to avoid emotional attachment to a product and realize that it is not good business management to waste money on business units with no future.

> *If you pick the right people and give them the opportunity to spread their wings and put compensation as a carrier behind it you almost don't have to manage them.*
>
> *—Jack Welch, former CEO, General Electric*

Summary

Planning is key to successful business management and to your personal career management. Learn how to objectively describe your current status. Be specific about your future goals. Outline specific steps that will take you from your current status to your future goals. Be prepared to make changes to your plans as the situation changes, but never underestimate the value of planning for organizations of all sizes and types and for yourself.

Questions for Discussion

1. What are the basic steps in planning, regardless of the size and type of organization? How could you apply these steps to planning for your own future?
2. How would you apply SWOT analysis to a study of some familiar organizations such as your school, church, or club?
3. A good goal is one that is SMART (Specific, Measurable, Attainable, Relevant, and Timely). How would you apply the concept of SMART to your personal goals in life?
4. Select a familiar company and match that company's strategy with one of the common strategies of low-cost provider differentiation, concentration, acquisition, globalization, or conglomeration. Explain why you think the company has chosen that particular strategy.

Chapter 5

Organizing: How To Build An Effective Organizational Structure

Imagine you have been given the job of building an organizational chart for a small company or a new division of a large organization. Where do you start? What choices of types of organizational structure should you consider? Are some organizational structures better than others? Would your chart be tall and skinny, or short and fat? Would you centralize power and authority, or decentralize it? This chapter addresses such questions.

In the successful organization, no detail is too small to escape close attention.

—Lou Holtz, former football coach, Notre Dame

In the Beginning

Before the Industrial Revolution, teams of craftsmen worked on building a product, such as a buggy or a sewing machine, and stayed with the product as it was being assembled until the final product was put together. In the early 1900s Henry Ford and others introduced the concept of the assembly line where the product moved along a belt or chain and each worker was assigned a work station where he sat or stood still while the product moved along the assembly line from worker to worker. Workers at the beginning of the line often were so far removed from the end of the line that they really did not even see the finished product. Communication between workers was difficult in the noisy factory, where workers were required to stay at their work stations. This approach, called the *separation of labor*, resulted in workers developing great skill at a very limited number of tasks. It created great efficiency and manufactured products much faster than previously thought possible. However, managers were the only ones who could walk from work station to work station communicating to workers and to the other managers. In a complicated assembly process—for example, the assembly of an automobile—specialized departments developed where engine parts were assembled, or the car body was painted or the seats were made. Some structure was needed to coordinate all these separate workers and tasks.

> *A place for everything, and everything in its place.*
>
> *—Isabella Mary Beeton, author of books on household management*

Max Weber's Bureaucratic Structure

Max Weber (1864–1920) was a German sociologist and economist who was fanatic about order. His ideal form of organization for a business or a governmental agency was a hierarchical organization delineated by clear lines of authority, written rules, and administrators who strictly enforced the rules.

Building an Organizational Chart

The abbreviated organizational chart shown below includes boxes that represent different jobs within the organization and their relationship to each other. At the top is the Chief Executive Officer with

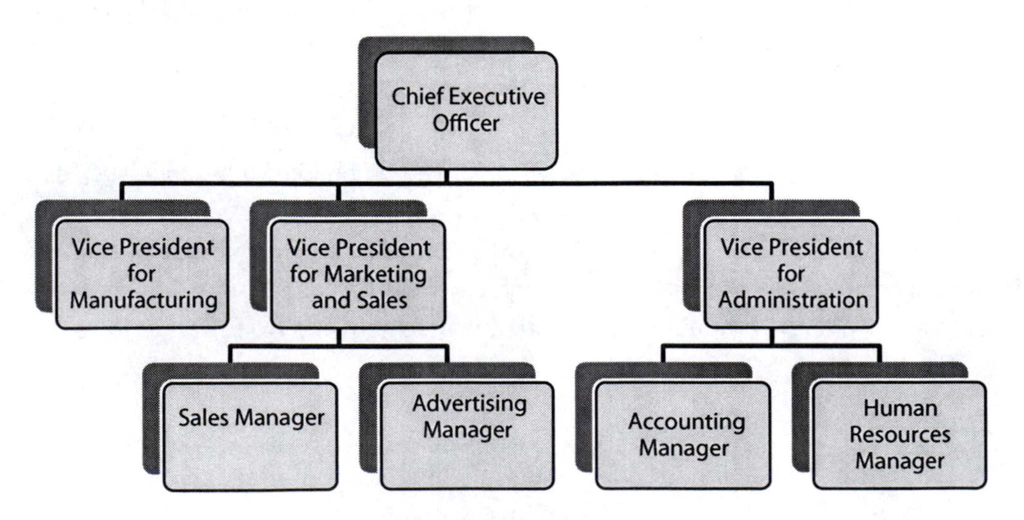

the highest level of authority. At the next level are the Vice Presidents of the major divisions within the firm. At the lowest level on this chart are the mid-level managers. The lines connecting the boxes represent lines of authority and communication. For example, the Accounting Manager reports to the Vice President for Administration, who, in turn, reports to the Chief Executive Officer. Not shown are the workers who report to the managers.

A *tall organizational chart* typically means there are many layers of managers between the workers and the CEO. A recent trend has been toward a *short, fat chart* with fewer layers and a broader span of control (more workers reporting to each manager). The other recent trend in organizational structure has been a movement away from the more formal and rigid structure toward one that is flexible and informal. When the organizational structure is rigid and inflexible, it is called *mechanistic*. A more modern and more flexible structure is referred to as *organic*. An organic structure is more informal, and uses teamwork where managers work more like coaches than bosses. Strange as it may seem, some people don't like the organic, informal approach, and prefer the clarity of authority of the old-fashioned, mechanistic way. Many companies today have various combinations of these two basic approaches.

Over the past several years, many American businesses have attempted to reduce the layers of management in an attempt to streamline the structure, so the organizational charts of many U.S. companies have recently grown shorter—that is, there are fewer layers and each manager has a broader span of control with more people reporting to him or her. Large corporations such as GE and GM used to have around 25 to 30 levels in their organizational charts, but today have much fewer.

To understand a discussion of the various types of organizational structures and the pros and cons of each, it is necessary to understand several terms. *Differentiation* is a term used to describe how a large organization is composed of many different units that work on different kinds of tasks using diverse skills and work methods. *Integration* means these differentiated units are put back together so that work is coordinated into an overall product. The assignment of different tasks to different people or groups is called the *division of labor*. *Specialization* is the process in which different individuals and units perform different tasks and develop high skills at those tasks. *Coordination* refers to the procedures that link the various parts of an organization to achieve the organization's overall mission.

Span of control refers to the number of subordinates who report directly to a manager or supervisor. A tall organizational structure typically implies a narrow span of control while a flat organizational structure will have wider spans. The span of control can be wide when the work is clearly defined and unambiguous. Because subordinates know what they are supposed to do, it is not necessary to have as many managers closely overseeing their activities. Also, the span can be wide if the subordinates are highly trained and have access to needed information, the manager is capable and supportive, jobs are similar and performance measures comparable, and when subordinates prefer autonomy to close supervisory control. When one or more of these conditions is not present, then a narrow span of control is more ideal. In an effort to cut costs, many businesses recently have gone to a wide span of control, but have not properly considered the disadvantages and have not properly prepared their supervisors and their employees to handle the decreased supervision. Loss of managerial control is often the result. So, as a manager, do not force your supervisors to manage more workers without considering the pros and cons and properly preparing both the workers and the supervisors.

Delegation is the assignment of new or additional responsibilities to a subordinate. As a manager, you must learn how to properly delegate, because it is through delegation that you use the talents of others to get more work done. New managers often find it hard to delegate; they may prefer to just do the work themselves because they are afraid the work will not be done correctly or on time. However, to be a successful manager, you must learn to properly delegate. A key aspect of proper delegation is understanding the concepts of responsibility, authority, and accountability. *Responsibility* means a person is assigned a task and is supposed to carry it out. *Authority* means a person has the power and the right to make decisions, give orders, draw on resources, and do whatever else is necessary to fulfill the responsibility of his or her mangerial position. *Accountability* means the subordinate's manager has the right to expect the subordinate to perform the job, and that manager has the right to take corrective action if the subordinate fails to do so. The manager has the responsibility to check and follow through to make certain the subordinate has properly performed the assigned task.

New managers often complain that they are being held accountable and must take responsibility, but do not have as much authority as they think they need to make decisions, give orders, hire, fire, reward, and in all ways use their managerial power to get the job done. Part of the problem lies in the difference in how most schoolwork is expected to be done, versus how work in the business world is expected to be done. At school most students do their own work and do not have others do it for them. In fact, it would be called cheating if you were discovered working together on some school assignments, or worse, you hired someone to do the work for you. However, in the work world, managers are expected to do much more than they could possibly do by themselves. To be a successful manager, you must learn how to let others do the work while you do the work of a manager. As you develop as a manager and can prove to others that you can motivate others to work with the necessary speed, accuracy, and concern for quality, then your authority will likely be gradually increased. Be patient. This takes time. However, you must not fall out of your role as manager and back into your more comfortable role as a student or as a worker and just do the work yourself. You may need to demonstrate to others how the job must be done and it is okay to pitch in and help, especially when a worker is experiencing difficulty with the task, but it is not okay to fail to properly delegate.

Centralize versus Decentralize

In a highly *centralized organization*, important decisions are made at the top of the organizational structure with little or no input from below. In contrast, in a *decentralized organization* many decisions are made at lower levels and people further down the organizational hierarchy feel empowered. All the power is not concentrated at the top but is distributed more evenly throughout the organizational structure with many decisions made close to where the actual work is being done.

Many organizations have moved back and forth between a centralized and a decentralized approach. Organizations especially tend to move toward the centralized model during hard times. At other times, the switch is due to a change in leadership at the top. If the previous CEO was dismissed for some failure and that CEO had presided over a decentralized approach, the new CEO is likely to reverse that course to compensate for the errors of the previous CEO. It is likely the new CEO was hired specifically to reverse the course set by the previous CEO. In still other cases, the executives at the top may say they are in favor of decentralization, but their actions show this is just talk. If they say they favor decentralization but keep all the budget decisions at the top, then they are just talking the talk and not walking the walk. In many organizations there is a lot of that.

Line versus Staff

In the terminology of organizational structure, a *line* position is one where the manager has direct responsibility for a principal activity of the firm. In contrast, a *staff* position is one that provides specialized or professional skill and advice in support of the line departments. In your climb up the organizational ladder, be careful not to get stuck for long in a staff position. People in the line positions tend to look down on those in staff positions and people without line experience are seldom promoted to executive-level positions. In general, staff people give advice; line people actually make the decisions regarding budgets, purchases, staffing, etc. However, be careful when you first get into a line position, because your legal liability is also likely to go up. For example, if you are the one with the line authority to make hiring and firing decisions, you are much more likely to get sued by someone who has been fired and is mad—which is about 100% of the time.

No matter how you fire people, the result is always the same. They will hate you.

—Donald Trump, entrepreneur and television personality

Four Basic Types of Organizational Structures

There are an unlimited number of possibilities for organizing large businesses, but there are four basic types of organizational structures: functional, divisional, matrix, and network. We will briefly examine the pros and cons of each.

Functional

The *functional organization structure* is organized around basic business functions such as purchasing, manufacturing, marketing, finance, information technology, and human resources. It groups people together that are similarly educated (all marketing people are in the marketing department, all accounting people are in the accounting department, etc.). This can produce very strong functional departments with lots of specialists who enjoy working together on related tasks. Very small organizations of less than 25 employees are seldom organized functionally. However, as an organization grows much larger, it is common for such functional grouping to gradually grow. Universities typically use a functional organizational structure grouping teachers of English in the English Department, teachers of accounting in the Accounting Department, etc. College teachers typically prefer to be grouped with others who teach similar subjects. Around most universities, departments consist of about 25 professors. When a department gets a lot larger than 25, it is often split into two departments. Other organizations have similar rules of thumb in terms of expected size of a department.

The U.S. Army has traditionally used an organizational structure composed of a squad (9–10 soldiers commanded by a sergeant), a platoon (16–44 soldiers led by a lieutenant), company (62–190 soldiers commanded by a captain), battalion (300–1,000 soldiers led by a lieutenant colonel), brigade (3,000–5,000 soldiers commanded by a colonel), division (10,000 to 15,000 soldiers commanded by a major general, corps (20,000–45,000 soldiers commanded by a lieutenant general, and army (50,000+ soldiers commanded by a lieutenant general or higher. Immediately after World War II, many American business organizations followed similar patterns and often employed former military officers to become managers in factories, laboratories, and offices. The general idea was that, since the United States was successful in winning World War II, the organizational structure used by the U.S. Army must be a good way to structure other types of organizations. In the 1960s and 1970s, the army style faded, and several other approaches were introduced. However, this general approach is still popular in many industries. Unfortunately, the idea of the first-level manager ordering employees around like a staff sergeant commanding an army squad has not completely died.

Divisional Organizational Structure

The *divisional organizational structure* is really a collection of types of divisional groupings. Common ones include divisions based on product, customer, or geographic region. If a business makes several different and unique products requiring specialized skills, then organizing into divisions based on type of product makes sense. If, for example, a company makes aircraft parts, farm equipment, and heavy construction equipment, it is logical to organize the company into these three divisions because each division is so unique.

Another logical approach to the divisional organizational structure is to organize into divisions based on the firm's major customer types. Some companies sell some of their products directly to the ultimate consumer but also sell to other businesses. For example, Goodyear Tire & Rubber Co. sells car tires to people like you and me. They also sell to automobile manufacturers such as Ford Motor Co. I don't know about you, but I've never bought more than four tires at a time, while Ford Motor Co. buys tires by the thousands. Also, as a new model of car is being designed, the design of the tire is part of that new design process. To sell to a major automobile manufacturer such as Ford or General Motors, Goodyear has to work with the designers of upcoming car models to produce tires that meet the car manufacturer's exact specifications. In such cases, it makes sense to have one division for Original Equipment Manufacturers (OEMs) and another division for consumers.

Yet another common approach to divisional organizational structure is by geographic region. For example, a company that operates around the world may have divisions such as North America, South America, Europe, Asia, and Africa. A smaller company working just within the United States may have divisions such as West Coast, Middle America, and East Coast. This approach may be necessary if each geographic area is unique and requires specific changes to products, services, or processes. However, if a company sells exactly the same thing to customers everywhere, then it makes less sense to use a geographic divisional structure.

Matrix Organizational Structure

The *matrix organizational structure* is a combination of the functional and divisional structures where some employers report to two managers—a functional manager plus a divisional manager. Many huge corporations use a matrix organizational structure simply because they are so complex that nothing else will really work for them. To read a matrix organizational chart, you must read it from top to bottom for one dimension and from left to right for another. Often, it reads like a functional structure vertically and a divisional structure horizontally. Resource utilization is efficient, because key resources can be shared across several important programs or products at the same time. As a new employee, you may find the matrix structure annoying, because you will have to report to two bosses, one vertically and one horizontally. However, it can also be a good way for you to learn how things operate from two points of view. Also, it may provide you with more career options since you can more forward either through the functional route (for example, being an accountant who moves up to higher and higher levels of accounting responsibility) or the department route (for instance, being an accountant who also gets the opportunity to move into marketing or other areas within the department). Finally, learning how to operate with two bosses can be a valuable learning experience in gaining diplomacy that may serve you well later as you move up the corporate ladder.

Network Organizational Structure

A *network organization* is a collection of organizations that work together to produce a good or a service. It looks more like a web than a pyramid. Examples of network organizations include arrangements among designers, suppliers, producers, distributors, and customers, where each independent unit is able to pursue its own distinctive core competency, yet work effectively with the other members of the network. Often the glue that holds such a complex network together is the computer network that provides the communication structure.

The big advantage of the network organizational structure is flexibility. It is especially well suited to organizations where much of the work can be done independently by experts. If properly structured, the network approach can enhance innovation; provide a quick response to threats and opportunities; and reduce costs and risks. The overall network must choose collaborators that are excellent at what they do and provide complementary strengths. The overall network must also make certain that all parts of the network fully understand the overall goals. Each party in the network must trust all the other parties to deliver their individual goods and services at the required level of quality, on time, and within budget. As a new manager, the network structure may seem confusing at first, but it can offer you a great opportunity to see many more different parts of the organization. You are not as isolated into silos as with the more traditional organizational structures.

The Informal Organizational Structure

Most organizations have two organizational structures: the formal one as written on charts, and the everyday relationships of men and women working together within the organization. In some organizations, especially those with rigid structures and multiple layers of authority, enterprising employees have figured out ways around the stodgy bureaucracy. They know how to "get things done." As a new employee, it is wise to learn about both the formal and the informal organizational structures where you work. There will be times when understanding each, and being effective in using each, will be important for your advancement within the organization. So, study the formal organizational charts, but also ask around. Find out what personal relationships are vital to making things happen within the organization.

Summary

The organizational structure should help the organization achieve its goals. It should make communication easier among the various departments and divisions. It should address the need to serve customers better than our rivals. As a new employee, it is important to get the "lay of the land." Understand the organizational structure of your organization. Learn how all the pieces are put together. Do not become one of the many who merely complain about the stodgy old bureaucracy. Learn how it works and how you can be effective within it.

Questions for Discussion

1. Select an organization you are familiar with such as your college or the place where you work. Draw its organizational structure, and describe the type of structure (functional, divisional, matrix, or network).
2. Describe a situation you have experienced, either as the supervisor or the subordinate, where a problem of delegation occurred. What should have happened to make the lines of authority and responsibility clearer for all?
3. If you have experienced an organization changing from a highly centralized to decentralized organizational structure, or vice versa, what issues arose? How were those issues resolved? How should they have been resolved?

Part I

READINGS

Motivating Employees

By Sharlyn J. Lauby

Lee Iacocca once said, "When I must criticize somebody, I do it orally; when I praise somebody, I put it in writing."

That's one method to motivate employees, but different needs motivate different people. Some employees crave power, others want money. Some employees desire constant praise, others want to be left alone. It's crucial for managers to figure out what motivates each employee.

Motivation is defined as a psychological force that determines the following:

- The direction of a person's behavior: This refers to the many possible behaviors in which an employee could engage. For example, an employee who knows what to do to satisfy a customer's needs should not have to ask for his or her manager's permission to act.
- A person's level of effort: Effort refers to how hard people work. Some employees exert a high level of effort to provide superior customer service.
- A person's level of persistence in the face of obstacles: Persistence refers to whether, when faced with roadblocks and obstacles, people keep trying or give up. If an employee did not have a customer's order in stock, for example, would he or she give up and apologize to the customer, or would the employee persist and locate the order at another store?

This issue starts where *Infoline* No. 259108, "How to Motivate Employees," starts: with a primer on motivational theories that have been updated and expanded. Based on these theories, this *Infoline* then presents ways to integrate motivation into the workplace, strategies to motivate employees, and common mistakes managers make.

Motivational Theories

Several motivational theories exist that can provide insight into how best to motivate employees, whether you are a manager or a trainer of managers. View the following theories as complementary, each focusing on a different aspect of motivation. By considering all of the theories together, you garner a valuable understanding of the intricacies associated with motivating a workforce.

Maslow's Hierarchy of Needs

Psychologist Abraham Maslow proposed that all people seek to satisfy five basic kinds of needs:

- physiological
- safety
- belongingness
- esteem
- self-actualization.

Those needs constitute a hierarchy of needs, with the most basic or compelling needs at the bottom (see the sidebar *Maslow's Hierarchy of Needs* for an illustration and ideas on how to use the hierarchy to motivate employees). Maslow argued that a person must have his or her lowest-level needs met before he or she would strive to satisfy needs higher in the hierarchy. Once a need is satisfied, it ceases to operate as a source of motivation. The lowest level of unmet needs in the hierarchy is the prime motivator of behavior. If or when that level is satisfied, the needs at the next highest levels in the hierarchy motivate behavior.

Herzberg's Motivation-Hygiene Theory

Researcher Frederick Herzberg proposed a theory that focuses on two factors:

1. Outcomes that can lead to high levels of motivation and job satisfaction.
2. Outcomes that can prevent people from being dissatisfied.

According to Herzberg's Motivation-Hygiene Theory, people have two sets of needs: motivation needs and hygiene needs.

Maslow's Hierarchy of Needs

Psychologist Abraham Maslow proposed the idea that everyone seeks to satisfy five basic kinds of needs: physiological, safety, belongingness, esteem, and self-actualization. The most elemental of an individual's needs are physiological: food, drink, shelter, and sexual satisfaction. The second step up the hierarchy is the need for safety, for shelter, and for protection from physical and emotional harm. The third level of needs are social ones—for love and a sense of belonging from parents, siblings, or extended families. The next level of need is for esteem. Needs here are both internal (for example, self-respect and autonomy) and external (for example, status and attention). Finally, an individual works to gain self-actualization, which is a "knowing" about Life and its meaning for the individual and a sense that she or he fits into the paradigm. Ways that managers can satisfy these employee needs follow:

- Physiological

  Provide a compensation system that enables an employee to buy food and clothing and to have adequate housing.
- Safety

  Provide job security, adequate health benefits, and safe working conditions.
- Belongingness

  Promote good interpersonal relations and organize social functions, such as company picnics and holiday parties.
- Esteem

  Grant promotions and recognize accomplishments.
- Self-Actualization

  Give employees the opportunity to use their skills and abilities to the fullest extent possible.

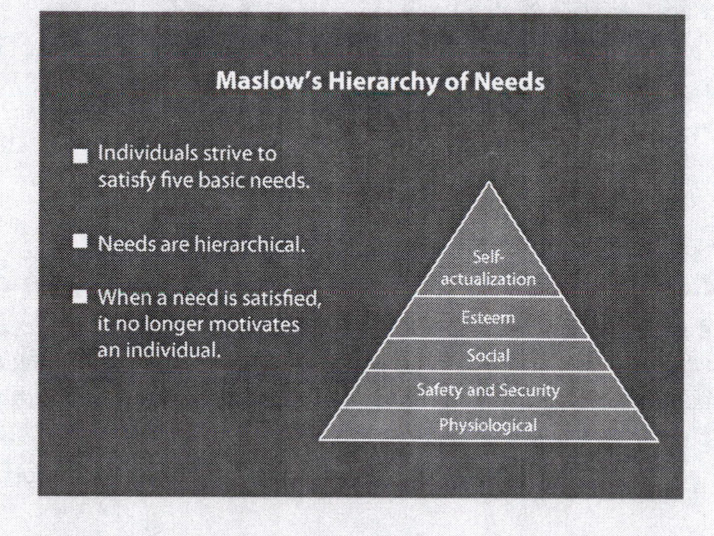

Adapted from Maureen Orey and Jenni Prisk's *Communication Skills Training.*

Hygiene Needs

Associated with the physical and psychological context in which work is performed, hygiene needs refer to extrinsically motivated behaviors performed to acquire material or social rewards, or to avoid punishment. The consequences of an extrinsically motivated behavior are the source of the employee's motivation, not the behavior itself. Hygiene needs are satisfied by pleasant and comfortable working conditions, pay, job security, good relationships with co-workers, and effective supervision.

Herzberg's theory contends that when hygiene needs are not met, workers will be dissatisfied. However, satisfying hygiene needs alone does not lead to highly motivated employees or high levels of job satisfaction within a workforce. For motivation and job satisfaction to be high, an employer must meet motivation needs.

Motivation Needs

Motivation needs are related to the work itself and how challenging that work is. Outcomes such as interesting work, autonomy, responsibility, growth and development on the job, and a sense of accomplishment and achievement help to satisfy motivation needs. Intrinsically motivated behavior, therefore, is behavior that the employee performs for its own sake; the source of motivation is actually performing the work. Some ways to motivate intrinsically are to provide opportunities for growth and achievement and to recognize people's achievements.

You can motivate people in three manners: intrinsically, extrinsically, or both. It depends on a variety of factors:

- personal characteristics such as personalities, abilities, values, attitudes, and needs
- the nature, or characteristics, of the job
- the nature of the organization—its structure, culture, control systems, human resources, and reward systems.

McClelland's Theory

Psychologist David McClelland extensively researched the following needs:

- achievement—the extent to which an individual has a stong desire to perform challenging tasks well and to meet personal standards for excellence
- affiliation—the extent to which an individual is concerned with establishing and maintaining good interpersonal relations, being liked, and having the people around him or her get along with each other
- power—the extent to which an individual desires to control or influence others.

To some degree, you'll notice the presence of each of those needs in all employees; yet, in the workplace, the level of importance of each need depends upon the position occupied by an employee:

- A high need for achievement and power is an asset in frontline and middle management.
- A senior-level manager needs to possess a strong desire for power.
- A high need for affiliation, contrarily, may not be desirable in senior-level managers. That need might lead them to try too hard to be liked by their employees, rather than doing all they can to ensure that employees' performance is as high as it can and should be.

McGregor's Theory X and Theory Y

In his 1960 management book, *The Human Side of Enterprise*, Douglas McGregor influenced the history of organizational management when he proposed the two motivational theories by which managers perceive employee motivation. He referred to those opposing motivational theories as Theory X and Theory Y. Each theory assumes that management's role is to organize resources—including people—to best benefit the company. However, beyond that commonality, the theories are quite dissimilar.

Theory X

A manager who ascribes to Theory X assumes the following:

- Work is inherently distasteful to most people, and they will attempt to avoid work whenever possible.
- Most people are not ambitious, have little desire for responsibility, and resist change.
- Most people are self-centered and prefer to be directed. They must be closely controlled and often coerced to achieve organizational objectives.
- Most people are gullible and unintelligent and have little aptitude for solving organizational problems.

Here, motivation occurs only at the physiological and security levels of Maslow's hierarchy. Theory X assumes that the primary source of most employee motivation is monetary, with security a strong second.

Under Theory X, management approaches to motivation range from hard to soft. The hard approach relies on coercion, implicit threats, micromanagement, and tight controls—essentially an environment of command and control. The soft approach, however, is to be permissive and seek harmony in the hope that employees, in return, will cooperate when asked. However, neither of those extremes is optimal. The hard approach results in hostility, low output, and extreme employee demands; the soft approach results in a workforce with an increasing desire for greater reward in exchange for diminishing work output.

You might think that the optimal approach to management would lie somewhere between those extremes. McGregor, however, asserts that Theory X management styles hinder the satisfaction of higher-level needs. The only way that employees can attempt to satisfy higher-level needs at work is to seek more compensation; thus, they focus on monetary rewards. Consequently, in a Theory X environment, people use work to satisfy their lower needs; they seek to satisfy their higher needs during their leisure time.

McGregor suggests that a command-and-control environment isn't effective because it relies on lower-level needs for motivation. In modern society, those needs are mostly satisfied, so they no longer act as motivators. You would expect employees in such an environment to dislike their work, avoid responsibility, have no interest in organizational goals, resist change, and so forth, thus creating a self-fulfilling prophecy. From that reasoning, McGregor proposed an alternative: Theory Y.

Theory Y

In strong contrast to Theory X, a Theory Y manager makes the following general assumptions:

- Work can be as natural as play if the conditions are favorable. Under those conditions, people will seek responsibility.
- People will be self-directed and creative to meet their work and organizational objectives if they are committed to them.
- People will be committed to their quality and productivity objectives if rewards are in place that address higher needs such as self-fulfillment.
- The capacity for creativity spreads throughout organizations.
- Most people can handle responsibility because creativity and ingenuity are common in the population.

Under those assumptions, employees have an opportunity to align their personal goals with organizational goals by using their need for fulfillment as the motivator. Employees can be most productive when their work goals align with their higher-level needs.

The higher-level needs of esteem and self-actualization are continuing needs in that they are never completely satisfied. As such, it is through those needs that you can best motivate employees.

McGregor stressed that Theory Y management does not imply a soft approach. Recognizing that some people may not have reached the level of maturity assumed by Theory Y, he suggests that those employees may need a system of tighter controls that a manager can relax as each employee develops. For more tips on applying Theory Y management, see the sidebar *Applying Theory Y Management* at right.

Vroom's Expectancy Theory

Yale School of Management professor Victor Vroom proposed the Expectancy Theory of motivation. This theory has evolved into one of the most popular work motivation theories because it focuses on all three parts of the motivation equation: inputs, performance, and outcomes. Its premise is that motivation is high when employees believe that high levels of effort lead to high performance, and high performance leads to the attainment of desired outcomes. Expectancy Theory identifies three major factors to determine a person's motivation:

- Expectancy

  Expectancy refers to the probability that a person's effort will yield a reward. For example, how motivated would you be to prepare for a test if you thought that no matter how hard you studied you would earn a "D"? Employees are motivated to put forth a high level of effort only if they think that doing so leads to high performance. In other words, for people's motivation to be high, expectancy must be high.
- Instrumentality

  Instrumentality refers to a person's perception that they will actually get the reward. Managers must ensure that employees receive the rewards that they are promised. Employees are motivated to perform at a high level only if they think that high performance will lead to—or is instrumental in attaining—outcomes (rewards). Outcomes can be pay, job security, or a feeling of accomplishment. Employees must have both high expectancies and instrumentalities, but the theory acknowledges that people differ in their outcome preferences.
- Valence

  Valence refers to how important the outcome is to a person. To motivate, you must determine which outcomes have high valence for your employees and ensure that those outcomes are provided when employees perform at a high level.

An example of Vroom's Expectancy Theory can be found in organizations where sales activity has a direct correlation to sales results. While commissions or bonuses might provide a basic reward, companies will often create additional incentives (or interim rewards) to recognize the Link between effort and performance. These incentives are commonly introduced as short-term programs to sell a particular product or service.

Additionally, many companies also are turning to employee incentive programs where points or company money is issued, so employees get the opportunity to select the reward that suits them best. An individual might save his or her points to get a watch or expensive item for him or herself or to purchase items for his or her children. The premise of these programs is to provide what is important to the employee.

Applying Theory Y Management

If Theory Y holds true, you can use these management principles to improve employee motivation:

- Decentralization and Delegation
  Decentralizing control and reducing the number of management levels creates an environment in which managers have more subordinates. Thus they are forced to delegate some responsibility and decision making to their employees.
- Job Enlargement
  Broadening the scope of an employee's job adds variety and opportunities to satisfy ego needs.
- Participative Management
  Consulting employees in the decision-making process taps their creative capacity and provides them with some control over their work environment.
- Performance Appraisals
  Requiring employees to set objectives and participate in the evaluation of those objectives allows them to feel involved in the appraisal process.

Properly implemented, a work environment such as the one described above results in a workforce that is highly motivated because employees work to satisfy their higher-level personal needs through their jobs.

Adams's Equity Theory

Your employees' perceptions concerning the fairness of their work outcomes relative to their work inputs is the focus of the Equity Theory. Formulated in the 1960s by workplace and behavioral psychologist J. Stacy Adams, this theory suggests that motivation is influenced by the comparison of one's own outcome-input ratio with the outcome-input ratio of another person or group of people. Note that Adams stressed that perception, rather than objective outcomes a person receives or the inputs a person contributes, is what is important in determining motivation in this case.

This theory is based on the assumption that employees ask two questions about their work:

- What do I receive in return for what I give?
- What do others receive for what they give?

The Equity Theory contends that employees create mental ratios about their work situations in order to answer those questions. Equity occurs only when employees believe that the ratio of their outcomes

Avoiding Inequity

Managers are charged with the responsibility of making sure that inequity does not occur within their work teams. They can incorporate interpersonal activities or procedural skills into their daily interactions to help employees feel that equity exists in the workplace.

Interpersonal Activities	Procedural Skills
Team management: Allowing employees to work on projects as a team can break down barriers.	Ethical behavior: Conducting oneself in an appropriate manner can build trust in employees.
Participative management: Including employees in the decision-making process can allow them to provide valuable input.	Consistency: Being aware of things that have been done in the past, so the scales don't tip too far in one direction or another, can forestall the perception of arbitrariness.
Empowerment: Giving employees the freedom to make decisions can boost their self esteem (not to mention improve customer relations).	Inclusiveness: Being nonjudgmental and unbiased and appreciating the differences each person brings to the workplace provides individuals with a sense of fair treatment.
Management by objectives: Having employees and management mutually agree upon goals can help employees get to the next level.	Accountability: Being responsible for one's actions and taking ownership of activities provides individuals with the sense that what they do is important.

received (pay, benefits, job satisfaction) to their inputs given (education, knowledge, experience, effort) is equal to the same ratio of a "comparison other" (who may or may not be like the employee).

Inequity, however, occurs either when employees believe they are receiving less or more for their efforts than the comparison other. According to this theory, balance is important, and employees are uncomfortable with either of those two imbalances. For some examples of how to avoid inequity in the workplace, see the sidebar *Avoiding Inequity* at left.

When imbalance is perceived, employees might

- work less because they believe others are overcompensated
- work harder because they believe that they are overcompensated in relation to others
- convince others to work less hard to restore equity
- convince others to work harder to restore equity
- reassess their perception of equity
- change their comparison other.

Self-Efficacy Theory

Self-Efficacy Theory relates to a person's belief about his or her ability to perform a behavior successfully. Even with the most attractive consequences or reinforcers hinging on high performance, people are not going to be motivated if they do not think that they can actually perform at the required high level.

Similarly, when people control their own behavior, they are likely to set difficult goals that will lead to outstanding accomplishments, but only if they think that they have the capability to reach those goals. Thus, self-efficacy influences motivation both when managers provide reinforcement and when workers themselves provide it—the greater the sense of self-efficacy, the greater the motivation and performance.

Eleanor Roosevelt once said: "No one can make you feel inferior without your consent." The following are some things managers can do and encourage employees to do to improve the situation:

- Mentoring: Peak performance requires skills and abilities. Help employees develop the skills and attitudes that they need to succeed.
- Behavior modeling: You've all heard the old saying, "practice what you preach." Well, it's true ... if you want others to act a certain way, you need to practice that behavior yourself. Making sure that you have a positive outlook and self-image can have a significant effect on yourself and the people you come into contact with.
- Setting achievable goals: It is important to set realistic, achievable goals and work toward accomplishing them. It is equally important to celebrate successes. As you get more comfortable with goal setting, you can introduce stretch goals.
- Take compliments graciously: Learn to accept "thank you" and "great job" with grace. Some people just don't want to believe the nice comment. Smile and say thank you in return.

Skinner's Behavioral Reinforcement Theory

According to psychologist B.F. Skinner, people learn to perform behaviors that lead to desired consequences and learn not to perform behaviors that lead to undesired consequences. Translated into motivation terms, Skinner's theory means that employees will be motivated to perform at a high level to the extent that they obtain outcomes that they desire.

This theory provides four tools—positive reinforcement, negative reinforcement, punishment, and extinction—that you can use to motivate high performance and prevent workers from engaging in behaviors that detract from organization effectiveness.

- Positive Reinforcement

  Giving employees the outcomes that they desire when they perform behaviors that contribute to organizational effectiveness is considered positive reinforcement. Those outcomes are the rewards that a person desires such as pay, praise, or a promotion. One example of an inexpensive reward system is provided in the sidebar *Positive Reinforcement: The CandyGram.*
- Negative Reinforcement

  Negative reinforcement also can encourage behaviors that contribute to organizational effectiveness. Managers might choose to use negative reinforcement to eliminate an undesired outcome when a specific behavior is performed. Examples of negative reinforcement include management criticism, unpleasant assignments, or job-elimination threats. When negative reinforcement is used, employees are motivated to perform behaviors because they want to stop receiving the undesired outcomes.

- Punishment

  The act of administering an undesired or negative consequence when a dysfunctional behavior is performed is punishment. Punishments take various forms: pay cuts, suspensions, discipline, and termination. They also can have unintended side effects such as resentment, loss of self-respect, and a desire for retaliation. Managers should use punishment only when necessary.

- Extinction

  Extinction is the process of eliminating whatever reinforces an undesired behavior. For example, if you have a co-worker who likes to come into your office and talk about nonwork topics, what can you do? While you like the person and enjoy the conversations, those breaks put you behind schedule, and you have to work late to catch up. By acting disinterested in the nonwork topics, you discourage the behavior.

Managers can get into trouble if they use only positive reinforcement and refrain from negative reinforcement. It is important for a manager to identify the right behaviors to reinforce. An effective manager will ensure that the reinforced behaviors are ones over which employees have control and that the behaviors contribute to organizational effectiveness.

Positive Reinforcement: The CandyGram

In *Getting Them to Give a Damn,* author Eric Chester specifically addresses recruiting and retaining a younger, emerging workforce. But he presents at least one idea that will work for employees of any age.

The North Carolina Department of Environment and Natural Resources encourages employees to participate in "CandyGram," a nominally priced recognition program. To recognize a co-worker, employees attach a note to one of the following edible items:

LifeSavers candies	For a person who has been a real "lifesaver"
Strawberry jam	For a person who has helped you out of a "jam"
100 Grand Candy Bar	For a person who saves you a lot of money
Nestle Crunch Bar	For a person who was there for you during "crunch" time
Zero bar	For a person who completes a project with no mistakes—or "zero" errors
Mr. Goodbar	For a person who possesses a great attitude
York Peppermint Patty	For a person who is invaluable—"he or she is worth a mint!"

Adapted from Eric Chester's *Getting Them to Give a Damn.*

Ways to Integrate Motivation Into the Workplace

When examining your workplace environment, you'll discover two influences that have a great effect on the motivation of your employees:

- Management
  Instead of coming from some nebulous ad hoc committee or corporate institution, the most valuable recognition comes directly from one's manager. The sidebar *Rewarding Employees* at right provides examples and options of ways managers can reward their employees.
- Performance
  Employees want to be recognized for the jobs they were hired to do. The most effective incentives are based on job performance—not on nonperformance-related praise such as attendance or attire.

These influences should be considered when integrating motivation into job design, performance feedback, pay-for-performance systems, and relationship-building initiatives.

Job Design

J.R. Hackman and G.R. Oldham's job characteristics model explains in detail how you can make jobs more interesting and motivating for your employees.

According to Hackman and Oldham, every job has the following five characteristics that determine how motivating workers will find that job. These characteristics determine how employees react to their work and lead to such outcomes as high performance and satisfaction, and low absenteeism and turnover.

1. Skill Variety.
   The extent to which a job requires an employee to use a wide range of different skills, abilities, or knowledge is referred to as skill variety. For example, the skill variety required by the job of a research scientist is higher than that required by the job of a food server.

2. Task Identity.
   Task identity refers to the extent to which a job requires a worker to perform all the tasks necessary to complete that job from the beginning to the end of the production process. For example, a crafts worker who takes a piece of wood and transforms it into a custom-made piece of furniture, such as a desk, has higher task identity than a worker who performs only one of the numerous operations required to assemble a television.

REWARDING EMPLOYEES

Research into why talented people stay in organizations is the basis for the following ways to show your employees that you appreciate them:

- Private Time With You

  Have lunch with an employee and ask questions like:
  - What can I do to keep you on my team?
  - What might make your work life easier?
  - What can I do to be more supportive or help you?
- Frank Talk About the Future

  Hold a career conversation in a quiet, private place— off-site, if possible. Ask the following questions to start:
  - What do you enjoy most about your job? The least?
  - Which one of your talents haven't I used yet?
  - What jobs do you see yourself doing in the future?
- Representing the Company

  Give employees the chance to attend an outside conference or seminar designed for their affinity group.
- Professional Growth

  Let employees choose from a list of potential projects, assignments, or tasks that could enrich their work.
- Recognizing Family

  Give employees a prepaid phone card during the holiday season, or give a free pass for X number of days or hours off to attend children's school programs or sport activities.
- Professional Interests

  Give a subscription to an employee's favorite business magazine and satisfy employees' need for information.
- Submit to Pruning

  Ask the employee with whom you never agree to engage in some straight talk about how you might work together better. Listen carefully and don't defend yourself. Then take a step toward changing at least one behavior.
- A Unique Perk for Fun

  Give an employee a "kicks" coupon that entitles him or her to spend up to X amount of money to take a break or have some fun at work. It could involve the entire team.
- A Priceless Introduction

  Ask the employee for the name of someone in the organization that he or she would like to meet, chat with, and learn more about. Provide an introduction and encourage the employee to decide how to spend the time.

- A Personal Trainer Session

  Consider a gift certificate for an employee to have a lunch with you or another mentor of his or her choice.
- A New Door

  Brainstorm an opportunity hit list with an employee about growing, learning, and stretching in some way. Prioritize the list and then open the door!
- Blending Work and Passion

  Have a "Passion Breakfast" for all employees, a team, or one-on-one. Ask, "What do you love to do?" "At work?" "Outside of work?" Brainstorm and commit to helping them build more of what they love into their workday.
- An Exception to the Rules

  Give a "Bend the Rules" pass that involves and encourages going against the status quo. Bend as much as you can when employees make their requests.
- Genie in a Bottle

  Ask an employee to write down six ways he or she would like to be rewarded. Anything goes. The only rule is that half of the ideas have to be low or no cost.
- A Chance to Download

  Give 12 coupons for listening time—one for each month, in which an employee can talk about anything for 20 minutes. Your job isn't to understand, just to listen.
- Honoring Values

  Over a cappuccino, glass of wine, or cup of tea, try asking one of your employees any of these questions:
  - What do you think makes a perfect day at work?
  - Looking back, what has satisfied you the most?
  - What does the word success mean to you?

  Take notes and read them back to the employee. What did you both learn about his or her values?
- The Starring Role, For Once

  Give an employee a chance to lead a project you've been hoarding for yourself (you know which one). Offer the spotlight, yield, coach when necessary.

Adapted from Beverly L. Kaye and Sharon Jordan-Evans's "The ABCs of Management Gift-Giving," *Training & Development*, December 2000.

3. Task Significance.

The degree to which a worker feels his or her job is meaningful because of its effect on people inside the organization (such as co-workers) or to people outside the organization (such as customers) is task significance. A teacher who sees the effect of his or her efforts in a well-educated and well-adjusted student enjoys high task significance compared with a dishwasher who monotonously washes dishes as they come to the kitchen.

4. Autonomy.

Autonomy refers to the degree to which a job gives an employee the freedom and discretion needed to schedule different tasks and to decide how to carry out those tasks. Salespeople who have to plan their schedules and decide how to allocate their time among different customers have relatively high autonomy compared with assembly-line workers whose actions are determined by the speed of the production line.

5. Feedback.

The extent to which performing a job provides a worker with clear and direct information about how well he or she has completed the job is feedback.

For example, an air traffic controller whose mistakes result in a midair collision receives immediate feedback on job performance; whereas a person who compiles statistics for a business magazine often has little idea of when he or she makes a mistake or does a particularly good job.

Hackman and Oldham argue that these five characteristics influence an employee's motivation because they affect three critical psychological states. If the employee feels that his or her work is meaningful and that he or she is responsible for work outcomes and for knowing how those outcomes affect others, the employee will find the work more motivating, be more satisfied, and thus perform at a high level.

Managers can use the following tips when designing structure and jobs:

- When deciding which type of organizational structure to use, carefully analyze an organization's environment, strategy, technology, and human resources.
- When creating a more formal structure, meticulously define the Limits of each employee's job, create clear job descriptions, and evaluate each worker on his or her job performance.
- When creating a more flexible structure, enlarge and enrich jobs and allow workers to expand their jobs over time. Encourage workers to work together and then evaluate both individual and group performance.

- When using the job characteristics model to guide job design, recognize that you can enrich most jobs to make them more motivating and satisfying.

Performance Feedback

Performance management is the process used to identify, encourage, measure, evaluate, improve, and reward employee performance at work. As a feedback process, it serves an important role for both motivational and informational purposes, as well as acts as an improver of manager-employee relations. For example, supportive feedback can lead to greater motivation, and feedback discussions about pay and advancement can lead to greater employee satisfaction with the process.

One of the biggest challenges managers face is how to handle an employee's reaction to feedback. That is especially true when confronting poor performance issues. If you remember that detailed and specific feedback is more likely to result in increased performance, you'll ease the situation for both you and the employee.

When conducting performance feedback sessions, focus on the following:

- Create a supportive environment for employees to address concerns.
- Open the channels of communication for productive two-way dialogue.
- Build and maintain trust and respect with your employee.

Pay-for-Performance Systems

In *Keeping the People Who Keep You in Business*, author Leigh Branham reviews the role money plays in retaining the right people. He explains that while surveys rank pay behind factors such as meaningful work, meeting challenges, and opportunity for advancement, compensation places people in a socio-economic niche. It determines what they can and cannot buy. That makes compensation an emotional and important issue.

Managers and executives should look at compensation not as a way to drive performance but rather as a message to employees about what results they value. In 2000, Branham writes that about two-thirds of small- and medium-size companies offered some kind of variable pay, such as profit sharing or bonus awards, to their employees, compared with less than 50 percent in 1990.

Four linkages are needed to connect performance with rewards:

- Valuable results are measured.
- Measured results are accomplished.
- Accomplished results are rewarded.
- Rewarded results are valuable.

Many companies have switched to variable pay options as a way of updating their compensation practices. Here are some types of variable pay in use today.

- Special Recognition Monetary Awards
  This method awards cash payouts to recognize unplanned, significant individual or group contributions that far exceed expectations. They are most effective if given when the contribution is fresh in the minds of all employees and with visible fanfare.
- Individual and Group Variable Pay
  These programs are designed primarily for employees or teams who do not normally participate in incentive compensation programs (that is, technical positions, telecommuters, and so forth). For positions or projects that do not have a lot of interaction with others, this method of variable pay is also valuable.
- Lump Sum Awards
  If you want to reward individual employee performance when base pay is already above the competitive market rate for the job, create a lump sum awards program. This program allows an organization to reduce annual payroll and still reward top performers.
- Stock Options
  These plans offer employees the opportunity to purchase their for-profit common stock at some time in the future at a specific price. Stock options serve to tie employees to the organization because ownership tends to cause employees to be more aware of how their organization is performing.

You can use the described options as complements to existing pay structures to enhance performance and retention. Your company executives must evaluate the current pay practices and business goals, and decide to what degree they want to reward results. The key word here is *results*. Rather than rewarding employees for seniority, bigger budgets, and larger staffs, these plans focus on the achievement of outcomes. Some examples of the use of pay-for-performance systems and their effects are described in the sidebar *Case Study: Who's Doing It?*

Relationship-Building Initiatives

In *The Six Fundamentals of Success*, Stuart Levine identifies the need to invest in relationships. He introduces the concept of how gestures—such as congratulating co-workers—can lead to better relationships, both personally and professionally.

A few of the key concepts that he mentions include:

Case Study: Who's Doing It?

The following are some examples of pay-for-performance systems that have been used in various organizations to improve motivation:

- A national airline carrier gives each of its employees a $100 bonus check every time the carrier is ranked the nation's number one on-time airline.
- A health system made its 4,800 employees eligible to earn one to five percent of their annual salaries as a performance bonus if their business units achieved certain patient satisfaction and cost-per-discharge goals. In two years, the system had eliminated a chronic absenteeism problem, flattened its cost-per-discharge, and raised its patient satisfaction rate to the 95th-plus percentile.
- A tech company quadrupled its number of stock-option-eligible employees between 1993 and 1999. The company believes that move has helped it to significantly cut turnover among technical workers during that same period.

Adapted from Leigh Branham's *Keeping the People Who Keep You in Business.*

- Give Generously

  When you give generously in relationships, you create an energy that brings good luck back to you.
- Talk Face-to-Face

  A *Fortune* 500 CEO tells the tale of how he walks through his entire U.S. headquarters to wish all 2,000 employees a happy holiday. He has a piece of candy at every stop. (He claims to put on 10 pounds each holiday season.) Why does he do it? He wants to thank them face-to-face. He knows that during the next year he will have to email them to ask for their support, and it helps if his employees see him as a real person.
- Help Team Members Get Ahead

  Having a great team makes coming to work rewarding for a manager. But attracting bright, hardworking people can be a challenge at times. The best way for you to recruit go-getters is to earn a reputation as a manager whose employees move up in the organization. To help you hire for a motivational match, use the interview questions in the job aid at the end of this *Infoline.*
- Coach Your Team

  Coaching your team makes your life easier in two ways: It improves the quality of work, and, as a result, your department's overall performance. Coaching elicits excellence.

Strategies for Rewarding Employees

There are two keys to rewarding your employees. First, you must understand the basic needs that motivate employees. Second, you need to continually monitor your workers to determine if their needs are being met.

Understanding Needs

In *The Manager's Desk Reference*, authors Cynthia Berryman-Fink and Charles B. Fink relate that 99 percent of employees are motivated by one of the following seven needs:

- Achievement
  Employees want the satisfaction of accomplishing projects successfully. They want to exercise their talents to attain success. If the job is challenging enough, employees are self-motivated. Therefore, if you provide them with the right work assignments, your employees will consistently produce.
- Power
  People get satisfaction from influencing and controlling others. They like to lead and persuade and are motivated by positions of power and leadership. Give your employees the opportunity to make decisions and direct projects.
- Affiliation
  Employees derive satisfaction from interacting with others. They enjoy people and find the social aspects of the workplace rewarding. You can motivate employees by giving them opportunities to interact with others: teamwork projects, group meetings, and so forth.
- Autonomy
  Employees want freedom and independence. It can be to your benefit to allow employees to make their own choices, set their own schedules, and work independently of others.
- Esteem
  Individuals need recognition and praise. Whenever possible, give your employees ample feedback and public recognition.
- Safety and Security
  Employees crave job security, a steady income, health insurance, fringe benefits, and a hazard-free work environment. By providing predictable work with little risk or uncertainty, you motivate your workforce.
- Equity
  Employees want to be treated fairly. You can assume that they compare work hours, job duties, salaries, and privileges with their co-workers. If they perceive inequities, employees will become discouraged.

Some ways to recognize which need is the primary motivator for an employee include considering his or her personality type based on various personality inventories, listening empathetically, or simply asking questions about job satisfiers. The sidebar *Four Nonmonetary Rewards* at right—which is based on the seven needs—describes some no-cost ways to reward your employees.

Gathering Information

On an ongoing basis, you should monitor your workforce to obtain useful information (for instance on motivation and job satisfaction) for a variety of organizational initiatives. Two ways to gather information about your workforce are surveys and focus groups.

- Surveys

  Employee surveys are instruments you can use to assess worker perceptions about their work environment. Use surveys to collect data on a wide variety of topics such as, but not limited to, the following:
  - quality of management
  - organizational strategy
  - quality of work-life issues
  - employee morale and job satisfaction
  - effectiveness of compensation and benefit programs
  - employee development opportunities
  - employee retention and attrition issues
  - organizational communications.

- Focus Groups

  Focus groups are small groups of employees that you invite to participate in a structured discussion with a facilitator. Use them as follow-up to a survey or independently to discover how employees feel about a specific program or issue. Note that for both surveys and focus groups, you must
  - avoid misleading respondents about the reasons for the survey or focus group
  - explain who is being surveyed and what the data will be used for
  - use the data only for the reasons explained to participants
  - maintain strict confidentiality if you have made that promise to the participants
  - provide results to participants if you have made that promise.

Four Nonmonetary Rewards

Cash bonuses are great, but they are certainly not the only way to reward employees. In fact, other methods can be equally as effective. Here are four ways that you can recognize employees without dipping into your budget.

- Flexible Scheduling

  Once an employee demonstrates that he or she is a consistent contributor, relax some of the structure. Let employees exercise some judgment on when to take breaks and meals. You could expand this benefit to flexible work start times.
- Advancement Opportunities

  Let good employees know that you are looking out for their best interests. Continually look for promotional possibilities for your employees—even if that means letting them leave your department. Sure, you might lose a good employee, but the company still retains that good employee, and your remaining employees will know that you have their best interests at heart.
- Special Assignments

  Managers should give special opportunities to exceptional workers. Employees will see these opportunities as a welcome change of pace and the chance to learn new skills. Assignments can vary from sitting on a special task force to working on a new product launch.
- Public Praise

  Most people relish being recognized in front of their peers (however, be sure that anyone you praise publicly does enjoy that kind of recognition). As a manager, you can benefit from these moments by praising exceptional performers.

Adapted from George T. Fuller's *The Supervisor's Big Book of Lists.*

Common Manager Mistakes

If you aren't getting the motivational mileage that you should as a manager, perhaps you are making one of the following five management mistakes.

- Misplacing Ownership

  Do you think motivation is the job of the human resources department? Although many companies give their HR departments some responsibility for formal rewards and recognition programs, that doesn't mean you are off the hook. In many situations, employees find that informal recognition from their managers for a job well done means more to them than a formal company program.

- Misaligning Incentives

  It is a mistake to give each of your employees the same incentive. No single action will motivate all employees. It's your job to determine the unique motivators for each employee and to provide an appropriate motivator when recognition is deserved.

- Saving Recognition

  It's inappropriate to save recognition for special occasions. When you observe your employees performing at a high level, recognize that success—regularly and often.

- Playing Favorites

  Managers should neither give handouts nor play favorites. You should not give recognition when none is warranted. That act not only cheapens the value of the incentive but also you, as a manager, lose credibility. In your interactions with employees, credibility is one of the most important qualities that you can build. Lose that, and you could lose everything.

- Misspeaking Praise

  When praising employees, don't just say, "Good job." Be specific so that your employees know exactly what they did to receive recognition. This simple act—providing detailed praise—helps to develop the skills and abilities of your workforce.

The mind is a muscle. If the minds of your employees go unchallenged, they will start to atrophy. Your workforce is full of creative people ready for an interesting, invigorating challenge. If you want to keep your top performers, you'll need to create new projects or opportunities for them. This *Infoline* will help you achieve that.

Job Aid

Finding the Motivational Match

Employees will not stay with a company very long if they are not motivated to do their jobs. It is important to discover what motivates individuals before they even start with the organization, during the interview process. The following list of interview questions can help determine an employee's motivational match for a position.

1. Tell me about a time when you handled a project that you found satisfying. What was the situation and why was it satisfying?

2. Tell me about a time when you worked on a project that you found dissatisfying. What was the situation and why was it dissatisfying?

3. Give me examples of job experiences that you felt were satisfying.

4. Do you have short-term and long-term goals for yourself? Are they realistic? Did you accomplish them last year?

5. What kinds of things can a manager do to motivate his or her staff?

6. Describe a situation when you were able to have a positive influence on the actions of others. How did you do it? What were they able to accomplish?

7. How do you motivate yourself to do unpleasant tasks?

8. Give me an example of a time you went above and beyond what was asked of you.

9. How would you define success for someone in your profession?

References & Resources

Books

Berryman-Fink, C., and C. B. Fink. *The Manager's Desk Reference*. New York: AMACOM, 1991.

Branham, L. *Keeping the People Who Keep You in Business*. New York: AMACOM, 2001.

Chester, E. *Getting Them to Give a Damn*. Chicago: Dearborn Trade Publishing, 2005.

Dell, T. *Motivating at Work*. Revised Edition. Menlo Park, CA: Crisp Publications, 1993.

Fournies, F. *Why Employees Don't Do What They're Supposed to Do and What to Do About It*. New York: McGraw-Hill, 1999.

Fuller, G.T. *The Supervisor's Big Book of Lists*. Englewood Cliffs, NJ: Prentice Hall, 1994.

Garber, P. R. *99 Ways to Keep Employees Happy, Satisfied, Motivated, and Productive*. Mystic, CT: Ransom & Benjamin, 2001.

Gostick, A., and C. Elton. *The 24-Carrot Manager.* Layton, UT: Gibbs Smith, 2002.

Jones, G., and J. George. *Contemporary Management*. 3rd edition. New York: McGraw-Hill/Irwin, 2003.

Levine, S. R. *The Six Fundamentals of Success*. New York: Doubleday, 2004.

McGregor, D. *The Human Side of Enterprise*. New York: McGraw-Hill, 1960.

Nelson, B. *1001 Ways to Energize Employees*. New York: Workman Publishing, 1997.

———. *1001 Ways to Take Initiative at Work*. New York: Workman Publishing, 1999.

———. *1001 Ways to Reward Employees*. New York: Workman Publishing, 1994.

Nelson, B., and P. Economy. *Managing for Dummies*. New York: John Wiley & Sons, 1996.

Orey, M., and J. Prisk. *Communication Skills Training.* Alexandria, VA: ASTD Press, 2004.

Woods, R. H. *Human Resources Management.* 2nd edition. Orlando, FL: Educational Institute of the American Hotel & Lodging Association, 1997.

Infolines

Austin, Mary. "Needs Assessment by Focus Group," No. 259401 (revised 1998).

Long, Lori. "Surveys From Start to Finish," No. 258612 (revised 1998).

Sharpe, Cat. "How to Motivate Employees." No. 259108 (revised 1997).

Reports and White Papers

Grensing-Pophal, L. "Engaging Employees From A to Z." SHRM White Paper, 2002.

Poe, A. C. "Doing More With Less: Motivating Your Workforce in Uncertain Economic Times." SHRM White Paper, 2002.

Ragan Communications. *The Motivational Manager.* Available through Amazon.com.

———. *The Manager's Intelligence Report.* Available through Amazon.com.

Miscellaneous

Envision Software. "Theory X and Y." www.envisionsoftware.com, 2005.

Society for Human Resource Management. "The SHRM Learning System" Module Three, Human Resource Development, 2004.

Society for Human Resource Management. "The SHRM Learning System" Module Five, Employee and Labor Relations, 2004.

Motivating Creativity in Organizations: On Doing What You Love and Loving What You Do

By Teresa M. Amabile

Arthur Schawlow, winner of the Nobel prize in physics in 1981, was once asked what, in his opinion, made the difference between highly creative and less creative scientists. He replied, "The labor of love aspect is important. The most successful scientists often are not the most talented. But they are the ones who are impelled by curiosity. They've got to know what the answer is."[1] Schawlow's insights about scientific creativity highlight the importance of *intrinsic motivation*: the motivation to work on something because it is interesting, involving, exciting, satisfying, or personally challenging. There is abundant evidence that people will be most creative when they are primarily intrinsically motivated, rather than extrinsically motivated by expected evaluation, surveillance, competition with peers, dictates from superiors, or the promise of rewards.[2]

Interestingly, this Intrinsic Motivation Principle of Creativity applies not only to scientific creativity, but to business creativity as well. Often, financial success is closely tied to a passion for the work itself. Michael Jordan, who by the mid-1990s was the most financially successful basketball player in history, insisted on a "love of the game" clause in his contract—securing for him the right to play in "pick-up" games whenever he wished. Robert Carr, a primary developer of the first pen computer, was captivated by the opportunity to do something spectacular that had never been done before. When entrepreneur Jerry Kaplan described the idea to him, Carr reacted with intense excitement: "Jerry, it's not a question of *whether* I want to do this. I *have* to do this. This is important. This is profound. ... It's not very often that opportunities like this come along—something really big, a chance to really make a difference. Maybe once a decade or so. I think you've got one here."[3]

When Steve Wozniak invented the micro-computer, he demonstrated creativity in new product development; for all intents and purposes, such a thing had not existed before. When Walt Disney created Disneyland, he demonstrated creativity in new service development; he essentially invented a new form of entertainment. Although most people think of creativity in business as limited to the creation of something new to sell, there are other forms as well. When Fred Smith developed the concept for Federal Express, he certainly was not inventing a new service or a new product; humans had been delivering messages and packages to each other for thousands of years. In this instance, the creativity resided in the system for delivery: a hub system, where all packages were flown to Memphis on the same day, sorted, and distributed for air delivery the next day. Creativity exists in less famous, more humble, examples as well: the ad campaign that revitalizes a dying brand, or the product line extension that captures additional market share.

At its heart, creativity is simply the production of novel, appropriate ideas in *any* realm of human activity, from science, to the arts, to education, to business, to everyday life. The ideas must be novel—different from what's been done before—but they can't be simply bizarre; they must be appropriate to the problem or opportunity presented. Creativity is the first step in innovation, which is the successful implementation of those novel, appropriate ideas. And innovation is absolutely vital for long-term corporate success. Because the business world is seldom static, and because the pace of change appears to be rapidly accelerating, no firm that continues to deliver the same products and services in the same way can long survive. By contrast, firms that prepare for the future by implementing new ideas oriented toward this changing world are likely to thrive.[4]

Individual Creativity

To some extent, intrinsic motivation resides in a person's own personality.[5] Some people are more strongly driven than others by the enjoyment and sense of challenge in their work. For example, Pablo Casals was driven by passion for the cello from the day he first heard the instrument played: "I had never heard such a beautiful sound before. A radiance filled me. I said, 'Father, that is the most wonderful instrument I have ever heard. That is what I want to play.'"[6] The novelist John Irving, in explaining his motivation to write for up to 14 hours in a single day, said, "The unspoken factor is love. The reason I can work so hard at my writing is that it's not work for me."[7]

Although part of intrinsic motivation depends on personality, my students, colleagues, and I have discovered in 20 years of research that a person's social environment can have a significant effect on that person's level of intrinsic motivation at any point in time; the level of intrinsic motivation can, in turn, have a significant effect on that person's creativity. Einstein described the dampening effect of a militaristic classroom environment on his own intrinsic motivation when he said, "This coercion had such a deterring effect upon me that, after I had passed the final examination, I found the consideration of any scientific problems distasteful for an entire year."[8] He later concluded, "It is a very grave mistake to think that the enjoyment of seeing and searching can be promoted by means of coercion and a sense of duty."[9]

Much of the evidence on this connection between the social environment, intrinsic motivation, and creativity comes from controlled laboratory experiments.[10] In one such study, for example, college students were presented with a simple artistic creativity task—making a paper collage with a standard set of materials.[11] Half of the students were randomly assigned to a condition where they were offered a reward (money) for making the collage, and half were simply given the collage activity to do. In addition, half within each group were given a choice; they were asked whether they would agree to make the collage in order to get the money (in the choice/reward condition), or they were simply asked whether they wanted to make the collage (in the choice/non-reward condition). Students in the no-choice condition were not offered any choice in the matter; those in the no-choice/reward condition were simply presented with the reward as a bonus, and those in the no-choice/non-reward condition were simply given the collage task.

The results were quite clear and striking. The students who had essentially made a contract to do the activity in order to get the reward (choice/reward condition) exhibited strikingly lower levels of creativity in their collages than the other three groups. The "means-end" work environment—"Do this task as a means to the end of getting this reward"—appears to have undermined their creativity. In contrast, however, those students who received the reward as a bonus showed no diminishment in creativity. In fact, their creativity was *higher* than those of the other groups. And, in keeping with the Intrinsic Motivation Principle of Creativity, students' creativity was correlated with their reported interest in the collage activity; the more interested they were, the more creative their collages were judged by art experts. Thus, it was not the *fact* of reward, but the *perception* of reward (resulting from the way in which it was presented) that made the difference.

Another experiment addressed the Intrinsic Motivation hypothesis even more directly. In this study, young creative writers were asked to fill out a short questionnaire before writing a poem.[12] The questionnaire was designed to have them focus on either their intrinsic reasons for being a writer (such as getting a lot of pleasure out of something good that you have written) or their extrinsic reasons for being a writer (such as getting rich and famous). (Participants in a control condition filled out an unrelated, non-motivational questionnaire.) They then wrote poems, which were later judged by experts in creative writing. The writers in the intrinsic condition and the control condition wrote poems that were judged as quite creative, on average. However, those who had focused for just a few minutes on the extrinsic motivations for their work wrote poems that were significantly less creative.

The Componential Theory of Individual Creativity

According to conventional wisdom, creativity is something done by creative people. Even creativity researchers, for several decades, seemed to guide their work by this principle, focusing predominantly on individual differences: What are creative people like, and how are they different from most people in the world? Although this person-centered approach yielded some important findings about the backgrounds, personality traits, and work styles of outstandingly creative people,[13] it was both limited and limiting. It offered little to practitioners concerned with helping people to become more creative in their work, and it virtually ignored the role of the social environment in creativity and innovation. In contrast to the traditional approach, the Componential Theory of Creativity assumes that all humans with normal capacities are able to produce at least moderately creative work in some domain, some of the time—and that the social environment (the work environment) can influence both the level and the frequency of creative behavior.

The theory includes three major components of individual (or small team) creativity, each of which is necessary for creativity in any given domain: expertise, creative-thinking skill, and intrinsic task motivation (see Figure 1).[14] The componential theory suggests that creativity is most likely to occur when people's skills overlap with their strongest intrinsic interests—their deepest passions—and that creativity will be higher, the higher the level of each of the three components. This is the "creativity intersection" depicted in Figure 1.

Expertise

Expertise is the foundation for all creative work. It can be viewed as the set of cognitive pathways that may be followed for solving a given problem or doing a given task—the problem solver's "network of possible wanderings."[15] The expertise component includes memory for factual knowledge, technical proficiency, and special talents in the target work domain—such as expertise in gene splicing, or in computer simulation, or in strategic management. For example, a high-tech engineer's expertise includes his innate talent for imagining and thinking about complex engineering problems, as well as focusing in on the important aspects of those problems; his factual knowledge about electronics; his familiarity with past work and current developments in high-tech engineering; and the technical skills he has acquired in designing, carrying out, and interpreting research.

Creative Thinking

This component provides that "something extra" of creative performance.[16] Assuming that a person has some incentive to perform an activity, performance will be "technically good" or "adequate" or "acceptable" if the requisite expertise is in place. However, even with expertise at an extraordinarily high level, the person will not produce creative work if creative thinking skills are lacking. These skills include a cognitive style favorable to taking new perspectives on problems, an application of techniques (or "heuristics") for the exploration of new cognitive pathways, and a working style conducive to persistent, energetic pursuit of one's work.

Creative thinking depends to some extent on personality characteristics related to independence, self-discipline, orientation toward risk-taking, tolerance for ambiguity, perseverance in the face of

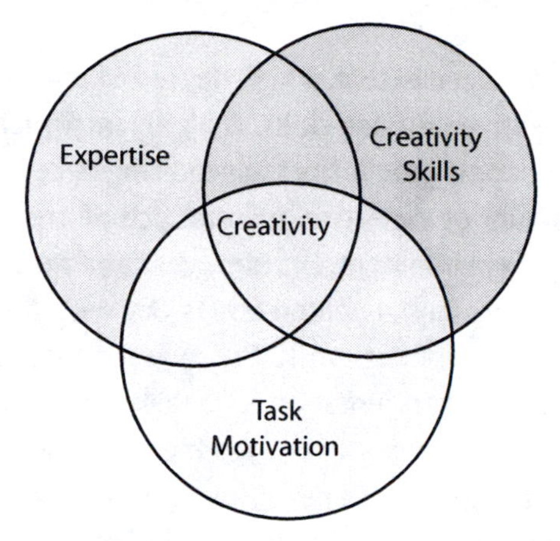

Figure 1 3 Component Model of Creativity

frustration, and a relative lack of concern for social approval.[17] However, creativity skills can be increased by the learning and practice of techniques to improve cognitive flexibility and intellectual independence.

An engineer's arsenal of creativity skills might include his ability to break out of a pre-conceived perception or expectation when examining testing results, his tolerance for ambiguity in the process of deciding on the appropriate interpretation for puzzling data, his ability to suspend judgment as he considers different approaches, and his ability to break out of strict algorithms for attacking a problem. He might also have learned to employ some of the creativity heuristics described by theorists: "When all else fails, try something counterintuitive;"[18] or "Make the familiar strange."[19] Finally, if he is productively creative, his work style is probably marked by an ability to concentrate effort for long periods of time[20] and an ability to abandon unproductive strategies, temporarily putting aside stubborn problems.[21]

Intrinsic Task Motivation

Although the two skill components determine what a person is capable of doing in a given domain, it is the task motivation component that determines what that person actually will do. Motivation can be either intrinsic (driven by deep interest and involvement in the work, by curiosity, enjoyment, or a personal sense of challenge) or extrinsic (driven by the desire to attain some goal that is apart from the work itself—such as achieving a promised reward or meeting a deadline or winning a competition). Although combinations of intrinsic and extrinsic motivation are common, one is likely to be primary for a given person doing a given task. A number of studies have shown that a primarily intrinsic motivation will be more conducive to creativity than a primarily extrinsic motivation.

Task motivation makes the difference between what an engineer can do and what he will do. The former depends on his levels of expertise and creative thinking skills. But it is his task motivation that determines the extent to which he will fully engage his expertise and creative thinking skills in the service of creative performance. To some extent, a high degree of intrinsic motivation can even make up for a deficiency of expertise or creative thinking skills. A highly intrinsically motivated person is likely to draw skills from other domains, or apply great effort to acquiring necessary skills in the target domain.[22]

Although a person's development of expertise and practice of creative thinking skills can be influenced to some extent by the social environment, the strongest and most direct influence of the environment is probably on motivation. Certainly, a person starts out with a level of intrinsic motivation that depends on his or her basic enjoyment of the work. But experiments like those described earlier have shown how a person's basic motivational orientation for a task, and resulting creativity on that task, can be influenced by even momentary alterations in the work environment. For example, an engineer may be highly intrinsically motivated to undertake a new project of his own design, but he may be singularly uninterested in a project handed to him by the director of the lab.

Motivational Synergy

The prevailing psychological model of the interaction between intrinsic and extrinsic motivation suggests an antagonism: as extrinsic motivation for an activity increases, intrinsic motivation must decrease.[23] But there is considerable evidence from field research that, under certain conditions, certain forms of extrinsic motivation may combine synergistically with intrinsic motivation, enhancing (or at least not undermining) the positive effects of intrinsic motivation on creativity.[24] For example, research in business organizations has uncovered several extrinsic motivators operating as *supports* to creativity: reward and recognition for creative ideas, clearly defined overall project goals, and frequent constructive feedback on the work.[25]

What determines whether extrinsic motivation will combine positively with intrinsic motivation, or detract from it, in influencing creativity? There are three important determinants: the person's initial motivational state, the type of extrinsic motivator used, and the timing of the extrinsic motivation.

First, the initial level of intrinsic motivation may play a crucial role. It may be that, if a person is deeply involved in the work because it is interesting or personally challenging, that degree of intrinsic motivation may be relatively impervious to the undermining effects of extrinsic motivators. Research has shown that a person's attitudes and motives will be most subject to external influences when those attitudes and motives are vague or ambiguous.[26] So, we might expect additive effects of intrinsic and extrinsic motivation when intrinsic motivation toward the work is already strong and salient. On the other hand, we might expect negative effects when intrinsic motivation is relatively weak. Thus, if an engineer is passionately interested in the development of the products he is working on, he may be relatively immune to negative effects of extrinsic motivators on his intrinsic motivation and creativity.

Second, the type of extrinsic motivation may make a difference. "Synergistic extrinsic motivators," including certain types of reward, recognition, and feedback, do not necessarily undermine intrinsic motivation; indeed, they may actually enhance some aspects of performance. These outcomes can result from reward, recognition, and feedback that either confirm competence or provide important information on how to improve performance; these are called *informational extrinsic motivators.*[27] Positive outcomes can also result from reward, recognition, and feedback that directly increase the person's involvement in the work itself; these are called *enabling extrinsic motivators*. For example, if a high tech firm recognizes outstanding performance by approving the allocation of additional technical resources to its engineers, the effects on intrinsic motivation are likely to be positive. On the other hand, constraint on how work can be done, as well as other types of reward, recognition, and feedback, will be detrimental to intrinsic motivation and performance. These "non-synergistic extrinsic motivators," which are *controlling extrinsic motivators*, may never combine positively with intrinsic motivation, because they undermine a person's sense of self-determination.[28] The engineer who works under stringent controls on how to approach a project, or for whom rewards signify attempts to control his behavior, will likely evidence decreased intrinsic motivation and creativity.

Third, the timing of extrinsic motivation may be important. Recall that creative ideas are marked by both novelty and appropriateness. While some stages of the creative process are most important in determining the novelty of an idea, other stages are more important in determining appropriateness. Synergistic extrinsic motivators may be most useful at those stages of the creative process where high degrees of novelty do not come into play—such as the gathering of background information or the validation of a chosen solution. Here, some level of outward focus, engendered by extrinsic motivation, may cue the problem-solver to the appropriateness of certain kinds of information or the workability of final solutions. However, it may be optimal to reduce all types of extrinsic motivators at those stages requiring the greatest novelty—such as the initial problem formulation or the generation of ideas.

The Intrinsic Motivation Principle

All of this research on motivation leads to the Intrinsic Motivation Principle of Creativity, which can be formally stated as follows: *Intrinsic motivation is conducive to creativity. Controlling extrinsic motivation is detrimental to creativity, but informational or enabling extrinsic motivation can be conducive, particularly if initial levels of intrinsic motivation are high.*

The Work Environment for Creativity

Although the experimental research is important in establishing causal connections between the social environment, motivation, and creativity, the most directly relevant information comes from interview and survey studies within corporations. It is through these studies that we began to understand the social environment in organizations and how it might impact creativity.

Recently, with my colleagues Regina Conti, Heather Coon, Jeffrey Lazenby, and Michael Herron, I studied the work environments surrounding project teams in a large company that we call High Tech Electronics International.[29] Our purpose was to determine whether and how the work environments of highly creative projects differed from the work environments of less creative projects. The primary research tool was an instrument called *KEYS: Assessing the Climate for Creativity.*[30] It consists of 78 items that constitute eight scales addressing different aspects of the work environment, plus two scales assessing the work outcomes of creativity and productivity.[31] Of the eight environment scales, six focus on Environmental Stimulants to Creativity—factors that should be positively related to creative work outcomes—including freedom, positive challenge, supervisory encouragement, work group supports, organizational encouragement, and sufficient resources. Two scales focus on Environmental Obstacles to Creativity—factors that should be negatively related to creative work outcomes—including organizational impediments and excessive workload pressure. (See Table 1 for scale descriptions.) Data on *KEYS* gathered over a 12-year period, with over 12,000 individual employees from 26 different companies, have established the reliability and validity of this instrument.[32]

High Tech is a United States company of over 30,000 employees providing diversified electronics products to international markets. The company has several divisions, with a large number of research and development projects going on within each division at any point in time. We conducted this study in three phases, across four divisions and a large number of projects. In Phase 1, we asked both technical and non-technical middle-level managers individually to nominate both the highest-creativity and the lowest-creativity project with which they had been involved during the previous three years in the company. For both projects, we asked them to select only from that set of projects in which creativity was both possible and desirable. This eliminated any low creativity projects that simply involved carrying out a routine task, and it allowed us to focus on differences between successful and unsuccessful attempts at creative project work. Instructions to the nominating managers defined creativity as "the production of novel and useful ideas by individuals or teams of individuals." These managers briefly described each nominated project (using a standard questionnaire) and completed a *KEYS* work environment assessment on each nominated project.

Phase 2 of the study was conducted to validate the creativity nominations of Phase 1, by allowing independent expert assessments of the level of creativity in the projects nominated in Phase 1. A group of experts from each of the four target divisions was asked to independently rate the projects nominated from that division on creativity and several other dimensions. These experts were unaware of the initial nomination status of the projects, and high- and low-creativity projects were randomly intermixed in the experts' rating questionnaires. (They were asked to skip the ratings for any projects with which they were not familiar.)

Phase 3 was conducted to validate any work environment differences between the high- and low-creativity projects discovered in Phase 1. We selected a sub-set of the projects from Phase 1, those that had been most strongly and reliably rated by the expert judges as either high in creativity or low in creativity. We then asked each member of those project teams to complete a *KEYS* survey to describe the work environment of his or her particular project. These respondents did not know that the study concerned creativity, or that their projects had been chosen for any particular reason. In fact, people were eliminated from participation in Phase 3 if they had participated in Phase 1. Furthermore, each respondent in Phase 3 focused on only one project, rather than the two contrasting projects for Phase 1 respondents. In this way, we attempted to eliminate any biases that might have arisen when the Phase 1 respondents explicitly contrasted the work environment of a project that they considered highly creative with one that they considered quite uncreative.

In Phase 1, the nominated high-creativity projects were significantly higher than the nominated low-creativity projects on all six work environment stimulant scales, and significantly lower on the two work environment obstacle scales. (See Table 1.) In addition, the high-creativity projects were higher on the two outcome scales assessing creativity and productivity.

In Phase 2, the expert ratings confirmed the initial nominations made in Phase 1: the previously-nominated high-creativity projects were indeed rated significantly higher on creativity than the previously-nominated low-creativity projects.

Phase 3 confirmed most of the findings from Phase 1 (see Table 1). Analyses of the responses from project-team members showed that the high-creativity projects were significantly higher than the low-creativity projects on four of the six work environment stimulant scales, and marginally higher on a fifth work environment stimulant scale. In addition, the high-creativity projects were marginally lower on one of the two work environment obstacle scales. Finally, as in Phase 1, the high-creativity projects were higher on the two outcome scales assessing creativity and productivity.

Table 1 summarizes the work environment findings from Phases 1 and 3 of this study at High Tech Electronics International. Clearly, although all aspects of the work environment may exert influence, some appear to carry more weight in the differentiation between high- and low-creativity projects. Somewhat surprisingly, three dimensions seem to play a relatively less prominent role in organizational creativity: resources, workload pressure, and freedom. However, the differences between high and low-creativity projects on five dimensions were striking. In particular, positive challenge in the work, organizational encouragement, work group supports, supervisory encouragement, and organizational impediments may play an important role in influencing creative behavior in organizations. Thus, this study clearly indicates that the work environment within which people work relates significantly to the creativity of the work that they produce.

Other researchers have also discovered aspects of work environments that appear to affect creativity and innovation. Our tentative finding of the positive impact of freedom or autonomy echoes a result obtained in a study of 200 R&D managers in eight semi-conductor companies, where independence among R&D personnel was identified as a key determinant of success.[33] Various organizational supports have likewise appeared in other findings. In a survey of 11 strategic business units, the presence of innovation norms emerged as the single most important predictor of the effectiveness of entrepreneurial strategy.[34] Using a critical incidents methodology, another study examined the treatment of new ideas in high-technology and health-services organizations by gathering data from several hundred managers.[35] Several features of successful innovations were identified, including: the earmarking of special funds for highly experimental research and development; the formal consideration of innovators' ideas, followed by feasibility studies; consideration of marketing issues in the

Table 1 Summary of Results from Study of High-Creativity and Low-Creativity Projects at High Tech Electronics International

KEYS Scale Name	*KEYS* Scale Description	Direction of Difference	Magnitude of Difference in Phase 1[a]	Magnitude of Difference in Phase 3
CREATIVITY STIMULANT SCALES				
Organizational Encouragement	An organizational culture that encourages creativity through the fair, constructive judgment of ideas, reward and recognition for creative work, mechanisms for developing new ideas, an active flow of ideas, and a shared vision of what the organization is trying to do.	High-Creativity higher	Strong[b]	Strong[b]
Supervisory Encouragement	A supervisor who serves as a good work model, sets goals appropriately, supports the work group, values individual contributions, and shows confidence in the work group.	High-Creativity higher	Strongb	Moderateb
Work Group Supports	A diversely skilled work group in which people communicate well, are open to new ideas, constructively challenge each other's work, trust and help each other, and feel committed to the work they are doing.	High-Creativity higher	Strong[b]	Strong[b]
Sufficient Resources	Access to appropriate resources, including funds, materials, facilities, and information.	High-Creativity higher	Moderate[b]	None
Challenging Work	A sense of having to work hard on challenging tasks and important projects.	High-Creativity higher	Strong[b]	Strong[b]
Freedom	Freedom in deciding what work to do or how to do it; a sense of control over one's work.	High-Creativity higher	Strong[b]	Moderate[c]
CREATIVITY OBSTACLE SCALES				
Organizational Impediments	An organizational culture that impedes creativity through internal political problems, harsh criticism of new ideas, destructive internal competition, an avoidance of risk, and an overemphasis on the status quo.	Low-Creativity higher	Strong[b]	Moderate[c]
Workload Pressure	Extreme time pressures, unrealistic expectations for productivity, and distractions from creative work.	Low-Creativity higher	Weak[b]	None
CRITERION SCALES				
Creativity	A creative organization or unit, where a great deal of creativity is called for and where people believe they actually produce creative work.	High-Creativity higher	Strong[b]	Strong[b]
Productivity	An efficient, effective, and productive organization or unit.	High-Creativity higher	Strong[b]	Moderate[b]

Notes:

a. "Strong" designates effect sizes (partial eta-squared) of .21-.54. "Moderate" designates effect sizes of .10-.20. "Weak" designates effect sizes of .05-.09. "None" designates effect sizes of less than .05.

b. Statistically significant.

c. Marginal ($.06 < p < .15$)

early stages of decision-making about an idea; substantial modification of most original ideas prior to final adoption; adequate funding and consistent monitoring of such projects; and initial small-scale implementation of the new idea.

How the Work Environment for Creativity Changes During Significant Organizational Events

In another recent study, Regina Conti and I set out to determine how the environment for creativity and innovation might change in an organization that is undergoing rapid transition.[36] Several months after our earlier study at High Tech Electronics International, the company's management announced a major (15–30%) downsizing. We returned and proceeded to collect *KEYS* data at three additional points in time: half-way through the downsizing, just as the downsizing had ended, and four months after the end of the downsizing. In addition, we conducted interviews with surviving employees at each of these three time periods. The results showed a striking pattern. All of the Environmental Stimulants to Creativity declined during the downsizing, but appeared to rebound as the downsizing came to an end. The most dramatic declines were seen in challenge, work group supports, and organizational encouragement—three of the dimensions which, according to the previous study, carry the most weight in differentiating between high and low creativity. Moreover, these same three dimensions showed the weakest rebound by four months after the downsizing ended. Although workload pressure remained unchanged during the downsizing, the Environmental Obstacle of organizational impediments increased significantly; however, this factor declined as the downsizing ended. Importantly, both creativity and productivity (as assessed by *KEYS)* declined during the downsizing; only productivity had rebounded to a significant degree by four months after the downsizing. In addition, potentially longer-term effects on creativity were suggested by a decline in the per-capita invention disclosures logged by the company's engineers during the downsizing. Invention disclosures are the first step in patent applications and, in a company like High Tech Electronics, patents are the lifeblood of its future innovative product streams.

Additional questionnaire and interview data collected as part of the downsizing study allow some insight into mechanisms by which these negative effects might have occurred. Surprisingly, the degree of actual downsizing that people experienced in their own department did not relate strongly to their perceptions of the work environment or to reported work behaviors. However, regardless of how much downsizing had gone on in their own department, people were less creative and reported poorer work environments when the stability of their own work-group had been disrupted. Moreover, the degree of *anticipated* downsizing strongly related to a large number of perceptions and behaviors. The more downsizing that people expected in the coming months, the poorer the work environment in the department, the lower the morale, and the less creative their approach to their work. However, even in those departments anticipating considerable downsizing, people responded more positively on all of these dimensions when they felt that their own management was trustworthy, communicated honestly with them, and listened to their concerns.

The downsizing study suggests that, given the potentially devastating effects on surviving employees' motivation and creativity, managers should attempt to avoid downsizing if possible. If that is not possible, they would do well to carry it out in a timely fashion (thus reducing the negative effects of anticipated downsizing), with good, clear, all-directional communication about the reasons behind the action and the processes being used. Moreover, attention should be paid to the stability of groups where a high level of creative productivity is desired. If those groups are disrupted by the downsizing, the new teams might be helped by team-building interventions.

Research Summary

On the basis of our two studies at High Tech Electronics International, we now know that the work environment within an organization—which is strongly influenced by management at all levels—can make the difference between the production of new, useful ideas for innovative business growth and the continuance of old, progressively less useful routines. We also know that management actions that result in significant changes within the organization, such as downsizing, can have dramatic and potentially long-lasting effects on creativity.

These results, as well as the results of many other studies, have led to a comprehensive Componential Theory of Creativity and Innovation in Organizations.[37] The aim of this theory is to adequately capture all of the major elements influencing creativity and innovation within organizations. The organizational theory is built on the foundation of the Componential Theory of Individual Creativity and incorporates that theory.

The Componential Theory of Organizational Creativity and Innovation

Figure 2 presents a simplified schematic diagram depicting the major elements of the componential theory, integrating individual creativity with the organizational work environment.[38] The three upper circles in the figure depict the organizational components (features of the work environment) that are considered necessary for innovation. The three lower circles in the figure depict the components of individual creativity.

The central prediction of the theory is that elements of the work environment will impact individuals' creativity (depicted by the solid arrow). The theory also proposes that the creativity produced by individuals and teams of individuals serves as a primary source for innovation within the organization (depicted by the dotted arrow). The most important feature of the theory is the assertion that the social environment (the work environment) influences creativity by influencing the individual components. Although the environment can have an impact on any of the components, the impact on task motivation appears to be the most immediate and direct. The three components of the organizational work environment include all aspects investigated in the study of high- and

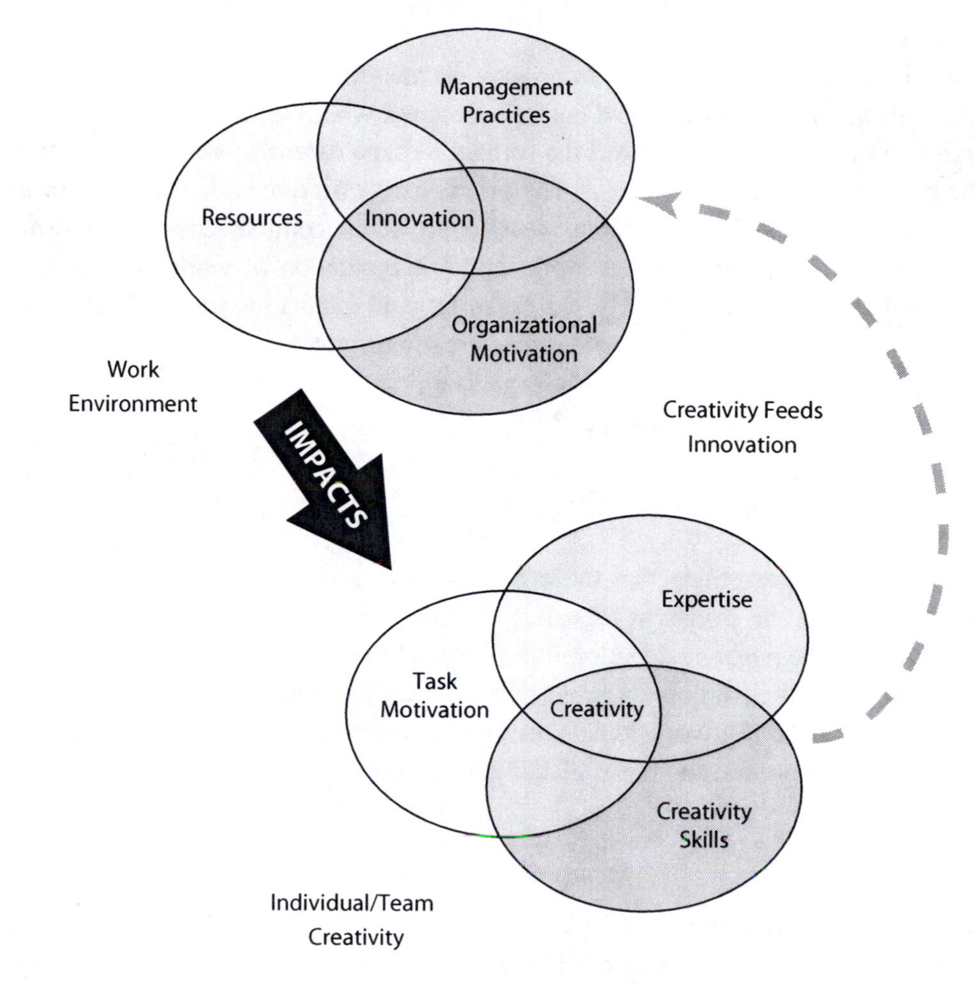

Figure 2 Impact of the Organizational Environment on Creativity

low-creativity projects at High Tech Electronics International, combined into conceptually coherent categories.

Organizational Motivation to Innovate

This component is made up of the basic orientation of the organization toward innovation, as well as supports for creativity and innovation throughout the organization. The orientation toward innovation must come, primarily, from the highest levels of management, but lower levels can also be important in communicating and interpreting that vision. In the studies at High Tech, this component was manifested in differences on Organizational Encouragement and (in the negative direction) Organizational Impediments. On the basis of these studies and work by other researchers, it appears that the most important elements of the innovation orientation are: a value placed on creativity and innovation in general, an orientation toward risk (versus an orientation toward maintaining the status quo), a sense of pride in the organization's members and enthusiasm about what they are capable of doing, and an offensive strategy of taking the lead toward the future (versus a defensive strategy of simply wanting to protect the organization's past position).[39] The primary organization-wide supports for innovation appear to be mechanisms for developing new ideas; open, active communication of information and ideas; reward and recognition for creative work; and fair evaluation of work—including work that might be perceived as a "failure."[40] Notably, the organizational motivation toward innovation includes the absence of several elements that can undermine creativity: political problems and "turf battles," destructive criticism and competition within the organization, strict control by upper management, and an excess of formal structures and procedures.[41]

Resources

This component includes everything that the organization has available to aid work in the domain targeted for innovation. In the studies at High Tech, it was manifested in differences on the Sufficient Resources scale and (in the negative direction) the Workload Pressure scale. These resources include a wide array of elements: sufficient time for producing novel work in the domain, people with necessary expertise, funds allocated to this work domain, material resources, systems and processes for work in the domain, relevant information, and the availability of training.[42]

Management Practices

This component includes management at all levels, but most especially the level of individual departments and projects.[43] In the High Tech studies, this component was represented by the Challenging Work, Work Group Supports, Supervisory Encouragement, and Freedom scales. Several earlier researchers and theorists have suggested that creativity and innovation are fostered by allowing a considerable degree of freedom or autonomy in the conduct of one's work[44] although, as noted, the high-low creativity study at High Tech did not provide strong support for this assertion. Some earlier work has suggested the importance of appropriately matching individuals to work assignments, on the basis of both skills and interests, to maximize a sense of positive challenge in the work.[45] Several aspects of project supervision appear to be important, starting with an ability to clearly set overall project goals while allowing procedural autonomy.[46] In addition, project supervision is likely to foster creativity when it is marked by clear planning and feedback, good communication between the supervisor and the work group, and enthusiastic support for the work of individuals as well as the entire group.[47] Finally, management practices for creativity include the ability to constitute effective work groups that represent a diversity of skills, and are made up of individuals who trust and communicate well with each other, challenge each other's ideas in constructive ways, are mutually supportive, and are committed to the work they are doing.[48]

Implications for Management

The Componential Theory of Creativity, and the research that underlies it, suggest a number of management implications concerning the motivation for creativity in business and the effect of the work environment on that motivation.

- Because human motivation is so complex and so important, the successful management of creativity for the next century must include management education about the types of motivation, their sources, their effects on performance, and their susceptibility to various work environment influences.
- We cannot hope to create a highly and appropriately creative workforce simply by "loading up" the intrinsic and the extrinsic motivators in the work environment, without paying attention to the *type* of extrinsic motivators and the context in which they are presented.
- Because a positive sense of challenge in the work is one of the most important predictors of creativity, it is imperative to match people to work that utilizes their skills, stretches their skills, and is clearly valued by the organization. As much as possible, all work should be designed to maximize intrinsically motivating aspects.
- Organizations must demonstrate a strong orientation toward innovation, which is clearly communicated and enacted, from the highest levels of management, throughout the organization.
- Organizations should orient themselves toward the generation, communication, careful consideration, and development of new ideas. This includes fair, constructive judgment of ideas, non-controlling reward and recognition for creative work, mechanisms for developing new ideas, and an active flow of ideas. It excludes turf battles, conservatism, and excessively negative criticism of new ideas.
- Work groups should be constituted of diversely skilled individuals with a shared intrinsic motivation for their work and a willingness to both share and constructively criticize each other's ideas. These groups should be led by supervisors who clearly set overall goals for projects but allow operational autonomy in achieving those goals. Performance feedback should be highly informational and work-focused.
- People should be given at least adequate resources to carry out their work, and at least minimally sufficient time to consider alternative approaches.

Organizational leaders and managers must begin to think of human motivation at work as a complex system where it *is* possible to achieve synergy between persons and their work environments, and between the different types of motivation. The system is complex, but it is not unknowable. We already know much about how to nurture the motivation for creativity, and we are learning more every day.

Summary

Maintaining your own creativity in your work depends on maintaining your intrinsic motivation. This means two things. You should do what you love, and you should love what you do. The first is a matter of finding work that matches well with your expertise, your creative thinking skills, and your strongest intrinsic motivations. The second is a matter of finding a work environment that will allow you to retain that intrinsic motivational focus, while supporting your exploration of new ideas.

Managers who learn these lessons will recruit for people who already have that spark of passion for their work (as well as the requisite skills and experience), but they will also nurture that spark by creating a work environment that downplays the obstacles and fosters the stimulants to creativity. Only then will their organizations be poised to lead through innovation.

Notes

1. "Going for the Gaps," interview in *The Stanford Magazine* (Fall 1982), p. 42.
2. T.M. Amabile, *The Social Psychology of Creativity* (New York, NY: Springer Verlag, 1983); T.M. Amabile, *Creativity in Context: Update to the Social Psychology of Creativity* (Boulder, CO: Westview Press, 1996).
3. J. Kaplan, *Startup* (New York, NY: Penguin Books, 1994), p. 30.
4. Importantly, it has been found that innovation within organizations has additional benefits aside from the creation of new products, services, and processes. In a study of 288 bank employees, the degree of innovation within a group was a significant negative predictor of turn-over among employees in the group. M. McFadden and E. Demetriou, "The Role of Immediate Work Environment Factors in the Turnover Process: A Systemic Intervention," *Applied Psychology: An International Review*, 42 (1993): 97–115. In a similar study of 314 nurses, job satisfaction was significantly predicted by innovation. S.E. Robinson, S.L. Roth, and L.L. Brown, "Morale and Job Satisfaction among Nurses: What Can Hospitals Do?" *Journal of Applied Social Psychology*, 23 (1993): 244–251.
5. T.M. Amabile, K.G. Hill, B.A. Hennessey, and E. Tighe, "The Work Preference Inventory: Assessing Intrinsic and Extrinsic Motivational Orientations," *Journal of Personality and Social Psychology*, 66 (1994): 950–967.
6. A.E. Kahn, *Joys and Sorrows: Reflections by Pablo Casals* (New York, NY: Simon and Schuster, 1970), p. 35.
7. T.M. Amabile, *Growing Up Creative* (New York, NY: Crown, 1989), p. 56.
8. A. Einstein, "Autobiography," in P. Schilpp, *Albert Einstein: Philosopher-Scientist* (Evanston, IL: Library of Living Philosophers, 1949), p. 18.
9. Ibid., p. 19.
10. See Amabile (1996), op. cit.
11. T.M. Amabile, B.A. Hennessey, and B.S. Grossman, "Social Influences on Creativity: The Effects of Contracted-For Reward," *Journal of Personality and Social Psychology*, 50 (1986): 14–23.
12. T.M. Amabile, "Motivation and Creativity: Effects of Motivational Orientation on Creative Writers," *Journal of Personality and Social Psychology*, 48 (1985): 393–399.

13. For example, F. Barron, "The Disposition toward Originality," *Journal of Abnormal and Social Psychology*, 51 (1955): 478–485; F. Barron, *Creativity and Personal Freedom* (New York, NY: Van Nostrand, 1968.); D. W. MacKinnon, "The Nature and Nurture of Creative Talent," *American Psychologist*, 17 (1962): 484–495; D.W. MacKinnon, "Personality and the Realization of Creative Potential," *American Psychologist*, 20 (1965): 273–281.
14. T. Amabile, "The Social Psychology of Creativity: A Componential Conceptualization," *Journal of Personality and Social Psychology*, 45 (1983b): 357–377; Amabile, (1983) op. cit.
15. A. Newell and H. Simon, *Human Problem Solving* (Englewood Cliffs, NJ: Prentice-Hall, 1972), p. 82.
16. Termed "creativity-relevant skills" in Amabile (1983), op. cit., and "creativity-relevant processes" in Amabile (1996), op. cit.
17. Barron (1955), op. cit.; D. Feldman, *Beyond Universals in Cognitive Development* (Norwood, NJ: Ablex, 1980); S. E. Golann, "Psychological Study of Creativity," *Psychological Bulletin*, 60 (1963): 548–565; R. Hogarth, *Judgement and Choice* (Chichester: Wiley, 1980); MacKinnon (1962), op. cit.; M. I. Stein, *Stimulating Creativity*, Vol. 1 (New York, NY: Academic Press, 1974).
18. A. Newell, J. Shaw, and H. Simon, "The Processes of Creative Thinking," in H. Gruber, G. Terrell, and M. Wertheimer, eds., *Contemporary Approaches to Creative Thinking* (New York, NY: Atherton Press 1962.)
19. W. W. Gordon, *Synectics: The Development of Creative Capacity* (New York, NY: Harper & Row, 1961).
20. D. Campbell, "Blind Variation and Selective Retention in Creative Thought as in Other Knowledge Processes," *Psychological Review*, 67 (1960): 380–400; Hogarth, op. cit.
21. H. Simon, "Scientific Discovery and the Psychology of Problem Solving," in *Mind and Cosmos: Essays in Contemporary Science and Philosophy* (Pittsburgh, PA: University of Pittsburgh Press, 1966).
22. See, for example, the work of S. Harter ["Effectance Motivation Reconsidered: Toward a Developmental Model," *Human Development*, 21 (1978): 34–64] and C. Dweck ["Motivational Processes Affecting Learning," *American Psychologist*, 41 (1986): 1040–1048].
23. See, for example, E.L. Deci, "Effects of Externally Mediated Rewards on Intrinsic Motivation," *Journal of Personality and Social Psychology*, 18 (1971): 105–115; M.R. Lepper, D. Greene, and R. Nisbett, "Undermining Children's Intrinsic Interest with Extrinsic Rewards: A Case of the "Overjustification" Hypothesis," *Journal of Personality and Social Psychology*, 28 (1973): 129–137; M. R. Lepper and D. Greene, *The Hidden Costs of Reward* (Hillsdale, NJ: Lawrence Erlbaum Associates, 1978); E. L. Deci and R. M. Ryan, *Intrinsic Motivation and Self-Determination in Human Behavior* (New York, NY: Plenum, 1985).
24. T.M. Amabile, "Motivational Synergy: Toward New Conceptualizations of Intrinsic and Extrinsic Motivation in the Workplace," *Human Resource Management Review*, 3 (1993): 185–201.
25. T.M. Amabile, R. Conti, H. Coon, J. Lazenby, and M. Herron, "Assessing the Work Environment for Creativity," *Academy of Management Journal*, 39 (1996): 1154–1184; T.M. Amabile and S.S. Gryskiewicz, *Creativity in the R&D laboratory*, Technical Report Number 30 (Greensboro, NC: Center for Creative Leadership, 1987); T.M. Amabile and N. Gryskiewicz, "The Creative Environment Scales: The Work Environment Inventory," *Creativity Research Journal*, 2 (1989): 231–254.
26. D. Bem, "Self-Perception Theory," in L. Berkowitz, ed., *Advances in Experimental Social Psychology*, Vol. 6 (New York, NY: Academic Press, 1972).

27. Deci and Ryan (1985) op. cit.
28. Ibid.
29. Amabile et al. (1996), op. cit.
30. T.M. Amabile, *KEYS: Assessing the Climate for Creativity* (Greensboro, NC: Center for Creative Leadership, 1995).
31. *KEYS* was developed on the basis of several earlier studies of the work environment for creativity, in particular a critical-incidents study of 120 R&D scientists. Amabile and Gryskiewicz, op. cit.
32. Amabile et al. (1996) op. cit.
33. A. Abbey and J.W. Dickson, "R&D Work Climate and Innovation in Semiconductors," *Academy of Management Journal*, 26 (1983): 362–368.
34. R.D. Russell and C.J. Russell, "An Examination of the Effects of Organizational Norms, Organizational Structure, and Environmental Uncertainty on Entrepreneurial Strategy," *Journal of Management*, 18 (1992): 839–856.
35. A.L. Delbecq and P.K. Mills, "Managerial Practices That Enhance Innovation," *Organizational Dynamics*, 14 (1985): 24–34.
36. T.M. Amabile and R. Conti, "What Downsizing Does to Creativity," *Issues and Observations* (Greensboro, NC: Center for Creative Leadership) 15 (1995): 1–6.
37. T.M. Amabile, "A Model of Creativity and Innovation in Organizations," in B. Staw and L.L. Cummings, eds., *Research in Organizational Behavior*, Vol. 10 (Greenwich, CT: JAI Press, 1988).
38. Ibid.
39. Amabile and Gryskiewicz, op. cit.; L.L. Cummings, "Organizational Climates for Creativity," *Journal of the Academy of Management*, 3 (1965): 220–227; J. Hage and R. Dewar, "Elite Values Versus Organizational Structure in Predicting Innovation," *Administrative Science*, 18 (1973): 279–290; R. G. Havelock, *Planning for Innovation* (Ann Arbor, MI: Center for Research on Utilization of Scientific Knowledge, University of Michigan, 1970); R.M. Kanter, *The Change Masters* (New York, NY: Simon and Schuster, 1983); J. R. Kimberly, "Managerial Innovation," in P.C. Nystrom and W. H. Starbuck, eds., *Handbook of Organizational Design* (Oxford: Oxford University Press, 1981); C. Orpen, "Measuring Support for Organizational Innovation: A Validity Study," *Psychological Reports*, 67 (1990): 417–418; S.M. Siegel and W.F. Kaemmerer, "Measuring the Perceived Support for Innovation in Organizations," *Journal of Applied Psychology*, 63 (1978): 553–562.
40. Amabile and Gryskiewicz, op. cit.; S.J. Ashford and L.L. Cummings, "Proactive Feedback Seeking: The Instrumental Use of the Information Environment," *Journal of Occupational Psychology*, 58 (1985): 67–80; Cummings, op. cit.; J.E. Ettlie, "Organizational Policy and Innovation among Suppliers to the Food Processing Sector," *Academy of Management Journal*, 26 (1993): 27–44; Kanter, op. cit.; P.R. Monge, M.D. Cozzens, and N.S. Contractor, "Communication and Motivational Predictors of the Dynamics of Organizational Innovation," *Organizational Science*, 3 (1992): 250–274; J.G. Paolillo and W.B. Brown, "How Organizational Factors Affect R&D Innovation," *Research Management*, 21 (1978):12–15.
41. Amabile and Gryskiewicz, op. cit.
42. Ibid.
43. This component was termed "skills in innovation management" in the original presentation of the model. Amabile (1988), op. cit.

44. Amabile and Gryskiewicz, op. cit.; F.M. Andrews and G.F. Farris, "Supervisory Practices and Innovation in Scientific Teams," *Personnel Psychology* (1967); G. Ekvall, *Climate, Structure, and Innovativeness of Organizations: A Theoretical Framework and an Experiment*, Report 1, The Swedish Council for Management and Organizational Behaviour, 1983; N. King and M.A. West, "Experiences of Innovation at Work," SAPU Memo No. 772, University of Sheffield, Sheffield, England, 1985; D.C. Pelz and F.M. Andrews, *Scientists in Organizations* (New York, NY: Wiley, 1966); Paolillo and Brown, op. cit.; Siegel and Kaemmerer, op. cit.; M.A. West, *Role Innovation in the World of Work*, Memo no. 670, MRC/ESRC Social and Applied Psychology Unit, University of Sheffield, Sheffield, England, 1986.
45. Amabile and Gryskiewicz, op. cit.
46. L. Bailyn, "Autonomy in the Industrial R&D Laboratory," *Human Resource Management*, 24 (1985): 129–146.
47. Amabile and Gryskiewicz, op. cit.
48. T.L. Albrecht and D.T. Hall, "Facilitating Talk about New Ideas: The Role of Personal Relationships in Organizational Innovation," *Communication Monographs*, 58 (1991): 273–288; Amabile and Gryskiewicz, op. cit.; Ekvall, op. cit.; Monge et al., op. cit.

Moral Person and Moral Manager: How Executives Develop a Reputation for Ethical Leadership

By Linda Klebe Treviño, Laura Pincus Hartman, and Michael Brown

Plato asked, which extreme would you rather be: "an unethical person with a good reputation or an ethical person with a reputation for injustice?" Plato might have added, "or would you rather be perceived as ethically neutral—someone who has no ethical reputation at all?" Plato knew that reputation was important. We now understand that reputation and others' perceptions of you are key to executive ethical leadership. Those others include employees at all levels as well as key external stakeholders.

A reputation for ethical leadership rests upon two essential pillars: perceptions of you as both a moral person *and* a moral manager. The executive as a moral person is characterized in terms of individual traits such as honesty and integrity. As moral manager, the CEO is thought of as the Chief *Ethics* Officer of the organization, creating a strong ethics message that gets employees' attention and influences their thoughts and behaviors. Both are necessary. To be perceived as an ethical leader, it is not enough to just be an ethical person. An executive ethical leader must also find ways to focus the organization's attention on ethics and values and to infuse the organization with principles that will guide the actions of all employees. An executive's reputation for ethical leadership may be more important now than ever in this new organizational era where more employees are working independently, off site, and without direct supervision. In these organizations, values are the glue that can hold things together, and values must be conveyed from the top of the organization. Also, a single employee who operates outside of the organizational value system can cost the organization dearly in legal fees and can have a tremendous, sometimes irreversible impact on the organization's image and culture.

MORAL PERSON + MORAL MANAGER = A REPUTATION FOR ETHICAL LEADERSHIP

These ideas about a dual pillar approach to ethical leadership are not brand new. As the opening quotation suggests, the emphasis on reputation goes back to Plato. Chester Barnard addressed the ethical dimension of executive leadership sixty years ago. Barnard spoke about executive responsibility in terms of conforming to a "complex code of morals"[1] (moral person) as well as creating moral codes for others (moral manager).

If Plato and Barnard had this right, why bother revisiting the subject of ethical leadership now? We revisit the subject because, in our 40 structured interviews (20 with senior executives and 20 with corporate ethics officers), we found that many senior executives failed to recognize the importance of others' perceptions and of developing a reputation for ethical leadership. To them, being an ethical person and making good ethical decisions was enough. They spoke proudly about having principles, following the golden rule, taking into account the needs of society, and being fair and caring in their decisions. They assumed that if they were solid ethical beings, followers would automatically know that. They rejected the idea that successful ethical executives are often perceived as ethically neutral. Furthermore, they assumed that good leaders are by definition ethical leaders. One senior executive noted, "I don't think you can distinguish between ethical leadership and leadership. It's just a facet of leadership. The great leaders are ethical, and the lousy ones are not."

However, a *reputation* for ethical leadership can not be taken for granted because most employees in large organizations do not interact with senior executives. They know them only from a distance. Any information they receive about executives gets filtered through multiple layers in the organization, with employees learning only about bare-bones decisions and outcomes, not the personal characteristics of the people behind them. In today's highly competitive business environment, messages about how financial goals are achieved frequently get lost in the intense focus on the bottom line. We found that just because executives know themselves as good people—honest, caring, and fair—they should not assume that others see them in the same way. It is so easy to forget that employees do not know you the way you know yourself. If employees do not think of an executive as a clearly ethical or unethical leader, they are likely to think of the leader as being somewhere in between—amoral or ethically neutral.

Interestingly, perceptions of *ethically neutral leadership* do not necessarily arise because the leader *is* ethically neutral. In fact, many of the senior executives we spoke with convinced us that it was impossible for them to be ethically neutral in their jobs, given the many value-laden decisions they make every day. Rather, the perception of ethically neutral leadership may exist because the leader has not faced major *public* ethical challenges that would provide the opportunity to convey his or her values to others. As one executive noted, "They haven't had to make any decisions on the margin ... once you're faced with [a major public ethical dilemma], you bare your soul and you're one or the other [ethical or unethical]." On the other hand, a reputation for ethically neutral leadership may exist because the leader has not proactively made ethics and values an explicit and evident part of the leadership agenda. Executives must recognize that if they do not develop a reputation for ethical leadership, they will likely be tagged

Figure 1 The Two Pillars of Ethical Leadership

as "ethically neutral." As a result, employees will believe that the bottom line is the only value that should guide their decisions and that the CEO cares more about himself and the short-term financials than about the long-term interests of the organization and its multiple stakeholders.

Figure 1 provides a summary of our study's findings.

Pillar One: Moral Person

Being an ethical person is the substantive basis of ethical leadership. However, in order to develop a reputation for ethical leadership, the leader's challenge is conveying that substance to others. Being viewed as an ethical person means that people think of you as having certain traits, engaging in certain kinds of behaviors, and making decisions based upon ethical principles. Furthermore, this substantive ethical core must be authentic. As one executive put it, "If the person truly doesn't believe the ethical story and preaches it but doesn't feel it ... that's going to show through. ... But, [a true ethical leader] walks in [and] it doesn't take very long if you haven't met him before [you think] there's a [person] with integrity and candor and honesty."

Traits

Traits are stable personal characteristics, meaning that individuals behave in fairly predictable ways across time and situations and observers come to describe the individual in those terms. The traits that executives most often associate with ethical leadership are honesty, trustworthiness, and integrity. A very broad personal characteristic, *integrity* was the trait cited most frequently by the executives. Integrity is a holistic attribute that encompasses the other traits of honesty and trustworthiness. One executive said that the average employee would say that the ethical leader is "squeaky clean." They would think "I know that if I bring an issue to him or her that I can count on their honesty and integrity on this because I've seen their standards and that one, integrity, is one that's very important to them."

Trustworthiness is also important to executives. Trust has to do with consistency, credibility, and predictability in relationships. "You can't build a long-term relationship with a customer if they don't trust you." Finally, *honesty*, *sincerity*, and *forthrightness* are also important. "An ethical leader ... tends to be rather candid, certain, [and is] very careful to be factual and accurate. ... An ethical leader does not sugarcoat things ... he tells it like it is."

Behaviors

"Your actions speak so loudly, I can't hear what you're saying." That is the sentiment expressed by one executive. Although traits are clearly important to ethical leadership, behaviors are perhaps more so, and these include: "The way you act even when people aren't looking." "People are going to judge you not by what you say but by what you do." "People look at you and understand over time who you are personally as a result of their observations." Important behaviors include "doing the right thing," showing concern for people and treating people right, being open and communicative, and demonstrating morality in one's personal life.

First and foremost, executives said that ethical leaders *do the right thing.* One retired CEO talked about the founder of his firm, a man who "was known for his strong belief that there is only one way to do business and that's the right way."

Second, executive ethical leaders *show concern for people* through their actions. They treat people well—with dignity and respect. "I think [the ethical leader] treats everybody with dignity—meaning everybody—whether they're at the lowest level or higher levels ... everyone gets treated with dignity and respect. I've also found that if you treat people with dignity and respect and trust, they almost invariably will respond in that fashion. It's like raising children. If you really don't trust them, they don't have much to lose by trying to get away with something. If they feel you trust them, they are going to think long and hard before they do something that will violate that trust." Several of the executives used the military example. "In the military, the troops eat before the officers. ... Leaders take care of their troops. ... A leader is selfless, a leader shares credit, a leader sees that contributors are rewarded."

Being open means that the executive is approachable and a good listener. Employees feel comfortable sharing bad news with the ethical leader. One executive said, "An ethical leader would need to be approachable so that ... people would feel comfortable raising the tough issues ... and know that they would be listened to." Another put it this way: "In general, the better leaders that I've met and know are more than willing to share their experiences of rights and wrongs, successes and failures." These leaders do not kill the messenger who brings bad news. They encourage openness and treat bad news as a problem to be addressed rather than punished.

Finally, *personal morality* is associated with ethical leadership. We asked explicitly about personal morality because our interviews with executives took place during the Monica Lewinsky scandal in the Clinton Presidency and the topic was prominent in everyone's mind. When we asked whether personal morality was linked to ethical leadership, most executives answered yes. "You can not be an ethical leader if your personal morality is in question. ... To be a leader ... what you do privately reflects on that organization. Secondly, to be a leader you have a greater standard, a greater responsibility than the average person would have to live up to."

Decision Making

In their decision-making role, executive ethical leaders are thought to *hold to a solid set of ethical values and principles.* They aim to be *objective and fair.* They also have a perspective that goes beyond the bottom line to include *concerns about the broader society and community.* In addition, executives said that ethical leaders rely upon a number of ethical decision rules such as the golden rule and the "*New York Times* Test." The "*New York Times* Test" says that, when making a decision, ethical leaders should ask themselves whether they would like to see the action they are contemplating on tomorrow morning's front page. This question reflects the ethical leader's sensitivity to community standards.

To summarize, the "moral person" pillar of ethical leadership represents the substance of ethical leadership and it is an important prerequisite to developing a reputation for ethical leadership because leaders become associated with their traits, behaviors, and decisions as long as others know about them. With the moral person pillar in place, you should have a reputation for being an ethical person. You can think of this as the *ethical* part of the term "ethical leadership." Having a reputation for being a moral person tells employees what *you* are likely to do—a good start, but it does not necessarily tell them what *they* should do. That requires moral managing—taking the ethics message to the rest of the organization.

Many of the executives we interviewed thought that being an ethical person who does the right thing, treats people well, and makes good decisions was necessary *and* sufficient for being an ethical leader. This is not surprising because executives know other executives personally. They have served under them, worked with them, and observed their behavior at close hand. Therefore, in their minds, an executive's ethical traits, behaviors, and decisions are automatically associated with a reputation for ethical leadership. However, some of the executives and even more of the ethics officers noted that being an ethical person was not enough. To develop a reputation for ethical leadership with employees, leaders must make ethics and values a salient aspect of their leadership agenda so that the message reaches more distant employees. To do this, they must be moral managers as well as moral persons. As one executive expressed it: "Simply put, ethical leadership means doing the right thing, and it means communicating so that everyone understands that [the right thing] is going to happen at all times ... I think that most of the people I've been in business with adhere to the first but do less well with the second. And, in my experience, it is something that has to be reinforced constantly ... the second part is the hardest."

Pillar Two: Moral Manager

In order to develop a reputation for ethical *leadership*, a heavy focus on the leadership part of that term is required. The executive's challenge is to make ethics and values stand out from a business landscape that is laden with messages about beating the competition and achieving quarterly goals and profits. Moral managers recognize the importance of proactively putting ethics at the forefront of their leadership agenda. Like parents who should explicitly share their values with their children, executives need to make the ethical dimension of their leadership explicit and salient to their employees. Executives who fail to do this risk being perceived as ethically neutral because other more pervasive messages about financial success take over. One CEO put it this way: "We do some good things [turn down unethical business opportunities, develop people, champion diversity], but compare the number of times that we recognize those [ethical] achievements versus how much we recognize financial achievements— it's not close. I mean, I cringe ... saying that ... I'm not saying we don't work at these other things, but ... the recognition is still very much on financial performance and ... it's true in almost all organizations ... And that's what's wrong. That's what's out of kilter."

Our study identified a number of ways moral managers can increase the salience of an ethics and values agenda and develop a reputation for ethical leadership. They serve as a role model for ethical conduct in a way that is visible to employees. They communicate regularly and persuasively with employees about ethical standards, principles, and values. Finally, they use the reward system consistently to hold all employees accountable to ethical standards.

Role Modeling through Visible Action

Role modeling may seem similar to the "doing the right thing" category above. However, role modeling emphasizes *visible action* and the perceptual and reputational aspects of ethical leadership. Some ethical behaviors will go completely unnoticed while others will be noticed and will contribute to a reputation for ethical leadership. Effective moral managers recognize that they live in a fishbowl of sorts and employees are watching them for cues about what's important. "You are demonstrating by your example on and off the job, in other words, 24 hours a day, seven days a week, you're a model for what you believe in and the values." In addition, "if you're unethical ... people pick up on that and assume because you're the leader that it's the correct thing to do ... that not only are you condoning it, but you're actually setting the example for it."

The effective moral manager understands which words and actions are noticed and how they will be interpreted by others. In some cases, visible executive action (without any words at all) is enough to send a powerful message. One executive offered the following as an example of the power of executive action. "Some years ago, I was running one of our plants. I had just taken over and they were having some financial troubles. ... Most of our management was flying first class. ... I did not want ... my first act to be to tell everybody that they are not gonna fly first class anymore, so I just quit flying first class. And it wasn't long before people noticed it and pretty soon everybody was flying coach. ... I never put out a directive, never said a word to anybody ... and people noticed it. They got the message. ... People look to the leader. If the leader cuts corners, they say its okay to cut corners around here. If the leader doesn't cut corners, we must be expected not to do any of that around here."

Negative signals can also be sent by visible executive action and moral managers must be particularly sensitive to these. For example, what kind of signal does it send when your organization's ethics policy prohibits employees from accepting any kind of gift from a prospective client and then employees see a group of senior executives sitting in a client's box enjoying a professional football or basketball game? Unless the CEO is wearing a large sign that says "we paid for these tickets," the message is clear. Ethics policies do not apply equally to everyone. It becomes much easier for an employee to rationalize receiving gifts. According to one interviewee, many executives "wouldn't think twice about it because you don't intend to do anything wrong." However, employees are generally not aware of your *intent*. They see the actions and make inferences based upon them.

Communicating about Ethics and Values

Many executives are uncomfortable talking about ethics and wonder about those who do. In our interviews, some executives expressed concern about the leader who talks about ethics too much. "I distrust people who talk about it all the time. I think the way you do it [ethical leadership] is to demonstrate it in action ... the more a person sermonizes about it, the more worried I am ... sometimes you have to talk about it, but mostly you don't talk about it, you just do things." However, moral managers need to talk about ethics and values, not in a sermonizing way, but in a way that explains the values that guide important decisions and actions. If people do not hear about ethics and values from the top, it is not clear to employees that ethics and values are important. You may not feel comfortable talking about ethics if it means discussing the intricacies of Aristotle or Kant. However, talking about ethics with your employees does not mean that at all. It means talking about the values that are important to you and the organization. It is a bit like teaching children about sex. Parents can choose to avoid the uncomfortable subject, hoping that their children will learn what they need to know in school; or, they can bring an expert home who knows more than they do about the physiology of the human reproductive system.

However, what parents really want their children to know about and adopt is a set of values the family believes in such as love, respect, and responsibility. To be most effective, that message must come from parents, in words and in actions. Similarly, the message about the values guiding decisions and actions in business should come from senior leaders.

The Reward System

Using rewards and discipline effectively may be the most powerful way to send signals about desirable and undesirable conduct. That means rewarding those who accomplish their goals by behaving in ways that are consistent with stated values. "The most senior executive should reward the junior executive, the manager, the line people who make these [ethical] decisions ... reinforcement is very important."

It also means clearly disciplining employees at all levels when they break the rules. A financial industry executive provided the following two examples. "If there's a situation within the corporation of sexual harassment where [the facts are] proven and management is very quick to deal with the wrongdoer ... that's leadership. To let the rumor mill take over, to allow someone to quietly go away, to resign, is not ethical leadership. It is more difficult, but you send the message out to the organization by very visible, fair, balanced behavior. That's what you have to do."

"If someone has taken money, and they happen to be a 25-year employee who has taken two hundred dollars over the weekend and put it back on Monday, you have to ... fire that person. [You have to make] sure everybody understands that Joe took two hundred dollars on Friday and got [fired] ... [they must also] be assured that I did have a fact base, and that I did act responsibly and I do care about 25-year people."

Another financial industry executive talked about how he was socialized early in his career. "When I was signed ... to train under a tough, but fair partner of the firm ... he [said] there are things expected from you ... but if you ever make a transaction in a client's account that you can't justify to me was in the best interest of the customer, you're out. Well that kind of gets your attention."

An airline executive said, "we talk about honesty and integrity as a core value; we communicate that. But then we back it up ... someone can make a mistake. They can run into the side of an airplane with a baggage cart and put a big dent in it ... and we put our arm around them and retrain them. ... If that same person were to lie to us, they don't get a second chance ... When it comes to honesty, there is no second chance."

The moral manager consistently rewards ethical conduct and disciplines unethical conduct at all levels in the organization, and these actions serve to uphold the standards and rules. The above reward system examples represent clear signals that will be noticed and that demonstrate clearly how employees are held accountable and how the leader backs up words with actions.

In summary, to develop a reputation for ethical leadership, one must be strong on both dimensions: moral person and moral manager. The ethical leader has a reputation for being both a substantively ethical person and a leader who makes ethics and values a prominent part of the leadership agenda.

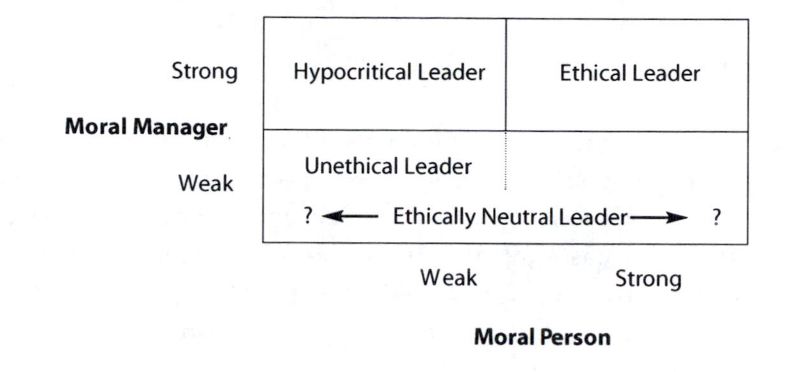

Figure 2 Executive Reputation and Ethical Leadership

What Does Ethical Leadership Accomplish?

The executives we talked with said that ethical leadership was good for business, particularly in the long term, and avoids legal problems. "It probably determines the amount of money you're spending in lawsuits and with corporate attorneys ... you save a lot of money in regulatory fees and lawyer fees and settlement fees." They also said that ethical leadership contributes to employee commitment, satisfaction, comfort, and even fun. "People enjoy working for an ethical organization" and it helps the organization attract and retain the best employees. "If the leadership of the company reflects [ethical] values ... people will want to work for that company and will want to do well." Finally, employees in an organization led by an executive ethical leader will imitate the behavior of their leader and therefore the employees will be more ethical themselves.

Next, we combine the two pillars of ethical leadership into a two by two matrix that can help us think about the kinds of reputation an executive can develop (see Figure 2). As noted, the combination of strong moral person and strong moral manager produces a reputation for ethical leadership. However, what happens if the leader falters in one of these areas? The matrix suggests the following possibilities: one may develop a reputation as an unethical leader, a hypocritical leader, or an ethically neutral leader.

The Unethical Leader

A leader who is perceived to be weak on both dimensions will develop a reputation for unethical leadership. A number of executives we spoke with named Al Dunlap as a prime example of someone with a reputation for unethical executive leadership. *Business Week* recently published excerpts from John Byrne's book about Dunlap entitled *Mean Business.*[2] The article describes Dunlap as the "no-nonsense executive famous for turning around struggling companies—and sending their shares soaring in the process." However, Dunlap was also known for tirades against employees "which could reach the point of emotional abuse." "He was condescending, belligerent and disrespectful." "At his worst, he became viciously profane, even violent. Executives said he would throw papers or furniture, bang his hands on his desk, and shout so ferociously that a manager's hair would be blown back by the stream of air that rushed from Dunlap's mouth." He used the promise of huge rewards to get "employees to do things they might not otherwise do." In order to make the numbers that Dunlap demanded, creative accounting techniques were employed and "dubious techniques were used to boost sales." He also lied to Wall Street analysts. "Despite the chaos inside the company, Sunbeam's chief kept up a steady drumbeat of optimistic sales and earnings forecasts, promises of tantalizing new products, and assurances that the Dunlap magic was working." In the end, the lies could no longer cover up what was really going on. Wall Street abandoned the company and the board of directors fired Dunlap. Sunbeam was left crippled and the company continues to struggle today.

On the moral person dimension, Dunlap was found to be dishonest, he treated people horribly and made decisions based upon the financial bottom line only, disregarding the interests of multiple stakeholders in the process. On the moral manager dimension, his own behavior, communications, and the reward system were used to send a single consistent message. The bottom line was the only thing that mattered.

The Hypocritical Leader

A leader who is not perceived to be a strong ethical person but who attempts to put ethics and values at the forefront of the leadership agenda is likely to be perceived as a hypocritical leader who "talks the ethics talk" but does not "walk the ethics walk." In such cases, people tend to see the talk only as window dressing. They watch for actions to match the words and if there is a mismatch, the words are dismissed. As suggested above, some executives expressed concern about the leader who talks about ethics too much. In terms of the leader's reputation for ethical leadership, communicating about ethics and values, without the actions to match, is probably worse than doing nothing at all because talk without action places a spotlight on the issue that would not otherwise be there. As a result, employees become cynical and distrust everything the leader says. They also figure that they too can ignore ethical standards if they perceive that the leader does so.

The Ethically Neutral Leader

This category generated a lot of comment. Half of the executives rejected it out of hand. The other half recognized its existence and almost all of the twenty corporate ethics officers we talked with readily acknowledged it. On the moral person dimension, it is most appropriate to say that this person is perceived to be *not clearly unethical*, but also not strongly ethical. Consider what people say about ethically neutral leaders. In terms of traits, the ethically neutral leader is seen as more self-centered than other-centered. In terms of behaviors, ethically neutral leaders are less open to input from others and they care less about people. They are less compassionate. In terms of decision making, ethically neutral executive leaders are thought to have a narrower view than do ethical leaders. They focus on financial ends more than the means that are of interest to ethical leaders. They also are more likely to base decisions upon the short-term bottom line and they are less concerned with leaving the organization or the world a better place for the future. Interestingly, much of the emphasis seems to be on what the ethically neutral leader is *not* (not open to input, not caring, not focused on means, not concerned with leaving a legacy). This is important because it means that to perceive ethical leadership, followers need evidence of positive ethical traits, behaviors, and decision processes. Lack of awareness of these positive characteristics leads to the perception that the leader is ethically neutral. Clearly, employees must be aware of these positive attributes in order for them to infer the existence of ethical leadership.

When asked to talk about ethically neutral leaders, people said virtually nothing about moral managing (role modeling, communicating, the reward system). Given that employees make sense of the messages they do get, the ethically neutral leader's focus on the short-term bottom line gets employees' attention by default. If that is what the leader is focusing on, it must be the only thing that is important. One executive said, "Ethics hasn't been on the scorecard for what's important here ... It's kind of like quality. Quality is something that we slipped away from and someone had to say, 'It's important.' Maybe the same is true of ethics ... we need a Deming ... to remind us of how important it is."

Perhaps the most important outcome of ethically neutral leadership is that employees then think that ethics is not particularly important to the leader, "So they're left deciding on their own what's important in a particular situation." This means that they are acting without clear guidance about the ethics and values of the organization. The leader has not demonstrated it, has not thought through it, has not given an example of it, has not talked about it, and has not discussed it in an open forum.

Cultivating a Reputation for Ethical Leadership

Given the importance of ethical leadership, we offer the following practical steps executives can take to cultivate a reputation for ethical leadership.

Share Your Values: Who You Are as an Ethical Person

"Ethical leadership is not easy ... the temptations and the rewards for unethical behavior are great. So, ethical leadership requires a discipline, a mental and personal discipline that is not easy to come by." Some senior executives arrive in their leadership positions with all of the necessary cognitive and emotional tools to be an active ethical leader. Part of the reason many of them ascend to senior leadership positions is because they have a reputation for integrity, for treating people well and for doing the right thing. They have likely had a lifetime of personal and work-related mentors and experiences that have molded and reinforced their values. By the time they reach the executive level, these values are so solid, that when challenged, the leader holds to them without question.

On the other hand, senior executive positions have a way of challenging your values in ways you may not have been challenged before. If you think that this aspect of your leadership needs work, devote energy to developing this side of yourself. Read books. Attend workshops and seminars with other senior executives who share your concerns. Work with a personal coach. Talk with your spiritual advisor about how your values can be applied in your work.

It then becomes particularly important to share this side of yourself. Find out what employees know about you and how they think of you in ethical leadership terms. You may be a strong ethical person, but your employees may have no way of knowing that. Most people do not have an accurate view of how others see them, especially when it comes to ethics. Surveys consistently find that most people think of themselves as above average and more ethical than their peers. However, the only way to honestly assess where you stand in terms of others' perceptions is to ask for candid input. A leader should "always have someone who can tell the emperor that he has no clothes." So, ask those closest to you. You can also survey your employees to find out how much they know about you as an ethical leader. Be open to what you learn and do not be surprised if employees say they simply do not know. For example, if you have not been outspoken on ethics and values issues, or you have not managed a highly public crisis that provided an opportunity for employees to learn about your values, you may be surprised to learn that employees do *not* know much about this aspect of your leadership. They may even see you as "neutral" on the ethics dimension. Talk to your communications people and your ethics officer, if you have one, about how you might successfully convey your values to employees on a regular basis. Figure out a way to open the lines of two-way communication on ethics and values issues. Ask employees to share the ethical dilemmas they face and to let you know what kind of guidance they would like from you.

Assume the Role of Moral Manager: Chief *Ethics* Officer of Your Organization

"Ethical leadership means that the person, the leader, who is exercising that leadership is well-grounded in a set of values and beliefs that we would view as being ethical. However, in a leadership sense … it means that the leader sets an example because ethical leadership doesn't just mean that leader, it means the entire organization. If there isn't an observed ethical leadership at the top, you won't find it in the organization."

As noted, moral management requires overt action on the part of the executive to serve as a role model for ethical behavior in highly visible ways, to communicate about ethics and values, and to use the reward system to hold people accountable. James Burke, former CEO of Johnson & Johnson provides an excellent example of highly visible action that gets everyone's attention. Soon after Burke assumed the presidency of Johnson & Johnson, he brought together 28 senior managers to challenge the age-old corporate credo. He asked them to talk about whether they could really live by the document that had been hanging on corporate walls for years. "If we can't live by this document then it's an act of pretension and we ought to tear it off the walls, get rid of it. If we can live with it but want to change it that's okay too, if we can agree on what the changes should be. And, we could also leave it the way it is." According to Burke, people "stayed up all night screaming at each other." When they were done, they had updated the credo. They then took it to J&J sites around the world, released a revised credo in 1979, and committed the organization to it. Less than three years later, the Tylenol poisoning occurred and lots of folks were waiting to see whether management would live up to the credo values. As every student of business ethics and corporate crisis management knows, they did, and the case is now held up as a premier example of good business ethics. Burke does not take credit for J&J's success in handling the corporate crisis. He attributes the success to the value system that had been articulated. However, clearly he was responsible for guiding the organization through the values articulation process and for making the credo prominent in the corporate culture and consciousness. As another executive put it, "all the written statements in the world won't achieve ethics in an organization unless the leader is perceived as being very serious and committed."

Following the Tylenol crisis, in 1985 Burke launched the credo survey process. All employees were surveyed regarding the company's performance with respect to the credo. Based upon the results, managers held feedback and problem-solving sessions with their employees and developed action plans to address problems. The survey process continues today on a biannual schedule under Burke's successor, Ralph Larsen, and remains a valuable way to keep attention focused on the credo and the values it represents.

To better integrate the Credo into the reward system, Larsen instigated a "standards of leadership" program which holds leaders at all levels accountable to the credo values. "At the important succession planning meetings, when upward mobility in the company is discussed, 'Credo Values' is first on the agenda. 'Business Results' is next in line. The following behaviors associated with Credo values are noted: 'Behaving with honesty and integrity. Treating others with dignity and respect. Applying Credo values. Using Credo survey results to improve business. Balancing the interests of all constituents. Managing for the long term.'"[3]

Finally, violations of Credo policy are handled swiftly and clearly. In one incident that involved infiltration of a competitor's sales meeting, President Larsen wrote the following to his management, "Our behavior should deeply embarrass everyone associated with Johnson & Johnson. Our investigation revealed that certain employees had engaged in improper activities that violated our policies. These actions were wrong and we took steps, immediately, to discipline those involved and guard against a recurrence of this kind of activity."[4]

Conclusion

Being an ethical leader requires developing a reputation for ethical leadership. Developing a reputation for ethical leadership depends upon how others perceive the leader on two dimensions: as a moral person and as a moral manager. Being a moral person encompasses who you are, what you do, and what you decide as well as making sure that others know about this dimension of you as a person. Being a moral manager involves being a role model for ethical conduct, communicating regularly about ethics and values, and using the reward system to hold everyone accountable to the values and standards.

Ethical leadership pays dividends in employee pride, commitment, and loyalty—all particularly important in a full employment economy in which good companies strive to find and keep the best people.

NOTES

1. C. Barnard, *Functions of the Executive* (Cambridge, MA: Harvard University Press, 1938 and 1968), p. 279.
2. J.A. Byrne, "Chainsaw," *Business Week*, October 18, 1999, pp. 128–149.
3. L. Foster, *Robert Wood Johnson* (State College, PA: Lillian Press, 1999), pp. 645–646.
4. Ibid., p. 646.

Part II

Foundations of Great Leadership

Chapter 6

LEADING: THE ART AND SCIENCE OF INSPIRING OTHERS

When someone asks you to name a great leader, what names come to mind? Do you think of a political leader such as President Obama, President Bush, President Lincoln, etc.? Do you think of religious leaders such as the pope, Martin Luther King Jr., and others? Maybe the person who comes to mind is your father or mother, or a favorite relative, teacher, or business leader.

Now consider why you think that person is a great leader. What is it about that person that causes you to hold him or her in that high regard? Almost every author in the field of leadership attempts to offer his or her own unique definition of leadership. Considering so many definitions of leadership often confuses or upsets the reader, because most of us believe we already know what leadership is. Perhaps, like pornography, we can't precisely define it, but we believe we know it when we see it.

The human mind is like an umbrella—it functions best when open.

—Walter Gropius (1883–1969), famous German architect

Most people agree, leadership is important, but they disagree about what it is. As you begin this chapter, open your mind to the possibility that there may be many new and worthwhile things to learn about leadership.

Leadership Defined

Leadership is the art and science of ethically and effectively guiding others toward a positive goal. Leadership is an *art* because so much depends upon the perception of the followers. Like a great painting, some think it is great, while others think it is trash. The one you consider a great leader, others may call a tyrant. For example, you may consider the current president of the United States to be a great leader and others may totally disagree. The same can be said regarding most leaders in government, religion, education, and business. Someday, perhaps people will have such a debate about you.

> *A boss creates fear, a leader confidence.*
>
> *A boss fixes blame, a leader corrects mistakes.*
>
> *A boss knows it all, a leader asks questions.*
>
> *A boss makes work drudgery, a leader makes it interesting.*
>
> *—Russell H. Ewing*

Leadership is a *science* because it has been scientifically studied for decades, and much is known about what does and does not work. We will examine key scientific findings about leadership later in this chapter. To be a leader, all you really need are followers; however, to be a *great* leader, you need much more.

Great leaders are *effective* at getting results, but not at the expense of their *ethics*. All this effort must be directed toward a *positive goal*. For example, Hitler was effective, but hardly a great leader. He lacked ethics, and his efforts were not directed toward a positive goal.

A great leader does much more than boss others around.

Finally, leadership is not about you; it is about what *others* accomplish under your leadership. You can't simply declare yourself a great leader. This is something others must willingly say about you. People speak of great leaders with respect.

Authors disagree about the precise definition of leadership, but most agree it is important. Most large organizations, both for profit and not for profit, fail when there is a failure of leadership. It is easy to find failed leadership; in fact, it seems to be all around us. The good news is, if you learn how to become a great leader, you will be in great demand. As evidence that great leadership is in such short supply, consider that scientists agree enough food is produced on our planet to properly feed and nourish everyone. However, approximately every five seconds someone on this planet dies of hunger or a disease related to hunger. Most who die are tiny children, certainly too young and frail to have a job. Food is not lacking. Transportation is not lacking. Desire to help is not lacking. What is lacking is leadership.

Leaders make decisions about priorities. Leaders focus the attention of their followers on what they believe is important. For example when a government decides to spend taxpayer money on wars, there is less to be spent on feeding the hungry and clothing the naked. Choices must be made, and leaders have a responsibility to make choices that benefit others, not just themselves.

Doing the Right Thing

> *Managers do things right. Leaders do the right thing.*
>
> —*Warren Bennis, organizational consultant and author*

What is the relationship between management and leadership? Many authors have used this approach to distinguish leadership from management.

What does it mean to say that managers do things right, while leaders do the right thing? In general, such a definition gets across the general concept that management is somewhat more involved with short-term matters regarding control and maintenance of the status quo, while leadership is more long term in scope and involved with vision, motivation, and implementation of organizational change. Bennis's definition is widely quoted and useful, but it is also true that most leaders within large organizations have come up through the ranks by demonstrating good management. Think of leadership and management as overlapping Venn diagrams. While management may be more concerned with keeping within a cost budget and a time schedule, really good managers are also inspiring leaders, and really good leaders do not ignore budgets and schedules. Your goal should be to be both a *great* manager and a *great* leader.

Top-level Management versus Leadership

Top-level management and leadership are often considered the same. Surely a top-level manager such as a CEO ought to be both a manager and a leader. However, there are times when even the lowest-ranking member of an organization may be called upon to lead. A manager holds an organizational position with the title of Manager. Leaders may or may not hold any official title. People often are forced to follow the directions of a manager or risk losing their job, but people voluntarily follow a true leader.

Spending a lot more time distinguishing between good top-level management and leadership is mostly a waste of time. There is much overlap, and people who qualify for top-level formal leadership positions have typically had to demonstrate good management in order to be considered for such higher-level positions. A good organizational leader was probably first a good manager. With the proper attitude, teaching, and experience, a good manager can learn to also become a good leader. Decide now to become a life-long learner about the fascinating topic of leadership. It is one of the most interesting and important topics you could possibly study.

Leadership and learning go together. To become a great leader, you will need to learn many things, but learning about the nature of leadership itself is most critical.

Leadership—Leading the Ship

Let's look take a closer look at the word "leadership" itself. First, according to Webster, when a word ends with the suffix *–ship*, it means the quality, condition, or state of being—as in hardship or friendship.

Leadership and learning are indispensable to each other.

—President John F. Kennedy

Therefore, leadership means the quality, condition, or state of being a leader. Now think of the second half of the word—"ship," as in a large boat. A leader is the captain of the ship. The captain guides the ship from one location to another, avoiding dangerous obstacles, and keeping all passengers, cargo, and crew safe.

How does the ship's captain do it? In order to properly lead, the ship's captain must have access to certain controls or access to those who do. The captain's station on the ship, or pilot's cockpit on a plane, needs to provide a variety of dials and gauges that inform the captain of many important variables, such as ship's speed, direction, and the status of important systems like air pressure, oil pressure, engine temperature, etc.

The pilot of an airliner is also a leader in need of many controls. Have you even taken a good look inside the cockpit of an airliner? There are hundreds of dials, gauges, and meters. For an airline pilot, some gauges, such as the altimeter, are critical, while others are only important if something is outside certain boundaries. Knowing how high you are above the ground is much more important than knowing the air temperature in the passenger cabin.

An airline pilot has the critical responsibility of avoiding a deadly crash landing. If the pilot fails and the plane crashes, the black box recorder is studied by experts for days to determine the exact reading of hundreds of sensors and gauges. The importance of each measure depends on the situation. Leadership is like that. Some measures are vital all the time, and some only in certain emergency situations or when something is terribly wrong. When things do go wrong, it is often some minor issue that, unfortunately, was not detected by the leader in time to take corrective action.

Good leaders see problems early and take corrective action. One of the ways they make it look easy is by addressing problems when they are small rather than waiting until they get out of hand. They do this by being focused. An airline pilot must focus on the responsibility of getting the passengers to their destination safely. He or she cannot be distracted by the hundreds of other things going on and therefore fail to notice some problem developing with an engine or some obstacle that needs to be avoided.

Let's take the example to an even more familiar place, the driver's seat of your automobile. When you move from the passenger seat to the driver's seat, you are assuming a position of leadership. You are now responsible for the lives of the other people in the car. You will need a clear idea of where you are going and how to get there safely. Information from a variety of gauges and dials such as the speedometer plus a clear view out the windshield and mirrors allows you to see and judge distances ahead, behind, and to the sides. Some parts of the car are so critical (such as the steering wheel and the view out of the windshield) that you need to give them constant attention.

In a driver's training class, you were probably taught to never take your eyes off the road and to keep your hands on the steering wheel at all times and even to position them at 10 o'clock and 2 o'clock. You were also probably taught when approaching an intersection to look to the left and then to the right and then back again to the left before proceeding into the intersection. Because crossing a busy intersection is so dangerous, new drivers are taught to be especially cautious about looking both ways before entering the intersection.

> *One of the true tests of leadership is the ability to recognize a problem before it becomes an emergency.*
>
> *—Harold S. Geneen, (1910–1997), CEO of AT&T, 1959–1977*

Other things, such as the oil pressure light and the engine coolant temperature gauge, need your attention only periodically, such as when the oil pressure is dangerously low or the coolant is dangerously hot. Under normal circumstances, some measures such as oil pressure and coolant temperature are of little interest. However, once oil pressure drops below some dangerous level, then to ignore it will result in disaster for your car, and perhaps everyone in it or near it. Often people refer to such warning lights as "idiot lights," because they only light up when something is very wrong and even an idiot should be smart enough to notice, stop, and take corrective action. Many idiot lights replaced gauges and dials that were too frequently ignored because drivers got so used to them being within normal ranges. Instead, idiot lights flash to get your attention that something is seriously wrong.

People who attempt to define leadership too narrowly run the danger of implying some important measures can be ignored. For example, we have observed some leaders who seem to ignore their own arrogance. Unfortunately, there is no idiot light to warn you that your positive self-confidence and pride have edged over into the arrogant range.

Followers will allow a leader with obvious talents some measure of personal pride, up to a point. We may even think a rather elevated sense of pride is necessary for someone to have the courage to accept the challenge of leadership. We expect the leader to courageously step forward to take command. Also, the "perks" of some leadership positions are seductive, making it easy to believe you really are special and your pride is justified. However, when that pride reaches an annoying level of arrogance, then many followers will view the leader in an extremely unfavorable light. At some point, it is similar to an overheated car engine. If unnoticed or ignored, the result will be disastrous.

Leadership is about piloting the "ship" or organization. A good leader puts the safety and well-being of all aboard the ship above self. A good captain keeps an eye on the ship's gauges, knows which gauges are most important in different situations, and knows what action to take, especially in emergencies. A good captain goes down with the ship—is the last to abandon a sinking ship. A good example of such leadership occurred on January 15, 2009, when Chesley Burnett "Sully" Sullenberger III successfully landed US Airways Flight 1549 in the middle of the Hudson River. The plane had lost all power, and Sullenberger had to act fast and with supreme skill to save the lives of his 115 passengers and crew. After piloting the plane to a safe landing in the Hudson, but while the plane was rapidly sinking, he walked the length of the passenger cabin twice to make sure everyone had evacuated before leaving the plane.

Great leaders are willing and able to take on great responsibility. Within a few years, many readers of this textbook will be given leadership opportunities within large corporations. You will be responsible

One way of looking at this might be that for 42 years I've been making small, regular deposits in this bank of experience: education and training. And on January 15 the balance was sufficient so that I could make a very large withdrawal.

—Chesley "Sully" Sullenberger III, airline pilot and hero

for budgets of millions of dollars; the hiring, training, and evaluation of hundreds of people; and the image and reputation of your organization as seen by investors, customers, suppliers, and citizens in the surrounding community. Exactly how many gauges are needed to properly control the piloting of a large corporation is unknown, but the "cockpit" should look more like that of an airline pilot than that of a soapbox derby racer.

Brief definitions of leadership erroneously lead students to believe leadership is simple, but leading a large organization is complex. Many of the "gauges" you will need are actually your followers and their abilities and willingness to provide honest, timely, and pertinent information to their leader.

Leadership Lessons from *The Emperor's New Clothes*

Often, we can find profound wisdom in the simplest of tales. All leaders should read and take to heart the moral in the children's story, *The Emperor's New Clothes*, by Hans Christian Andersen. Recall the evil tailors decided to trick the foolish and vain emperor by telling him they had a new type of cloth that was visible only to those who were loyal and worthy of their position in the king's court. Since the king and all the members of his court were afraid to admit they might not be totally *loyal* and *worthy* of their positions, none admitted they couldn't see the cloth. The evil tailors pretended to sew and eventually told the king his new robes were ready. They collected a huge sum for their "work" and suggested the king hold a parade to show off his new robes as they quickly packed up and moved out. It was only the honesty of a little child (who was too young to know or care about being totally loyal or worthy of his position) that finally revealed that the king was, in fact, parading around totally naked.

This story is played out daily in real life. People hesitate to tell the leader the truth, especially if it might call into question their *loyalty* or *worthiness* for their position. They are even more reluctant to tell the leader bad news, especially if the leader has, in the past, punished the bearer of such bad news. By daily recalling the moral of *The Emperor's New Clothes*, leaders should remember to seek out dissenting opinions and bearers of both good and bad news.

Many leaders we have known think they do, but often they don't. Instead, they enjoy surrounding themselves with "yes-men" and "yes-women," who constantly sing the praises of the leader. Vanity reigns supreme—but not forever. At some point, the king's nakedness is revealed, and the embarrassment is great.

Some Native American tribes were known to include at least one official "contrarian." A *contrarian* typically acts and thinks in a way contrary to popular or accepted opinion. In the 1970 movie *Little Big Man* starring Dustin Hoffman, the role of a Native American contrarian called Younger Bear was played by Cal Bellini. Younger Bear said hello when he meant goodbye, rode his horse backwards, washed with dirt, and did just about everything exactly opposite of everyone else, but the contrarian was thought to bring good luck to the tribe. In real life the chief and elders of the tribe knew they could rely on the tribe's official contrarian to provide a different, and valuable, point of view. In our modern society, the term contrarian often refers to a financial adviser who suggests buying stocks that the rest of the financial community shuns. In general, the contrarian sees opportunities where others see only the risk. Unfortunately, in many bureaucratic organizations, contrarians are not tolerated, and this leaves leaders blind to the insights a contrarian provides.

What Leadership Research Teaches Us

Professor Richard Boyatzis at Case Western Reserve University says, "Research is the source of our integrity?" Do you agree? What is the source of your integrity? Perhaps you aren't convinced of the importance of academic research. You are not alone. Some people outside the academic community, and some inside it, criticize academic research. In fact, when people say something is "academic," they often mean that it really doesn't count; perhaps it is interesting in theory, but useless in practice.

Some, but not all, of the academic literature about leadership is, unfortunately, useless in practice. We've all heard the phrase, "publish or perish," and it is usually understood to mean that academics are forced to publish a certain number of academic articles in obscure journals that are only read by other academics or by their students who are forced to read them as part of their course assignments.

Good research, however, is very practical. It is easy to see the value of research in areas such as medicine or rocket science. The academic discipline of business is not rocket or medical science. However, scholars in the academic area of business do conduct research and publish their results in academic journals. Academic journal articles become much of the source material for college textbooks. When professors decide what should and should not be taught in college courses, the decision is frequently based upon what has become accepted knowledge through the process of research as reported in the journals.

There is nothing so practical as a good theory.

—Kurt Lewin (1890–1947), considered the father of modern social psychology

We should be honest about what we teach. That is what Boyatzis means when he says, "Research is the source of our integrity." We should not teach myths. We should teach truths. Research is how we tell one from the other. It's far from perfect, but it's the best we've got.

It's not what we don't know that hurts, it's what we know that ain't so.

—Will Rogers, humorist and social commentator

Good research is based on critical thinking and the scientific method. The methodology of a good study about leadership should be similar to what one would expect to find in research studies published in the most respected academic journals. Such articles must pass rigorous inspection, and should be based on appropriate theory, proper sample size, and the proper statistical tests should be used to test clearly stated hypotheses. Other researchers should be able to replicate the study and obtain similar results. The aim should be to prove or disprove statements about leadership so those who are teaching about this topic will be able to separate unproven myths from scientific fact.

Will Rogers hit the nail on the head with respect to the field of leadership. People insist they know what good leadership is, but often it simply isn't so. Among the myths that are often presented as scientific fact in the books and articles found in the common press are the following:

Myths About Leadership

1. Leaders are born, not made.
2. Future leaders can be identified early in life by observing a few key traits.
3. A more participative leadership style will produce followers who are more productive and more highly satisfied.
4. The best leadership style is contingent on a few key factors, such as the type of relationship that exists between the leader and the followers, the type of task to be done, and the positional power of the leader.
5. The best leaders help their followers align their personal goals with the goals of the organization, and thereby produce an environment where both individuals and the group are highly successful.
6. The best leaders are either born with charisma or develop their charisma and use it to make large and dramatic changes in organizations.

You probably believe that some, if not all, of the above listed myths are true. None, however, stand up well to rigorous scientific testing. You are not convinced, you say? You have observed leaders, both good and bad, and you have formed your opinions. Do you feel the same way about taking medicines? Instead of taking only such medication that has been thoroughly tested in scientific laboratories, prescribed by your doctor (who has a medical degree), and available in your local drug store, do you rush off to another country to buy your medicine from someone operating out of a cheap hotel? If you answered "no" to that question, then why would you want to accept cheap myths about something as important as leadership?

In this chapter, we examine a few of the major studies about leadership, both to learn which ideas have withstood the bright light of scientific investigation and which might seem logical, but have not been scientifically verified. While we know of no official count of the number of published research studies regarding leadership, it must be in the thousands. *Bass & Stogdill's Handbook of Leadership Theory, Research, & Managerial Applications* is a summary of such studies—a massive book consisting of 1,182 pages. If it took 1,182 pages to summarize the research on leadership, imagine how many pages of detail exist.

Among the various theories of leadership you will find:

1. *Great Man Theory*—Leaders are born leaders or sent by God to lead.
2. *Leadership Trait Theory*—Potential great leaders can be identified early by certain traits.
3. *Ohio State Studies*—Concern for people versus concern for task, usually accompanied by recommendations to be more concerned for people or more humanistic.
4. *Contingency Theory*—Which leadership approach to use depends on elements of the leader's personality, plus the task, workers, and power of leader.
5. *Path-Goal Theory*—Leaders lead by helping followers align their goals with goals of the organization.
6. *Transactional Theory*—Leaders use pay and other rewards to trade off with followers to get them to do what is expected of them.
7. *Transformational Theory*—Leaders inspire their followers to change to implement really major organizational shifts or sea changes. Vision is the thing.
8. *Charismatic Leadership Theory*—Leaders use their charm and personal persuasive powers over others to lead others. Sometimes charismatic and transformational leadership theories are combined into charismatic transformational leadership, a powerful combination indeed.
9. *Servant Leadership*—Very commonly prescribed in the not-for-profit sector, but gaining some ground in the for-profit world. Turn the organizational chart upside down and think of the leader as servant to others.
10. *Leader-Member Exchange Theory*—Leaders work with a close inner circle of followers who share the leader's position. Benefits and power goes to those in the inner circle. Those in the out-group are not trusted, and their power is minimized. Leadership is all about relationships between the leader and the followers.
11. *Authentic Leadership*—Leadership comes from the consent of the governed. Leaders only have authority as it derives from those being led. It is closely related to the concept of democratic government of the people, by the people, and for the people.
12. *Various combinations of the above.*

The above list should be thought of as a group of overlapping Venn diagrams. Proponents of each theory or approach to leadership have a tendency to include within their favorite approach all the good things from other theories and exclude all the bad. This adds to the confusion about leadership research. However, the above list also illustrates how researchers have found this area fascinating and have attempted many combinations of variables in a failed attempt thus far to find the one approach that works best in all situations.

Given all the attention scholars have paid to leadership, it would be reasonable to assume we would know a great deal about what researchers have been able to prove regarding leadership. Unfortunately, much of leadership remains a mystery, some would say an art. That is not to say, however, that we know nothing. Some leadership approaches clearly work better than others in certain circumstances.

The main purpose of this chapter is to briefly summarize some of the main findings about this topic, so popular with researchers. Any attempt to briefly summarize this massive amount of research can easily be criticized for omissions. The perfect approach to leadership simply does not exist; perhaps it never will. Leadership will likely always remain partially an art, because the perceptions of followers are such an essential component and people's perceptions are never totally predictable. Each person is unique. At this point, those aspiring to develop their leadership potential have to be satisfied with what we do know and must be careful not to accept as fact what is merely myth. Assuming we know it all is the source of arrogance, whereas research is the source of our integrity.

Hero or Great Man Theories—Are Leaders Born Special?

From the earliest recorded histories until today, many people have believed certain men—and once in a while a woman—were sent to earth by God(s) or aliens from outer space to lead large groups of people in support of some great cause. The *Great Man Theory* or *Hero Theory* is a myth that assumes leaders are born, not made. In many cultures, people believed these leaders were part divine. Throughout history, emperors such as Julius Caesar have assumed titles that amounted to being called the son of God. The *divine right of kings* is the belief that kings and queens derive their right to rule from the will of God. Therefore, the monarch is not subject to the will of the people. There have been many legends about leaders who were thought to be sons of a human woman and a divine father. In other cases, the leader may have been born of human parents, but a god or gods or some superpower intervened in some way to give this child superhuman powers. Such people are destined from birth to become leaders.

Although there is not a shred of scientific evidence to support this Great Man Theory, many people still believe leaders are born. They think some people are born with natural leadership ability. Some believe in fate and say certain people are destined to be leaders, others are born to be followers, and still others are uninvolved and are neither leaders nor followers. Many of us hope there will be a superhuman hero who will arrive to save the day with their super strength. When the hero fails, the people often turn the hero into a scapegoat to be sacrificed for the benefit of the group. People simply won't let this myth die, and prefer to continue looking for a different savior or hero. It is as though we still believe in Superman—"faster than a speeding bullet, more powerful than a locomotive, and able to leap tall buildings in a single bound."

> *When men are most sure and arrogant they are commonly most mistaken.*
>
> *—David Hume, Scottish philosopher (1711–1776)*

The 2003 election of bodybuilder and movie star Arnold Schwarzenegger as governor of California could be viewed as an example of hero worship. Schwarzenegger was elected, despite the fact he had no experience in elected office and his qualifications were mostly in the areas of bodybuilding and playing an action hero in the movies. However, Governor Gray Davis, the person reelected only a few months earlier, was perceived as weak and unable to solve the huge budget problems plaguing California, so California voters removed Davis from office and elected a new governor with absolutely no relevant experience and very questionable credentials. What Schwarzenegger did have was an image of power and strength. Of course, that image was created mostly by Hollywood moviemakers, but sometimes perceptions are more important than truth. The long-term success or failure of Schwarzenegger's tenure as governor of California will be determined by history, but regardless of that outcome, we should not conclude that the way for you to prepare for leadership is to spend all day lifting weights to build up your muscles.

People may hate to admit it, but many of us still hope some superhuman hero will rescue us from all our problems. We seem to want our leaders to be powerful and stand for "truth, justice, and the American way," as Superman did. We have to be careful not to fall into hero worship.

The turmoil in the Middle East provides another example of people hoping for a superpowerful leader who will protect them from their enemies and bring honor and respect to their individual nations. For centuries that area of the world has been marred with violence, and the people have been forced, for their own safety, to align with the toughest leader. To align yourself with the second toughest leader in such a violent environment is to greatly increase your chances of death.

> *The most dangerous leadership myth is that leaders are born—that there is a genetic factor to leadership. This myth asserts that people simply either have certain charismatic qualities or not. That's nonsense; in fact, the opposite is true. Leaders are made rather than born. Failing organizations are usually over-managed and under-led.*
>
> *—Warren Bennis*

Similarly, Vladimir Putin, currently prime minister of Russia, was elected partially because of his reputation for toughness. Many assumed anyone of lesser physical strength, courage, and cunning would not survive the threats of the Russian Mafia and other tough opponents. Lyndon Baines Johnson, 36th President of the United States, expressed his views on power as, "I do understand power, whatever else may be said about me, I know where to look for it, and how to use it."

What seems strange is the preponderance of research evidence in the United States supporting a softer, more participative form of leadership, and at the same time seeing several leaders recently elected primarily because of their toughness. The idea of the leader as a superhero with strength and cunning—even if a bit unethical—dies hard. Many people still want their leader to be stronger than the competition's leader. Our leader should protect us, even if he or she bends the rules a little. We have a fundamental desire for safety. If our safety is threatened, we throw out the soft, intellectual, fair, consensus builder, and bring on the tough guy. However, when the threat is gone, many will want to toss out the tough guy. In numerous organizations, we see leaders come and go in a see-saw pattern of tough guy, then soft guy, then back to tough guy, and so on.

Another reason the Great Man Theory still is believed—despite mountains of research evidence to the contrary—is that people who write history books seem to believe that history is all about what certain great leaders have done. According to this concept, many historians have claimed that if it had not been for Winston Churchill, Germany would have won World War II. Of course, that completely discounts the thousands of soldiers' lives that were sacrificed to win that war. Winston Churchill was, undoubtedly, a great leader, but he was not the only important leader in World War II. Much of the German army was actually defeated in Russia when Hitler overextended his supply lines, and the severe Russian winter caused many Nazis to die of cold and starvation in the snow.

History is written by the victors. Today, Churchill is remembered primarily for his role in rallying the citizens of England to have courage during the bombing of London. Instead of seeking shelter in a safer environment, he elected to stay in London so the people could see him walking the streets and hear him on the radio: vowing that the British people will never surrender.

Try to imagine being in London hearing bombs exploding all around you and straining to hear Churchill's words over the radio. At the time, most of Europe had already fallen to Nazi advances, and many assumed England would soon surrender. Churchill's words provided much-needed inspiration during desperate times. However, as the war was ending in 1945, Churchill was defeated and Clement Attlee became prime minister. Then, in 1951 when a war against Communist forces appeared imminent, Churchill was again elected prime minister. The English wanted Churchill's leadership in wartime, but apparently not in peacetime. Many organizations do likewise, and select one type of leader in stormy times and a totally different kind during calmer times.

Another example often cited as a great hero responsible for changing the course of history is Martin Luther King Jr. While practically everyone would agree he was a great leader, there were thousands of others who also risked their lives to bring greater civil rights to African Americans. Thousands of ministers, mostly African American but some white, risked their lives by speaking out for civil rights. However, it is Martin Luther King's *"I Have a Dream"* speech that is so often quoted.

To this day, many still feel a lump in their throats when they recite those famous words. The fact that King used the phrase *"I have a dream"* rather than the less dramatic *"I have an objective, or goal, or concept"* is often cited as an example of how a leader can reach inside followers and touch the inner spirit. Dr. King, like many famous leaders, had a flare for the dramatic. He did more than manage or motivate: he inspired.

Some of the rationale behind people freely selecting leaders on the basis of hero worship may be explained by the psychological concept of transference. *Transference* was first described by Freud, and later by Carl Jung in *The Psychology of Transference*, as a tendency to unconsciously redirect or transfer our feelings for one person to another. For example, children raised in a family where the father was a good provider for the family but was also abusive, often transfer their mixed feelings for their father to other leaders. They expect leaders to protect them and provide for them, but also seem to accept the abuse. Psychologists often find their patients become erotically attracted toward their therapist, attributing to the therapist feelings they may wish were present. Some wives look for husbands who are much like their fathers—or how they hoped their fathers would be. Sometimes we get so carried away with the charisma or engaging personality of the "hero" that we follow them blindly. Or we "create" a hero out of someone who is actually rather like almost all humans, someone with both good and bad traits.

Another danger of the Great Man Theory of Leadership is the tendency to expect our leaders to be perfect. In Walter Isaacson's recent best seller, *Einstein: His Life and Universe*, he reveals that several universities turned down Einstein's application for a faculty position. Einstein's family life and personal appearance were often a mess, and in several areas Einstein was far from a genius. For example, he never learned to drive a car because he considered it too complicated. However, he changed the world of physics and showed intellectual leadership in ways that have forever changed our understanding of the relationship between energy, mass, and the speed of light. Just imagine how embarrassed those universities must have felt later to know they had passed up the opportunity to have a Nobel Laureat on their staff. Further, we are indeed fortunate that Hitler rejected Einstein from the German scientific community because of Einstein's Jewish ancestry and that Princeton University offered him a position, causing him to immigrate to the United States and eventually become a U.S. citizen. Just imagine what Hitler might have done had Germany developed the atomic bomb before the United States. Einstein had lots of flaws, some real and some only perceived by madmen such as Hitler, but today he stands as an example of how someone can be the world's foremost leader in one area and deficient in another. In

When we allow freedom to ring, when we let it ring from every tenement and every hamlet, from every state and every city, we will be able to speed up that day when all of God's children, black men and white men, Jews and Gentiles, Protestants and Catholics, will be able to join hands and sing in the words of the old Negro spiritual, "Free at last, free at last. Thank God Almighty, we are free at last."

—Rev. Martin Luther King, civil rights leader

looking to others for leadership, do not require perfection in any human being—it doesn't exist. For yourself, if you have flaws—and who doesn't?—take heart; all great leaders also had flaws.

For students of leadership, the greatest harm done by accepting the concept that leaders are born with some gift that predisposes them to be leaders is that it discourages students from thinking for themselves and taking the study of leadership seriously. If leadership is something you are born with, then there is no point in studying it or working to develop your leadership abilities. Either you have it or you don't. While it is true that some of us are born more gifted than others, there isn't any serious researcher who currently supports The Great Man approach to leadership. But despite this lack of evidence, the idea that some people are born leaders persists.

Trait Theory—Can You Predict Who Will Be a Good Leader by Their Traits?

Trait Theory and the Great Man Theory are like Venn diagrams that overlap about half way. With *Trait Theory*, we do not have to believe our leader was sent from the gods, but we do believe leaders are special people recognized by a specific set of traits. Perhaps the traits were developed by the leader through a combination of education and experience and not from divine intervention, but still the traits amount to the description of a hero. Leaders were believed to be brave, intelligent, strong, charismatic, articulate, truthful, trustworthy, likeable, and extraordinarily effective at getting things done. At the extreme, these traits almost make the person glow, and some people are attracted to them like moths to a flame.

Since the 1920s, several studies have tried to explain leadership in terms of traits of personality and character. By 1950 most researchers had given up on finding some set of traits that described either how to achieve positions of great leadership or to describe which traits were necessary to produce great results once the leadership position was attained. Clearly, some traits such as honesty, trustworthiness, persistence, etc., are good traits for any human to have. At the time of his death in 1790, Benjamin Franklin was working on a list of virtues he thought most important for young people to cultivate:

Benjamin Franklin's 13 Virtues:

1. *Temperance—Eat not to dullness; drink not to elevation.*
2. *Silence—Speak not but what may benefit others or yourself; avoid trifling conversation.*
3. *Order—Let all things have their places; let each part of your business have its time.*
4. *Resolution—Resolve to perform what you ought; perform without fail what you resolve.*
5. *Frugality—Make no expense but to do good to others or yourself; i.e., waste nothing.*
6. *Industry—Lose no time; be always employed in something useful; cut off all unnecessary actions.*
7. *Sincerity—Use no hurtful deceit; think innocently and justly, and, if you speak, speak accordingly.*
8. *Justice—Wrong none by doing injuries, or omitting the benefits that are your duty.*

9. *Moderation—Avoid extremes; forbear resenting injuries so much as you think they deserve.*
10. *Cleanliness—Tolerate no uncleanliness in body, clothes, or habitation.*
11. *Tranquility—Be not disturbed at trifles, or at accidents common or unavoidable.*
12. *Chastity—Rarely use venery but for health or offspring, never to dullness, weakness, or the injury of your own or another's peace or reputation.*
13. *Humility—Imitate Jesus and Socrates.*

Since 1790 many others have attempted to compose lists of the traits, values, or virtues young people should develop if they aspire to become good human beings. William J. Bennett, former Secretary of Education under President Reagan and Director of the Office of National Drug Control Policy (the Drug Czar) under President George H. W. Bush, authored *The Book of Virtue*. In it he encourages us to teach our children such virtues as self-discipline, compassion, work, responsibility, friendship, courage, perseverance, honesty, loyalty, and faith. A big danger is building oneself into a teacher of morality is that others will find pleasure in exposing your own weaknesses—in Bennett's case, high-stakes gambling.

A person who is a good human being is also likely to be a better leader than someone who, other things being equal, is a bad human being. However, this knowledge is simply common sense. There really isn't very much you can do with it. For example, how would this help you to develop a training program for future leaders? What would it tell you to include or exclude from a leadership course?

Sometimes the list of traits proposed for the future leader sounds like the traits for a Boy or Girl Scout. No one wants to argue against such traits as being physically strong, mentally awake, and morally straight. The problems arise with doing anything with this information. While people may answer a questionnaire indicating they want their leader to be, for example, helpful, moral, friendly, and open to suggestions, when the going gets rough, we still expect our leader to be tough, to get results, and most of all to protect us. Our desire to have leaders who protect us can override our desire to have leaders who are kind, gentle, and friendly.

To go back to using U.S. presidents as examples, President Jimmy Carter was considered by many to be a kind, religious, ethical, and generous person. However, he was roundly criticized for not dealing more effectively with inflation in the economy and more harshly with the Iranians who held a group of Americans hostage for several months, only to release them on the very day Carter was turning over the reins of the presidency to Ronald Reagan.

In general, people assumed the incoming President Reagan would be tougher on the Iranians and that they had decided to release

On my honor I will do my best to do my duty to God and my country and to obey the Scout Law; to help others at all times; to keep myself physically strong, mentally awake, and morally straight.

—The Boy Scout Oath

the Americans so they wouldn't have to face a tougher U.S. president. Carter came out of the situation looking very weak and Reagan very strong. Whether those were the facts or not, we may never know. However, perceptions are sometimes more important than facts. When the going gets tough, being strong often wins over being kind, especially when followers are full of fear for their personal safety or the safety of their loved ones. Sometimes people are simply seeking someone with enough power to protect them or get them what they want.

Having the Bearing of a Leader

People often say someone has the "look" or "bearing" or "manner" of a leader. No doubt it does help to carry yourself with a sense of confidence—shoulders back, chest out, head up, voice strong, etc. Of course all this can be overdone and the person crosses the line from dignified to arrogant. Each leader has to find the proper balance between arrogance and confidence. We want our leaders to show confidence, but not too much. The balancing act is tricky. There will be times, as a business leader, when you will need to rely on the power of your position to get things done. There will also be times when you will likely be scared, but it may not be a wise thing to let it show. If you have been entrusted with a position of leadership, it is likely your followers need you to be a leader more than a buddy.

Just as there are books and consultants that can teach you how to dress for success, there are guidelines for establishing an atmosphere of power and authority in office design. While many management and leadership scholars will suggest power and authority are old fashioned and ineffective aspects of good leadership, there is also a danger in being too informal and unconsciously establishing an atmosphere where others simply ignore you and appeal to someone further up the chain of command. Excessive employee appeals going over your head will give those above you the idea you can't handle the job.

In general, the trait theory suggests leaders can be made, or at least developed given reasonable raw material. Leaders do not have to be born from special parents or be specially sent from gods. However, it was important they either be born with the "right stuff" or work to develop such traits through education, experience, hard work, and sacrifice. That "right stuff" looked a lot like the Hollywood image of a hero, i.e., the rugged he-man type who was strong, honest, courageous, and willing to fight for what is right. This rugged individualism may be great for Hollywood movies, but many leaders have to work as members of cooperative teams and need to motivate others to actually perform almost all of the actual tasks. Even Arnold Schwarzenegger wasn't strong enough to solve all of California's problems all by himself.

Another problem with the "he-man" image of leadership is that women have a difficult time fitting into such a role. Many perceive women in general as having a more nurturing disposition. When women attempt to step out of that nurturing role and act tough, some people are repulsed. What may work well for many men is likely to fail with many women.

Throughout history, there have been many examples of highly successful leaders who are women. One of the most interesting controversies today revolves around the role some say was played by Mary Magdalene and other women in the early Christian movement.

Some historians are now claiming that the early Christian church decided to downplay the role of women in order to gain wider acceptance in a middle-Eastern culture that, even today often views women as having few rights and little formal power. For a popular fictional story based on this issue, see Dan Brown's *The Da Vinci Code*, and for a nonfiction book on the same theme, see Elaine Pagels's *Beyond Belief: The Secret Gospel of Thomas*. Both books suggest the Christian church has, for approximately two thousand years, hidden the role played by Mary Magdalene and other women during the period immediately following the death of Jesus in order to gain acceptance within the Roman Empire. Whether this is true or not, we may never know. However, as students of leadership you need to be aware of the strong feelings held by some that women simply have no place in positions of power and leadership. Further, if you are female, you need to decide for yourself how you are going to deal with this attitude. Research does suggest it is harder for a woman who acts tough to be accepted. This is one more outdated idea that dies hard.

Ohio State Studies on Leadership

In the late 1940s a series of academic studies of leadership began with pioneering work that was done at Ohio State University. The general idea was to split leadership into a focus on task versus a focus on people. The question being addressed was whether it was better for a leader to focus on pushing followers to produce results by being stern and demanding, or to focus on building relationships with followers by being more friendly and kind.

Similar studies were done at the University of Michigan and still more were done at the University of Texas and elsewhere. It seems like each school was trying to put a slightly different spin on what was really the same thing, i.e., how much emphasis should a leader place on pushing people to get results and how much on getting people to like the leader—a task orientation versus a people orientation. The task-oriented leader was pictured as tough and used punishment and rewards to get the job done. The people-oriented leader was shown as someone who was kind, considerate, friendly, and more concerned about building relationships than getting the most work done.

What several of those researchers assumed was that a high emphasis on both task and people would be the best of all worlds, i.e., someone who was friendly toward people yet got results. Unfortunately, the world is not that simple, and research has produced conflicting results. While it was clear that a leader who scores high on the people-orientation scale (however the various researchers tried to measure that) seemed to produce slightly higher levels of job satisfaction among followers, the relationship between leadership style and level of output was mixed. Workers with a friendly but tough boss felt better, but didn't necessarily turn out more work. Researchers were disappointed. Clearly other factors had to be considered. Which factors would be the most important?

> *Whatever women do they must do twice as well as men to be thought half as good. Luckily this is not difficult.*
>
> *—Charlotte Whitton, first mayor of a major Canadian city, Ottawa (1896–1975)*

Leadership scholars moved on to look at specific characteristics of the work itself and workers. The thought was that some types of work and workers require closer supervision. For example, highly educated, competent workers in such areas as research, it was assumed, would work best with a minimum of supervision. In contrast, poorly educated assembly-line workers in a car factory would have to be watched closely and leaders in such an environment need to be tough.

While there is a certain amount of common sense in this theory, actually confirming it in a controlled experiment proved nearly impossible. Highly educated workers may be involved in complex work requiring much supervision, whereas uneducated workers may have a job that is so simple little supervision is needed. For example, medical interns, despite their many years of education and training, are not allowed to do complex surgical procedures on live patients without supervision, whereas your friendly Maytag repairman is sent out to people's homes all by his lonely self to repair your dishwasher. It wasn't sufficient to simply consider the educational level of the follower; the task itself also had to be considered. Again researchers have been disappointed. No exact formula produced the proper mix of ingredients to guarantee both highly satisfied and highly productive workers. In general, highly educated workers doing creative work typically prefer loose supervision. However, the tougher question always involves the question of which leadership approach to use to produce the greatest number and highest quality of results.

Why is leadership research so difficult? Think about your own work experiences and that of those you know personally. Why do some people go to work and slack off while others work so hard? There are almost as many reasons as there are people. People are like snowflakes, each one is unique. Some people are desperate to feed their family and will put up with just about anything to save their children from starvation. The next person working at the same job may be working simply because sitting around the house after retirement was just too boring, but might quit at the slightest provocation. Some people want a boss that will protect them from the enemy, or at least from the fierce competition in the marketplace, so they actually look for a "tough" boss. Some people want a boss they can call by their first name, while others would never respect someone who was so informal. Some employees enjoy having a boss who will ask for their input, but some expect their boss to know all the answers, thinking, "If the boss has to ask me, why should he be the boss?"

Consider your own approach to doing your college homework assignments and preparing for tests and term papers. Some of you probably spread the work out somewhat evenly throughout the semester, while others of you wait until the last minute and then go into panic mode. No doubt some of you have found you do your best work in panic mode. Athletes talk about peaking too early in the season. We

A new breed of leader is emerging, and that breed is female.
—Esther Wachs Book, author of Why the Best Man for the Job Is a Woman

each have to find what works best for us and adapt to the situation, whether as leaders or as followers. As leaders you will need to find for yourself what works best given many contingencies. That is basically what contingency theories of leadership are all about. The best form of leadership is contingent upon several factors.

Contingency Theories—It All Depends, but on What?

On the most basic level, contingency theory says "It depends." Of course that, by itself, doesn't help us very much. However, it does point out one important truth. There is no single way to lead all types of people in all types of tasks.

Fred Fiedler, a psychologist who was born in Vienna in 1922, immigrated to the United States in 1938, taught at the University of Illinois, and authored *A Theory of Leadership Effectiveness* in 1967, suggests the appropriate leadership approach is contingent upon three key factors: (1) Leader-member relations; (2) Task structure; and (3) Positional power. Fiedler is convinced individuals cannot change their basic leadership approach. Therefore, the organization must select the most appropriate leader to accomplish a particular task.

Leader-member relations have to do with the degree of confidence, trust, and respect employees have in their leader. *Task structure* concerns the degree to which the job assignments of workers are structured or unstructured. *Position power* has to do with the leader and his or her power over variables such as hiring, firing, discipline, promotions, and salary increases.

Fiedler focused on the problems any leader faces when taking on a new task. A leader knows intuitively that each task requires a different strategy and a different set of leadership tools. You need to recognize and appreciate the various tools a leader might use and understand the strengths and weaknesses of those tools so that you can choose wisely.

One of the trickiest aspects of conducting leadership research is to determine what type of a leader an individual actually is. We all have a tendency to tell a researcher what is politically correct. Since it is usually not considered politically correct to admit that we are not a "people person," the researcher needs to get at the issue indirectly. Fiedler used something he called the *Least Preferred Co-worker* (LPC) scale to indirectly get at people's leadership orientation. Subjects were asked to think of a co-worker they would least like to work with, and then describe that person's characteristics. The general idea is that what you say about others says more about you than it tells about the person you are describing.

A person who describes the person they would least like to work with in a kind and friendly manner is more likely to be kind and friendly himself. From a scale of 1 through 8, the leader was asked to describe their least preferred co-worker using terms such as:

Unfriendly	1 2 3 4 5 6 7 8	Friendly
Uncooperative	1 2 3 4 5 6 7 8	Cooperative
Hostile	1 2 3 4 5 6 7 8	Supportive
Guarded	1 2 3 4 5 6 7 8	Open

Usually 16 such terms would be used, and the scores would be totaled and averaged. A high Least Preferred Co-worker score suggested the leader is more people oriented. A low score meant the leader was more task oriented. People with high LPC scores get satisfaction out of interpersonal relationships, whereas those with low LPC scores get satisfaction out of successful task performance.

Fiedler divided tasks into highly structured versus unstructured tasks. A highly structured task is one where the job to be done is described by the leader to the employees in detail, perhaps with a detailed and elaborate job description. Assembling a complicated electronic device would be an example of a highly structured task. Teaching, especially at the graduate level, would be an example of the opposite.

Position power has to do with the leader's power to hire, fire, discipline, and reward employees. For example, the leader of a non-union construction crew has more positional power than a chairperson in a department of tenured college faculty.

One of the most remarkable conclusions of Fiedler's research is that the task-oriented leadership style was often more effective than the leadership style providing more consideration for human relations. In general, the task-oriented leader fared better in both extremely favorable and unfavorable conditions. The relationship-oriented leader performed best only in moderate or middle-ground situations where none of the variables were at extreme points. These are disappointing results for those who are absolutely sure a more friendly style of leadership is always better. In fact, it was the task-oriented leader who came out on top, both when position power was strong and when it was weak. Such a leader also fared better when the task structure was high and when it was low. The task-oriented leader also was more successful when the leader-member relations were good and when they were poor. The friendlier people-oriented leader only scored highest when all such conditions were moderate.

One conclusion we can draw from all this is that the people-oriented leader often runs into trouble at the extremes. When all the conditions are moderate, people seem to favor the more friendly leadership

An individual's leadership style depends upon his or her personality and is, thus, fixed.

—Fred Fiedler, expert on the study of leadership

style. However, when conditions are not moderate, followers prefer the more task-oriented leader. Recall how the voters in England elected Winston Churchill as their prime minister during wartime and defeated him in peacetime.

Fiedler believes leaders cannot change their basic style, and suggests instead trying to match the person's leadership style to the appropriate set of followers and task assignments. While there have been many who have questioned his work, most agree Fiedler has made it clear that there is no one leadership style that works best in all situations.

Path-Goal Theory of Leadership—Does This Way Get Us Both What We Want?

Robert House, who earned his PhD at Ohio State but then went on to teach at the Wharton School of the University of Pennsylvania, is credited with developing the Path-Goal Theory of Leadership, which assumes the leader's primary job is to help followers find the path to their own goals. House disagrees with Fiedler in that House thinks leaders can change their leadership approach to meet the situation as determined by a combination of employee factors and environmental factors. However, House proved the leadership situation is even more complicated than previously thought.

According to House, leader behavior can be directive, supportive, participative, or achievement oriented. Environmental factors that need to be considered are the task structure, the formal authority system, and the work group. Employee factors of greatest importance include locus of control, experience, and perceived ability. Finally, he measured outcomes on the dimensions of performance and satisfaction.

Path-Goal Theory draws heavily on research about what motivates employees, especially Expectancy Theory. It is seldom used in on-the-job leadership training programs because of its complexity. However, all students of leadership need to understand that human motivation is complicated. As a leader you must chose behaviors that complement or supplement what is missing in the work setting. Good leaders find out what their followers need in order to reach both the goals of the followers and of the organization and clear the barriers to such goal attainment. For example, some followers have a high need for affiliation and prefer a more supportive style of leadership. In contrast, followers who are themselves dogmatic and authoritarian and have to work under conditions of uncertainty prefer a more directive style of leadership that promotes clarity and structure.

Especially central to Path-Goal Theory is the concept of locus of control. People with an *internal locus of control* believe they are in charge of the things that occur in their life. People with an *external locus of control* believe that chance, fate, God, or other outside forces determine life's events. Path-Goal Theory recommends a participative leadership approach for subordinates with an internal locus of control, but a more directive approach for followers with an external locus of control.

House and others have shown that leadership consists of many dimensions. It isn't all about the leader. You also have to at least consider the work situation and the workers. The formula for leadership success is not as simple as it was originally thought. As a future leader, you can't assume that all you have to do is develop your leadership talents and everything will work out okay. You will have to adapt to changing work situations and changing employees, among other things. Predicting the levels of satisfaction and performance of your followers is not as easy as once thought.

Charismatic Transformational Theory—Let's Follow the Exciting and Charming Leader

Charismatic Transformational Leadership is based on the concept that a person with charisma has that indescribable something we often call charm or magnetism that fosters obedience and loyalty. Someone who appears charming to some may be repulsive to others. However, in general, a charismatic leader is one who excites others to willingly follow him or her. Usually the person is physically attractive, is very good at making motivational speeches, and has a reputation for getting things done.

The "transformational" aspect of the charismatic transformational leader relates to getting really big things done. Instead of making small incremental change, the transformational leader inspires others to make sea changes, changes that completely alter the nature and scope of the organization. Perhaps he or she causes the organization to drop making the product that has been its mainstay for years and go into a totally new line of manufacturing. Perhaps a manufacturing concern is changed into a financial services firm. Taking a local firm global could be a transformational change.

Putting the two descriptions together, we get a charming leader who is effective at implementing big change. Charismatic leaders challenge the status quo, create a compelling vision, build from a base of shared values, encourage and enable others to act, often by modeling the way themselves and by touching others in a heart-to-heart manner. Charismatic leaders arouse strong emotions in others. Some have suggested this type of leadership is especially effective when the followers are relatively weak or lack self-confidence. Some charismatic leaders tend to have a strong need for power, possess a high degree of self-confidence, and hold strong convictions regarding their own beliefs.

Transactional Leadership—Let's Make a Deal

A transactional leader clarifies for followers what needs to be done in order for the followers to get specific rewards. It is somewhat like a business transaction where one person gives up something to get something of equal or greater value in return: "You do this for me and I will do something nice for you."

Many business leaders are actually applying transactional leadership theory when they advocate for incentive-based pay, piece rate, or commission. They believe you get what you pay for. To get workers to produce more, make their pay depend on their rate of output. Those who disagree say such an approach degrades people; it treats people like a trained animal that rolls over and plays dead to get a treat. Further, it assumes people are only interested in material things.

Some suggest such an approach also fosters greed and may even result in unethical behavior. For example, some blame the recent scandals at Enron and other major corporate disasters on excessive attention to executive incentive pay based on quarterly earnings per share and the price of the corporation's stock. Instead of making executive decisions in the best long-term interests of all the stakeholders, such compensation packages tempt executives to do whatever it takes to inflate the quarterly earnings per share to temporarily drive up the price of the firm's stock. Unscrupulous executives then cash in their stock options and quickly leave before the truth comes out. When the general economy is booming, such a day of reckoning may be postponed for years.

At some point, excessive compensation packages not only buy your talent, they may buy your soul. The Transactional Leadership approach has such a dark side. We may agree that a merit-based pay system, cash bonuses for achieving goals, and stock option plans are all good things in moderation. However, the example of Enron suggests even good people can be sorely tempted to do very bad things when the compensation systems seems rigged to so richly reward such behavior.

Another problem with the transaction approach arises when the leader runs out of rewards. This can be the situation when an individual worker does exceptional work, but the organization as a whole is doing poorly. There may not be the funds to provide the earned reward. The inability of the leader to live up to the leader's end of the bargain can seriously undermine the transactional relationship. The followers believe they have lived up to their end of the bargain, but the leader has let them down. Employees become like bears in Yellowstone National Park being fed by tourists. Everything seems okay until the tourists run out of treats and then the bears attack, convinced there is more food hidden somewhere in the tent.

An especially troublesome consequence of some forms of transactional leadership is that it can lead to an attitude that the means to the end do not matter. "Just show me the bottom line and I don't care how you got there," is the message that may be implied. However, when it comes to ethics, how you get there does matter.

In general, the transactional leadership approach, while sometimes effective, has severe limitations. People do work to earn money, but money isn't everything. The relationship between most leaders and their followers is more complicated that the simple business transaction of "You do what I ask and I'll pay you this amount of money." However, leaders certainly have to be aware of the importance of following through on what has been promised. Transactional leadership can be effective up to a point, but this approach is seldom inspirational. For example, consider the brave firefighters and police officers who rushed up the stairs of the burning World Trade Center towers on September 11th, 2001 while others were rushing to get out. Such heroes are not motivated by pay. Many of the executives screaming and running away were paid hundreds of times more than the rescue workers rushing in. Some careers are intrinsically more rewarding than others and truly extraordinary feats are often performed by those who are intrinsically motivated.

The transformational leader goes beyond the simple level of a business transaction and inspires followers to do things many may have thought impossible. However, if the transformational leader fails

organizations, it simply doesn't fit in business. Business leaders have to perform in the arena of global economic competition and cut-throat ambition. How can they be effective acting like a servant?

Greenleaf counterargues that servant leadership is actually the most powerful form of leadership because the servant leader has nothing to lose. He reasons that servant leadership starts with a personal choice: the choice to serve. Such a person adopts an attitude of service to others over self.

In contrast, a person who first aspires to formal leadership lives in fear that their lofty position may be taken away. He or she may compromise their values in order to gain or maintain such a position of formal power. The servant leader has no such fear. Instead of worrying about what he or she has to do to keep a highly desired position such as CEO, president, etc., the servant leader can focus on what is really needed to be of service.

Perhaps the argument centers on the concept of inner strength. For someone with a strong sense of who they are, why they are here, and what important mission they hope to accomplish, the outer trappings of power and authority can be viewed as mere tools to accomplish a more important goal. Many will agree that the concept of servant leadership sounds great in theory. However, many also rightly point out how much of the world both expects and respects power. In general, the concept of servant leadership is more commonly accepted in the not-for-profit world. All of the world's major religions, however, teach humility and warn of the dangers of power and pride.

The difference manifests itself in the care taken by the servant—first to make sure that other people's highest priority needs are being served.

The best test, and the most difficult to administer, is: do those served grow as persons; do they, while being served, become healthier, wiser, freer, more autonomous, more likely themselves to become servants?

And, what is the effect on the least privileged in society; will they benefit, or, at least, will they not be further deprived?

—Robert K. Greenleaf

Summary

Some of the differences in leadership that researchers attempt to distinguish are of questionable value. If a writer has a particular type of leadership he or she wants to promote, then that leadership theory appears to take on all the positive attributes one would hope for in the perfect leader. You should take from each theory what could work for you. Do not assume there is one, and only one, best approach to leadership.

What is important for students of leadership to understand is that there have been many proposed theories of leadership. Scholars started out with the belief that leaders were born in some special, perhaps divine, way or were gifted with talents far beyond the average human. Over time, that idea lost favor, and people tried to assemble a list of leadership traits that could either be something you have from birth or something you have developed through education, experience, and practice. More recently researchers have discovered there were several other dimensions to be studied including several characteristics of the followers, types of tasks to be accomplished, and the various levels of power and authority and resources available to the leader. As a minimum, when you get your next leadership opportunity, examine the situation to see what tools you have to work with and what issues regarding the variables mentioned in this chapter are present in this situation. If you are going to offer your followers rewards for doing what you ask, what rewards do you control? If you are expected to be a visionary leader, what is the long-term vision, and how can you best express it so everyone sees it clearly and shares your enthusiasm for it?

It is also important for students of leadership to know some of the basic terminology researchers commonly use in articles and books about leadership theory. I want to encourage all students to become lifelong scholars of leadership. The fact that scholars have not, to date, fully defined exactly what constitutes good leadership and cannot recommend a particular course of action that will guarantee you will always be successful and honored as a great leader, actually makes continued study of leadership even more interesting. What does seem clear is that more research is needed on this important, yet poorly understood, topic. Further, it is clear that great leadership involves not only a combination of leadership attitudes and actions, but also a complex combination of situational circumstances especially involving the particular task at hand, the followers and their skills, motivation of the followers, their level of experience, plus more than a good measure of luck and timing.

Questions for Discussion

1. Leadership has been defined as the art and science of ethically and effectively guiding others toward a positive goal. Discuss how leadership is an *art*. How is it a *science*? Why must *ethics* be included in the definition? Why must a *positive goal* also be included in the definition?
2. Explain the concept of a contrarian, and discuss why good leaders should consider their viewpoints.
3. This chapter includes several theories or approaches to leadership. Which one is your favorite? Why? Which one is your least favorite? Why?
4. Imagine you have just been given a position requiring leadership. What key variables discussed in this chapter should you study before deciding which approach to leadership would work best in this setting?

Chapter 7

Controlling: How Businesses Measure for Results

As a manager, you will be held responsible for controlling various aspects of the organization's operations. Some controls are organization-wide and primarily financial, while others are designed to control specific operations at lower levels within the organization. As future managers, you need to know what the primary control mechanisms are and how to use them and interpret them.

Management is often described as being composed of planning, organizing, leading, and controlling. How do managers control? What are the various approaches to controlling? What are the basic steps in setting up a control process? How are budgets used to control? How do managers analyze a firm's financial condition? All these questions will be addressed in this chapter.

Drive the business or it will drive thee.

—Benjamin Franklin

Why Organizations Control

Large organizations are often criticized for being too controlling and killing individual creativity and initiative. Why is it that large organizations put so much emphasis on control systems? When organizations grow beyond a few dozen or so employees, it is simply too difficult for any one manager to know for sure what is going on. Formal reports start to take the place of informal chats. Companies that fail to put proper control systems into place typically suffer from lax management, an absence of written and implemented policies and procedures, a lack of agreement about standards, the lack of regular reviews that compare actual results to standards, bad information about the condition of the organization and its operations, and sometimes even a lack of ethics in the organization's culture. When companies issue stock to the public and are listed on one of the major stock exchanges, then the Securities and Exchange Commission of the U.S. government demands the filing of certain reports every three months plus an annual summary. As a manager, if you file false reports to the SEC, you could be put in prison. Have I convinced you yet that the stuff in this chapter is important?

Basic Terms of Control Systems

To understand control systems you have to know a few terms unique to this area. *Control* is defined as any process that directs the activities of individuals toward the achievement of the organization's goals. *Bureaucratic Control* is the use of rules, regulations, and formal authority to guide the performance of employees. *Market Control* is control based on pricing mechanisms. If something gets too costly, then the market will show purchasers that the same product or service is available elsewhere at a lower cost. A never-ending argument is how much control the government should impose on businesses versus letting the market regulate them. *Clan Control* is a term used to describe control employees impose on themselves based on agreed-upon norms, values, shared goals, and trust. If the employees of an organization have great pride in their organization, clan control can work wonders without the need for either bureaucratic or market controls. Finally, a *standard* is defined as an expected performance. Often a control standard is defined not only in terms of how many items are to be produced within a day, week, or month but also what are the maximum allowable defects within those items.

Basic Steps in Setting Up a Control Process

As a manager you will be expected to: (1) Set up performance standards; (2) Measure actual performance and compare that performance to the standards; (3) Take corrective action if the actual falls short of the standards; (4) Praise and reinforce performance of your employees that is better than the established standards; and (5) Repeat steps 1–4 indefinitely.

Standards should meet or exceed the expectations of customers. If your organization's customers are other large businesses, then the purchasing agents for those businesses will likely demand you produce what they want in the quantity and quality the buyer expects, or your organization will lose their business. In some industries, national or even international standards have been established and any supplier that wants to do business within that industry has to meet those standards to even be considered a viable supplier.

Six Sigma is a term used to describe a control process standard of less than 3.4 defects per million. Sigma is the Greek letter used to denote a standard deviation from the mean in a normal distribution. Moving out from the mean six standard deviations leaves approximately 3.4% of the area under the normal curve. Six Sigma is a data-driven, customer-focused, and results-oriented methodology that uses statistical tools and techniques to systematically eliminate defects and inefficiencies to improve processes. It involves finding out the root cause of the problem by first defining the problem statement and project goal and then measuring the current performance baseline. After identifying the root cause of the defects, then take specific steps to eliminate them and put in place control measures to sustain the improved process. Finally, Six Sigma involves validating the performance of the new procedure and its ability to meet customer needs. Proponents of Six Sigma claim the benefits, in the long run, include cost reduction, productivity improvement, market share growth, customer satisfaction and retention, cycle time reduction, defect reduction, and work culture improvement. Several corporations enroll key employees in a Six Sigma training program, where those who achieve the highest level are awarded the "black belt" in Six Sigma certification.

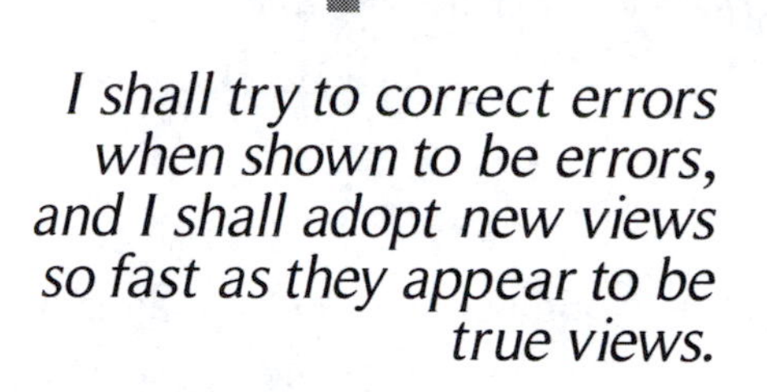

Following closely on the heels of Six Sigma is the concept of *Lean Manufacturing*, which focuses on eliminating waste by making labor-related activities more efficient, repeatable, and impactful. The concepts were developed primarily in Japan and especially at Toyota. A key concept is that the customer will not pay for your mistakes. The customer only wants to pay for the value of the product or service they receive. The value of the product is defined from the customer's point of view, not from the internal manufacturing point of view. *Value* is defined as any action or process that a customer would be willing to pay for. The expenditure of resources for any goal other than the creation of value for the end customer is a waste, and thus a target for elimination.

Budgets as Control Devices

Budgets are a key component of many organizational control systems. An organization prepares a budget for the upcoming year that lists all the expected revenues and expenses for the year. At the end of each month, that budget is updated with the actual revenues and expenditures for that month listed and compared to the portion of the annual budgeted revenues and expenses expected for that month. In some cases, it makes sense to simply take the annual figures and divide by 12 to determine the monthly targets. However, in many instances, the flow of revenues and expenses is not expected to be the same each month. For example, if you are in the toy industry, you will expect to have peak revenues in the weeks just before Christmas. If you are in an agricultural business, expenses may peak during planting season and revenues during harvest season. Budget meetings at the end of each month will focus attention on revenues that are below expectations and expenses that are above. Typically, the managers responsible for each area are asked to explain why items vary from the budget and must

A budget should reflect the values and priorities of our nation and its people.

—Mary Landrieu, U.S. senator

give assurances that things will be better controlled next month. In some cases, managers that are not able to control such revenues and expenses are dismissed.

Large organizations often have many different budgets, each focusing on a particular aspect of resource allocation and organizational priorities. Major budget categories common to most businesses include the sales budget, production budget, project cost budgets, cash budget, capital budget, and operating budget. The *Sales Budget* is defined as that budget that contains forecasts of sales by month, sales area, and product. The *Production Budget* forecasts the units to be produced each month per product. Within each production budget, the costs are divided into fixed and variable costs. *Fixed Costs* are those costs that will remain the same regardless of how many units are produced this month. *Variable Costs* are those costs, such as raw materials used, that go up as the level of production goes up. The *Project Cost Budget* is focused on each major project the organization is undertaking. For example, if an organization is designing a new product that may take several weeks in research and development followed by weeks in engineering, then those costs would be summarized and controlled using a Project Cost Budget. The *Capital Budget* contains the planned costs to build or buy large items such as a building or large equipment that would not be a part of the ordinary monthly costs of doing business. The *Operating Budget* is typically the budget that lists the revenues and expenses related to the regular and ongoing operations of the organization. The *Master Budget* is the budget of budgets. The Master Budget is where all the other budgets are combined.

Financial Control

Business organizations are required to maintain records that describe the financial activities and conditions of the business. Such statements usually include the Income Statement, Balance Sheet, and the Cash Flow Statement. We will shortly be using figures from these key statements to calculate a series of ratios used to determine the financial health of an organization.

The *Income Statement* is defined as the report that measures a company's revenues and expenses over a specific accounting period such as a quarter (three months) or a year. It is also known as the *Profit and Loss Statement or P and L.* The exact format of this statement can vary somewhat, but it typically starts with the total revenue (sometimes called total sales or gross sales or gross revenue) at the top of the report and ends with net income at the bottom—the so-called "bottom line." Between the top line of revenue and the bottom line of net income the report lists the cost of goods sold and the various expenses in categories ranging from advertising and selling expenses to administrative and miscellaneous expenses and taxes. Think of the Income Statement as representing a stack of money that is divided into slices or categories. Of course, a key measure is the amount of net income left after all expenses have been paid.

The *Balance Sheet* is the financial report summarizing a company's assets, liabilities and stockholders' equity at a specific point in time. The Balance Sheet must follow the following formula:

Assets = Liabilities + Stockholders' Equity

It is called a balance sheet because the two sides of the equation must be equal or in balance. A company has to pay for all the things it owns (assets) by either borrowing money (liabilities sometimes called debts) or by getting it from shareholders (shareholders' equity). Both assets and liabilities are further subdivided into short term and long term items. A short term or current asset is either cash or something (such as inventory) that can quickly be converted into cash. A long-term asset is a building or a large piece of equipment that, although valuable, would be difficult to convert into cash quickly. Similarly, a short-term liability is something that needs to be paid this year. Long-term liabilities are debts owed that must be paid back over several years. Owners' equity is determined by subtracting all liabilities from assets to see what is left. A balance sheet is said to be in good shape if the company is not too much in debt. Exactly how much debt is okay depends on several items such as the value of the firm's assets and the firm's ability to pay the interest and payments on the debt. Most major U.S. corporations owe millions in debt, but this is not typically a problem as long as the corporation can easily handle the interest expense and the payments. If money can be borrowed at a low interest rate (for example 5%) and used by the corporation to produce high earnings (for example 15%), then many corporations will readily accept those terms and borrow money to expand the business. Of course, excessive borrowing can get you or me or any organization into deep trouble. We will shortly examine some ratios that are used to evaluate whether a company is too heavily in debt.

The *Cash Flow Statement* is defined as the report that provides information regarding all cash inflows a company receives during a quarter or a year and all cash outflows the company has used to pay for things during that same period. If a company lands a major contract and records the expected income from that contract in the Income Statement, it will appear to investors that the company has lots more money than before the contract. However, the company may not actually receive the cash from the contract until a later date so the company's profit figure shows an increase, but the company's cash position will not change until the cash from the contract is actually received. It is vitally important for managers to carefully manage cash flow within any organization. If an organization runs out of cash, they will not be able to pay their employees, suppliers, or their taxes. Employees, suppliers, and government agencies get very upset when that happens.

A budget tells us what we can't afford, but it doesn't keep us from buying it.

—William Feather, American publisher and author

Happiness is a positive cash flow.

—Fred Adler, American businessman

Organizations must keep enough cash on hand to pay such bills or else have an arrangement with their bank to cover such expenses with a loan when cash temporarily runs low.

The typical financial analysis involves 20 to 30 ratios, but we will consider six key ratios every investor should know about a company before making an investment in that company. You should also know these ratios about a company before deciding to take a job with that company, especially if taking that job means you will need to move far away from your present home. Imagine how bad you would feel if you went to the trouble and expense of moving your family from Ohio to California to accept a new job and after a few weeks found that your employer was in such bad financial condition that your payroll check would not cash at your bank.

Working Capital Ratio (Sometimes Called Current Ratio) = Current Assets/Current Liabilities

The *Working Capital Ratio* (*also called Current Ratio*) is calculated by dividing current assets by current liabilities. If ABC Company has current assets of $10 million and current liabilities of $5 million, then the Working Capital Ratio is $10 million/$5 million or a ratio of 2 to 1, which is considered good. If they have current assets of $8 million and current liabilities of $10 million, then the Working Capital Ratio is $8 million/$10 million or 4 to 5 (0.80), and this organization may have trouble meeting their current liabilities or debts. The key is to have at least as many current assets as current liabilities or a Working Capital Ratio of 1.00. A current ratio of 1.0 means the organization has just as much value in current assets as they have in current liabilities.

What happens to a company when the current assets fall below the level of their current liabilities? The short answer is the organization may not be able to pay its bills. In some cases, the organization may have already established a line of credit with their bank so they can continue to print their checks to their employees and suppliers and pay their taxes. However, if the organization does not have a good enough credit history, the bank may not be willing to offer such a line of credit. In that case, the organization cannot pay their employees, their suppliers, and their taxes, and bankruptcy is a likely next step. There are a few large retail businesses that regularly have a current ratio slightly below 1.0 and have no trouble. This is often the case when a retail business has most of its annual sales during the holiday season. The positive flow of cash into the organization during the weeks before Christmas may more than offset the negative flow of cash during the other months. However, for most other businesses, a current ratio of less than 1.0 should be a warning sign that the business may have trouble paying its bills. That is especially bad news if you are an employee and need to cash your paycheck to pay your bills.

Capitalism without bankruptcy is like Christianity without hell.

—Frank Borman, former NASA astronaut

Quick Ratio = (Current Assets – Inventory)/Current Liabilities

The *Quick Ratio* (*also called the Acid Test*) subtracts inventories from current assets before dividing by current liabilities. The concept is to show how well current liabilities are covered by cash and by items that can easily and quickly be converted into cash. Some businesses can quickly convert their inventory into cash by holding a big sale and offering customers bargain prices. However, some businesses have to worry about something going wrong with their inventory (such as meat that spoils or causes customers to get sick) and is suddenly worthless. A company that makes tires may suddenly experience a situation where their tires blow out and customers experience accidents. A company that makes medical drugs may suffer losses if new medical research indicates their pills actually cause customers to have heart attacks or strokes. So, it is a good idea to use the Quick Ratio to see if the company can still pay its bills even if their inventory suddenly becomes useless.

As with all these ratios, it is best to also consider trends. If an organization's quick ratio is falling, dig further. Try to find out why the quick ratio is getting worse. Also, compare this company's quick ratio to that of other companies in the same industry. Is this a problem that is just affecting the one company, or is there an industry-wide problem?

With both the current ratio and the quick ratio, it is important to imagine you have gone to the organization's warehouse, opened the doors, and examined the inventory. Do not think of inventory as merely a number that you see on the Balance Sheet. What is it? In some situations, a company's inventory may be no big deal. For example, eBay has zero inventory, yet is a highly successful company. eBay has no inventory because they are simply in the business of bringing together (electronically) buyers and sellers. They operate an electronic auction house. eBay never actually owns the items that are offered for sale on eBay. Other businesses may sell services and thus have little or no inventory of products to sell to customers. So, you cannot just mechanically calculate these ratios and thoughtlessly make judgments about the organization's financial health. You also have to apply common sense.

Earnings Per Share (EPS) = Net Income/Shares of Stock Outstanding

Earnings Per Share is defined as the net income divided by the average number of common shares outstanding during the year. If a company has net income of $2 billion and has 100 million common shares outstanding, then EPS = $2,000,000,000/100,000,000 = $20. In the recent recession, many organizations failed to generate a positive net income so the Earnings Per Share were zero. Clearly, this is a bad sign. Earnings Per Share of zero or close to zero are not good for investors, employees, or anyone who cares about the financial health of the organization. However, many businesses have temporarily experienced short periods of low or zero net income and still survive. The key word in the previous sentence is "short," No organization will survive for long if they fail to earn positive Earnings Per Share.

The question of what constitutes good EPS is more difficult to answer. Again, it is a good idea to look at trends and at the competition. Of course, it is best if the EPS are trending upward and are higher than the competition. If you are studying an organization and find their EPS are trending downward, investigate further. Either sales have been decreasing or expenses have been increasing or both.

Price-Earnings Ratio (P-E Ratio) = Stock Price/Earnings Per Share

Price-Earnings Ratio is defined as the price per share of stock divided by the Earnings Per Share. In the above example, if the price of a share of stock in that company is $400 and EPS are $20, then the Price-Earnings Ratio = $400/$20 = 20 times. A general rule of thumb is that stocks are overpriced if they are selling for much more than 20 times earnings. However, during a recession, few companies had a P-E Ratio of 20. However, in general, if a share of stock is selling for far more than 20 times its annual earnings, the stock is said to be overpriced. The common sense rule is to buy stock low and sell high. So, if the price of the stock gets too high priced (in the above example over $400 per share), then it is not wise to buy it. Of course, there is always the outside chance that the company is doing so well that the stock will go even higher, but the odds are low. As with all these ratios, examine trends and compare the company to other companies in the same industry facing similar economic conditions.

Debt-to-Equity Ratio = Total Liabilities/Shareholders' Equity

Debt-to-Equity Ratio is defined as the company's total liabilities divided by shareholders' equity. If a company has $10 million in total liabilities and owners' equity of $40 million, then the debt-to-equity ratio = $10 million/$40 million = 0.25. Even though a debt of $10 million would look huge to you or me, to a company with owners' equity of $40 million, it is nothing to worry about.

Recall Shareholders' Equity is found on the Balance Sheet and is calculated by taking the organization's Total Assets and subtracting Total Liabilities. Shareholders' Equity represents the value of the organization's assets the stockholders own after all the debts are subtracted. In general, the lower the Debt-to-equity Ratio, the stronger the company is said to be in terms of its equity position.

What should you make of a company with a high Debt-to-equity ratio? It depends. If the company is rapidly expanding and has borrowed heavily, in the long run that may be a good thing. However, if the company has borrowed heavily to build a fancy new executive headquarters building, then you should question the wisdom of its executive team. Also, it is important to consider the trend and the Debt-to-equity positions of rivals.

Return on Equity (ROE) = (Net Income – Preferred Dividends)/Common Shareholders' Equity

Return on Equity is defined as net income minus preferred dividends divided by common shareholders' equity. Some corporations have preferred shareholders that get their dividends before the common shareholders. These preferred shareholders may have been the original investors in the firm or were investors that provided much needed money to the firm during difficult times within the firm and are therefore granted preferential treatment, such as higher dividends. However, the Return on Equity figure considers just the regular, or common, shareholders. If a business has net earnings of $150 million and dividends to preferred shareholders of $50 million and common shareholders' equity of $300 million, then the Return on Equity = ($150 million - $50 million)/$300 million = 100/300 = 0.33 for a ROE of 33%. The higher the ROE, the better the company is at generating profits for the shareholders.

The ROE ratio is widely used by investors as an important measure of a company's earnings performance. In general, investors like to see a ROE in the 15–20% range. Again, trends are important to consider, as are the ROEs of rivals of approximately the same size in the same industry.

Watch the costs and the profits will take care of themselves.

—Andrew Carnegie (1835–1919), Scottish industrialist

Other Important Financial Ratios to Consider

Many financial analysts consider two dozen or more financial ratios when they are attempting to determine the financial health of a company. Those financial ratios that fall within acceptable ranges and have been relatively stable over recent years can be somewhat ignored so you can focus on those that appear to be out of line. A good reference to consider is http://www.investopedia.com/university/ratios/. It lists 30 measurements that are the most relevant to the investing process, organized into six main categories as listed below:

1. Liquidity Measurement Ratios
   a. Current Ratio
   b. Quick Ratio
   c. Cash Ratio
   d. Cash Conversion Cycle
2. Profitability Indicator Ratios
   a. Profit Margin Analysis
   b. Effective Tax Rate
   c. Return on Assets
   d. Return on Equity

    e. Return on Capital Employed
3. Debt Ratios
    a. Overview of Debt
    b. Debt Ratio
    c. Debt-Equity Ratio
    d. Capitalization Ratio
    e. Interest Coverage Ratio
    f. Cash Flow to Debt Ratio
4. Operating Performance Ratios
    a. Fixed-Asset Turnover
    b. Sales/Revenue per Employee
    c. Operating Cycle
5. Cash Flow Indicator Ratios
    a. Operating Cash Flow/Sales Ratio
    b. Free Cash Flow/Operating Cash Ratio
    c. Cash Flow Coverage Ratio
    d. Dividend Payout Ratio
6. Investment Valuation Ratios
    a. Per Share Data
    b. Price/Book Value Ratio
    c. Cash Flow Coverage Ratio
    d. Price/Earnings Ratio
    e. Price/Earnings to Growth Ratio
    f. Price/Sales Ratio
    g. Dividend Yield
    h. Enterprise Value Multiple

The http://www.investopedia.com/university/ratios/ website provides the formula, an example calculation, and an explanation of each measure. Many of the online financial services websites such as http://www.google.com/finance# and http://www.reuters.com/finance/markets/us provide all the calculations for these ratios for any company on the stock exchange and compares them to the company's industry, sector, and the S&P 500.

Summary

Management has been defined as planning, organizing, leading, and controlling organizations. Control is defined as any process that directs the activities of individuals toward the achievement of the organization's goals. Some control is done through rules (bureaucratic), prices (market), culture (clan), or by standards (expected performance). Six Sigma and Lean Manufacturing are relatively modern approaches to reducing errors, waste, and defects in processes. Budgets are used to compare the amount spent during a specific time period to what was expected and authorized to be spent during that time period. Analysts commonly use two dozen or more financial ratios and measures to objectively consider the organization's financial health. You should do likewise before accepting a job with a potential employer because you do not want to have moved to take a job only to find out that the company is about to go bankrupt.

The surest way to ruin a man who does not know how to handle money is to give him some.

—George Bernard Shaw (1856–1950), Irish critic and playwright

Questions for Discussion

1. Management has been defined as consisting of planning, organizing, leading, and controlling. Discuss this definition and the important role of controlling. Use an example from your work experience or from your readings.
2. Discuss how the various general types of control (bureaucratic, market, and cultural) differ. Give examples from your work experience or from your readings.
3. Select a company on the New York Stock Exchange that interests you. Using the ratios described in this chapter, plus any other ratios listed on www.investopedia.com/ratios and calculated on www.reuters.com, analyze the company's financial health. If time permits, also calculate recent trends, and compare your company's ratios to similar companies in the same industry. Would you like to invest your savings in this company's stock? Why or why not? Would you like to work for the company? Why or why not?

Chapter 8

Human Resource Management: How to Properly Hire, Evaluate, and, When Necessary, Fire Employees

This chapter examines the Human Resource Management (HRM) role in the organization and focuses on those aspects of HRM that are most important for you as a future manager. It also examines several laws that were passed to try to end discrimination in the United States. Unfortunately, some managers look at those antidiscrimination laws as restricting their ability to properly hire and fire employees. That is the wrong way to look at these laws. The manager still has plenty of power. However, instead of basing your decisions about hiring and firing on things such as race, color, sex, age, etc., you must base them on the job description and the objective evidence you have observed and documented. Do not fire someone while you are mad at them. Terminating an employee is something that must be done using your very highest level of professionalism. This chapter explains how.

As a future GREAT manager and GREAT leader, you need to know how to properly hire and fire employees. Of course, the hiring part can be a lot of fun and the firing part can be gut wrenching. However, you need to know how to do both. Far too many beginning managers just hire their friends and relatives or those they like personally. When you reach the level of authority where you are making decisions about hiring employees, you will be amazed at the number of friends and relatives that will

I am convinced that nothing we do is more important than hiring and developing people. At the end of the day you bet on people, not on strategies.

—Lawrence Bossidy, former chief operating officer at GE

show up on your doorstep expecting you to hire them just because they are a friend or relative. DO NOT DO IT! This is a reason many managers fail at their job.

Functions of the Human Resource Management Department

The *Human Resource Management (HRM)* function within large organizations is typically responsible for the list of responsibilities such as: Planning workforce needs; recruiting the best applicants; hiring the best; training those you hired; providing performance feedback; providing fair compensation and benefit; and, when absolutely necessary, firing properly.

The HRM function begins with planning the number and types of employees needed in the future. Then those types of future employees must be recruited. Next, you select the best from the list of qualified applicants and hire them. Your job is far from done. You must train the newly hired employees. After those newly hired employees have been on the job for a specified period, your job as manager is to provide objective feedback to them regarding their performance. Managers have the responsibility to provide their employees fair compensation. When all else fails, it is also management's responsibility to terminate employees who have failed to correct their mistakes and have continued to fail to meet clearly explained standards of performance. Managers who are afraid to do all of these tasks should resign as managers. They do not deserve the title and the big bucks and they are doing their organization a disservice.

It all starts with the organization's strategic plan. Where does the organization plan to be in five to ten years? What employees will the organization need to hire over the next few years to get the workforce needed to not only replace employees who might retire or otherwise leave the organization, but also build up the workforce with the types of talented employees needed to reach the new objectives? How many new employees will we need in categories such as accounting, sales, engineering, supply chain management, information systems, etc.?

The *job analysis* is a detailed examination of each position within the organization and should result in a job description and a list of job specifications for each position. The *job specification* lists what education, skills, talents, etc., the organization needs to look for in applicants for each position. The *job description* lists the specific tasks and responsibilities the organization expects the employee in each position to perform. The job description is absolutely critical to several other tasks to be discussed later in this lesson. Many managers find that writing detailed job descriptions is a boring job, and unfortunately, many put off the task or fail to do it altogether. That can be a disastrous mistake.

A key decision the organization must make is whether to promote from within (*internal recruitment*) or to go outside (*external recruitment*). Typically, the decision centers on whether the organization thinks it needs new blood. This may well be the case if the new strategic plan calls for a change of direction for the organization. For example, when B. F. Goodrich decided to leave the tire business and focus primarily on the aerospace business, clearly new and different skills were needed in their workforce. However, many organizations find that promoting from within promotes employee morale. If an organization is following a strict policy of promotion from within and does only internal recruiting for all but entry-level jobs, then it needs to have a well-developed employee training program designed to develop their talent from within.

As a manager, you may well find yourself with the responsibility to read through a large stack of résumés and narrow that stack down to some small number of applicants who will be invited to come to the organization's location for interviews. The key to doing the review of résumés properly is to stick to the requirements of the job. If the job specification says that the person needs a particular level of education or a particular skill or a particular set of prior experiences, then eliminate those résumés that fail to meet such specifications.

Later in this chapter, we will examine several federal and state laws that make it illegal to discriminate in hiring. In your role as a manager, you will likely be held responsible for doing the hiring subject to these laws. Many managers find these laws discouraging and restricting, and some complain bitterly about them. Do not be one of them. Instead, focus on hiring to fit the job specifications. Later, we will discuss some of the specific laws that make it illegal to discriminate in hiring because of race, color, religion, age, sex, national origin, and disability. Managers absolutely must know those laws and obey them. Failure to do so is illegal and may result in lawsuits costing you and your organization millions of dollars.

While you are narrowing down the stack of résumés to a small number to go on to the next step in the hiring process, it is important not to just hire someone based solely on the résumé. Studies have revealed that one out of three job applicants falsify something on their résumé. In most cases, it is minor and is simply exaggerating a bit. However, if you hire someone based on just their résumé and later find that person exaggerated on their résumé and you then fire them because of that, be aware that if they sue you for wrongful termination, the judge in the courtroom will probably be aware of the statistic that one in three people falsify something on their résumé. If that judge doesn't know that statistic, you can count on the employee's lawyer to so inform the judge and the jury. Among the common slight falsifications typically seen on résumés is making the résumé look like the person graduated from college when they only attended, were responsible for some big improvement at their previous place of employment when they really were only there when it happened, extend their length of employment at previous organizations to "fill in" any holes in their times of employment, especially if that "hole" included time in prison. Some applicants will include in the salary the person received at the previous organization the dollar amounts all sorts of "benefits" such as the cost of health insurance, the employer's contribution toward retirement, and tuition reimbursement. The salary figure may have also included some "one-time only" compensations or bonuses in such a way to make it look as though such bonuses were a part of the person's base pay. The reason applicants like to exaggerate their previous salary is to help in their negotiations for their new salary.

Later in this chapter, we will consider several laws that apply to the hiring process. To avoid even the appearance of violating these laws, during the interview you should *NOT* ask:

- How old are you?
- How many children do you have?
- Are you married?
- Do you have any physical or mental disabilities?
- Are you a U.S. citizen?
- Have you ever filed a lawsuit against your employer?
- Have you ever been arrested?

In short, the law says you are not to discriminate on the basis of a long list of things. The list of questions you should NOT ask really has to do with avoiding the appearance of gathering data that could be used to discriminate against the applicant in some illegal category. For example, asking the applicant how old they are might cause the applicant to assume you are going to discriminate against him or her because of their age. Asking how many children the applicant has may lead the applicant to assume you are going to discriminate against him or her because of having children. This could also lead to charges of sex discrimination if you only ask this question of women and not men. The same idea holds for the rest of the questions. The last question, "Have you ever been arrested?" is wrong because being arrested is not the same as being guilty. In America you are innocent until proven guilty.

Further questions you should *NOT* ask during the interview include:

- What is your maiden name?
- What provisions have you made for child care?
- Do you have AIDS?
- Have you ever had cancer, high blood pressure, heart problems?
- Have you ever abused alcohol?

The list of forbidden (or at least unwise) questions continues. Most are seen as just roundabout ways of asking things that are none of your business and likely to cause an applicant to think you are discriminating against him or her in some illegal manner. For example, asking a woman to provide her maiden name is really the same as asking her whether she is married. Asking about provisions for child care is implying you might not hire her if you think she may have to stay at home at times to care for her children. Since these are questions you would not likely ask of a man, you are opening yourself up to charges of sexual discrimination.

While you might think it is important to ask about AIDS, cancer, high blood pressure, heart problems, or alcoholism, the law says you cannot discriminate against someone who has a disability. Put yourself in the shoes of someone who has an illness or disability. Wouldn't you need to somehow make a living? Instead, focus your questions on the requirements of the job and the person's ability, or lack of ability, to do those specific things. After the person has been hired, then the HRM department will have the newly hired person fill out forms necessary for filing tax information and for the determination of benefits such as health insurance. At this point, it is okay to ask some of the above listed questions because the decision to hire has already been made.

What you *CAN* do:

- Have applicant fill out an application form and check against résumé
- Check references
- With applicant's permission, do background check of:
  - Educational institutions attended
  - Prior employers
  - Court and police records
  - Credit rating

Instead of complaining about the questions you should NOT ask, a good manager will focus on asking questions based on the qualifications needed for the job. You can require the applicant to fill out an application form that asks the questions you really need to know to choose the best applicant for the job. For example, if a particular speed of typing is required to properly perform the job, it is certainly okay to ask the person how fast he or she can type and even to require a typing test. If a certain level of skill at programming in a particular computer language is required, then it is entirely proper to ask the applicant about such skills and even to require a demonstration of the applicant's skill level.

When I'm hiring a cook for one of my restaurants and I want to see what they can do, I usually ask them to make me an omelet.

—Bobby Flay (1964–), American celebrity chef and restaurant owner

It is common today to ask the applicant's permission to do all sorts of background checks such as checking the schools attended to see if the person really did earn the degree he or she says they earned. It is also common to check sources such as LexisNexis to see if the person has a criminal record. Finally, it is also common today to check on the applicant's credit rating. In some cases, this is done because the person will be responsible for handling a lot of money. In most cases, however, it is done simply to see if the person has a bad credit rating as this is sometimes a clue that something else, such as drug addition, might be a problem. Many drug addicts spend more than they make and therefore get into credit trouble.

So, the word to the wise is, don't be stupid about the questions you ask. Don't open yourself up to charges of discrimination. You don't have to. Focus on the tasks listed on the job description. You have every right to ask the applicant questions about his or her ability to do those tasks. Think of all these other questions as just getting you off the track. Getting off the track is likely to get you into unnecessary trouble with the law. Remember, when someone is turned down for a job and then sees someone else they think is less qualified get that job, they are likely to be mad, and some will take their anger to their lawyer, who has promised to "make them pay." Recently, average verdicts against employers in such cases have approached $500,000 with some going much higher.

Training

Once you hire the best applicant, then it is your responsibility, as a manager, to train that person. Training usually begins with an *orientation session* where the new hire learns about the history of the organization, plus an overview of the current aspects of the company. This orientation session also teaches the person about the various benefits offered such as some choice of health insurance, vacation days, sick days, etc. So many organizations today expect their employees to work in teams that it is a good practice to actually have training sessions teaching employees how to properly work within and manage teams. *Diversity training* is used to teach new employees about the importance of diversity as a source of strength in the workforce. It also should teach them how to communicate with employees who are different from them. It is especially important to mention what is considered improper ways to speak to each other. *Sexual Harassment Training*, to try to prevent sexual harassment in the workplace, is also vitally important. New employees need to know how sexual harassment is defined, where to report incidences of sexual harassment, and what procedures to follow to minimize the harm caused by sexual harassment in the workplace.

Finally, *job training* must eventually get to helping the new employee do his or her job correctly, keeping up-to-date with changes in hardware and software and new procedures, and preparing the employee for potential promotion. At the highest level of training is training designed to prepare the organization's next generation of managers and leaders, often called *training in management and leadership*, and includes many of the same topics found in this book.

Providing Objective Performance Feedback

As a manager, it is also your responsibility to provide your employees with objective feedback regarding their performance. Unfortunately, many organizations fail to do this or do it poorly. A poor way is to base your feedback on traits. *Trait appraisals* typically include such subjective items as "Employee is a hard worker" or "Employee is reliable." However, research shows that managers are typically not very good at judging such traits. They are too biased and based simply on opinion. Often, hard evidence is not noted, so there is no backup data to support whatever grade the manager gave the employee on such traits. In short, do not use trait-rating scales in performance evaluation. There are much better options. Behavioral appraisals are much better than trait appraisals. In *behavioral appraisals*, the manager bases the employee's performance evaluation on particular behaviors that can be directly observed. Instead of rating the employee on trustworthiness, for example, the behavioral approach is to indicate whether the employee has accurately counted money (or whatever he or she is supposed to count and handle) and recorded cash transactions into the organization's computer system. Does the money in the cash register match with what the cash register printout says should be there? In general, the idea of a behavioral appraisal is to base everything on specific behaviors that can be objectively observed and recorded. It is always best to have more than one person doing the observing and you need to check to make sure the various people observing the employee's behavior agree on what they have observed. This approach takes a lot more time than simply marking a list of traits, but it is much more effective and much easier to defend in a lawsuit.

An even better approach is to base the employee's performance appraisal on results, called *results appraisal*. For many jobs, there may be many ways to reach the desired result. As long as the employee gets the required result, and as long as the way he or she got that result is legal and ethical and in accordance with company policies, then the employee should get a good performance appraisal. Some areas, such as sales, are especially well suited for this type of performance appraisal. However, many jobs cannot be evaluated based on results because what the employee works at just does not directly affect results.

In some cases, one of the best approaches, called *Management by Objectives* (*MBO*), is to have sessions where the manager and the employee sit down periodically and jointly agree on objectives to be achieved over the next few months. Then, the performance appraisal can be based upon whether those objectives have been met. MBO became popular over 30 years ago and is still used in many organizations. The major advantage of the MBO approach is the involvement of the employee in the process.

Over 20 years ago, 360-Degree Feedback became popular. The general idea of *360-Degree Feedback* is to get observations on the employee's performance from people above, below, and beside that employee. Research has shown it to be good for general development of the employee, but not good when used to determine raises, promotions, or dismissal. Why is that so? Usually, the observations are done anonymously. While this may be good for protecting those under that employee from recrimination, it does not give the employee the opportunity to challenge the observation. There may be arguments going on between employees that have nothing to do with job performance, but such disagreements may spill over into this type of performance appraisal. Also, if all the employees know that the money available for raises is some fixed sum for the total raises within the organization, then they may be reluctant to give others a high performance rating because they feel that may take raise money away from them. In general, 360-degree feedback should be used only to help an employee improve their performance, and not to determine raises or promotions or terminations. It is simply too subject to abuse.

Perhaps you are working now and your boss has "sort of" forgotten to provide you with a performance appraisal. This often happens because many managers simply hate to do appraisals. Some managers hate doing appraisals because they believe they are inherently destructive, create divisions, and undermine morale; they unleash negative energy and the organization gets nothing in return; they make people angry, jealous, and cynical; and sometimes top management doesn't back up a tough manager when they make negative appraisals, so the tough manager is left looking bad while the employee gets off scot-free.

The criticism of excessively high performance appraisal is somewhat analogous to the way some people have criticized colleges for allowing grade inflation. Job performance appraisal inflation is also a common problem. While there are many problems with performance appraisals, as a manager, you simply cannot ignore your responsibility to do them and to do them properly. If you "cop out" and just give everyone good ratings, then your employees will not take them seriously and will not respect you as a manager. This becomes an especially troublesome situation when the employees know that one or more employees are not doing their work properly and you, as their manager, simply do not do the responsible thing and remove the bad apple from the barrel. The reason a rotten apple has to be removed from a barrel of apples is that leaving it in the barrel will cause the rest of the apples to also become rotten. So, despite all the problems inherent in employee performance appraisals, as a manager, it is simply part of your duty. That is why you get the big bucks. Do performance appraisals on all your employees on time and according to the rules. Base the appraisal on objective behaviors or results that have been well-documented.

Guidelines for conducting a proper employee performance appraisal:

- Base it on job analysis
- Use it to remind everyone of performance standards
- Use specific performance-related behaviors
- Document the appraisal carefully
- Use more than one rater
- Have an appeal process
- Consider the legal issues

So, you need to do employee performance appraisals based on the job analysis. What does the job description say the person is supposed to do? What are the criteria for determining whether the person in the job is doing those things well or poorly? What are the performance standards? If you base your employee performance appraisals on objective observations of your employee's behavior in relation to their job descriptions, then you are normally on safe ground. Document your appraisals carefully in writing. Whenever possible, use more than one rater. Inform the employee of what you have observed, and explain why she is getting a particular rating. Many organizations provide the employee with an appeal process the employee may use if he thinks their evaluation is unfair. If the employee performance appraisal is going to

It is an immutable law in business that words are words, explanations are explanations, promises are promises, only performance is reality.

—Harold S. Geneen (1910–1997), former president of ITT

lead to the dismissal of the employee, be sure to consult with the organization's legal staff before going through with the termination.

Firing Properly

Now, imagine that you have done all the proper steps, but you have an employee that still is just not performing his or her job properly. Firing should never be your first option, but when all else has failed and you are left with no other choice, do it properly. Do not get angry and fire the person while you are mad. You have to be careful. You certainly don't want to tell the person they are fired and later find that you have not done all the prerequisite steps, and you therefore have to take the employee back. Instead, make sure that when you tell someone that they are fired, they stay fired. So, before telling them they are fired, you should tell them what they are doing wrong, show them how to do the job correctly, give them a reasonable amount of time to improve, and then—if all else fails—terminate the employee as quickly and as professionally as you can.

Document your reasons for firing. Remember, it must be for a good reason, and the reason should relate to the person's specific job description. The evidence should be well documented. There is no reason to shout or be mean to the individual being fired. Getting fired is bad enough. Be sensitive to the person's feelings. Everyone makes mistakes. Remember that managers often get fired. So, treat the person being fired the same way you would want to be treated if you were the one being fired. Recall the old saying, "What goes around comes around." If you treat your employees ruthlessly, don't be surprised when someday you get the same treatment.

Other guidelines to follow in properly firing an employee include:

- Meet in a private office, but have a witness.
- Use about 15 minutes.
- Provide a written explanation of severance benefits.
- Provide outplacement service if appropriate.
- Employee needs to hear it face-to-face from the manager.
- Tell the person in the first sentence that they are being fired—no confusion.
- Do not allow debate.
- Be at your highest level of professionalism.
- Have security force available.

Tell the person being fired to come to your office at a specified time. Have someone else with you in the office who will be willing to truthfully testify as to what was said. Keep in mind that every word said may someday be repeated in a court of law. Be extremely professional. Do not beat around the bush. Get right to the point. Tell the employee right away that, "The purpose of this meeting is to officially inform you that you are being terminated from this organization." Do not leave any doubt in the person's mind. Be kind, but be clear. The whole meeting should take about 15 minutes. Many organizations have a printed document that outlines any severance benefits allowed. For example, the individual needs to know how long their health insurance stays in effect. They may be entitled to some retirement or pension benefits. They may be entitled to unemployment benefits. In some cases, the employer may provide some outplacement services such as help with their résumé and some training in searching for another job. However, if the person is being fired for some very negative behavior, such outplacement services may not be appropriate.

Do not tell the individual they are being fired via e-mail, phone, or memo. Tell the person face-to-face. If you are not brave enough to do this, then do not become a manager. This is part of the job. This is not the place for you and the employee to engage in any debate. If you have been following proper procedure up to this point, there should have been several meetings before this termination meeting, during which such discussions have already taken place. The time for any debate is now over.

Do not be surprised if the employee gets angry. Be prepared in case he gets violent. Have two security guards outside your door with instructions to enter immediately if called. Some managers have a panic button hidden under their desk or someplace handy. Such a button should be used to summon security guards if the individual is threatening in any way. Stop such behavior before it becomes dangerous. It is also common practice for others in the organization to be notified that a termination is taking place at a particular time, and during that time, the terminated employee's computer password is disabled, locks are changed on the person's office door, and any sensitive materials removed from her office. In some cases, the employee's personal things are being packed up, and the person is escorted by security guards from the building directly to their car. Of course, such drastic measures are not always needed, but never forget the wise words of Donald Trump: "When you fire someone, the result is always the same; they will hate you." It is better to be safe than sorry.

Key Laws

Now, our attention turns to several laws that are especially important to consider while hiring, promoting, and/or terminating employees. There are numerous local, state, and federal laws that may come into play. However, the laws we will now consider are the most likely ones to impact these managerial responsibilities.

National Labor Relations Act of 1935

Before the 1930s, many workers were simply at the mercy of their employers, and unfortunately, some of those employers were ruthless. It was common for workers to be forced to work a 12-hour shift and to work six or seven days per week for wages so low it was impossible for those workers to support their families. During the Great Depression, when approximately 25 percent of the workforce was unemployed, some bosses were especially cruel. Workers in many mines and factories were so badly treated that something had to be done.

Major events happened in General Motors factories in Flint, Michigan, where workers decided to remain seated at their work stations when their shift was over. By staying at their seats, they prevented other workers from coming in and taking their jobs. Managers at the General Motors factory in Flint called on the governor of Michigan to send in National Guard troops with guns to force the workers out of the factory. Women were bringing food and drink into the factory for the workers. Most of the women were wives, mothers, or sisters of the sit-down workers. The young men who were in the National Guard did not want to open fire on the women. The stalemate forced General Motors managers to sit down with the representatives of the striking workers. This marked the beginning of the United Auto Workers (UAW) organization. As a result of the sit-down strikes against General Motors in Flint, Michigan, and similarly organized efforts elsewhere, labor unions gained membership and strength and negotiated for a 40-hour work week, higher wages, and safer working conditions. In 1935, *The National Labor Relations Act*—also known as the *Wagner Act*—was passed, declaring that employees have a legal right to form a union if they vote to do so. The law further stated that managers who interfere with that right are in violation of the law. The Wagner Act also established the National Labor Relations Board, with the authority to investigate cases of management preventing workers from forming unions. See www.nlrb.gov for details. So, as a manager, if you hear your employees talking about forming a union, do not threaten to fire them for doing so, or you could be guilty of an unfair labor practice.

The best way for any organization to prevent their employees from forming a union is to listen to their grievances and treat their employees with respect. Remember the old saying, "All roads lead to management." If the employees are not doing their jobs properly, whose fault it that? Was it not the managers who did the hiring, the training, the promoting, and determined the wages and benefits? So, if a large number of your employees are upset, listen to what they have to say, and do your best to treat them fairly.

Only a fool would try to deprive working men and women of their right to join the union of their choice.

—Dwight D. Eisenhower (1890–1969), 34th president of the United States

Taft-Hartley Act of 1947

The Wagner Act was passed in 1935 while the Democrats were in the majority. In 1947, after President Roosevelt died and the Republicans gained power, there was an effort to overthrow much of the Wagner Act. *The Taft-Hartley Act of 1947* was passed to outlaw the "closed shop." A *closed shop* is a place of employment where employees are forced to join a union before being hired. In other words, if you were not already a member of the union, you could not get a job there. The Taft-Hartley Act of 1947 outlawed the closed shop, but did not outlaw the "union shop." At a *union shop*, workers are not required to be a member of the union before they are hired, but after they are hired, they are required to either join the union and pay union dues or at least pay their fair share to the union. The concept is that the union is negotiating for wages, benefits, and working conditions for all workers, and therefore all workers should be required to pay their fair share of what it costs to run the union. Unfortunately, over the years, unscrupulous people came into power in some unions and corruption became common, giving unions a bad reputation. However, managers should learn from history and realize that treating their employees unfairly eventually has consequences. The Golden Rule is best.

Equal Pay Act of 1963

The Equal Pay Act of 1963 makes it illegal to pay women much less for doing exactly the same job as a man. The old-fashioned reasoning was that it was the man who was responsible for providing for his family, so he should get more money than a woman. People used to think that if a woman was working, it was thought she was not providing for a family—perhaps she was single or was simply working so the family could have extras such as a better house, car, or vacation. However, women lobbied their congressmen and –women, and eventually, the Equal Pay Act of 1963 made it illegal to pay a woman less than a man for doing essentially the same work. The Equal Pay Act was to be enforced by the *Equal Employment Opportunities Commission* (*EEOC*). Unfortunately, studies conducted by the National Organization for Women (NOW) show that women's pay is still far below that of men for similar jobs. According to a recent study by NOW, women today are getting about 78 percent of what men get at similar jobs. Women still have a ways to go to fully achieve the goals of the Equal Pay Act of 1963.

Title VII of the Civil Rights Act of 1964

The biggest law of all regarding discrimination is the Civil Rights Act of 1964. Of special interest to all managers is the part of that law called *Title VII of the Civil Rights Act of 1964*, which makes it illegal to discriminate in hiring on the basis of race, color, religion, gender, or national origin. One of the main reasons this law is so important to the study of management is that most wrongful termination lawsuits involve this law. As a manager, you may say that you fired someone because they did not do their job properly. However, the person terminated is likely to charge that you have fired him or her because of race, color, religion, gender, or national origin. If you have failed to follow the firing procedures previously discussed, and the fired person falls into one of these categories, then you are open to possible

> *To live anywhere in the world today and be against equality because of race or color is like living in Alaska and being against snow.*
>
> *—William Faulkner (1897–1962), American writer and winner of the Nobel and Pulitzer prizes*

legal action. This is why it is so important that you have good job descriptions, that you hire based on what the job requires, that you promote based on objective evidence of job performance, and that you terminate based on objective, documented evidence of the employee's failure to properly do what the job description says the employee is supposed to do.

Age Discrimination Act of 1967

The Age Discrimination in Employment Act of 1967 makes it illegal to discriminate in employment decisions against persons age 40 and above. So, if, as a manager, you fail to hire someone who is 40 and instead hire someone who is under 40 who has fewer qualifications for the job, then you are open to legal action against you. This is especially tricky because you are not supposed to ask someone how old they are—you are just supposed to hire the person with greater qualifications, regardless of age. Of course, if you are smart enough to qualify for a job in management, you are certainly smart enough to notice when the applicant graduated from high school, and since most people graduate from high school at approximately age 18, you should be able to easily calculate the person's age without asking. Perhaps the good news is that everyone will eventually enter into this protected class—unless you die before reaching 40 years of age.

Americans with Disabilities Act of 1990

The Americans with Disabilities Act of 1990 makes it illegal to discriminate in employment decisions against people with physical or mental disabilities. It was amended in 2008 to provide clarity about what is included. Disability is defined by the ADA as "... a physical or mental impairment that substantially limits a major life activity." The determination of whether any particular condition is considered a disability is made on a case-by-case basis. Certain specific conditions are excluded as disabilities, such as current substance abuse and visual impairment that is correctable by prescription lenses. Essentially, as a manager, you should not discriminate against someone who is capable of doing the job, but has some physical or mental disability. Again, the key is the job description.

Family and Medical Leave Act of 1993

The Family and Medical Leave Act of 1993 permits workers (either female or male) to take up to 12 weeks of UNPAID leave for pregnancy and/or the birth of a new child, adoption, or foster care of a new child, illness of an immediate family member, or personal medical leave. Notice the employer is not required by this law to provide a PAID leave. Also, you should notice that the length of the leave is only 12 weeks. In most of the rest of the industrialized nations, the provisions for such medical leaves are much more generous. For example, in Canada, it is 16 months at 80 percent of full pay; France, 16 weeks at full pay; Germany, 14 weeks at full pay; and England, one year at 90 percent of full pay. Women of

America, it is time you let your congressional representative know what you think about this, and also let them know that you vote.

Lilly Ledbetter Act of 2009

The Lilly Ledbetter Act of 2009 amends Title VII of the Civil Rights Act of 1964 and says the 180-day limit to file an equal-pay lawsuit resets with each new discriminatory paycheck. It overrides *Ledbetter v. Goodyear Tire & Rubber Co.*, 2007. For many years, Lilly Ledbetter worked for Goodyear Tire & Rubber Co. While she suspected that she was getting less pay then men with essentially the same level of responsibility and authority, she did not find out for sure until several years had passed, when someone with knowledge of the company's payroll secretly gave her the facts. She filed a lawsuit using the Equal Pay Act of 1963 as her basis for legal action. Ledbetter's case went all the way to the U.S. Supreme Court; she lost. The U.S. Supreme Court said that the law required her to file a claim within 180 days of the act of discrimination. The Court also suggested that the U.S. Congress should consider changing this law, and that is what the U.S. Congress eventually did. Now, each unfair paycheck is considered a new event of discrimination. This was a major change because many employees have no idea what other employees are paid, so they have no basis for filing a claim of discrimination. The Lilly Ledbetter Fair Pay Act of 2009 makes it easier to file such a claim. While Lilly Ledbetter was unable to get any money from her lawsuit against Goodyear, she did make it easier for anyone else to get justice.

State Laws Regarding Employ at Will

Several states have *Employ-at-Will* laws saying, "In the absence of a written employment agreement or a union contract, an employment agreement is terminable at will by either the employer or the employee for any reason that is not contrary to law." While on the surface this may sound fair to both the employer and the employee, think about it. Such laws imply an employer can fire the employee for any reason. When that happens, the employee no longer gets paid and is also likely to lose many other benefits such as their family's health care insurance. When an employee quits, what does the employer lose? The employer loses nothing. It is not fair at all.

Also, to be truthful it should not be called employ at will, but rather fire at will. It is not really about hiring. It is about firing. The intention of such laws is clear. It is to protect the employer. However, there is a catch. Federal law trumps state law. So, as a manager, do not think that because you are in a so-called employ-at-will state that you can just fire anyone you please for any reason at all or for no reason. The so-called employment-at-will states are still part of the United States of America, and the federal laws regarding discrimination apply in all 50 states. Instead, base any termination on documented, objective observation of the employee's failure to properly do the tasks as set forth in the job description.

State Laws Regarding Right to Work

Another law aimed at undermining unions is the so-called right-to-work state law currently on the books in over 20 states—mostly the states that made up the old Confederacy during the Civil War. The general idea was to kill off any union organizing by saying it was illegal to force workers to join a union or to pay union dues. Pro-union people refer to this law as the right-to-work-for-less law. On the other hand, those in favor of this law say that such a law encourages businesses to locate in the state and thereby encourages more jobs in right-to-work states.

Unfortunately, this debate still rages on. However, GREAT managers and GREAT leaders know that the way to deal with employees is to treat them with respect. Base your employment decisions on the job descriptions and the objective evidence. Carry out your managerial responsibilities with knowledge of the law and with an attitude of fairness and justice. Just because you may be able to get by with being a bully and a bigot is no excuse. Bigotry and prejudice are wrong. Using your power as a manager to be a bigot is an abuse of power. Do not be a bigot.

> *The quality of employees will be directly proportional to the quality of life you maintain for them.*
>
> *—Charles E. Bryan*
> *former head of the International Machinists' Union*

Summary

When it is part of your responsibility to hire and fire employees, you MUST know what the various laws have to say about it. Basically, the way to stay out of trouble with the law is to base your decisions on the job description. If the job description says in writing that the employee must do a specific task, and you have documented evidence that the employee has not done that specific task or has not done it correctly, and he or she has been informed of that issue and has been shown how to do the task correctly, and the employee has been given a reasonable amount of time to improve or correct their performance, then you are generally on safe grounds to terminate that employee. However, it is always advisable to have sound legal counsel before firing anyone. Also, always remember to conduct these activities at the very highest level of professionalism. Take this responsibility seriously.

Discussion Questions

1. Describe any experiences you have had regarding being hired, promoted, or fired. Were the guidelines described in this chapter followed? If you were the manager, what would you have done differently?
2. Locate a Human Resources Manager at your school or at an organization convenient to you and ask him or her to describe to you what plans they have for future staffing and how those plans were determined. Does the organization plan to recruit internally or externally? What reasons did the HRM manager give for their choice?
3. Consider the list of questions that a manager should NOT ask job applicants. Which question seems the most controversial to you? Are there other ways an HRM manager can determine the answer to that question without arousing suspicions of discrimination?
4. Have you experienced a work situation where you were scheduled to receive a report regarding your job performance, but the manager postponed or completely ignored doing the job review? What might have been that manager's reasons for not doing the appraisal? How would you handle the situation if you were the manager?

Chapter 9

Teamwork: Working Together Effectively

The way a team plays as a whole determines its success. You may have the greatest bunch of individual stars in the world, but if they don't play together, the club won't be worth a dime.

—*Babe Ruth (1895–1948), first baseball player to hit 50 home runs in one season*

Why Study Teamwork

Your first opportunity to manage others is likely to come as a team leader. Teamwork is a process of cooperative work that most organizations use to increase productivity, reduce costs, improve quality, enhance speed, and capture the creativity and innovation of their employees. Working within a team allows you to get to know others in the organization and to learn about other parts of the organization outside your own work area. Therefore, teamwork is important for organizations and for your development as a manager, so let's find out how to build effective teams.

Perhaps your experience working in teams for class work has not been positive. Students often complain about being assigned to a team for course assignments, saying they would rather work alone. Much of what you do in school is done alone. In fact, working with someone else may, in some circumstances, be considered cheating. However, business schools have learned from the corporate recruiters who come to campus to interview prospective employees that teamwork is extremely important. When I am called by a prospective employer to give my recommendation of a former student, I am almost always asked if the person works well on a team. Today, almost all organizations use teams to manage projects,

> *Individual commitment to a group effort—that is what makes a team work, a company work, a society work, a civilization work.*
>
> —*Vince Lombardi (1913–1970), football coach*

make group decisions, and run the company. So, like it or not, you will almost certainly be working in and eventually managing teams. Get as much teamwork and team management experience as you can while in school, so you can stand out as you enter the job market. Convince your teachers that you work well as both a team member and as a team leader, and then ask them to put that in a letter of reference for you.

Purge the Social Loafer Early

The biggest complaint students have about team assignments is that the teacher gives everyone on the team the same grade regardless of which team members did all the work. They resent the "social loafer" who does no work but hangs on to get the grade that was actually earned by the most serious student on the team. At work a social loafer is a team member who fails to do his or her fair share of the work but expects to reap the team's reward. Dealing properly with a social loafer is the first lesson to learn in team management.

The secret is to assign some small task to be done by everyone on the team by a particular deadline early in the project. Typically, the social loafer will quickly identify himself by not meeting that task deadline. This is the point where the social loafer should be removed from the team. It does not work to wait until the night before a major team assignment is due and then to protest to the teacher or manager that certain members have not done their assigned part. Most teachers will accommodate a request to remove the social loafer from the team if the request is made based on facts and early in the project schedule; the same is true for most bosses. The key is to make the request early and based on facts. Whether the team is for a classroom assignment or for work, social loafers need to be purged from the team as early as possible.

Team versus Working Group

A *Working Group* is a collection of people tossed together to work on some project. In contrast, a *Team* is a small collection of people carefully chosen for their complementary skills who trust one another and are committed to a common goal, a common approach, and have agreed to hold each other mutually accountable. A common cliché in sports is, "There is no 'I' in team, but there is a 'u' in suck." The individual must put his or her selfish interests aside for the good of the team. Effective team managers form teams, not just working groups. They do it by inspiring each team member to work for the overall good of the team. They convince the other team members that through teamwork, "*T*ogether *E*veryone *A*chieves *M*ore."

Teams Overcome Silo Effect

The current emphasis on teamwork in the business setting is a reaction to the "silo" concept of the past. On a farm, a silo is a tall round building made of strong blocks or other tough material and designed to hold feed for cattle. It is somewhat like a huge thermos bottle. It keeps the contents from spoiling by not allowing air or water into the silo. In the business world, the term silo is not used so positively. Instead, it is used to describe a situation where the workers in one department perform in isolation their part of a process on some product or service, and when that department is done with their task, toss the item over the wall of their "silo" into the next department, or "silo." Instead of working together as a team, the workers remain within their various silos and seldom collaborate with anyone outside their silo and are not concerned with what goes on outside their individual silo walls.

In designing a new automobile, for example, the designers may work on the shape of the car for months. When they are satisfied that the new shape is appealing, they will toss it over their silo wall into engineering for them to create the motor and drive train and other parts of the car. Eventually, the newly designed and engineered car gets tossed into the sales department, where the salesmen and saleswomen may exclaim, "How do you expect us to ever sell this monstrosity?" When the employees in the finance department finally get a look at the newly designed and engineered car, they may complain, "This car won't sell because it will cost too much." Think about how these problems could have been addressed at the beginning of the design process if only the design team had included members from the sales and finance departments from the start.

I am a member of a team, and I rely on the team, I defer to it and sacrifice for it, because the team, not the individual, is the ultimate champion.

—Mia Hamm, American female soccer player

How Groups Become Teams

The typical stages in building a team are:

1. Forming—Deciding who is on the team
2. Storming—Ironing out differences about team goals and roles
3. Norming—Agreeing on shared team goals and processes
4. Performing—Getting the job done as a team
5. Adjourning—After job is done the team can dissolve

Finding good players is easy. Getting them to play as a team is another story.

—Casey Stengel (1891–1995), professional baseball manager

Forming. To build a successful team, each step must be done carefully with the end goal in mind. Too often, students form their teams based primarily on friendships. While it may at first seem more pleasant to have a team composed of your closest friends, the better approach is to look for complementary skills and experiences. If the assignment involves an in-depth financial analysis, for example, then it would be a good idea to include on your team at least one member with a finance major instead of a team of all marketing majors. Getting rid of the social loafers early is also part of the "forming" step in team building. The goal is to form a team of people with complementary skills, a positive attitude, and a commitment to a common goal. Do not rush this step; it is the most critical step in the team-forming process.

Storming. Each team member must have a unique role to play, must understand what it is, and must know how to do it. Imagine a baseball team with nine players but no defined roles. If the players have not ironed out who is the pitcher, who plays first base, etc., then imagine the confusion when it is time to take the field. A team of employees in a business is no different. At first it is normal for members to disagree about some fundamental issues such as exactly what is expected of the team, what are the time deadlines, what resources are needed and whether they are available, what are the quality standards that must be met, and exactly who is responsible for each task. Again, do not rush this process. To continue with the baseball team analogy, do not force the "team" to run out on the baseball diamond until these differences are worked out. Some disagreement is normal and healthy, but such differences need to be settled as soon as possible.

Norming. In sociology, a *norm* is defined as the agreed-upon behavior within a group. In a team, these norms are strengthened and take on the aspects of rules that the team members mutually agree to follow. The process starts with agreeing upon some basic goals and processes, but over time assumes much more power within the team. In some highly effective teams, all it takes is a quick glance from one team member to another to transmit the rule or process. Good team members are very aware of the norms of the team and will go to great lengths to avoid violating those norms. Those norms are the glue that holds the team together. When these norms are strong, close external supervision is not needed. The team members will quietly enforce the norms within the team. Building a strong set of norms takes time, so don't rush this step either.

Performing. Finally, we have reached the stage of actually getting the task done. The major point is to notice that this is Step 4. Far too often, people want to jump immediately into this step before Steps 1–3 are properly completed. This almost always results in failure. It may temporarily look like success, because some minor task is quickly completed. However, in the long run it is much better to properly form, storm, and norm the team than to worry about quickly completing the first task. But business teams must eventually produce results. The business team is not just about fun; performing the task properly is what it is all about.

Adjourning. Once the task is done, the team can disband. This is the main difference between a team and a department. A department is more permanent. Teams typically have a relatively short life. They are a more flexible way of organizing people. They are built to perform a particular task and can be disassembled and re-formed with different people to best suit the next project to be performed.

Build for your team a feeling of oneness, of dependence on one another and of strength to be derived by unity.

—Vince Lombardi (1913–1970), famous football coach of the Green Bay Packers

When you get your first opportunity to be a team manager, remember to give your team sufficient time to go through each of these five stages. Others may charge out of the starting gate, but your goal should be to demonstrate your mastery of team management and, in the long run, your results will be better than the quick charger.

Reasons Why Teams Fail

There are lots of reasons why teams fail. Think back over your own experiences with sports teams and other teams you know. Just as it is hard to be a good football or basketball coach, it is hard to be a good business team manager. You must address each of the following reasons why many groups often fail to become successful teams:

1. Lack of vision.
2. Ineffective communication.
3. Lack of role clarity.
4. Low morale.
5. Low productivity.
6. Lack of trust.

Lack of vision. In sports, the vision for the team is often clear—win the conference trophy or the tournament. In business, the vision may not be quite so obvious. We all know that a major goal for any for-profit business is to make a profit. However, many projects conducted within a business are only remotely connected to that vision. Also, the corporate-wide goal of increasing Earnings Per Share or Return on Investment or some similar financial target is not likely to excite employees, especially those who are not shareholders. Instead, the vision must be expressed in terms that do excite employees. The typical approach is to express the corporation's vision using a sport's analogy such as "We're number 1." Business managers use expressions from the sports world to put excitement and understanding into otherwise drab financial goals. As a manager, the better you are at phrasing financial goals into more

People who work together will win, whether it be against complex football defenses, or the problems of modern society.

—Vince Lombardi (1913–1970), football coach

generally understood terms, the better you will be at motivating your employees to work together toward a shared vision.

In addition to being clear and exciting, a good vision statement also makes it clear what the organization will and will not do. It should point the organization in a clear direction and help employees make decisions about what to do or not to do. Far too many vision statements are so general that they do not provide any direction at all. Ask, how does this vision statement help this organization know which turn to take at every decision point?

Ineffective Communication. Inexperienced managers often tell their employees what the vision is just once, and then expect everyone to understand it and work together to achieve it. When that does not happen, some managers get frustrated and angry at their employees. However, the problem is often management's fault. The vision for an organization's future must be communicated over and over, because the people within an organization are constantly moving about within the organization. Some get promoted or transferred to another job, some retire, some leave for a job at another organization, some are terminated, and new employees are hired. One wise manager compared this communication problem to giving a speech to a parade. The speaker stands in one place, but the audience keeps moving. You cannot assume everyone in the parade heard the same thing. Also, the people in the parade were busy marching, playing musical instruments, guiding horses, etc., and may not have had the time to pay close attention to the speaker. Workers within an organization are also busy doing their own jobs and may not have fully heard or fully comprehended what the manager was trying to describe as the future state of the organization and why obtaining that future state is so important to everyone within the organization. I do not recall ever hearing a manager say that he or she communicated too much. The goals of the organization and the goals of a particular team must be crystal clear and repeated so often that every team member can repeat them from memory and knows how his or her individual role contributes to that broader goal.

Lack of Role Clarity. Each team member must know exactly what is expected of him or her, what resources can be used to accomplish the task, what time schedule must be met, and what quality standards are demanded. As a team manager, it is your job to spell all this out to each team member, make sure each team member knows exactly how to perform each task, and follow up to make certain all tasks are being completed within budget, on time, and at or above the expected quality standards.

Low Morale. We have all seen sports teams with low morale. It is usually visible just in the way the members hang their heads or slouch their shoulders. A team with high morale seems to walk taller, head back, chest out, a smile on their faces and a sparkle in their eyes. What does it take to build this type of morale? The answer is usually small wins. Confidence comes primarily from success. A series of small wins results in a growing feeling that this is a winning team.

The single biggest problem in communication is the illusion that it has taken place.

—George Bernard Shaw (1856–1950)

Rosabeth Moss Kanter has studied confidence within organizations and has authored several books on the topic, including *Confidence: How Winning Streaks and Losing Streaks Begin and End*. She describes how an airplane that has lost power and is rapidly losing altitude reaches a point where, no matter if power is suddenly restored and the world's best pilot is in charge; the plane is destined to crash. This "death spiral" is something that has to be avoided at all costs. She describes some of the professional sports teams she has studied that have been losing for so long that even though the owners hire a new coach, replace all their players, build a new stadium, and even begin to win a few games, will still likely return to their losing ways. The team has entered the "death spiral," and it is almost impossible to reverse the course. As a team manager, you will need to establish not only the ultimate goal but also intermediate goals along the path that can be celebrated when accomplished. Projects that take several months, or even years, to complete need to have many shorter-term targets. Team members must be praised for the accomplishment of each intermediate objective. Build confidence within your team.

Low Productivity. Regardless of the other aspects of a team, if the productivity is low, the business team is considered a failure. It is not like some childhood league where all the children get a trophy at the end of the season and everyone tries to minimize the consequences of a losing season. The opposite is true in business. The people who invested in the business expect a good return on their investment and are not that concerned about how much "character building" went on at the business this year. The bottom line (net profit) is an important line, and any manager who fails to produce results, either from a team or from any sort of organization, should not expect to keep his or her job for long. As Peter Drucker, the famous author of management textbooks, declared, "Management is not about giving speeches, it is about getting results."

Lack of Trust. When you see a basketball team or any team where all the team members totally trust each other, it is a thing of beauty. Trust is hard to obtain; you have to earn it. It comes mostly from doing what you say you are going to do, over and over again. As a student training to become a manager, you need to be taking steps now to eventually become a trustworthy person. A person worthy of trust is someone you can count on, especially when the going gets tough. In study after study across nations and cultures, the one thing that stands out as the attribute followers most want in their leaders is trust. You cannot wait until late in life to develop into a trustworthy person. Start today by being a trustworthy student. Do what is expected of you in a trustworthy manner. When you get your opportunity to lead a team, give the team the opportunity and the time necessary to learn to trust you and each other.

How to Build an Effective Team

There are ten essential steps in the building of an effective team:

1. Focus on goal.
2. Give members time to socialize.
3. Provide clear performance goals and tasks.
4. Show how task is meaningful.
5. Put skilled members on team.
6. Stress teamwork versus star power.
7. Keep team small.
8. Be a cheerleader for the team, especially to those outside the team.
9. Tie rewards to team effort.
10. Manage conflict.

When you get your first opportunity to manage a small team of employees, remember these ten steps. Each takes time to accomplish. Make sure you, as the team manager, fully understand the goal the team is expected to accomplish. Do not be so impressed with your promotion to team manager that you lose focus on the goal the organization expects of the team.

Good team management is not all work and no play. You must be serious about accomplishing the organization's goal for the team, but that does not mean there should be no socializing. The act of socializing is important for any team. Of course, it should not be carried too far, but some socialization among the team members is a good thing.

Once you clearly understand the performance goals and expectations of the team, it is your duty, as the team manager, to communicate clear performance goals and tasks to each member of the team and to the team as a whole. Further, you must show the team how important those goals are to the organization and how accomplishment of those goals will help both the organization and all the team members. New managers often find it difficult to realize it is not about you; it is about getting results through the best efforts of others under your guidance and motivation.

> *If you can laugh together, you can work together.*
>
> *—Robert Orben (1927–), U.S. magician and comedy writer*

You need to have skilled members on the team, but you must stress how teamwork is even more important than star power. In sports we often see a team composed of good, but not superstar, players who, if they have good teamwork, can win over a team of superstars. Of course the best situation is to have superstars that are also super team members—a rare event indeed.

Some managers will attempt to add as many members to the team as possible, because they think their power as a manager depends on the number of employees under their command. However, research shows most teams are better kept small, usually less than ten. So resist the urge to keep adding members. Communication is so critical to good teamwork that going beyond ten members on the team complicates communication. Get the "right" number on the team, not the biggest number.

You must be the cheerleader for the team. Arrange things so there will be frequent small wins, and use each win to celebrate the team's accomplishment. You are the team's spokesperson and the one who shows outsiders what a great team you have. Do not be shy about this. Build pride among the team members. People like to be part of an organization that makes them feel proud. Use that concept to inspire each team member to do his or her best for the good of the team.

As the manager, you must do all you can to tie rewards to the accomplishment of the team. This is difficult for teachers to do when they assign teams to prepare reports for a class assignment. Typically, the teacher grades the term paper and gives each member of the team the same grade. Unfortunately, there is no place on the typical college transcript to record team grades. However, in business it is often possible to reward the entire team for their results. It may also be possible to reward each team member separately for his or her contribution to the team and to punish those who have not pulled their fair share of the weight. The business manager has many carrots and sticks in his or her arsenal of job-related rewards and punishments. Pay raises, opportunities for advancement, more desired job assignments, a better office, more opportunity for future training, more opportunity for travel, and many more extrinsic rewards are possible. Also, do not forget intrinsic rewards as described in the chapter on motivation. People strongly desire an opportunity to make a difference. Letting each team member know how vital his or her performance was to the team outcome is one of the best things you can do to inspire future trust in your management and willingness to go the extra mile to accomplish the goals you set for them.

Most teams experience some conflict, and it is your responsibility as their manager to properly manage conflict. It is usually not a good idea to merely try to avoid it. It seldom works to sweep conflict under the rug. As Joe Gingo, President, CEO, and Chairman of A. Schulman Inc., says, "Put the dead fish on top of the table. Don't try to hide what stinks. Instead, face it." Manage it so that arguments do not get out of hand. Keep everyone focused on the goal the organization expects of the team. Keep the discussions about the processes and procedures. Do not let it get personal, insulting, or demeaning to any team member. Let the team members know that you are the manager, and you will be the one to take the responsibility for any punishment or reward for any team member. Channel the energy into the goal to be accomplished. Often, strong feelings represent an attitude of caring. Use that to move the team in the right direction and to foster an attitude of high quality and no acceptance of sloppy work.

Coming together is a beginning. Keeping together is progress. Working together is success.

—Henry Ford (1863–1947), industrialist and pioneer of the assembly-line production method

Teamwork can be fun, and being a good team manager can be rewarding. Do not minimize the importance of this early opportunity to show your managerial potential. Not everyone who goes to work for a large organization gets that opportunity. Make the most of it.

SUMMARY

Students of management and leadership need to study how best to work within and manage teams because today's business organizations have found that teamwork can increase productivity, reduce costs, improve quality, enhance speed, and capture the creativity and innovation of their employees. A team differs from a working group in that a team is a carefully selected collection of people chosen for their complementary skills and are committed to a common goal. The stages in building a team include forming, storming, norming, performing, and adjourning. Each step takes time, so do not expect to toss together a group of employees and have them instantly form into a highly productive team. Some major reasons teams fail include lack of vision, ineffective communication, lack of role clarity, low morale, low productivity, and the lack of trust. To become an effective team manager, you must be aware of these issues and take steps to avoid each. Instead, you should take the steps of focusing on the goal, giving members time to socialize, providing clear performance goals and tasks, showing members how the task is meaningful, putting skilled members on the team, stressing teamwork versus star power, keeping the team small, being a cheerleader for the team, tying rewards to team effort, and managing conflict within the team.

QUESTIONS FOR DISCUSSION

1. Describe both a good and a bad team experience you have had, either at work or at school. What were the causes of each? What suggestions from this chapter could have been used to improve teamwork?
2. Describe how you would properly manage each of the five stages of team building (forming, storming, norming, performing, and adjourning).

3. Research shows teams typically fail because of lack of vision, ineffective communication, lack of role clarity, low morale, low productivity, and lack of trust. Describe how a great team leader would address each of these challenges.

Chapter 10

Writing as a Manager and Leader

Would you like to be able to give speeches that inspire others? Would you like your written communications to be top-notch? Chapters 10 and 11 provide guidelines that can help you do just that. Being able to speak and write with the best can be a big help as you graduate and enter the world of the professional business manager. It can be what sets you apart and gets you noticed so you have a better chance of reaching your leadership potential. Even more importantly, being able to communicate with the best will help you be successful once you obtain that desired position. Most people agree they have problems with communication. Most organizations suffer from poor communication. Why is it so difficult to communicate? How is communicating as a manager or leader different from other types of communication?

One learns peoples through the heart, not the eyes or the intellect.

—Mark Twain

The Mark Twain quote above talks about how one "learns peoples." Management is a people-oriented business and managers definitely need to know how people receive, understand, and act upon the manager's communication. Communicating as a manager requires a whole new level of communication, not mere communication from one mind to another, but also from one heart to another.

Win hearts and you have all men's hands and purses.

—William Cecil Burleigh (1521–1598), English statesman

Managers have to do more than communicate facts, but communicate facts they must. Let's first look at the traditional model of communication. You have likely studied this model in other courses, but now look at it in terms of communicating as a manager. How do you communicate a vision for your organization's future? How do you communicate so you inspire?

Shannon & Weaver's Communication Model

Many courses in communication begin with the traditional model of communication developed by Shannon and Weaver (1949). It consists of five elements:

1. An *information source*, which produces a message. That could be you, the leader.
2. A *transmitter*, which encodes the message into signals. For example, your brain and mouth.
3. A *channel* that carries or transmits your voice to the intended receiver. The phone lines, for example.
4. A *receiver*, which "decodes" (reconstructs) the message from the signal. The phone and ears of your followers.
5. A *destination*, where the message arrives. The minds of your followers.

In many cases, a sixth element, *noise*, is introduced as a dysfunctional element. *Noise* is defined as any interference with the message traveling along the channel resulting in the signal being received incorrectly. For example, the sound of a train going by!

People Are More Complex than Phones

Shannon and Weaver were engineers working for Bell Telephone Labs. Their model was intended to represent the efficiency of telephone wires. If a telephone system gets the message sent from the transmitter to the receiver in exactly the same condition as it was produced by the information source, then the telephone system has properly done its job. (If you need more detail, a Google search of "Communication Theory Shannon & Weaver's Model" will provide numerous articles and drawings of this famous model.)

However, our focus is on the interpretation of the message by the "destination," which is not some mechanical device, but rather a human being. Shannon & Weaver's model is linear and ends with the receiver obtaining the message as sent. We want to complete the feedback circle from leader to follower and back to leader and extending out to action. Leaders need to communicate not just to inform, but also to cause followers to actually change their behavior, a task much more daunting than merely informing.

COMMUNICATE THE "MUSIC" BEHIND THE WORDS

When human beings interpret any message, an extremely complex process happens. We have all experienced the situation where two people are given exactly the same message and each interprets it differently. How do we know that what we think we have communicated clearly actually gets received and interpreted as we hope? Furthermore, how do we communicate more than just the facts? How do leaders also communicate a sense of importance, urgency, and spirit? Someone expressed it as, "How do you communicate the music behind the words, so you not only inform but inspire?"

KNOW YOUR AUDIENCE

The most important thing for a leader to consider when communicating is—*who is the listener?* What set of experiences, education, attitudes, values, motivations, and feelings does the listener bring into the process? What does the listener think of the speaker? You must know your audience and how they feel about you. For example, do they trust you?

When you really distrust someone, do you really listen to them? If your feelings are so negative about the person, you probably just turn the person's voice off inside your head. Have you ever experienced someone doing that to you?

> *Who you are rings so loudly in my ear I cannot hear what you are saying.*
>
> *—Source unknown*

We need to consider not only possible noise on the transmission channels, but also noise within the mind of the receiver. In the workplace, one of the biggest factors producing noise is the relative power between the transmitter and the receiver. If you fear the person, your perception of what they are saying is very different than if the same words are coming out of someone you love and trust.

OUR PERCEPTIONS FILTER OUR COMMUNICATIONS

Suppose, for example, your boss has just threatened to fire you. Imagine you have been at this job for ten years, you are married with a family to support, and you have a child with a chronic disease that requires expensive medical treatment which is currently covered by the firm's medical insurance. Even if it was only an idle threat, once issued the relationship between you and your boss will never be the same. Practically everything he or she says from this moment on will be filtered by your perceptions of how getting fired will affect you and your family's future. Such thoughts will act like a perception filter altering all future communications between you and your boss.

We all notice and accept stimuli from a source consistent with our perception and ignore or are blind to inconsistent stimuli. If our main perception of our boss is that of a threat to our family's survival, then

Perception is the process by which individuals make sense of their world.

—Chuck Williams (1915–), founder, Williams-Sonoma Co. and cookbook author

all future stimuli coming from that boss will have to first pass through that perceptual filter before we understand and act on it.

The Psychological Contract

Scientists suggest a psychological contract exists between the employer and employee. This implied contract refers to the employee's perceptions of what they owe their employer and what their employer owes them. For example, most of us expect our employer to reward our hard work and positive results with continued employment and a fair market wage.

Can you see how a threatened firing is a train wreck on the communication channel? It has been my experience that this, or something near to this, happens frequently in the workplace. Bosses threaten to fire people and then wonder why everyone can't seem to work together as a team. It is like a bomb has exploded blowing apart the psychological contract, and the boss is wondering why his whispered communication was somehow lost in the blast.

Communication Ought to Build Community

The root word of *communication* is "common." It is also the root word of community and communion. It is about sharing. It is about a relationship. It is much more complicated than the simple transmission of voice. We communicate with our whole being, not merely our voice. A community is a group of people who share things in common. A community of neighbors shares a common street or area. A community of workers shares tasks. Hopefully there is also a sharing of interests, values, and goals. Good leaders create good communities.

As George Bernard Shaw pointed out, "The single biggest problem in communication is the illusion that it has taken place." George Bernard Shaw's quote points out the need to not merely send a message but to also make certain the communication was complete. Many of us erroneously assume we have communicated when we have merely transmitted. The message may have been accurately written or spoken, transmitted, and received. These conditions are necessary, but not sufficient for effective leadership communication. Getting the message properly transmitted is only the beginning.

Don't Assume Your Message Is Properly Interpreted

As a manager and a leader, one of the worst mistakes you can make is to assume that what you have said or written is what is received and interpreted. For example, as a manager, you may have asked your employees to cut costs, but what they heard was that layoffs were coming. Perhaps such a thought did not even enter your mind. How did it enter the minds of your employees? Your employees will remember

Communication leads to community, that is, to understanding, intimacy, and mutual valuing.

—*Rollo May (1909--1994), psychologist and author of* Love and Will

previous communications about cutting costs. If they ever personally experienced being laid off as a result of cost cutting, that memory will never fade. It will be a perceptual filter that your current message regarding cost cutting will pass through before an interpretation is made.

Your listeners are not machines. They have emotions and memory. Business leaders frequently complain that even their simplest statements are often misunderstood. Perhaps they haven't looked carefully at the perception filter that exists between the leader and the followers. The same holds true for feedback. Good feedback is when you learn that your instructions have been carried out according to your expectations and with the expected results. The noise here may be your followers' reluctance to admit disappointing results or less than full compliance. You may be thinking all you need is accurate and timely data about the results, and they may be thinking about protecting their jobs. Instead of honestly admitting they did not fully comply with your instructions or that something failed in the implementation phase, a scapegoat may be presented. "The unexpected harsh weather delayed the project." "The needed supplies did not arrive on time." "Some of the key employees were ill." They see this as protecting their jobs while you see it as making excuses.

Again, the problem is caused by a perceptual filter. If the followers perceive the leader as a threat to their job security, then that perception produces a filter through which any feedback from follower to leader must pass. It is human nature to look for a scapegoat to carry the blame instead of clearly communicating a failure. Even worse is when followers fashion the feedback in such a way that the leader believes everything is okay when in fact serious problems exist. Perhaps the followers hope they can fix the problem and the leader will never have to know it existed.

Technical, Semantic, and Effectiveness Problems

There are at least three types of problems your message will likely encounter: (1) the *technical* problem—how accurately your message was transmitted; (2) the *semantic* problem—how accurately the meaning was conveyed; and (3) the *effectiveness* problem—how your message affected behavior. While each can cause a breakdown in communication, we need to focus on effectiveness—why didn't our message create the response we expected? The problem is similar to that of a teacher who gives a great lecture and later is amazed the students didn't learn what was "taught." We measure what was taught not by what the teacher said, but by what the students actually learned.

Problems in Common to Teaching, Learning, and Leading

Teaching, learning, leading, and communicating have much in common. Recently, educators have begun to focus on how teaching and learning are not the same. It is the student who must do the learning. The teacher's role is as a facilitator. In a learner-centered environment, the center of attention shifts from the teacher to the learner. Learning is not just about memorizing and parroting back facts and figures; it is also about changing behaviors and attitudes. So is leading.

How the Brain Changes

James Zull, Professor of Biology at Case Western Reserve and author of *The Art of Changing the Brain*, relates a time when he delivered a lecture that was so well prepared and delivered that the students applauded—an all too rare event for most of us professors. Dr. Zull left the classroom on Cloud Nine. His thoughts were that he had just given the very best lecture of his career. He assumed he had taught and the students had learned.

> *The art of teaching is the art of assisting discovery.*
>
> *—Mark Van Doren (1894–1972), American Pulitzer Prize–winning poet*

The next class period, Zull's euphoric feeling was destroyed when he gave a quiz and found his students really didn't understand what he had said. Many had misinterpreted what he thought he had taught so successfully. Almost none could actually use what he had taught in an application. He was disappointed the students had not learned what he had expected, despite his delivery of a lecture they had applauded. His lecture had not changed the students' behavior in the way he had hoped. The best lecture of his life didn't produce the effect he wanted.

Managers often experience the same problem. They believe they have communicated clearly—perhaps even brilliantly—but the effect is not what was desired. In Professor Zull's case, he turned his attention to how the brain learns, and the result was his book, *The Art of Changing the Brain*.

Professor Zull admits he seldom lectures any more. Instead, he uses a teaching style that combines experiential and conversational learning—even in large sections. Experiential learning is learning by doing. Conversational learning is learning in a format of casual conversation. The combination calls for active learning within a non-threatening atmosphere.

As a biologist, Professor Zull learned that cells communicate differently when the atmosphere is relaxed. When the brain is relaxed, it produces more of a chemical called serotonin. When brain cells communicate in an atmosphere rich in serotonin, the connections between communicating nerve endings build a coating around the connections similar in effect to the insulation around an electrical wire. There is actually a microscopically observable difference between learning under stress and learning while relaxed. Zull hypothesizes that we can remember things longer when we learn in a relaxed atmosphere because of the coating the brain puts along the communicating nerve endings.

Learning So We Remember

How do we remember? Why are some things easy to remember and other things nearly impossible? Have you ever been amazed at what you have forgotten and what you have remembered? Many older adults admit they have forgotten most of what they learned in school.

Those courses best remembered typically involved some activity or experience such as conducting an experiment, writing and presenting a paper, or working on a project in cooperation with the professor. Especially memorable are courses where the teacher did something to really make the student feel like the teacher really cared about the student as a person—there was a heart-to-heart connection. In contrast, many lecture courses are, over time, almost totally forgotten.

Think about your own educational experiences. Which ones do you still vividly remember several years later? Which ones were purged from your memory a few minutes after the final exam? Now imagine yourself in a position of leadership responsibility. You do not want to merely transmit information. As a manager, you need to teach your employees. You need to change attitudes and behavior. You need to motivate others to action. How are you going to communicate to get the desired results?

> *Learning is not a spectator sport.*
>
> *—Source unknown*

The first thing a teacher has to remember in preparing to teach any subject is that teachers teach people. It is as important to understand your students as it is to understand your subject matter. The same is true for managers and all leaders. You first lead people. To better communicate with your subordinates, first understand them as individuals.

Chapters 10 and 11 examine ways leaders communicate with followers and vice versa. Chapter 10 focuses on writing and Chapter 11 on speaking, but throughout both chapters I hope to provide hints on how to communicate in a more heart-to-heart manner to inspire, motivate, and produce the results you want. Keep in mind, however, that communication is far from an exact science and no process is foolproof. Both the sender and the destination are infinitely complex human beings. Both must take full responsibility for verifying the message sent was properly received and interpreted.

Employers Demand Better Communication

The issue of improving communication is especially troublesome to employers of recent business school graduates. Advisory boards to business colleges have long called for those schools to produce graduates with better writing and speaking skills. In response, many business colleges have changed their curriculum to include more courses in English and speech. Unfortunately, this has not produced the desired results.

Business leaders are still complaining that recent business school graduates are ineffective in their writing and speaking skills. The concern they raise goes deeper than learning grammar, spelling, and basic techniques of speaking. Communications that are technically correct are not necessarily heart-to-heart communications, and therefore do not change the values or behaviors of the receiver. Leaders need to not only be heard; they also must be taken seriously.

For many years, my favorite example of someone who murdered English grammar, but nonetheless communicated effectively as a leader, was Mike Ditka, former coach of the Chicago Bears. Now you see him on television providing "color commentary," discussing football strategy, and advertising various products. Over the years, Mike's grammar has improved. However, the effective communication I have in mind is when he was able to motivate the Chicago Bears to win the 1985 Super Bowl. In that setting, it was not proper grammar but rather heart-to-heart, emotional, spiritual communication that transcended ordinary speech. He was able to take a bunch of rather self-centered individuals and turn them into a winning team, a feat most leaders would love to accomplish.

Being good with words is not the same as being perfect with grammar, but many courses on written communication focus more on rules of grammar than on using words to inspire. You can probably think of someone who might have a difficult time passing an English grammar course, but deserves an "A+" in the area of motivating others through effective speaking. Therefore, this chapter will not be a rehashing of English grammar rules. Modern word processors provide most of the help you will need in the technical areas of spelling and grammar. Failure to use such checkers is simply inexcusable. There are times when your computer's grammar checker is simply wrong and there are some errors it will miss, but it catches most obvious mistakes.

I never teach my pupils; I only attempt to provide the conditions in which they can learn.

—Albert Einstein (1879–1955)

Some Handy Writing Aids

Every person who cares about writing needs to study Strunk and White's classic book, *The Elements of Style*. This little reference book has been at the side of most good writers since it was first published in 1959. It cuts right to the quick and addresses common problems most writers face regarding spelling, grammar, and other aspects of writing style. Also, you will find helpful *The Careful Writer* by Theodore M. Bernstein, plus *Pocket Fowler's Modern English Usage* published by Oxford Paperback Reference. Always on my desk is the latest edition of *Webster's New World College Dictionary.* More recently, I have started using Purdue University's Online Writing Lab called the OWL at http://owl.english.purdue.edu. Go to the Site Map on the OWL for a listing of just about every English issue you are likely to ever face, click on the issue that concerns you, and see the English rule followed by examples of proper English usage.

Later, we will examine the art of speaking as a manager and a leader. It is easier to touch the heart through speech than through writing, because you can use gestures and tone. Your followers can not only hear you, but can also "see" what you mean. The written page is stark in comparison. However, a good speech begins with good writing; therefore, we will first examine some techniques of good writing.

Good Writing Begins with Good Reading

What do you read, and why?

Too many of us have gotten out of the habit of setting aside time each day to read. Students and leaders have plenty of excuses for not taking the time each day to read. Mark Twain said, "The man who does not read good books has no advantage over the man who can't read them." As Mark Twain's quote implies, if you don't read good books, for whatever reason, then you have very little advantage over someone who never learned to read.

The mind grows on what it feeds on so be careful what you feed both your body and your mind. Don't starve, either. Don't fill either with junk. Good writing begins with good reading. You must, after all, have something worthwhile to say. While reading is not the only way to collect worthwhile things to say, it certainly is one of the best.

When we get in the habit of reading material that is well written, we also begin to write and speak better. We tend to copy what we experience and like. Furthermore, learning to put our thoughts in writing forces us to think more exactly.

Read Good Literature about Management and Leading

Many business professionals fail to read broadly within their discipline. Instead of reading the quality material backed up by theory and research, there is a tendency to read what a select few gurus of management fads, such as Tom Peters, Steven Covey, and others have written. While much of what such writers have to say is truthful and helpful, most of it is merely one person's opinion. You may find such opinion of highly experienced and articulate people helpful, but don't limit yourself to just such literature. Every accomplished leader likely has his or her list of must-read books.

New books on such popular topics as leadership, ethics, emotional intelligence, change management, and business strategy keep rolling off the presses. Watch for them and resolve to keep up to date on those areas of business literature that will be of greatest benefit to you in the future. You can ask Amazon.com to send you a message alerting you to newly published books on leadership or any topic that interests you.

If you feel inadequate to jump right into the more difficult areas right now, consider the series of books for "Dummies" or for "Complete Idiots" that are so popular today. Most are excellent at providing the beginner with an overview of an area. I especially recommend *Leadership for Dummies* by Loeb and

Kindel. Another strong recommendation is *The Complete Idiot's Guide to Understanding Ethics* by Ingram and Parks. Of course, anyone looking for help in writing well should not miss *The Complete Idiot's Guide to Writing Well* by Laurie Rozakis.

The Secret to Good Writing is Rewriting

> *Reading maketh a full man; conference a ready man; and writing an exact man.*
>
> —*Francis Bacon (1561–1626), English philosopher*

Most writers believe the secret to good writing is to polish your writing by revising and rewriting. With today's word processing technology, it is easy to do much of your own editing. You can now go through a dozen or more rewrites in the time it used to take to do one.

Proofread your work, but let it cool off first. Let it sit for at least an hour; otherwise, you will see what you *hope* is on the page rather than what is actually there. When you proofread, read first for meaning. As you do so, keep in mind the following questions:

1. What is the central theme, and what does each piece contribute?
2. So what? Why is this important?
3. Who cares?
4. How can this be used?
5. Can this be said more precisely?
6. Am I touching readers' hearts in addition to their minds?

Do something else for an hour or so and then proofread it a second time for mechanics, looking for such things as:

7. Missing or mismatched headings and subheadings.
8. Missing words.
9. Incorrect numbers. (This is especially important in business reports where the readers are likely to be trained to look for inaccuracies in the numbers.)
10. Missing citations and references.
11. Typographical errors.
12. Repeat until well cooked.

Spelling and grammar checkers will not pick up missing words or words that are correct as to spelling and grammar but just don't fit. Better yet, have someone else you can trust to be careful and honest proofread your work, but only after you have proofread it yourself at least twice. It never ceases

If we encountered a man of rare intellect, we should ask him what books he read.

—Ralph Waldo Emerson (1803–1882), American writer and poet

to amaze me how often students turn in term papers and other important papers containing errors their computerized spelling and grammar checker had to flag. There is simply no excuse for that. Furthermore, there is no excuse for turning in business reports with similar errors; many readers will simply assume your poor writing is a reflection of poor thinking and/or a careless attitude.

Beginnings and Endings

Readers form a first impression within a few seconds. The final sentences have a major impact upon the reader's final impression of your writing. Plato is said to have rewritten the first sentence of *The Republic* 50 times. Hemingway took 39 tries before he was satisfied with the last page of *A Farewell to Arms*. Neither had the benefit of a word processor.

Communication works for those who work at it.

—John Wesley Powell (1834–1902), U.S. explorer and writer

Take the time to get the beginning and ending right both mechanically and emotionally. For the beginning, ask, "Would this make me eager to read the rest?" For the ending, ask, "Does this leave the reader with the right knowledge and motivation to carry out what is needed?" Remember, leaders must accept responsibility for clearly communicating their call to action, and the best way is to communicate heart to heart. Communicate accurately and with spirit. Take your leadership communication responsibilities seriously; others will, for better or worse.

A business report typically ends with a "call to action." Think about what action you want the reader to take upon reading your report. If your report is more than a couple of pages long, quickly summarize your key points and conclude with a statement about what needs to be done now.

Management means, in the last analysis, the substitution of thought for brawn and muscle, of knowledge for folklore and superstition, and of cooperation for force.

—Peter Drucker (1909–2005)

Many politicians now end their speeches with "God bless America." While some may be sincerely making a request to God, many are simply using this phrase as a way of saying "I'm done now and I hope you applaud." Another such phrase is "Thank you for listening." The point is you must give some thought to the way you end any written or spoken communication. Ask yourself what it is you want the audience to do at the end, and make certain you set up the situation to maximize the probability you will get that result.

Getting Material from Newspapers, Journals, and the Internet

The dogmas of the quiet past are inadequate to the stormy present.

—Abraham Lincoln

While technology has shortened the time between writing a book and seeing it in print, it still commonly takes more than a year to get a manuscript produced by the major publishers. In addition to reading good books, read current journal articles. Be as up to date as possible. Also, you need to ask, what do the writers of business books read? Where do they get their ideas? Journal articles are a major source for book authors, especially books that are based on sound theory and research.

If you are serious about assuming the awesome responsibilities of organizational leadership, you must expand your journal reading to more than the standard fare of the *Wall Street Journal*, *Forbes*, *BusinessWeek*, *Time*, and *U.S. News & World Report*. Of course, you need to regularly read them and also some good national daily newspaper such as the *New York Times*, but you must also go beyond and get into the more meaty journals such as *Harvard Business Review*, *Leadership Quarterly*, *Academy of Management Review*, *Sloan Management Review*, *Business Horizons*, and others that address the latest scholarly findings within your specific discipline and industry.

Today, anyone who fails to take advantage of the wealth of current information available on the Internet is indeed foolish. While I am using Word, I have my computer set up so I can easily switch to a Google search. To find, for example, quotes that fit right in, I do a Google search using the key words "famous quotations," followed by the topic that I am currently writing about. For example, such a search using key words "famous quotations wisdom" just turned up this:

Of all the arts in which
The wise excel,
Nature's chief masterpiece
Is writing well

—John Sheffield (1649–1720), first duke of Buckinghamshire and poet

A great online general reference is www.refdesk.com, a source librarians use. Another is Arts & Letters Daily at www.aldaily.com. You should build your own collection of useful websites to aid your writing. Do not expect to do this all at once. The main point is to put together your personal reference list of online and print sources that will be most valuable to you.

Communication is the real work of leadership.

—Nitin Nohria, dean of Harvard Business School

If you expect to compete successfully with budding executives from around the world, read what they are reading. Imagine a contest of wits between someone who is truly well-read versus someone who spends their free time watching situation comedy shows on television. Consider the *New York Times* list of best sellers in the field of business non-fiction.

Once you have listened, observed, and read enough to feel confident you have something to say, how do you get it down on paper? Today, instead of the blank page, the challenge is to face a blank computer screen and know you need to start keying in something—but what?

It all has to do with being "centered." Be on task. Be focused. Know exactly what you are trying to say and to whom. Most writers feel a need to communicate their thoughts to others. Leaders need to become good writers so they can more clearly communicate to their followers.

Summary

Good writing begins with good reading. Fill your mind with good information that is based on more than one person's opinion. When writing for an audience of business leaders, be concise. Such readers are busy and hate to waste their time. Get to the point as quickly as possible. The first sentence should grab their attention and answer the question, "Why should I read the rest of this?" The ending should quickly summarize your main points and end with a call to action.

Questions for Discussion

1. Describe a book you have recently read that relates to the topic of management and/or leadership. What were the main points? How did the book change your behavior?
2. Recall a communication failure from either your work or your school experience. What was the cause of that failure? What would you do now to avoid or overcome that communication problem?
3. Explore the website http://owl.english.purdue.edu. Describe at least one item you found especially helpful for your writing.
4. Take a term paper or report you have recently written and proofread it using the set of questions listed in this chapter. Describe what you discovered as a result of proofreading in this manner.

Chapter 11

Public Speaking as a Manager and Leader

A good speech is first a well-written communication. The writer must have first studied the topic and have something important to say. That is why good speaking demands good writing and good writing demands good reading. However, the speech has to be delivered in person. You can't just mail it in.

To Speak as a Leader, First Overcome the Fear of Public Speaking

Studies suggest one of many people's worst fears is public speaking. In fact, some studies have even suggested there are people who fear public speaking worse than death. That is a little extreme, but it is true that many people are anxious about making major presentations in front of a large audience. However, as a future manager and leader, it is something you will be expected to do.

People who appear calm on stage may, in fact, be just as nervous as you or I. Everyone seems to have their own way of dealing with nervousness. For some people, their nervousness really shows. Perhaps they stutter or sweat or shake or get sick to their stomach. For others, the nervousness can be hidden. It might appear as tightness in the stomach, a dry mouth, weak knees, or any of a hundred other

According to most studies, people's number one fear is public speaking. Number two is death. Death is number two. Does that sound right? This means to the average person, if you go to a funeral, you're better off in the casket than doing the eulogy.

—Jerry Seinfeld (1954–), American comedian

You can conquer almost any fear if you will only make up your mind to do so. For remember, fear doesn't exist anywhere except in the mind.

—Dale Carnegie (1888–1955), American writer

manifestations of nervousness. Almost everyone has some nervous reaction to public speaking. We all have fears; what any future leader has to learn to do is cope with those fears. A certain amount of fear can be your motivator to invest the necessary amount of preparation into your speech. What has to be avoided is the excess of fear that either keeps you from stepping up to the challenge of public speaking or ruins what would otherwise be a great presentation.

Take a Deep Breath

One of the most challenging speaking assignments is to speak at the funeral of a relative or friend. At such times, emotions can be overwhelming and people will be very understanding. Taking two or three deep breaths before giving such a talk can get you through even some of the most challenging moments. Do not underestimate the importance of deep breathing exercises. Women about to give birth are often coached in the Lamaze technique to use deep breathing exercises to help them cope with the severe pain of childbirth. Deep breathing will not relieve all the sorrow or pain, but it can help you cope with fear.

Dale Carnegie's first publication, *Public Speaking and Influencing Men in Business*, was a collection of stories and tips he received from his students in a public speaking class he taught. He is most famous for *How to Win Friends and Influence People* and later *How to Stop Worrying and Start Living*. These books and his courses have helped thousands overcome their fears and take on the challenges of living a full and productive life. For more information, see http://www.dalecarnegie.com.

Thorough Preparation Is Essential

In this chapter, we suggest tips (such as deep breathing) that have been helpful in overcoming or coping with the fear of public speaking. However, there is no substitution for preparation. No gimmick or coping trick will make up for a lack of preparation about the topic of your speech. So it goes without saying that the first rule is to thoroughly prepare. Most students who really do poorly on an oral presentation have only prepared at a minimal level.

Some people argue that they do better at public speaking when they merely compose a list of key words or topics and do not actually memorize every word they plan to say. By suggesting you need to thoroughly prepare, we do not mean you should memorize every word. Instead, prepare so you know your topic so well you do not have to memorize everything you are going to stay. Instead, aim for a level of confidence about what you are going to say that you are able to put aside your notes and speak from the heart.

Prepare Like Musicians

One way to think about the right amount of preparation is to consider those who sing or play a musical instrument in front of large audiences. Have you ever been around such performers? Those who go on stage to play a long and difficult piece may have practiced that piece thousands of times. They have done it so many times the music is burned into their brain for life. Perhaps you have experienced having a song so entrenched in your brain that you can't get it out of your head no matter how hard you try.

Music majors really have it tough. In addition to extreme levels of talent, they must also practice countless hours. After graduating with a degree in music, there is certainly no guarantee anyone will offer them a job. Instead of simply signing up for job interviews with the college placement office, they often head off to a large city, work nights at restaurants or at other minimum wage jobs while practicing all day and hoping to get an audition along with hundreds of others with similar talents and skills. Business majors can learn a few things by observing music majors and can be inspired to put much more preparation into the presentations we are expected to make. After all, if the singer screws up, the worst that could happen is the audience boos and the singer goes back to practice more and try again. If you screw up as a business leader, it may cost hundreds of employees their jobs and thousands of investors their life savings. So, practice, practice—and then practice some more. Earn those big bucks.

What the music major is working toward is the point where he or she has so mastered the music that the musician's spirit takes over. Then the result moves from a mechanical presentation of the proper notes into the realm of a spiritual event. Music critics and audiences cannot explain exactly what it is, but they know it when it happens. The music touches their inner spirit.

Scholars at Harvard have conducted research on the relationship between a great actor on stage and the audience. Somehow they measured how, when a great actor is really at his or her best, the audience's respiration and heart beat are in sync with the actor's. You have probably experienced a time during a play or a movie when the actor would suddenly gasp and many people in the audience would also gasp or jump in their seats. The audience has temporarily forgotten they were merely watching a play. They had become so drawn in by the actors that they had become part of the play. Scholars of acting don't know exactly how to describe such levels of communication, but we all know it when it happens. The level of communication has risen above the simple correct reciting of the lines of the play. Instead, the actors and the audience experience a spiritual event together. Audience members, upon leaving the theatre, talk about how they were "carried away" by the performance. We forget we were simply sitting

The best way to sound like you know what you're talking about is to know what you're talking about.

—Source unknown

There are three things to aim at in public speaking: first to get into your subject, then to get your subject into yourself, and lastly, to get your subject into the heart of your audience.

—Alexander Gregg (1819–1893), Episcopal bishop

in a darkened theater watching professional actors recite lines. Rather, we feel inspired, uplifted, or have a sense we have just returned from a journey. The play did more than touch our minds. It touched our hearts, our inner selves, or perhaps our souls. This is the challenge of communication for leaders. Can you communicate on a spiritual level? Can you write and speak in such a way that others want to follow you?

Public Speaking Begins with (But Is Different From) Writing

You will recall the idea that good speaking begins with good writing. There are, however, many differences. All writing acknowledges the importance of pace and rhythm. But the reader has the advantage of progressing at the individual's speed and rereading what is not understood. The spoken word is accompanied by gestures and motions that emphasize the importance of overall appearance, just as the orderly presentation of the written word demonstrates the need for good grammar.

Take the example of TV newscasters. When you have the TV sound off, you still get some clues about the subject being discussed by looking at the reporter and the set. Business clothes and a clean desk suggest serious news. A golf shirt and slacks bring a casual air to the presentation and probably indicate a human interest story. Work clothes and an open neck often mean a report from some far-off place where dress is practical and casual.

Newscasters also are aware of the importance of emphasis as they issue their report. Radio announcers might get a lot of their news from the newspapers and other printed sources, but they use a different writing style, using fewer words and shorter sentences. Some key words stand out and carry much of the message. The broadcaster calls this "punching" their words so that they form key landmarks as the message goes out. In many cases, the reader won't remember details of the report so much as the key words presented in the broadcast. You can use the same technique to make certain parts of your presentation stand out in the memory of your listeners.

You may need to practice pausing before delivering the punch phrase. Maybe you will need to say it louder or with a different tone of voice. Some leaders repeat the key phrase over and over until the listeners can't help but remember it. Think about your key point and then think about what you can do to give it "punch." By all means, though, never deliver a speech in a monotone voice.

It's about the Audience

In writing a speech you have to write for the ear as well as the eye, constantly asking yourself, "Is this boring?" Look for ways to shorten sentences. Use simple words. Remember that a listener will get more out of a story than a lecture. Make your motto, "Show it," not "Tell it."

> *A speech is poetry; cadence, rhythm, imagery, sweep! A speech reminds us that words, like children, have the power to dance the dullest beanbag of a heart.*
>
> *—Peggy Noonan (1950–), speechwriter for President Reagan*

Leaders must be especially careful in the delivery of a speech. Leaders speak for the organization. Their most casual remark may eventually be reported in the newspaper, used in court, or influence investors. Financial data must be checked carefully and placed in the proper context. As a leader, the spotlight is on you. Some leaders, such as the president of the United States and candidates for that office, have to be aware of every word being recorded by the opposition. Business leaders must be especially aware of how not only the immediate audience will interpret what they say, but also how it will later be perceived by the competition, stockholders, financial writers, and others.

Proofread your written speech asking the same questions we suggested earlier for the proofreading of writing, but add the step of rehearsing the delivery. Many leaders prepare for key speeches by video recording their rehearsals. They review the recording, listening and watching for ways to improve not only the words but also the gestures, timing, and voice tone. Modern day smart phones and other electronic devices that include video recorders are now commonly available so there is no excuse for not video recording your practice session.

> *Be sincere; be brief; be seated.*
>
> *—Franklin D. Roosevelt (1882–1945), 32nd president of the United States*

It is vital to begin and end strongly. Many professional speakers will go over the beginning and the ending dozens of times until they feel it is just right. By all means, time it. Be certain to stay within your time limits. Even a great public speaker can quickly ruin a speech by running too long.

The most important message of this chapter is that leaders have a heightened responsibility to know their audience and to make certain their message is communicated accurately and clearly into the hearts and minds of their followers. As a business leader, you will no longer be speaking just for yourself, but will be the spokesperson for many. Put the proper time and effort into doing your best to become an effective public speaker.

Tips for Overcoming Fear of Public Speaking

Following are helpful tips for overcoming the fear of public speaking:

1. Prepare by reading the right books and journals.
2. Write the speech as carefully as you would an important written assignment.
3. Proofread using the questions listed in the previous chapter.
4. Polish by editing and rewriting over and over.
5. Learn as much as you can about the audience and address their needs.
6. Add emotional punch to key points.
7. Put special attention on the beginning and ending.
   - The beginning must address the question of why the audience should listen.
   - The ending must be specific about your call to action. Exactly what do you expect the audience to do once your speech is finished?
8. Prepare like a musician would for a concert. Rehearse over and over again until you could throw away the script.
9. Use repetition to emphasize and help the audience remember key points.
10. Video record yourself so you can observe your body language and hear your emotion in your voice.

Learn from the Masters of Public Speaking

During the 1950s, Bishop Fulton J. Sheen had the most popular show on television, *Life Is Worth Living*. It was not merely the most popular religious show, but the most popular show in all of television. All Bishop Sheen did was stand and talk for a half hour. There was no elaborate set, no band, and no beautiful women. It was just this priest standing there with no notes speaking directly into the camera. How could such a simple show become so popular?

> *Know that a word suddenly shot from the tongue is like an arrow shot from a bow. Son, that arrow won't turn back on its own; you must damn the torrent at its source.*
>
> —*Mevlana Rumi*

In one show, Bishop Fulton J. Sheen described how he prepared for his popular television show. Bishop Sheen refused to use a teleprompter or idiot cards. Instead, he researched his topic thoroughly, making many pages of notes. He went over and over the ideas for his speech until he was able to put the key ideas onto a small piece of paper about the size of an ordinary envelop. Before going before the camera, he would toss the paper away.

He explained the most important thing was to be sincere. Reading from notes, a teleprompter, or idiot cards subtracted from that sincerity. But most people, he explained, are afraid they will forget what they want to say. The notes are their crutch. His technique for dealing with the possibility of forgetting what he wanted to say next was to have a few humorous stories memorized so he could fill in gaps while his mind relaxed and he eventually remembered what it was he intended to say. He demonstrated by telling the following story:

> *Christians were being fed to the lions in the Roman Coliseum. As the lion approached one especially clever Christian, he hugged the lion and whispered into the lion's ear. The lion listened and then nervously walked away and sat back down in his cage. Caesar called for a new lion that had been kept away from food for two days. Again the Christian hugged the charging lion, whispered in his ear, and the lion nervously walked back to his cage and sat down. Caesar called for another lion that had been kept hungry for a week. Again the Christian hugged the lion, whispered something in his ear, and the third lion nervously went back to his cage.*
>
> *The Roman audience cheered the brave Christian and shouted for Caesar to release him. Caesar called the Christian over to his royal throne and told him, "I will release you, but only after you tell me what you whispered to those lions."*
>
> *The Christian replied, "Caesar, I simply told the lions that after their next meal they'd be required to give a speech."*

So learn from the masters at public speaking. Practice speaking without notes. Toss away the crutches and the training wheels and be brave. Think ahead about what you will do if you suddenly forget what you planned to say next. Have your coping mechanism ready for the moment when you need it. Use every opportunity to practice the skill of public speaking. If you regularly attend religious services, ask to be a reader. Join a club such as Toastmasters and become an active participant. Join a business club such as Rotary or Kiwanis and volunteer to make regular presentations in front of such audiences. When someone needs to volunteer to be the spokesperson for your department at work, step up to the plate.

Audiences Think Primarily about Themselves

Do not think of the members of the audience as being focused totally on you and wanting to pounce on you the moment you slip. Researchers have discovered that even in a darkened auditorium, when the spotlight is focused on the speaker or performer, most people in the audience are thinking primarily about themselves. They are worried about whether their hair is properly combed, their clothes are the proper style and fit, and what others in the audience are thinking about them. They are seldom focused totally on the speaker, even when the spotlight is. Think about this the next time you are in such an audience. Do not be overly concerned about what members of the audience are thinking about you while you are giving a public talk—they are probably thinking mostly about themselves. They won't mind your minor stumbles as long as you are knowledgeable, sincere, and deliver a message that touches their hearts.

Summary

Managers and leaders of all types need to be effective communicators. Good communication begins with good reading and good listening. Dedicate yourself to learning all you can about being a great manager and a great leader so that when you need to communicate you will have something intelligent to communicate to others. Practice good communication skills at every opportunity. If public speaking is something you find frightening, face your fears head on. Do not shy away from public speaking. Do just the opposite. There is no other way to get over your fear of public speaking. You are now spending your money, time, and energy taking college courses. What a shame it would be if your fear of speaking or writing would make it so others could not tell just how smart and talented you are. Do not waste all your effort by letting your fear of communicating hide all you have to offer.

Success is not measured so much by heights attained as by obstacles overcome.

—Source unknown

Questions for Discussion

1. Recall your best and your worst experiences at public speaking. What would you do now to overcome the challenges of your worst experience?
2. Before your next public speaking task, use a video recorder to record a practice session. Make a list of the things you did wrong, the errors you want to correct, and ways you could make your speech more sincere and heartfelt.
3. Watch a YouTube video of one or more winners of the International Public Speaking Contest. Make a list of what these prize-winning speakers did to make such outstanding presentations.

Part II

READINGS

The Six Sigma Approach to Improvement and Organizational Change

By Ronald D. Snee

Six Sigma is quickly becoming part of the genetic code of our future leadership.

—Jack Welch

The Supply Chain and Biopharmaceuticals

For a major U.S. biopharmaceutical manufacturer, it was the best of times and the worst of times. Though approval for their new blockbuster drug was expected in nine months, the company's manufacturing and quality assurance processes were not ready to manufacture product and generate required FDA (Food and Drug Administration) documentation in a reliable, repeatable fashion (McGurk 2004). Another company product already in production had historically suffered from supply problems. For both the old and new drug, the creation and review of "batch records" was also a major problem. These records, required by corporate standards and government regulations, track important steps in the manufacturing process. Failure to keep accurate batch records can result in high inventory costs, a potential plant shutdown, and delays in shipments of lifesaving drugs to patients awaiting treatment.

The stakes were enormous and the organization was at loggerheads. The manufacturing organization blamed Quality Assurance (QA) for inconsistencies in the records and the long delays in completing them. QA insisted that manufacturing should get the records right the first time instead of simply throwing in lots of undigested data and expecting QA to find the inconsistencies and correct mistakes.

Phase	Six Sigma Principles and Tools Helped ...
Define	Clearly identify the problem to be solved and associated financial impacts
Measure	Understand the process through various measurement tools
Analyze	Analyze data to determine root causes of problems
Improve	Develop and test potential solutions
Control	Sustain the gains by developing control plans to monitor key performance variables

Table 1 Six Sigma's DMAIC Methodology

Meanwhile, the clock was ticking toward approval of the new product, and problems persisted with the existing product.

The manufacturer decided to address the poor performance of its batch records review process—and the underlying organizational issues—through Six Sigma's powerful problem-solving methodology: Define, Measure, Analyze, Improve, Control (DMAIC) (see table 1).

In the *Define* phase of DMAIC, management created a cross-functional team of ten people drawn from operations, quality assurance, and documentation, and reached agreement on what success of the project would look like: a reduction of 50 percent in review time of the batch records for the two products in six months.

In the *Measure* phase, the project team mapped the batch record process and identified key measurement points that allowed them to track review cycle times through a complicated network of participants (the lab, operators, supervisors, manufacturing, quality assurance, and investigators reporting out-of-spec incidents).

In the *Analyze* phase, the team tracked and analyzed each of the subprocess cycle times and overall cycle time. In addition, the analysis uncovered the root causes of errors in the records, which was the other critical-to-quality (CTQ) criterion besides cycle time. The team identified five areas that needed to be addressed: lack of expectations and targets for the overall process and subprocesses, a single reviewer, lack of feedback through metrics, lack of training, and problems with the records themselves.

In the *Improve* phase, the team worked with management to develop target cycle times for each step in the process, set up a system to report progress on the targets, initiate training, create backup reviewers, and restructure the review process to focus more on exception resolution than routine data gathering. These improvements reduced cycle time by 55 percent for one of the products and by 36 percent for the second product, freed up $5.2 million in inventory, increased customer satisfaction, saved $200,000 in cost of capital, and achieved additional savings through reduced floor space and handling costs.

In the *Control* phase, the team initiated a continuous improvement process to manage and improve cycle time, reduce errors over time, and sustain the gains already made. In addition, management planned future evaluations of subprocess cycle times in order to look for further improvements.

This example illustrates a number of key features and advantages of Six Sigma. It begins with the premise that improvement happens project by project. Its methodology entails a carefully sequenced set of steps; it relies on rigorous empirical observation as well as statistics, and it seeks not merely to correct individual "defects" but also to get at the root causes of variation in processes and fix them once and for all. Moreover, though it involves manufacturing processes—which Six Sigma is best known for improving—the project actually focuses on a business process, indicating Six Sigma's wide applicability to *any* work process.

In this case, as in other successful implementations, the methodology can help overcome organizational silos and intramural conflict, create an organization-wide culture of quality, and disseminate training and the tools widely among employees, creating a permanent capability for continuous improvement and a training ground for future leaders of an organization (Snee, "Can Six Sigma," 2004). Within one year, the site went from a conflict-ridden, process-challenged facility to one that won the company's global award as a model of improvement.

The Basics: Answers to Frequently Asked Questions

What Is Six Sigma?

Six Sigma methodology arose at Motorola more than a quarter of a century ago as a statistically based, process-focused method of eliminating defects in manufacturing processes. It subsequently flourished at Allied Signal and achieved legendary status at General Electric (GE) under Jack Welch. GE, expanding the notion of "defect," recognized that Six Sigma could be applied not only to ailing manufacturing processes but also to any subpar process, enabling the company to drive relentlessly toward a goal of "zero defects" across all of its business processes. Millions of dollars of bottom-line savings resulted. Six Sigma moved quickly beyond manufacturing to administration, finance, business processes, new product development, and supplier performance—becoming the characteristic approach to quality and continuous improvement of organizations as diverse as 3M, Johnson & Johnson, Home Depot, J. P. Morgan, Chase & Co., Dupont, and W. R. Grace. Six Sigma continues today as a well-known approach to process and organizational improvement (Snee and Hoerl 2003, 2005).

Based on the scientific method and utilizing statistical thinking and methods (Hoerl and Snee 2002), Six Sigma builds on quality improvement approaches developed earlier. It seeks to find and eliminate causes of mistakes or defects in business processes by focusing on process outputs that are critically important to customers. Six Sigma projects also often focus on improving productivity, process yields, production rates, and process downtime. As a result, process performance is enhanced, customer satisfaction is improved, and the bottom line is impacted through savings and increased revenue. It is a strategic approach that works across all processes, products, and industries—and it is a significant catalyst for ongoing organizational change.

Six Sigma is also a measure of process performance. The methodology utilizes "process sigma" as a measure of process capability. A six-sigma process has a defect level of 3.4 parts-per-million (ppm) opportunities and a three-sigma process has a defect level of 66,807 ppm (Harry 1998). In many instances, a six-sigma process is considered world-class. Today, the performance of most processes is in the three- to four-sigma range.

The ability to produce products and services with only 3.4 defects per million opportunities yields a Six Sigma process. Of course, a Six Sigma level of performance should not be the goal for all processes. Some processes, such as airline safety, require a higher level of performance. For other processes, a lower level of performance may be acceptable. The appropriate level of performance is determined by a business decision that balances the cost of attaining the higher level of performance versus the benefits of a higher-performing process. Further, as customer needs and competitive pressures change over time, the appropriate process sigma level may change accordingly.

What Are the Distinctive Characteristics of Six Sigma?

There are at least four critical elements that, when combined, make Six Sigma a distinctive, highly value-added approach to organizational improvement:

1. *Six Sigma places a clear focus on getting bottom-line results.* In properly run Six Sigma programs, no improvement project is approved unless the bottom-line impact has been identified. Six Sigma initiatives have been known to produce average bottom-line results of >$175,000 per project and as much as $1 million per year per full-time Six Sigma practitioner.
2. *Six Sigma integrates the human and process elements of improvement.* Six Sigma emphasizes human elements like teamwork, customer focus, and culture change as well as the process aspects of improvement such as statistical process control, process improvement, and design of experiments.
3. *Six Sigma sequences and links the improvement tools into an overall approach.* The five-phase DMAIC improvement process—Define, Measure, Analyze, Improve, Control—sequences and links key improvement tools proven to be effective in improving processes. DMAIC creates a sense of urgency by emphasizing rapid project completion, typically in three to six months.
4. *Six Sigma provides a unique leadership development tool.* Companies such as Honeywell, GE, DuPont, 3M, and American Standard require that managers achieve Six Sigma Green Belt

(GB) certification and in some instances Black Belt (BB) certification for management promotion. These companies realize that the job of leaders is to help the organization move from one paradigm of working to another. Changing how we work means changing our processes. By providing the concepts, methods, and tools for improving processes, Six Sigma provides leaders with the strategy, methods, and tools for changing their organizations—a key leadership skill that heretofore has been missing from leadership development.

When and Where Is Six Sigma Used?

Across almost all major industries, the pressure to improve to the point of achieving flawless execution—every time—is relentlessly increasing. From financial services to telecommunications, executing on customer service has become one of the few remaining differentiators for products that are largely commodities. In consumer goods, giant merchandisers like Wal-Mart and Target continue to pressure suppliers to improve their performance year after year—or lose business. In the life sciences, with an unprecedented number of blockbuster drugs coming off patent and little in the pipeline to replace them, excellence in manufacturing has taken on more importance than ever. Identifying, investigating, adjudicating, and correcting manufacturing deviations costs pharmaceutical companies millions of dollars each year in reduced capacity and increased labor, inventory, and good manufacturing practices (GMP) compliance problems. In manufacturing generally, where Six Sigma originated, continuously improving manufacturing processes remains a critical imperative.

Within any of these organizations and in any area of the business, Six Sigma can be usefully applied to improve virtually any kind of processes, whether they are manufacturing, financial, supply chain, or customer service. The key is simply to recall the great insight from GE—that Six Sigma can be applied to any process that results in defects or faults, whether the defects or problems are in products, services, or transactions.

What Tools Are Used?

The broad use of DMAIC as an overall framework for improving existing processes adds predictability, discipline, and repeatability to improvement projects. Along with Define, Measure, Analyze, Design, Verify (DMADV; Creveling *et al.* 2002) for the development of new products and processes, DMAIC can constitute the improvement infrastructure of the organization, linking and sequencing the required tools regardless of their source. Sources can include Lean, which seeks to eliminate various forms of waste through such concepts as just-in-time manufacturing; and Total Quality Management (TQM), which seeks to integrate all organizational functions to meet customer needs and organizational objectives, as well as other improvement tool sets. It's worth remembering, however, that the tools don't make improvements; people do.

Table of Uses

Organization	*Project Length*	*Key Events*	*Number of Participants*
Specialties Chemicals and Materials Company Main businesses are catalysts, construction materials, coatings/sealants, and silica/absorbents Sales $2 billion/year	30 months	Executive Workshop	32 top executives
		3 Champion Workshops	15–22 Champions per workshop
		3 waves of Black Belt (BB) in 1999, 2000, and 2001	15–25 BBs per wave
Plants are in the United States, Canada, and Europe. Training done both in the United States and in Europe		6 waves of Design for Six Sigma (DFSS) training begins 11/01	15–20 persons per wave
		Green Belt (GB) training in the United States begins 02/01	15–20 persons per wave
Goal is to improve productivity and increase growth Strategy—Top down deployment led by the CEO. Projects reviewed monthly. CEO reviews initiative quarterly Bottom Line savings: $26M in 2000 and $50M in 2001 Work reported here is for 1999–2001; Six Sigma Initiative continues		Process Operator training begins 06/01 Advanced BB Training 02/01	10–15 operators per wave 20–25 BBs
Manufacturing Facility	3 years	Plant Leadership Workshop in 08/01	10–12 top managers
Plant is a supplier to pharmaceutical and food industries 120 employees		BB Training 2002	1 BB
		Champion Workshop 2003	10 managers
Goal was bottom-line savings of $1M/year, increased plant capacity, and improved teamwork Initiative was led by plant manager Mentoring sessions held with the GB biweekly First 10 projects produced $1.7M in savings Deployment was slow and deliberate by design		GB training 2003	10 GBs
		GB training 2004	6 GBs
Project Budgeting Process Improvement	9 months	Steering Team Workshop	10 senior managers
Director of project budgeting process for a clinical trials operations of a pharmaceutical company desires to increase the forecasting accuracy of the project budgeting process as well as increase the speed of the process and reduce the wasted time involved		3 Champion Workshops	8–10 Champions per workshop
Strategy—train 14 employees as GBs to get the needed process improvements now and in the future. GBs were located both in the United States and Europe. Training was done both in the United States and Europe		2 Organizational Awareness Training Sessions	100–150 persons per session
Mentoring sessions held with the GBs biweekly Steering Team reviewed projects monthly First six projects identified $2.2M in wasted effort and cost avoidance savings		GB Training	14 GBs trained

Major Deployment Phases

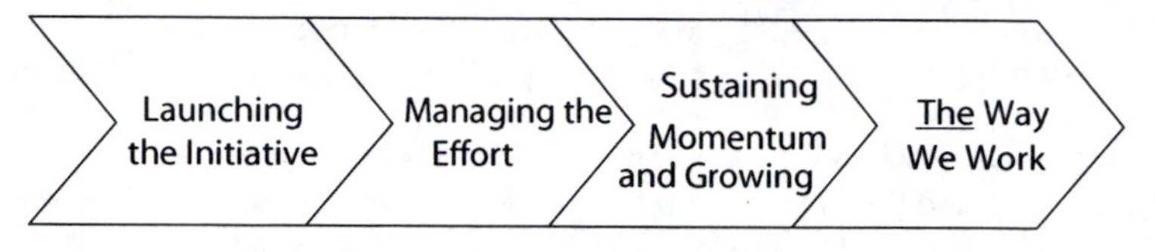

Major Transition Points

From Business as Usual to a Six Sigma Approach	From a New Launch to a Long Term Initiative	From THE Initiative to AN Initiative	From an Initiative to a Normal Part of the Job

Individual Project Methodology: DMAIC

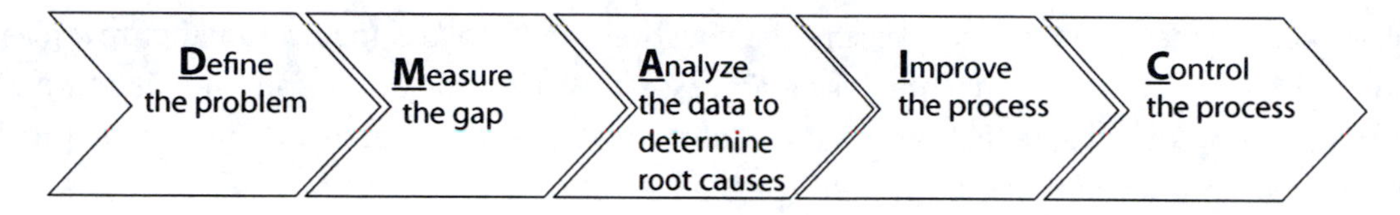

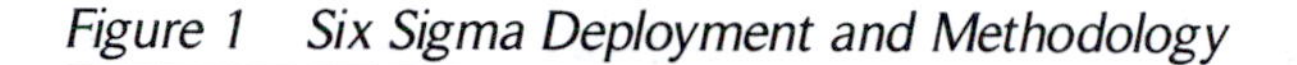
Figure 1 Six Sigma Deployment and Methodology

Getting Started

Organizations considering whether to initiate a Six Sigma program have a broad range of choices that range from large-scale deployment across the entire company through a comprehensive, all-embracing Six Sigma structure; to divisional, business unit, or departmental programs; to limited, small-scale pilot projects. However, total deployment may be beyond the budget and resources of some companies. On the other hand, initially confining Six Sigma projects to a single pilot project, or one area, risks quarantining it to the area it is in and eventually killing it. The key phases of deployment and DMAIC projects are summarized in figure 1.

By instituting Six Sigma projects in widely disparate areas, leaders can signal the entire organization that they are serious about it—it's not just for those folks over in manufacturing or Quality Assurance (Snee, "With All Deliberate Speed," 2004). For example, you might choose an operational process, a customer-facing process, and a business/managerial process, each in a different department, for initial Six Sigma projects. Moreover, having projects in disparate areas prepares the way for widespread and rapid propagation of Six Sigma later.

There are basically three different types of deployment: Full top-down deployment involving the whole organization, a single location such as a plant, and a process or function such as finance. Other examples of Six Sigma deployment can be found in Snee and Hoerl (2003, 2005).

Once a program—of whatever size—has been established, individual project teams should, in the early stages of improvement, harvest the "low-hanging fruit": correct obvious problems with a process,

Participant	General Responsibilities
Corporate Management	Create strategy and goals, define boundaries, provide resources
Unit Management	Establish project selection criteria that support strategy, select project Champions, and approve projects
Project Champions	Ensure proper project setup, regularly monitor progress, and remove barriers to success
Black Belts	Deploy Lean and Six Sigma methodology and tools, deliver process improvements and financial benefits, and access formal power structure as needed to remove barriers
Master Black Belts	Develop, coach, and counsel Black Belts and Green Belts and focus on mission-critical projects
Green Belts	Lead Six Sigma projects at the local level and assist in improving a process as a member of a team that is guided by a Black Belt
Functional Support Groups	Provide data and expertise for improvement, identify improvement opportunities, serve on project teams, and take local responsibility for process execution and improvement

Table 2 Roles, Responsibilities, and Relationships

fix broken measurement systems, and ensure the consistency of process inputs, whether raw materials in manufacturing or data in non-manufacturing processes. Work should also be streamlined through the reduction of complexity, waste, and non-value-added work. The later stages of improvement focus on optimizing and controlling processes by improving value-added work steps, shifting the process average and reducing variation around it, improving process flow, and reducing cycle time—in short, finding the "operating sweet spot."

Roles, Responsibilities, and Relationships

Six Sigma creates an infrastructure of permanent change agents who lead, deploy, and implement improvement projects. Borrowing terminology from the martial arts, Six Sigma programs train and mobilize practitioners known as Champions, Master Black Belts (MBBs), Black Belts (BBs), and Green Belts (GBs), each with differing roles and responsibilities in individual projects and in ongoing continuous improvement (see table 2).

This infrastructure of quality-conscious people, determined to make improvement stick and thoroughly trained in how to do it, provides the organization with a significant advantage over competitors with a less rigorous and systematic approach to improvement and organizational change.

Conditions for Success: The Path to Organizational Change

One of the most frequently encountered obstacles to the success of Six Sigma programs is the "Six Sigma won't work here" attitude, especially in non-manufacturing organizations. To overcome that attitude, it is critical to obtain some quick wins and, as additional improvements and benefits materialize, the organization's culture will change (Kotter 1996). Deployment should take place rapidly, with attention to critical elements of the launch, but without obsessive worry about defining every detail of the deployment. Taken together, the fundamental elements of Six Sigma deployment provide a path to organizational change that comes not as a result of the deployment but as a result of the benefits that Six Sigma produces, reinforcing its value and weaving it into the organization as *the* way to work. These key deployment elements, their significance, and their pitfalls include (Snee and Hoerl 2003):

- *Strategy and Goals:* Senior management sets the overall vision for Six Sigma deployment, chooses where to initially deploy Six Sigma, develops one- to two-year goals, including financial targets, and communicates the goals widely. Failure to state goals in financial terms often indicates a management team that is not serious about Six Sigma.
- *Process Performance Measures:* These measures, such as quality, delivery, and cost, define what's important for success and are used to select projects. Such measures provide strategic focus areas for the initial projects; and if all initial projects affect the measures, then the organization will have significant, tangible results when they are completed. The chief pitfall here is selecting each project independently rather than choosing projects on the basis of their relation to common, strategic measures of success.
- *Project Selection Criteria:* The process metrics are used to develop a set of more specific criteria for selecting projects. These may include such criteria as savings per project and expected time to project completion. Such criteria also communicate to the wider organization what types of improvement are important.
- *Project Identification/Selection System:* In a Champion Workshop, initial candidate projects are put in a "project hopper" (list of projects) and prioritized for assignment to a Black Belt or Green Belt. In the first wave or two of projects, the focus should be on hard, bottom-line results, because nothing goes further to establish the credibility of Six Sigma. In later phases of deployment, a permanent system is established to identify potential projects, prioritize them, and put them in the hopper so that there is a continual stream of fresh projects. Ultimately, the hopper should be managed as a "project portfolio," the composition of which matches the improvement and financial needs of the organization.
- *Deployment Process for Leaders:* A list of initial Champions is developed in an Executive Workshop. At an ensuing Champion Workshop, Champions develop the list of initial projects, as well as a list of candidate Black Belts to lead them. The pitfall here is selecting the Champions and Black Belts before identifying the specific projects they will lead, increasing the likelihood that important projects will be overlooked.
- *Roles of Leadership and Others:* Although there are generic job responsibilities for Champions, BBs, GBs, and so forth, leadership can tailor the roles for a specific function or business (see Table of Uses).
- *Curricula and Training System:* An overall training system is a must for each of the Six Sigma roles and, at launch, there must be a training schedule for the first wave of Black Belts. The pitfall here is undertaking a wave of mass training, which is usually ineffective and has little lasting impact. Instead, there should be a well-thought-out system that identifies the training needs of the roles and puts them together in a sustained way to continually satisfy training needs in the most efficient way.

- *Project and Six Sigma Initiative Review Schedule:* An effective review schedule involves short, usually 30-minute, weekly reviews by the Champion and monthly reviews with functional leaders, local management, or business leaders, as appropriate. Regular reviews show management's commitment and provide timely feedback to keep projects on course. The entire Six Sigma deployment should be reviewed quarterly by the appropriate corporate or business unit leaders. Failure to review the overall progress of the initiative at this level can slow the momentum of the Six Sigma effort and fail to detect if the initiative is bogging down.
- *Project Reporting and Tracking System:* This system documents the results of the projects and provides management with valuable information. A formal system isn't required during initial deployment, but it will ultimately maintain a record of all Six Sigma projects, generate managerial reports that include financial results as well as nonfinancial information such as number of projects in progress and completed, time to completion, status, and so on. The tracking component of the system documents the financial benefits of closed projects. The pitfall here is establishing an insufficiently rigorous tracking system that cannot provide accurate and credible results.
- *Audit System for Previously Closed Projects:* This system audits the financial and process performance impact of the improvements and the control plan of previously closed projects to ensure that the benefits of these projects are still being achieved. Failure to audit the control plan can lead to the improvements eroding over time.
- *Reward and Recognition Plan:* Human Resources should develop a reward and recognition plan that ensures the acquisition and retention of the best possible candidates for Six Sigma roles. Failure to reward Six Sigma roles in a way that attracts top performers to them can seriously undermine the long-term prospects for success.
- *Communication Plan:* A thorough communication plan, enacted through various media, is essential to support a Six Sigma initiative, especially in nonmanufacturing organizations that may harbor false impressions about the applicability of the approach. Leadership must clearly communicate why they chose to deploy Six Sigma, how it applies to the business, and where they expect it to take the organization both in business and in cultural terms. The pitfall here is setting unreasonable expectations. It is preferable to make more sweeping statements only after significant results are obtained.

Experience has shown that all of these elements of deployment are important. Paying insufficient attention to any of them can seriously limit the effectiveness of a Six Sigma program and leave the organization stuck in old, less-productive ways of doing business.

Theoretical Basis

From the long historical perspective, Six Sigma has its roots in the Industrial Revolution and the division of labor (Snee, "When Worlds Collide," 2004). In the late nineteenth and early twentieth centuries, Frederick W. Taylor introduced scientific management, initially grounded in time and motion studies and standardization of tools and procedures. In 1924, Walter Shewhart introduced control charts. In the 1930s, Shewhart and W. Edwards Deming developed the improvement approach known as PDCA (Plan, Do, Check, Act). All of these methods were developed in response to the need to reduce high variation in production processes.

Joseph M. Juran, who as early as 1928 had already written a pamphlet entitled "Statistical Methods Applied to Manufacturing Problems," made many contributions to the field of quality management. He was the first to incorporate the human aspect of quality management in what came to be known as Total Quality Management (TQM) and promoted such indispensable tools as Pareto charting and the project-by-project approach to improvement.

The ideas of Shewhart, Deming, and Juran were adopted extensively in Japan and began the revolution in quality. In the 1980s, Motorola executives, touring industrial sites in Japan, witnessed how the Japanese had achieved exemplary quality through the application of statistical tools—and Six Sigma was born. Developed throughout the 1980s by Motorola, it was adopted and famously expanded by GE to include any type of process. At the same time, TQM, just-in-time (JIT) manufacturing, Kaizen, Business Process Reengineering, Benchmarking, Lean Manufacturing, and other improvement methodologies were also developing and spreading to organizations all over the world. Today, Six Sigma encompasses the best practices from all of these methodologies.

Six Sigma has had a particularly fruitful relationship with Lean. Lean is based on the premise that work almost always involves waste: of correction (the quality of the worst component), overproduction, overprocessing, conveyance, inventory, motion, and waiting. Lean seeks to eliminate these various forms of waste through such concepts as just-in-time manufacturing. However, Lean does not address the effects of process variation, which Six Sigma, with its data-driven, rigorously statistical methods, can uncover and eliminate. In addition, Six Sigma is ideal for solving complex, multidetermined problems whose root causes are unknown. Often, Six Sigma and Lean are applied either concurrently or consecutively in an approach known as Lean Six Sigma (Snee 2005).

Six Sigma also fits well with ISO 9000 quality management systems and with the Baldrige Criteria for Performance Excellence. The key to their integration is the recognition that all three are process focused, data based, and management led. Six Sigma methods of project selection, reviews, and reporting can also be very effective in turning opportunities identified by a Baldrige assessment into sharply focused, high-impact projects that lead to lasting improvements.

Sustaining the Results

Six Sigma has a formal step in the DMAIC process—the control phase—that is specifically designed to implement controls that prevent improved processes from reverting to their previous levels of lower performance. Management reviews of projects—weekly by Project Champion and monthly by the management team—keep projects on track and also help ensure that the projects continue to generate benefits. At the level of the overall Six Sigma initiative, leadership undertakes quarterly reviews that monitor the progress of each of the elements of the deployment plan and, in particular, the contents of the project hopper.

The system for auditing the financial and process performance impacts and control plans of previously closed projects ensures that completed projects continue to generate the benefits that their improvement produced. If the audit finds that the benefits have eroded, action is taken to revisit the project, regain the benefits, and establish a more effective control plan. Moreover, having a cadre of people trained in Six Sigma ensures that the same disciplined, repeatable methodology will be brought to every project.

From the point of view of organizational development, one of the strongest spurs to maintaining momentum and sustaining the gains comes from the effect that the achievement of significant, measurable benefits has on the culture. People like to succeed, and when they get tangible results, they are eager to repeat the process. That is the simple but powerful principle of culture change underlying Six Sigma: Culture change doesn't produce benefits; benefits produce culture change.

Burning Questions: Project Selection

After the question of how to sustain gains, the burning question both for those who are new to Six Sigma and for those with ongoing programs is how to select projects. The high-level characteristics of a good Six Sigma project, in any area of application, include:

- Clear connection to business priorities and links to strategic and annual operating plans
- The potential to provide a major improvement in process performance and a major financial improvement
- A reasonable scope and a doable time frame of four to six months
- Clear quantitative measures of success, with the baseline measures and the goals well defined
- Clear importance to the organization
- The wholehearted support of management

A Final Word

Six Sigma isn't immune to criticism. It's sometimes said, for example, that Six Sigma offers little that is new or innovative in the way of tools. It's certainly true that many of the techniques of Six Sigma have been borrowed from TQM, Lean, and other quality and improvement programs. However, Six Sigma combines the tools with a disciplined methodology, teaches people when to use them, focuses on bottom-line results, and rigorously and successfully establishes a more effective way of working. Moreover, the insistence on "newness" is misplaced. The true test of an improvement methodology is a proven track record and, after a quarter of a century, it's safe to say that Six Sigma has passed with flying colors.

References

Creveling, C. M., J. L. Slutsky, and D. Antis, Jr. *Design for Six Sigma in Technology and Product Development.* Upper Saddle River, NJ: Prentice Hall, 2003.

Harry, Mikel J. "Six Sigma: A Breakthrough Strategy for Profitability." *Quality Progress* (1998): 60–64.

Hoerl, R. W., and R. D. Snee. *Statistical Thinking—Improving Business Performance.* Pacific Grove, CA: Duxbury Press, 2002.

Kotter, J. P. *Leading Change.* Boston, MA: Harvard Business School Press, 1996.

McGurk, Thomas L. "Ramping Up and Ensuring Supply Capability for Biopharmaceuticals." *BioPharm International* (January 2004): 38–44.

Snee, R. D. "Can Six Sigma Boost Your Company's Growth?" *Harvard Management Update* (June 2004): 2–4.

———. "Six Sigma: The Evolution of 100 Years of Business Improvement Methodology." *International Journal of Six Sigma and Competitive Advantage* 1, no. 1 (2004): 4–20.

———. "When Worlds Collide: Lean and Six Sigma." *Quality Progress* (September 2005): 63–65.

———. "With All Deliberate Speed: Weaving Six Sigma into the Fabric of the Organization." *Quality Progress* (September 2004): 69–71.

Snee, R. D., and R. W. Hoerl. *Leading Six Sigma—A Step by Step Guide Based on the Experience with General Electric and Other Six Sigma Companies.* New York: FT Prentice Hall, 2003.

———. *Six Sigma Beyond the Factory Floor: Deployment Strategies for Financial Services, Health Care and the Rest of the Real Economy.* Upper Saddle River, NJ: Pearson Prentice Hall, 2005.

Welch, Jack, and John Byrne. *Jack: Straight from the Gut.* New York: Warner Business Books, 2001.

Welch, Jack, with Suzy Welch. *Winning.* New York: Harper Business, 2005.

Organizations

American Society for Quality—www.asq.org
Tunnell Consulting—www.tunnellconsulting.com

On some level, most people know the steps they need to take to overcome their fear of public speaking. A combination of training and, like the Nike commercial slogan, "just doing it" is part of the formula for success. As the "sales guy," Richard Elmes says, "The presentation you give tomorrow will be that much better because of the speech you delivered today." Life is too short to be paralyzed by this fear. People need to hear what you have to say. Why rob them of that opportunity? Let's look at how you can use the 4 P's model to walk through the steps of becoming a more confident and competent speaker.

Prepare

When I first started as a corporate trainer, I spent days and days preparing for one presentation. I studied the material, tried to anticipate every question, and entered the room ready to be the expert. Of course, I soon realized that though I felt well versed in the material, I could never be totally aware of every fact and every question that might arise. The company had hired a coach to work with our team on presentation skills. He saw my tenseness that day, and before the program, he walked up to the lectern and said, gently, "Jennifer, you know this material. Now enjoy the experience and relax." His words have stuck with me over the years. The synergy of well-prepared material and, even more importantly, your attitude is a winning combination for presentation success.

Prepare the Material

1. Know Your Purpose

You should know the purpose of your program. Is it to inform, persuade, educate, or motivate? Do you know what you want people to leave with? Why should they care about what you have to say? What are the three big points you want to make? Focus in depth on these points, and use lots of examples. Do not overload your audience with numerous points. What do you want them to remember? This will be the basis of your talk. Your preference for introspection will allow you to reflect on this and think it through before putting pen to paper. Being prepared gives you the confidence to get up there and be with your audience. Many introverted professionals I know have said that people do not believe them when they say they are introverts because they look so at ease on the stage. It is the preparation that allows them to relax during the delivery.

2. Tell Me a Story

A few years ago, I heard Montel Williams deliver a keynote speech to a room full of administrative professionals. He told a story about promoting his secretary to president of one of his companies and introduced this woman to the crowd. It was a moving moment, and many of the people in the audience were visibly touched by his showcasing a living, breathing role model. There is power in examples. How many times have you heard a speaker, whether a motivational speaker or your CEO, engage a group by sharing a story? How often have you seen a leader make a point by sharing a personal experience? The use of stories to drive home a point is a skill you too can master.

Stories emphasize ideas a lot more powerfully than bullet points on a slide. The good news is that you can prepare and rehearse these stories to make a much stronger case. This can be done to motivate a team on a project that is lagging, or to influence customers to purchase your product. Today, stories are the key to a successful presentation.

Annette Simmons, a storytelling expert, says, "The human presence in communication is frequently elbowed out by criteria designed to make communication clear, bite sized and attention grabbing, but which instead oversimplifies, truncates and irritates. These 'sub goals' often obscure the real goal: human connection. Communication can't feel genuine without the distinctive personality of a human being to provide context. You need to show up when you communicate. The real you, not the polished, idealized you. The missing ingredient in most failed communication is humanity. This is an easy fix. In order to blend humanity into every communication you send, all you have to do is tell more stories and bingo—you just showed up. Your communication has a human presence."

We are not all natural-born storytellers (coming from someone who forgets the punch line of most jokes!), but you can learn to tell great stories. There are sources of stories all around us: the media, books, movies, television, etc. I think the most powerful stories, however, come from our own experience. This is especially true when we reveal our flaws. It is then that we connect with the audience.

I remember an experience several years ago when our family went whitewater rafting. My spouse, Bill, flipped out of the raft, and because I never really listened to our trusted, pony-tailed guide before the trip, I practically strangled Bill in the process of "rescuing" him. I often use that story (with more graphic details, of course) to make a point about the importance of listening. It certainly wasn't funny at the time, but in retrospect, with time to reflect and weave lessons like that into the story, people can relate to it, and I can make a point at the same time. You can do the same.

Follow a format that works. What is the point you want to make? What was going on in the scene? Include the smells, the sights, and the sounds. You can help the listener be there with you. I am so committed to tell stories in my work now that I keep a small notebook with me and jot down memories and observations. Just open your eyes and you will find stories waiting to be told.

3. No More PowerPoint Karaoke

Though PowerPoint is a great tool, it has become overused and over-relied on by many of us. Too many bullet points on a slide, reading the slide out loud when the audience can do it themselves, and not promoting audience engagement are some negative impacts of PowerPoint. Kevin Smith, a marketing manager at Dell Canada, put it well: "The audience showed up to hear the expert (that's you) talk about a solution to a problem that's causing them pain, not to hear you perform 'PowerPoint karaoke' by reading PowerPoint off of the slides."

Instead, consider using photos, other images, a single question, key words, and even audio to make your points. Cliff Atkinson has some great examples of how to construct these types of presentations on his Web site www.beyondbulletpoints.com. One benefits specialist resisted this approach. I suggested that her audience take notes on an outlined handout, and for her to make the material available online. You are better off providing only the three key points in your presentation on your slides. By writing down the points that are important to them, audience members will increase their retention, and they can get more details in their follow-up online. I don't think people can retain the myriad of benefits details she is providing. Your audiences will appreciate this approach and gain more from your program.

Prepare Yourself

I. Conquer Fear

Fear of public speaking is by no means limited to introverts. The fear that manifests in shaking heads, sweaty palms, and knocking knees is common across the leadership spectrum. Extroverts, because they are more comfortable in conversation, may think they can transfer their conversational skills to the stage. However, speaking to a group calls on different skills. Few people can ad lib when it comes to presentations, nor should they. The introvert's tendency to reflect is a benefit here. Using reflection to tackle the fear will help you be focused and prepared, allowing you to be more spontaneous when you are delivering a program.

To be a confident speaker, you need to get into the right mindset and use the nervous energy you feel. Being in the moment and getting involved with the audience is the key. This is particularly true when reactions come up that you didn't anticipate—and let's face it, you rarely can anticipate reactions. I was speaking at a program a few months ago when I noticed that I wasn't getting much of a reaction. So I decided to move around and get out from behind the lectern. It made all the difference. I was more in my comfort zone, and I think the audience then saw me as a person and not "the speaker." Be open to listening to your gut. This will allow you flexibility.

Scott Mastley, author of *The Confidence Zone* and a professional speaker, told me, "All speakers feel anxious before standing in front of the audience and beginning their talks, but the best speakers focus that nervous energy into a greater level of enthusiasm by reminding themselves of their previous successes, their preparation, and the great feeling that comes from delivering a message of value to people who appreciate it."

2. Visualization

Marny approached me after a class asking for advice. She said that as a pharmaceutical sales rep she has to do many briefings for doctors and other medical personnel. She is an introvert. Recently she had to do a talk in a large lecture hall, and despite the fact that she had learned to manage her nervousness in these smaller briefings, the large venue threw her for a loop. She said it felt scary and awful. What should she do in the future to handle her anxiety?

Visualization is a very powerful technique that I suggested Marny try the next time. Sports heroes such as Tiger Woods use it all the time. Many people tell me they had high school and college coaches who utilized this technique with great results.

Here is how it works. Go to a relaxed, quiet place before the program and imagine a great experience. First, relax your body and get the kinks out. Try listening to calming music on your iPod. Then picture yourself in the room, giving your presentation. Imagine responsive faces, smiles, questions being asked, and your clear compelling answers. The pleasant feeling that you experience in your visualization will last. Your brain essentially is being rewired to experience a calm and positive experience. Visualization is an art. You get better with practice. Some people tell me they are not ever able to visualize. If you are one of these people, don't worry. Not every technique works for everyone, and you can find other ways to calm your nerves, such as taking slow deep breaths.

3. Get Energy

Prepping your mind by pumping yourself up and visualizing success is important. It is also helpful to remember that the whole body needs to be involved. Taking slow, deep breaths prior to speaking relaxes you and helps you to calm mental chatter. A walk or other physical exercise helps you to get the blood going and energy flowing. This can help those with quieter temperaments who may be a little low-key in their presentation. You will feel alert and more alive if you take these steps.

The principles of eating a good breakfast and getting plenty of rest hold true when preparing for speaking. If you are doing a training session, bring healthy snacks that you can nibble on at breaks. Have plenty of water on hand to stay hydrated, and limit caffeine.

4. Rehearse

Practice your talk out loud with a tape recorder. You can also use a video recorder. Listen to how you sound, including the inflections, word emphases, pauses, and timing. It's okay to break your presentation practices into segments. Trying to do the entire presentation at once, and then review the whole thing at once, can get tedious. You will be amazed at how much rehearsing out loud helps. The words on the page will come alive, and you will be more natural when your actual presentation rolls around. By the way, speech coaches also recommend that you tape your program and listen to it afterward to keep improving the delivery, especially if this is a program you will present again.

Rey San Pascuel, a global demand manager, said that his company's communications manager said, "practice, practice, practice," and it made a difference. He said that you could tell who practiced by the smoothness of their delivery. Those who didn't practice fumbled and went over their allotted time.

5. Early, Early, Early

Wendy Kinney, an introverted referral marketing researcher who speaks, told me why she values being early. "I get there early. Really, really, really, really early. I can look over my notes again, or read a magazine, just sit and stare—but I am not stressing about being late or the traffic or the last phone call. And when the meeting planner gets there, they are happy not to worry about me, so they treat me well. I can help them a little (even if it is only to carry a bag), which makes them grateful and friendly and if there is anything about the room that needs to be changed it's no hassle."

Presence

So you have prepared. Now comes the moment to present. Let's consider how to best develop presence on the stage.

In speaking with numerous successful introverts about this, I heard three key themes emerge. They are (1) connect with your audience; (2) use your voice; and (3) use body language.

1. Connect with Your Audience

Marilynn Mobley, a senior vice president at Edelman, also coaches people on presentation skills and does media training. She says, "people love to eavesdrop," and advises "looking at one person in the audience because everyone else pays attention to what you are saying to that person ... so pick a person to lock eyes with as you make an important point, then move to another person, then another, and so on. You'll have great impact, not just on those with whom you lock eyes but with everyone else as well."

Richard Elmes, the sales trainer said, "When I shifted my focus from what I am doing or saying to what the audience is receiving, everything changed. I was less nervous and more effective."

Kathy Armstrong Lee, a communications and community affairs manager, gave a great illustration of how a CFO she saw learned to engage. "He literally couldn't move from behind the lectern—he read his presentation, head down into the microphone. Talk about a rest break—this was a complete snoozer! A year later, with coaching and practice, and a lot of effort at pruning the myriad details from his slides, he was confident enough to use a lavaliere microphone and walk the stage to punctuate his presentation. He described how aspects of what the audience was involved in contributed to the bottom line. He also gave the audience a call to action and a way to focus their efforts. The audience walked out buzzing about how they finally 'got it' and they were energized by his call to action—something he never had when just reading financial results."

2. Use Your Voice

Those of you who spend a lot of time on the phone have probably become adept at "reading" the voices you hear. You can tell if the person on the other end is rushed, tired, or really on their game. Or maybe they have learned to pretend.

How we breathe affects how we sound. Renee Grant Williams, a well-known voice coach, says, "Shallow breathing makes you sound breathy and weak. Tension around the neck stiffens the vocal chords making them rigid, unresponsive and vulnerable to damage. It cuts off the resonance and reduces resilience. ... You'll get a richer, fuller voice with a low abdominal breathing because your body and vocal chords are free to vibrate."

Pausing is one way to use your voice for impact. Introverts are less afraid of silence than extroverts, so use this to your advantage. A pause before your point gets your listeners' attention and prepares them for what is to come. A pause after your point lets the idea sink in. Renee Grant Williams also says, "Speech is silver, silence is golden and the power pause is pure platinum." Kevin Horst, a trainer who speaks, advises "pausing for what may seem to the speaker to be too many beats after you make a takeaway point, the one you want the audience to remember and act upon." Use this selectively with extroverts. One manager told me that her extroverted boss gets visibly impatient if she injects too many pauses. So, remember to flex to your audience.

Once you are aware that this element of communication can form up to 85 percent of a person's impression of you, you may decide to adjust your instrument. You have been asked to brief the boss about the Galileo project, and the baby got you up at 3:00 A.M. for a feeding. You want to crawl into bed. Try taking a few full breaths from your stomach, and slow it down. Watch your energy come back. You are acting "as if" and will be successful in showing energy and using your voice more effectively.

3. Use Body Language

The first time I was videotaped doing a training session, I had a flip chart marker in my hand and played catch with it. Hand to hand it went, and I was totally oblivious to the baseball game I was playing. I am sure few eyes and ears were tuned into my pearls of wisdom. They were watching the back-and-forth metronome action.

Wendy Kinney, the referral marketing researcher mentioned earlier, discussed the importance of posture in establishing her stage presence. Like a number of introverted leaders in this book, she said that she chooses who she wants to be that day and "steps into them. So I hold my head the way they would, hold my shoulders the way they would. When I first learned this technique, I often modeled Oprah Winfrey."

Some of the strategies we've talked about in the prepare and presence sections may fall under the push category for you. Here are a few more ideas taken from the mouths of introverts.

Get Serious about Increasing Your Skills

A common recommendation from people who have overcome their fear of speaking in public is, "Join Toastmasters!" Toastmasters (www.toastmasters.com) is a worldwide nonprofit organization with chapters in ninety-two countries. Their mission is to "help people become more competent and comfortable in front of an audience." With weekly opportunities to practice in a nonthreatening atmosphere with constant feedback, you will develop stronger public speaking skills. Of course, you have to keep attending to improve.

Get Creative

A little creativity goes a long way. Look for opportunities to liven up your presentations. I suggested earlier that you consider replacing bullet points on PowerPoint slides with images. I attended a program on humor given by Pat Haley, a former writer for *Seinfeld* who speaks to corporate groups. He shared family photos from the 1960s that had us howling. There are stories in photos that can be shared to make a point and draw the audience in. I still remember the photo of his brothers and sisters at Halloween. He pointed out that his sisters' witch costumes were recycled for the brothers as warlock outfits. You didn't have a choice in his family. Immediately, my mind flashed back on the unusual costumes of my youth and the lack of choice I had, especially the time Mom dressed me as a Russian sputnik space rocket. This kind of connection with your audience will help your presentation have the effect you want. Check out the Web sites online that actually sell the scanned family photos of others. You can also access *New Yorker* magazine cartoons and ask groups to think up their own captions. This solicits some out-of-the-box responses.

My colleague Marty Mercer, a masterful public speaker, told me about a push strategy he used at a recent conference where he spoke. He arrived the night before with his camera in hand. As he wandered around the hotel, he took various shots of attendees. That night Marty downloaded the photos and interspersed them into his slide presentation. He made some humorous comments and had his audience totally engaged and "with him" from the get-go.

Wendy Kinney also pre-plans audience participation. She chooses someone who likes the limelight. She says it is easy to tell who these people are. She listens for their stories and anecdotes and asks for permission to use their example to make her presentations come alive. She might say at lunch, "Oh, I'm going to ask you to share that story. It will come about 15 minutes in, will you do that?" Wendy claims that she feels like a magician who uses diversion, and the audience doesn't see how the trick works.

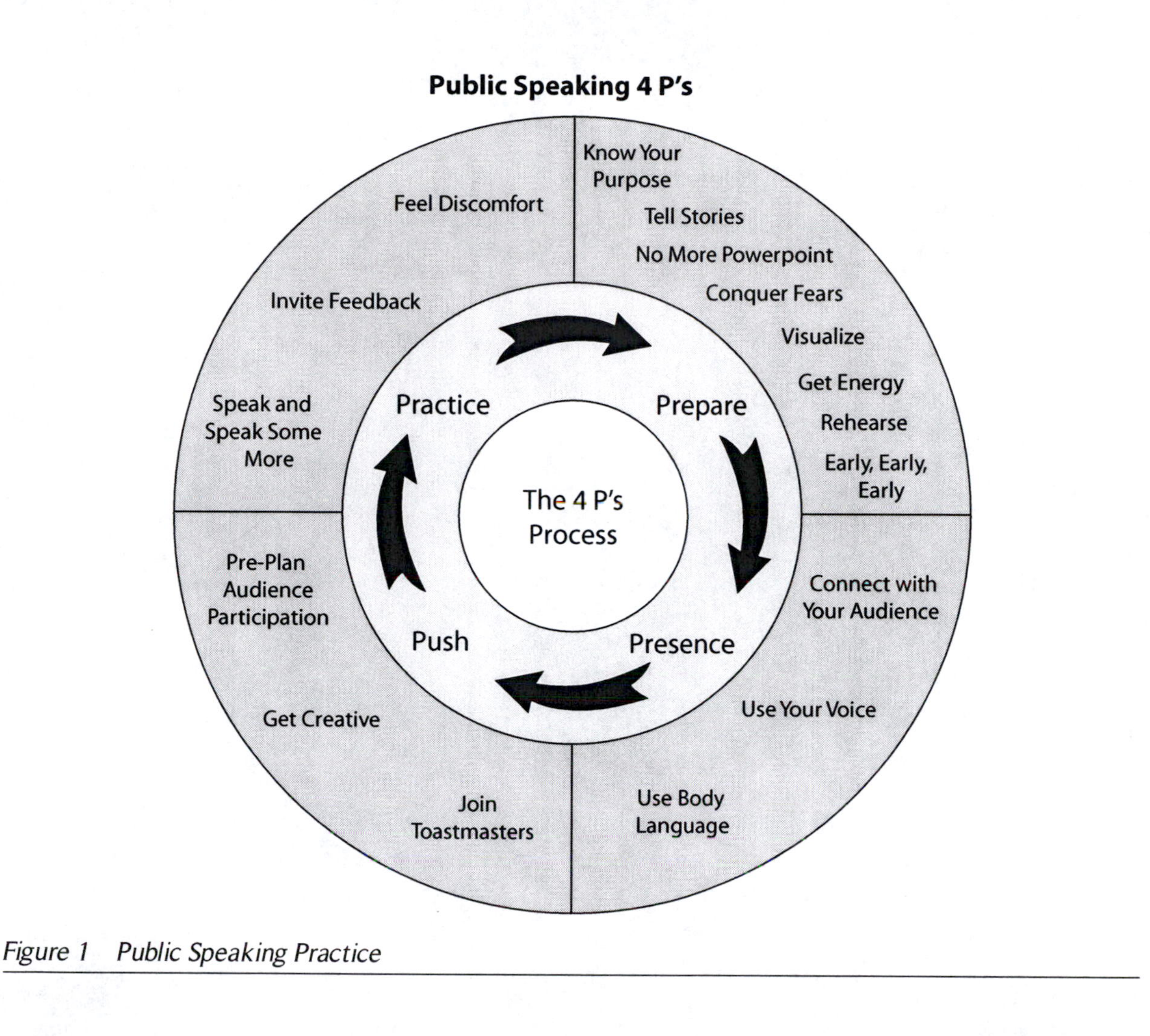

Figure 1 Public Speaking Practice

Practice

You can use tricks to speak with ease, but practice is the magic that will bring out your best. (See Figure 1.) What are the key steps that will move you to public speaking mastery? Speak and speak some more. Take every chance to speak in order to improve and increase your comfort level. How about offering to give a recap of a recent training class at your next staff meeting? What about sharing with the team what you learned about competitive trends in your industry when visiting exhibit booths at a recent conference? Why not tell your boss you are available to present a project status report to the team he usually meets with? Opportunities are all around you to get up and speak. Invite people to observe you and always ask for feedback. Yes, practice is hard and it is uncomfortable, but it is the *only* way to get better.

Part III

Applications of Great Management and Leadership in Today's Environment

Chapter 12

Managing for Diversity: Finding Strength in a Diverse Workforce

No one has been barred on account of his race for fighting and dying for America. There are no white or colored signs on the foxholes or graveyards of battle.

—President John F. Kennedy

Affirmative Action

As a manager, one of your responsibilities will be compliance with the U.S. government's program of Affirmative Action. In 1961 President John F. Kennedy issued Executive Order 10925 mandating affirmative action to ensure that applicants for jobs in federal agencies are considered without regard to race, color, creed, or national origin. President Lyndon Johnson extended this policy by issuing Executive Order 11246 demanding that all executive departments and agencies establish and maintain a positive program of equal employment opportunity. In 1964 the Civil Rights Act prohibited places of public accommodation, such as restaurants or hotels, from discrimination based on race; Title VII of the Civil Rights Act of 1964 prohibited employers from discriminating based on race, gender, or religion.

These laws and executives orders address two separate, but related issues. First, the law expressly prohibits discrimination. Second, the executive orders go a step further and strive to enhance diversity. Few issues are as controversial as affirmative action. Some readers may disagree with various aspects of these executive orders and laws, but as future managers, you need to put those disagreements aside and focus on what the law requires, and even more importantly, what constitutes good management. Most businesses want to sell their goods and services to people of all races, creeds, gender, etc., and one way

We have talked long enough in this country about equal rights.

It is time now to write the next chapter—and to write it in the books of law.

—President Lyndon B. Johnson

to enhance such sales is to employ people who look like and understand the customers you want to attract.

The controversy still rages all these years since the 1960s over whether affirmative action helps or hurts minorities. Supporters of affirmative action argue it is designed to remedy a long history of discrimination and ensure racial equality in the long run. Opponents of affirmative action say that a better approach is to be "color blind" when it comes to hiring people or admitting people to colleges or other prestigious organizations. These opponents suggest that affirmative action actually hurts minorities by making people assume that any minority in a high position got that position not based on their own merit, but rather on the basis of their color, thus undercutting the person's merits.

The 2008 election of Barack Obama as president of the United States has caused some to say there is no longer a need for affirmative action. However, others argue discrimination is still, unfortunately, a fact of life in the United States, and affirmative action needs to be improved, not eliminated. As future managers and leaders, you need to understand what the law requires and go beyond the prejudices of the past by treating diversity in the workforce as something positive. Notice that the title for this chapter is Managing *for* Diversity: Finding Strength in a Diverse Workforce. Managers who manage *for* diversity help their organization attract and retain a diverse workforce and give their organization a better perspective on a diverse marketplace, greater creativity and innovation in problem solving, and enhance the organization's flexibility. Having a workforce that is similar to the composition of your customer base is simply good business.

Affirmation Action is defined as taking positive steps to correct previous injustices and prejudices. *Prejudice* is defined as judging someone in advance, before an objective, fact-based review. Executive Order 11246 applies the requirement of affirmation action to any government contractor with 50 or more employees and $50,000 or more in government contracts. Most universities must comply because they receive federal grants totaling much more than $50,000 annually. According to the U.S. Department of Labor, "For federal contractors and subcontractors, affirmative action must be taken by covered employers to recruit and advance qualified minorities, women, persons with disabilities, and covered veterans. Affirmative actions include training programs, outreach programs, and other positive steps.

We all should know that diversity makes for a rich tapestry, and we must understand that all the threads of the tapestry are equal in value no matter what the color.

—Maya Angelou (1928–), American poet

These procedures should be incorporated into the company's written personnel policies. Employers with written affirmative action programs must implement them, keep them on file and update them annually." See http://www.dol.gov/dol/topic/hiring/affirmativeact.htm#lawregs for more details.

Until recently, the reaction of many in the business community has been to rather begrudgingly obey the law. However, a growing number of business organizations have recently decided to go beyond the minimum requirements of the law and to consider diversity in the workforce as a positive force leading to more customers and more creativity in organizational decision making. This chapter is about managing diversity so your organization benefits from the richness of talents and different perspectives of a diverse workforce.

THE CHANGING U.S. WORKFORCE

The discussion of affirmative action is often focused on African Americans. However, diversity is much more broadly defined. *Diversity* is defined as the condition of being different, not all alike. A major change in the U.S. workforce over the past few decades is the number of women graduating from college and entering professional fields previously dominated by men. Today, nearly 50% of the U.S. workforce is female and about one third of U.S. businesses are owned by women. These businesses employ approximately 20% of all U.S. workers. Almost 60% of all marriages are dual-income marriages, and one in four women makes more than her husband does. Despite all these advances by women, as of this writing less than 25 of the Fortune 500 largest U.S. companies have female CEOs. The *glass ceiling* is a metaphor for an invisible barrier that makes it difficult for women and minorities to rise above a certain level in many organizations.

If we cannot now end our differences, at least we can help make the world safe for diversity.

—President John F. Kennedy

About 14% of the U.S. workforce is Hispanic/Latino. This percentage is growing rapidly. Approximately 11% of the U.S. workforce is African American. Recent extensions of civil rights laws and rules have included military veterans and people with disabilities, so today diversity refers to far more than skin color; it includes religious affiliation, age, disability status, military experience, sexual orientation, economic class, educational level, lifestyle, gender, race, ethnicity, and nationality.

According to the National Center for Public Policy and Higher Education, the U.S. workforce (generally ages 25 to 64) is changing rapidly. From 1980 to 2020, the white working-age population is projected to decline from 82% to 63%, and the minority portion of the workforce is projected to double (from

Toxic language creates a hostile work environment—and that's now illegal ... just as sexual harassment was ruled by the courts to create a hostile work environment for classes of employees protected under EEOC and Title VII laws, so toxic language poses similar legal liabilities. Companies are being sued today for language used by bosses.

—Art Bell (1945–), American broadcaster and author

18% to 37%) The Hispanic/Latino portion is projected to almost triple (from 6% to 17%). These changes can be traced to two primary causes. Larger numbers of younger Americans are ethnic minorities and increasing numbers of white workers are reaching retirement age. Over the next 15 years the largest increase in the younger U.S. population is projected to be Hispanic/Latino. All this suggests that to become a *great* manager and a *great* leader in the United States, you should develop the skills to lead men and women of different colors, cultures, ages, abilities, and backgrounds. Do not remain stuck in the past. At a minimum, obey the law and remove from your thinking any toxic thoughts or language that your employees and/or customers are likely to find offensive. On the positive side, learning how to properly manage all types of diversity will help you advance in your career.

Dealing with Sexual Harassment

As future managers entering a business world where women constitute approximately 50% of the workforce, you need to be especially sensitive to issues of sexual harassment. The law defines *sexual harassment* as any unwanted and offensive action of a sexual nature. Managers need to be especially aware that, as managers, they are considered in the position of power. As such, managers are especially vulnerable to charges that they have been forceful toward others. Also, you need to understand that the law does not require there to actually be an act of sexual intercourse or even a kiss or a hug for there to be sexual harassment. Telling sexually oriented jokes falls into the category of being offensive to some. Praising someone for looking especially sexy or appealing is another. The workplace should not be the place where sexually suggestive or nude photographs are displayed, even in the back room, because some employees are likely to find them unwanted and offensive. The term *hostile environment* is used to describe a workplace where an employee is made to feel threatened or is offended. In general, managers should remove from the workplace anything that others are likely to find offensive.

While most of the cases of sexual harassment involve a man being sexually aggressive toward a woman, the law does not distinguish between the sexes in cases of sexual harassment. It is possible for a man to feel sexually harassed by a woman or for two people of the same sex to become involved in a sexual harassment lawsuit. What is even more important than which sex is involved is which person occupies a position of power. The term *quid pro quo* is used to describe a situation where one person, typically a manager, offers something to another, typically an employee, in exchange for a sexual favor.

An example would be where a manager promises a promotion to someone in exchange for a sexual favor, such as a date.

Until a few years ago, only the person actually doing the sexual harassment was held liable by the courts. However, today the organization employing that person is often held liable. To avoid such liability, organizations should have a clear policy stating that sexual harassment will not be tolerated. Training sessions should be mandatory for all employees from the CEO to the janitor. An effective way to enforce attendance at such training sessions is to inform the employees that their next paycheck will not be issued until they have completed the required prevention of sexual harassment training program. These training sessions should define sexual harassment clearly and explain how to report such actions without fear of retaliation. As a manager you must make it clear to your employees what actions will be taken to investigate and put a stop to all sexual harassment within the organization. Those who file a legitimate complaint must be assured that their complaint will be taken seriously and the proper actions will be taken to follow through. If a worker is found guilty of sexual harassment, the best managerial approach is immediate dismissal. Furthermore, serious cases must be reported to legal authorities. It is your duty as a manager to think of the harm sexual harassment can cause to your employee, the victim of such unwanted activity in the workplace and the harm that the loss of a sexual harassment lawsuit can cause to the entire organization. Do not consider sexual jokes, pictures, or suggestive chatter to be trivial. The law makes it clear. The workplace should be a place free from such things—as a manager, it is your responsibility to make it so.

Steps in Cultivating Diversity

Good managers go beyond what the law requires and turn diversity into a positive aspect of their organization. The following are important steps you can take to cultivate diversity in your workplace:

1. Get top management's support.
2. Conduct an organizational assessment.
3. Proactively work to attract a diverse group of qualified job applicants.
4. Train all employees to better understand and work with diverse employees.
5. Proactively work to retrain talented employees.

No effort to cultivate diversity in the workplace will work without top management's support. This should be reflected in the organization's statement of values and followed up with specific actions that demonstrate top management's commitment to creating a workforce that looks at diversity as a powerful and positive asset.

Some organizations have never actually conducted an organizational assessment to determine just how monolithic the organization is. A *monolithic organization* is one that employs few women, minorities,

Some people are very sensitive to sexual harassment, and some are a little more used to it. But when you feel that prickling feeling across the back of your neck, you know that some boundary has been crossed.

—Jan Johnson, author and speaker

or other groups that differ from the majority, and thus has a highly homogeneous employee population. In contrast, a *pluralistic organization* is one with a relatively diverse employee population as the result of a proactive effort to involve employees from different gender, racial, and cultural backgrounds. The ultimate goal should be a *multicultural organization* that highly values cultural diversity and actively seeks to utilize and encourage diversity. So, first determine where your organization now stands and then set a target for the type of organization you want to create.

Great managers realize it is not enough to sit back and wait for a diverse pool of job applicants to suddenly appear at your doorstep. Instead, you should take a proactive approach, especially in making your intentions known to the minorities you especially want to attract. For example, if you sincerely want to attract more females into your workforce, making the public aware of your child care facilities for your employee's children and your flexible working hours would be important. Your brochures should show photos including diverse employees to assure potential minority applicants that they would not be all alone at their workplace. Of course the best way to let people know that your organization is a *great* place to work is for your employees to voluntarily and truthfully spread the word.

I've learned that people will forget what you said, people will forget what you did, but people will never forget how you made them feel.

—Maya Angelou

Diversity Requires More Communication

An advantage of a monolithic organization where all the workers are alike is that communication is easier. However, with that advantage comes the disadvantage that everyone may be thinking the same way and innovation and creativity may be stifled. When you take proactive steps to recruit people who are different from your current workforce, you must follow up with training about the importance of diversity in the workforce and pro-actively work to prepare all your employees to better understand and accept the newly hired workers who are not like the current personnel. It is important to stress that this new proactive recruiting approach is not just to bring in more minorities to help out those minorities, but instead is a program designed to improve the organization overall and provide a sustainable competitive advantage for the business.

Finally, it is not enough to put more emphasis on recruiting and training for diversity. You cannot overlook the fact that other organizations may be doing the same thing and some are likely to recruit minorities away from your organization after you have gone to all the effort to recruit, hire, and train them. You have to show the minority employees how they can achieve a desirable career within your firm. Minorities must be recognized for their good work and promoted within the organization. Glass ceilings of all types must be eliminated. Getting and keeping talented minorities is a challenging and on-going effort. As a manager, it is part of your duty to make all employees feel respected and appreciated.

Going Overseas for Business/Career Opportunities

Another aspect of diversity is working in foreign countries with people of all nationalities. As you prepare to enter a highly competitive global marketplace, consider the opportunities provided overseas. This section describes how to prepare for such assignments, the advantages and disadvantages of overseas assignments, and particular dangers managers need to avoid as they work around the world.

How to Prepare for an Overseas Opportunity

Diversity also includes working overseas and working with people from overseas. In both cases, the most important thing that will help you in your career is to be sensitive to, and accepting of, differences in cultures. Educators in the field of international business used to put the highest priority on the study of foreign languages. Of course knowing one or more foreign languages is a good thing. However, American businesses have found that it is even more important that their managers be accepting of the diversity of cultures around the world.

The second most important thing that will increase your chances of gaining overseas work experience is to take the opportunity to travel outside the United States while in school. Business leaders say they are reluctant to spend the organization's funds to send a worker overseas only to find out that, after a few days, they are so homesick that they have to bring them back. You need to demonstrate to your employer that you are willing to spend time away from your home, family, and friends in your home country and that you can adapt to all the changes associated with international travel and being in a foreign location for an extended time. One of the best ways of doing that is to take advantage of your

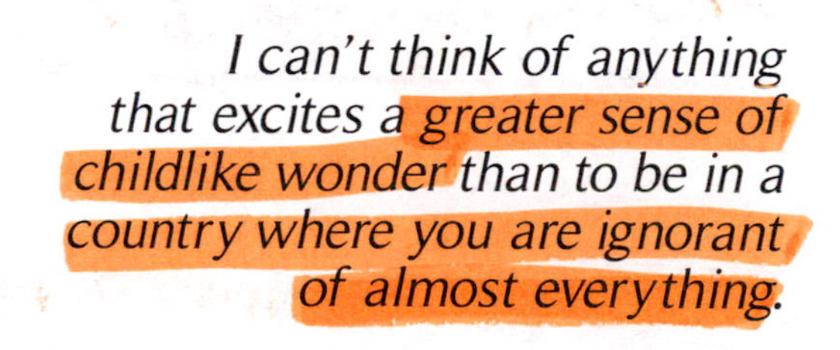

—Bill Bryson, (1951–), American author of humorous books on travel

> *Travel makes one modest. You see what a tiny place you occupy in the world.*
>
> —Scott Cameron (1946–), American author and painter

college's foreign exchange program. Typically, these programs involve a semester abroad so they are long enough to convince your employer that you can stay abroad more than a few days. Also, staying at a foreign college and taking classes provides you with a support structure during your initial overseas experience. You have a place to stay, a place to eat, things to do, and people who are familiar with the types of issues you will encounter. In most cases, your college has arranged so your tuition will be the same as it would be at your home university, and the travel and living accommodations will be reasonably priced. Imagine if you are in competition for an overseas job opportunity and your competition has participated in such a foreign exchange program and you have never been outside the United States. Which one do you think will get the job?

Third, have some knowledge or skill that is needed overseas. Businesses do not spend the money to send someone overseas unless that person's knowledge or skill is needed at that location. Perhaps you have extraordinary abilities in software design, financial analysis, marketing expertise, etc. Have some business knowledge that is universally valuable. Knowledge of a foreign language can be a help, but be sure that you can say something intelligent about how business is conducted internationally, even if you can only say it in English.

Leaving your home country to take an overseas assignment takes courage. Be willing to assume some risk. Learn all you can about the country where you are going. If you do not know the language, at least take the time to learn a few phrases, such as how to say "please" and "thank you" and "hello" and "goodbye" in their language. Most people appreciate your efforts to at least say a few words in their language. Do not, however, assume you are fluent in a foreign language until you have actually lived successfully among people who are native speakers of that language. Spoken language, especially as spoken by someone who has used that language since birth, is far faster than what is spoken in a typical foreign language classroom.

When you travel to another country, it is okay to love your native country and to be proud of your homeland's accomplishments. However, it is important to not overdo your pride in your native land and offend people from other nations. The phrase "ugly American" is a term used to refer to perceptions of arrogant behavior by Americans abroad, especially American business managers. Do not let that phrase describe you. People who judge others by the standards of their own culture, which they think

> *Travel is fatal to prejudice, bigotry, and narrow-mindedness.*
>
> —Mark Twain

is superior, are defined as *ethnocentric.* Be proud of your home country, but also be open to what all nations and cultures have to offer.

Foreign Corrupt Practices Act of 1977

All U.S. managers going overseas need to know about the Foreign Corrupt Practices Act of 1977, making it illegal for any U.S. citizen anywhere in the world to bribe a foreign official. If you are found guilty of violating this law, you may be fined up to $100,000 or up to twice the value of the benefit you were trying to obtain with the bribe, plus up to five years in prison. Also, it is illegal for such fines to be paid by the person's employer. Of course, it is impossible to put a corporation in prison but easy to imprison a manager, so it will be you sitting in prison for five years, not your corporation. So, regardless of how much bribery you may see going on, think twice before offering anyone a bribe to get their business.

The law states that it is not the amount of the bribe that is at issue, it is the intent. If the intent of the bribe is to get a foreign official to do something they would not normally do, then the dollar amount of the bribe is of no matter under the law. While you may think that no one will find out or report your bribe, recall that your business competition will be upset that your company got the contract and they did not. It is usually the manager from the business that lost the contract that reports the bribe. Also, consider that a good business deal should be able to stand on its own. A bribe is often a compensation for some flaw in the contract. See http://www.justice.gov/criminal/fraud/fcpa/ for details. In summary, it is against the law for you to offer a bribe to a foreign official—like it or not, you must obey the law or face the consequences.

Disadvantages of Some Overseas Assignments

In almost all cases, an overseas assignment helps a manager advance in his or her professional career. However, if the corporation's headquarters are in the United States and the division of the business that is overseas is of little consequence, then it is not a good idea to spend too many years at that overseas location. Some devious business executives have even been known to send their internal rivals overseas as a way of getting them removed from the "action."

Look at any potential overseas assignment as objectively as you can. Examine the credentials of those higher than you in the organization and notice whether they have spent time overseas. In some

No man is above the law and no man is below it; nor do we ask any man's permission when we ask him to obey it. Obedience to the law is demanded as a right; not asked as a favor.

—President Theodore Roosevelt

U.S. corporations it is practically a requirement to have some overseas experience before advancing into the ranks of executive. However, in other corporations it is of questionable importance. If it will broaden your business experience and help you to better understand the overall operations of the corporation, then it will likely increase your chances for advancement. Also, it can be a lot of fun.

Summary

This chapter has asked you to look at diversity in the workforce in a positive manner. At a minimum you need to know and obey the law. Do not discriminate against any employee on the basis of anything except their observed merit and results. Be aware that the U.S. workforce is rapidly changing. The percentage of women and Hispanic/Latino employees is growing rapidly. Diversity includes religious affiliation, age, disability status, military experience, sexual orientation, economic class, educational level, lifestyle, gender, ethnicity, and nationality in addition to the commonly considered consideration of race. Taking an overseas work assignment can introduce you to foreign cultures and help you further appreciate the positive aspects of diversity. Above all, respect *all* cultures.

Twenty years from now you will be more disappointed by the things you didn't do than by the ones you did. So throw off the bowlines, sail away from the safe harbor. Catch the trade winds in your sails. Explore. Dream. Discover.

—Mark Twain

Questions for Discussion

1. What experiences have you had with Affirmation Action, either at work or at school? Have you been the victim of discrimination? What further steps do you suggest for making the workplace a *great* place to work for people of all races, genders, etc.?
2. Have you ever experienced or observed sexual harassment at work or at school? How was the situation handled? After studying the chapter regarding sexual harassment, what changes would you implement if you were the manager in charge?
3. If you have traveled overseas through your work, your school, or your family, describe how that experience changed your understanding of various cultures. Would you recommend other students participate in an overseas student exchange program? Why or why not?

Chapter 13

Power: How to Get Power and Use It Properly

Knowledge without power is of remarkably little use.

—Jeffrey Pfeffer, Stanford professor and author of Power: Why Some People Have It—And Others Don't *(2010)*

Many students think power is a dirty word. They say, "I don't want to have to deal with office politics and power." Unfortunately, nothing gets done within large organizations without the use of power and political influence. So, if you want to be someone who makes a difference within a large organization, you will need to learn how to get, keep, and properly use power. But some of my students tell me they believe that if they work hard, play fair, and have a clear vision of a better future, things will work out okay. Good luck with that.

It is true that the grabbing of power and using it to get things done is not always an attractive process. At times it appears as though the powerful and despicable win over those who work hard, play fair, and have the best ideas. But good people can learn how to get and use power. If good people don't, evil ones will.

Power Is the Implementation of Change Despite Resistance

Getting things done often means getting new ideas implemented. New ideas almost always meet with resistance. Overcoming resistance requires power. *Power* is defined as the ability to implement change despite resistance. Being right isn't enough. Other people, good or bad, often have other ideas about how things ought to be done. Conflicting values, priorities, and ideas are commonplace within organizations. Things don't get done without effort.

Why Bad People Win

We often see people who are mean and nasty in positions of power and wonder, how did that happen? Why is it that people who obviously use power badly sometimes get promoted or win elections? Why do followers freely choose such people to be their leaders? Why do bad people so often win?

At times we are forced to choose between the lesser of two evils. War or the threat of bankruptcy can make us think we are threatened by an evil force. We seek out a bully to protect us from the even more threatening bully. The business world can be tough. Adam Smith's invisible hand of the marketplace often looks like a fist. We often feel the need to follow a leader who is tough, gets things done, and knows how to get and use power. At other times, followers are simply too meek and the bully wins by default. People may lack the courage to stand up to a bully. The bully may have overwhelming physical power.

People are fascinated with power, even when they know it is being used improperly. Even such notoriously evil people as Hitler and Stalin attracted loyal followers, perhaps out of fear, perhaps out of fascination. Today, as modern Russia tries to deal with the historical facts about Stalin, they point to other rulers who also governed with a cruel hand. According to an article in the *New York Times* on August 12, 2007, Russia points to the United States and notes how our reaction following the attacks on the World Trade Center towers on 9/11 was to move to concentrate power in the hands of the president as commander in chief. We may say we prefer a leader who is friendly and kind, but when we are overcome with fear, we seek protection. We want our bully to be bigger and stronger than their bully.

When a bully has held power for a long time, it takes a great deal of courage and power to stand up to him. Unfortunately, intimidation and terror are often effective. Even today, many nations are ruled by powerful dictators who think nothing of torturing or putting to death those who dare to disagree. Many large businesses today are led by power-hungry, egotistic, dictatorial executives who put their personal gain above all else while shamelessly destroying the careers of thousands, the retirement savings of thousands of investors, and undermining the trust and confidence in our economic system. But there have always been bullies; the mystery is why they are not being stopped. We expect bullies to be the way they are; why aren't the good people more willing to accept power and change things for the better?

> *Evil crucially expresses itself through power—the raw energy of politics, good and bad.*
>
> —*Lance Morrow, author of* Evil: An Investigation

The world is a dangerous place to live; not because of the people who are evil, but because of the people who don't do anything about it.

—Albert Einstein

PEOPLE FIGHT OVER POWER

Being in a position of leadership creates its own resistance. Other people want that position, some for the pay, others for the honor, still others to have a chance to make a difference in ways that matter to them. In our culture we honor those in positions of leadership, and consciously or unconsciously, many of us have a strong desire to achieve such positions. In fact, we often cast aside those in consideration for such top-level positions who do not express a sufficiently strong desire for the position. Members of a search committee may believe someone who does not express a strong desire for the position will lack the drive and determination to actually perform the difficult job. People often look for someone with a "commanding presence." They expect the potential leader to walk tall, chest out, and have a look of confidence. To obtain a high-ranking position, you may need to demonstrate a sufficient level of egotism; the trick is to not to overdo it.

When you do land that coveted leadership position, never underestimate the opposition. When a position such as company vice president or president, college dean, editor in chief, etc., becomes available, there may be hundreds of well-qualified applicants, many from within the organization. All the applicants (and many who may decide not to apply) feel they are the right person for the position. Only one is picked. Those who felt they deserved that position do not instantly stop feeling that they would have been the best choice. Loyalty to the new leader is far from automatic. When the chosen leader is announced, there may be ceremonial events that make it look as though everyone is happy the new leader has arrived. Do not be fooled; beneath the happy exterior lies an ocean of disappointment, resentment, and anger. When the opportunity is right, many will consciously or unconsciously undermine the chosen leader in hopes of having another chance at getting the position. Further, each applicant is likely to have several supporters who also represent potential pockets of resentment toward the new leader. At some future point when they sense they have gathered sufficient power, they are likely to overthrow the leader so they can put in place their own choice.

If we aspire to positions of leadership, even if for the most selfless of reasons, we must understand what power is, how to acquire it, how to put it to proper use, and how to deal with the inevitable loss of power.

Power has a life cycle: it begins small, grows, matures, and then declines and dies. However, to become a leader who gets things done, we need to follow the path to power. Evil people already seem to know the value of gaining power; it is the good people who shy away from the good use of power who need to be awakened. Power by itself, like money, is neither

The worst disease which can afflict executives in their work is not, as popularly supposed, alcoholism; it's egotism.

—Harold S. Geneen

good nor evil; it is the use to which power is put that makes all the difference. Learn how to gain power and put it to good use.

THE PATH TO POWER

The primary source of leadership power comes from followers. Even evil dictators cannot remain in power for long if enough "little people" decide to band together.

Karl Marx's famous quotation, "Workers of the world unite, you have nothing to lose but your chains", was meant to encourage the millions of ordinary workers to band together to overthrow oppressive owners and bosses. He observed the rich getting richer and the poor getting poorer, but also concluded the poor far outnumbered the wealthy. The poor could, if properly organized and united, overthrow the wealthy few, and hopefully establish a more just and socialistic state. Of course, we all know that the Communist regimes that eventually came to power in Russia and much of eastern Europe and China had their own forms of corruption, and most failed miserably. That failure, however, does not discredit the concept that the only legitimate source of power comes from the people. Government, whether of a nation, business, or nonprofit, ought to be *of the people, by the people, and for the people*.

In the American colonies, the leaders were also tired of oppression by the few (English royalty) over the many (the colonists). The Declaration of Independence declares "*Governments are instituted among Men, deriving their just Powers from the Consent of the Governed*." It further declares that when "*any form of Government becomes destructive of these Ends, it is the Right of the People to alter or abolish it*." The true source of leadership power comes from the followers who voluntarily give power to their chosen leader. You cannot legitimately declare yourself to be a leader; it is something others declare about you.

We have many sources of personal power, even before we gain organizational power from an official position. The child on the playground with the most power may actually be the one who is the strongest, tallest, or most athletic. In the classroom, much of the power goes to those best able to learn quickly and do well on tests. In life following college, a source of power is often emotional intelligence. It is a powerful thing to be aware of your own emotions and to have the self-confidence to use them effectively. If you can be calm and assertive when others are scared, you will gain power. It is even more powerful to be able to sense and influence the emotions of others and to use that knowledge ethically and effectively. The combination of intelligence, talent, skill, good health, good looks, charm, the ability to communicate persuasively, and self-assurance makes for a tough mix to beat. Add a strong sense of spirituality or recognition of a higher, loving power and you have one very powerful individual. Now the important question is how that powerful individual will use such power. Why is it so frequently wasted?

Regardless of individual power, people within organizations must gradually move through a series of steps to accumulate organizational power. To successfully resolve most of today's major problems requires organizational power. Accumulating the power to get things done within large organizations typically follows these phases: (1) stepping forward, (2) tasting power, (3) focusing, (4) using authority.

Phase 1: Stepping Forward

Some people seek power because of a high need for achievement, the lure of more money, or the need to feed an oversized ego. Others react to injustice or need to right a wrong. We are angry about the way those in power exploit their victims. The word "victim" comes from the Latin for a beast to be killed as a sacrifice to a god in a religious rite. Today, we think of victims as those who are powerless to protect themselves or those they love. They, like the sacrificial lamb, have done nothing to deserve the harsh treatment. If we know of someone who has suffered a great loss such as being swindled or robbed, we say they are a victim of a crime. In large organizations, there are often many who sincerely believe they are victims of those currently in power. Some actually are. Good people need to step forward to seek power to stop being victims themselves and to help those who are being victimized.

We see things that need to be changed. We hate to feel powerless to affect that needed change. We may feel that those in power are perpetrating an unfair act or promoting a position that is causing pain and suffering. Eventually our reluctance to seek power is overpowered by our sense that something has to be done. We make a conscious or unconscious choice to gather the power necessary to make a difference. We step forward, ready to accept the responsibility of leadership.

Some leaders are drafted. Victims come to potential leaders seeking help. They feel powerless and look to a prospective new leader as someone with the potential to bring change. The group is seeking someone who can create an organizational structure, obtain resources, and focus energies in the proper direction. The leader may not have sought power, but accepted it when offered. Perhaps others have already come to you and put their trust in you to help them through some difficulty or to right some injustice. In many cases the step is so gradual it is only upon looking backwards years later that the leader can begin to observe what happened. In other cases the change is instantaneous, such as when a soldier gains a battlefield commission because the officer in charge is killed in action. Whether dramatic or subtle, gradual or instantaneous, the change happens and you enter the world of leadership. To most, these first steps are scary.

The inability to get things done, to have ideas and decisions implemented, is widespread in organizations today.

—Jeffrey Pfeffer

Phase 2: Tasting Power

Suddenly you are part of the powerful group. You have been promoted, elected, chosen. You have joined the in crowd or the group with sufficient power to implement change. If you are experiencing your first taste of power, likely your first actions are tentative. You look around for someone you know who can show you the ropes. You quietly listen and avoid speaking up. You have to learn how to act in this new culture. You ask, what are the new ground rules? Where does the power lie within this group? What is

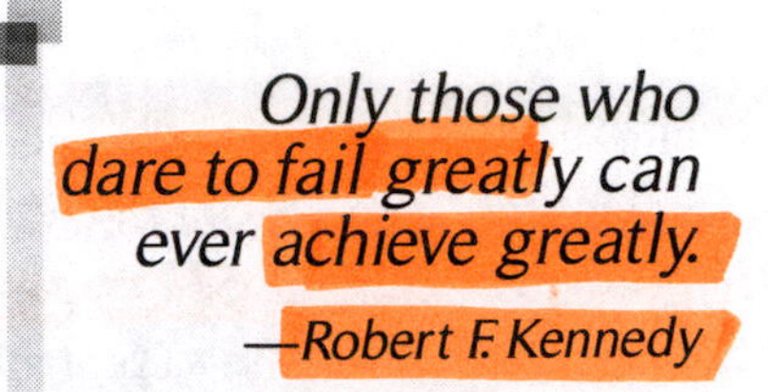

expected of the new person in the group? What do you really need to do to be accepted as one of the in group?

Despite all the uncertainty, most of us feel good about belonging to a more powerful group. Most people feel an increase in pride. You hold your head a little higher, walk a little straighter, and dress a little better. You try to fit in, observe, and learn. In many cases, the increase in pay and the nicer office aren't bad either. Others, especially others from the group you just left behind, treat you differently. Some will resent you. Others will shower you with false praise. Some will look to you with hope in their eyes. You can't forget you are in this new position for a reason. You want to be in this group because you sensed there was power within it. You want to make a difference, to bring change, to right a wrong. You no longer are willing to be a victim yourself. You want to help those who are victimized.

This is the time to find a mentor. This is the time to form alliances. This is the time to study and prepare. Become a student of people. Learn what makes others tick. Learn who can get things done and how. Find out how people feel about the issues. Listen intently, not just to what is said but to the music or emotions behind the words. Know what people are saying in the hallways so you will know in advance how votes will turn out. Become a student of body language and other subtle nuances of human behavior. Become sensitive to the feelings of others. Learn what others need and want; what motivates them. Learn how to get people to do what you think needs to be done without hurting feelings. Above all, develop the courage to do the right thing.

Phase 3: Focusing Personal Energy for Results

Your first managerial assignment is your opportunity to demonstrate your ability to produce results. In the business world, this is often an assignment to work with a team of others on a specific assignment with specific procedures, timetables, resources, and objectives. For many young managers, this is their first workplace experience where it is not okay to leave at quitting time. Many successful executives recall spending 60 or more hours per week on their first assignments. Being able to focus all your energies on the task at hand is a tremendous advantage, but it has a downside. This necessity to focus on the task and devote long hours makes it difficult for young women with small children to make their mark in the business world. Despite the enormous difficulties, women are coming on strong and moving up fast within many large organizations.

> *Courage is rightly esteemed the first of human qualities because it is the quality which guarantees all the others.*
>
> —Winston Churchill

A project that produces measurable positive results gains attention. Being known as someone with energy and focus that can produce results is a great source of power. Success begets success. Your next assignment is likely to be one with more responsibility. Eventually, you are likely to become recognized as an effective team leader. While you may still lack an official title designating power, your growing reputation is adding to your expanding storehouse of personal power. Are you ready for the next step?

Phase 4: Using Official Authority

Organizations bestow power on those with titles such as Division Director, Division Manager, Vice President, etc. Once you get over the thrill of the new business card, the new office, and being called by your new title, the weight of responsibility sinks in. Having a title means you are authorized to sign certain official documents. Your signature suddenly has more meaning—plus the legal responsibility. It carries power, but also risk and responsibility. You now have the power to spend a certain amount of the organization's money. You can purchase resources others need to carry out their jobs. Your recommendation results in someone being hired or promoted. You have authority over other people's salaries.

> *Courage, sacrifice, determination, commitment, toughness, heart, talent, guts. That's what little girls are made of; the hell with sugar and spice.*
>
> *—Source unknown*

You have become an *agent* for the organization, or some part of it. A corporation is simply a legal entity. Certain people, by reason of their titles or positions within that legal entity, act for the corporation. You are now one of them. You are the agent acting in the name of the corporation and your area of responsibility has greatly expanded. While technical ability is still important, your moral courage is becoming more and more important.

Now, if you make a mistake, not only you, but also your organization may get into trouble. For many young managers, their first true realization of the power of their title is when they must appear in court to explain why they signed a particular document. What may have seemed like a casual signing of your name now becomes extremely important. Hopefully, the organization will come to your defense—not because you are a nice guy and need help, but because the organization must act in self-defense. It must protect its agents as a matter of preserving the organization.

Does the Organization Make the Leader?

There are those who say it is the organization that creates, empowers, and perpetuates leaders out of a need to preserve itself. Once a new leader is chosen, the organization rallies around that leader, not so much for the sake of the leader, but for the sake of the organization. However, it is easy for the new leader to mistake this activity as being personal. The organization is creating and nourishing the leader because the organization requires a strong leader. However, the leader may start to believe his or her own press releases. The praise and perks are self-affirming. But the organization nourishes the CEO with high pay, a big office, and many perks, not for the benefit of the CEO, but for the good of the organization. These trappings of office are outward signs of power, and that the organization wants to show others it has a powerful leader.

Leaders might think of their job title and themselves as the same, concluding they deserve special treatment. Many people defer to the power of officeholders far more than they should. Do not confuse the differential treatment employees often give to those of a higher rank with true friendship and loyalty to you—it may all be just about the title. For example, some people say they strongly disagree and lack respect for the current president of the United States, but at the same time, respect the office of the presidency. Be careful that people do not say the same thing about you when you gain a prestigious title.

Growing into Leadership

Our fondest hope is that when people lacking sufficient leadership ability have leadership responsibility thrust upon them, they will grow into their position of leadership. It may be out of a sense of duty, pride, or responsibility that we often see rather ordinary people blossom into great leaders. They grow into the ability to use the power of their office to make a positive difference.

> *Power corrupts and absolute power corrupts absolutely.*
>
> *—Lord Acton (1834–1902), English historian*

The story of the rise to power of Lyndon Baines Johnson is especially interesting as a case study in the acquisition of power. Johnson moved from a strong supporter of segregation to become the person who single-handedly passed more civil rights legislation in less time and with greater effect than anyone else in U.S. history. (Source: Robert A. Caro, *The Years of Lyndon Johnson: Master of the Senate*. New York: Knopf, 2002)

As with most people who become so obsessed with power, Johnson did not always use it to help others, but instead to selfishly help himself. However, you simply can't argue with his claim that he knew how to get and use power. When it was time to pass a bill, he knew exactly whose arm to twist and how.

Perhaps Johnson's greatest moment in the Senate came when the opportunity to pass the Civil Rights Act of 1964 presented itself. He was exactly the right person in the right place at the right moment. Despite the fact Johnson had earlier sided with segregationists, when the moment came for this historic act to be considered, he knew exactly how to apply power. The passage of this act greatly increased the number of registered black voters and started in motion a series of civil rights laws. As President Johnson said "Whatever else people say about me, I know how to get and use power."

The dark side of power is when it is used to hurt others. While power by itself is neither good nor evil, the potential for evil is great. As Immanuel Kant, the famous German philosopher, said, "The possession of power inevitably spoils the free use of reason."

Those who penned our Constitution understood the danger of unlimited power and wisely divided the power of the government between the executive, legislative, and the judicial branches, and encouraged each branch to watch over the others. The founding fathers had felt firsthand the evil of the nearly unlimited power of the king of England.

Evil still exists; people still use power to rule by intimidation and fear and harm others. While we would like to think that atrocities such as Hitler's murder of six million Jews and Stalin's murder of ten million of his own people are things of the past, we must acknowledge the recent murders in Cambodia, Bosnia, Rwanda, and in America on 9/11.

In the world of business, the last few years have produced a litany of abuse of power. Perhaps the most serious consequence has been an erosion of confidence in governmental agencies and auditors to watch over and regulate commerce, thereby calling into question all actions of business executives and government officials. Some say it is as though we have let the fox guard the henhouse. Despite these great dangers, the power one gets from their title is a force that can be used to make a positive difference. Using power for good or evil is a matter of choice. By itself, the power of an official title is neither good nor evil; it is human intent that makes the difference.

REASONS PEOPLE MAKE UNWISE AND UNETHICAL CHOICES

It is not sufficient to say that those who choose the wrong path are simply bad people. Most leaders who have accumulated massive amounts of power achieved that success largely because others have, for years, viewed them as wise, capable, and ethical. Somewhere along the line, they chose to use that power unwisely, unethically, or illegally. What went wrong?

In many organizations the climb up the ladder of power is also the path to great wealth. Money, like power, is not bad by itself. However, the temptation is sometimes more than we can handle. We may have passed on thousands of opportunities to take more than we should. We may have performed wisely and ethically over and over—and then suddenly, we make an unethical choice. Even the strongest among us can slip and fall. Why is that so?

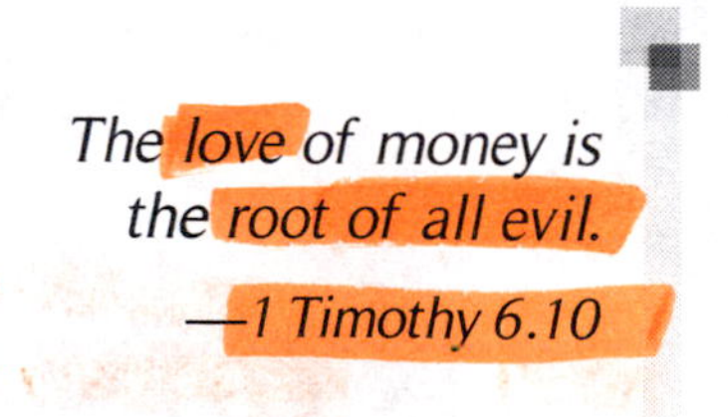

For some, the allure of money builds until it is overpowering. Perhaps it starts with getting by with a small indiscretion. Our followers may want so desperately for us to succeed that they cover for us. In some cases we step over the line ethically and justify it as doing something for a greater good. Eventually, we may begin to believe we are the ones establishing that line—we are the ones who decide what is ethical and what is not. The combination of so much temptation and so much power may just be too much. Perhaps we have a weaker moment, we are tired and under pressure, perhaps we drink a little too much, or perhaps we hunger for just a little more excitement in our lives. Even the president of the United States can forget that no man is above the law as evidenced by President Nixon's regrettable comment, "When the President does it, that means that it's not illegal."

We might even justify it by saying we are doing it for our families, not ourselves. Some business deals today are so lucrative they could set everyone in your family up for life. Who among us hasn't been tempted by the sight of some money or other treasure lying there in plain sight with nobody around? That may be what it appears to someone in a position to use their powerful position to transfer funds from the organization. With a simple signature, you may be able to move hundreds of thousands of dollars, and nobody will ever know. Well, at least that's what most crooks think until they get caught.

Still others who have taken the wrong turn say what they did was not as bad as what someone else did. They say everyone is doing it, so it must be okay. They blame society, their superiors, or their peers for establishing a culture where such behavior seemed acceptable, even normal or expected. Doesn't everyone cheat a little on their income taxes? Doesn't everyone fudge a little on their expense accounts? Doesn't everyone slip a few supplies into their pocket for use at home? Where does this slippery slope end? Once you have cheated a little, it is easier to cheat a little more. Almost everyone can find someone who has done worse, yet was punished less severely. We convince ourselves we aren't evil, we are just a victim. We are only evening the score.

In marketing we talk of the life cycle of a product. A new product is born and grows slowly at first. Then some products take off, and for a time, soar like a rocket. Eventually, even the best products seem to run out of fuel, slow down, and eventually fall back to earth. Power is like that.

Acquiring Power Through Personal Energy and Talent

Many who eventually gain great power began by exhibiting exceptional personal energy and talent. They stand out among their peers. They were the ones willing to put in the extra time and effort. They were the first to arrive in the morning and the last to leave at night. Others were amazed at their energy. Most of us are willing to grant such people a measure of power in recognition of their exceptional energy and talent.

> *I find the harder I work, the more luck I seem to have.*
>
> *—Thomas Jefferson, 3rd president of the United States*

Studies indicate many young executives are not exaggerating when they say they spend 60–80 hours per week on the job. They sacrifice time with family, friends, and time just to rest and relax. In return, others notice. They get results where others collect excuses. They acquire power through extreme expenditures of time, energy, and talent.

Getting Power Through Alignment and Focus

Focus is about the concentration of power into a small area. You may have first observed the power of focus when, as a child, you used a magnifying glass to focus the rays of the sun onto tiny scraps of paper to start a fire. We have all had to find ways to focus our efforts preparing for examinations, concerts, auditions, or initial work assignments.

The power to focus and concentrate can be both helpful and hurtful. Used properly, it can help you gain recognition, respect, and power. Used improperly, it can make you blind to other important issues. Some prospective leaders appear to be too smart for their own good. They are so talented and so interested in so many things that they fail to focus enough on what is highest in priority. This allows others who are less intelligent or talented to overtake them in achievement. We even use the fable of *The Tortoise and the Hare* to teach our children that the race is not always won by the swiftest. The little turtle just kept his head down and kept moving forward with a singular focus, while the rabbit jumped around all over the place and wasted energy and time.

Beginning managers often find once they reach the ranks of management, everyone is smart, works hard, and expects to be highly successful. So what? Spend your time getting results. Don't waste your time on extraneous stuff. Focus on the key success factors.

Using Power with Sensitivity

New managers need to be sensitive to the feelings of others. Most people resent being bossed around. We like to be asked, rather than told, what to do. Successful people need not talk down to others. Many followers will not be as full of energy, as talented, or as focused as you—the ambitious new manager—and that is okay. Most organizations cannot afford to employ an entire workforce made up of such people.

Most of the world's population is not willing to work 60 hours a week and that is okay, too. To many, work is simply a place to go to earn sufficient money to pay the rent and keep food on the table and that is okay. New managers often make the mistake of treating such people with disrespect or even contempt and that is not okay. They blame them for their department's poor performance. They call others lazy and stupid and threaten to fire them unless they adopt the work pattern they have chosen for themselves. When someone truly believes someone else is stupid and lazy, that other person senses it and resents it. Who wants to be thought of as stupid and lazy?

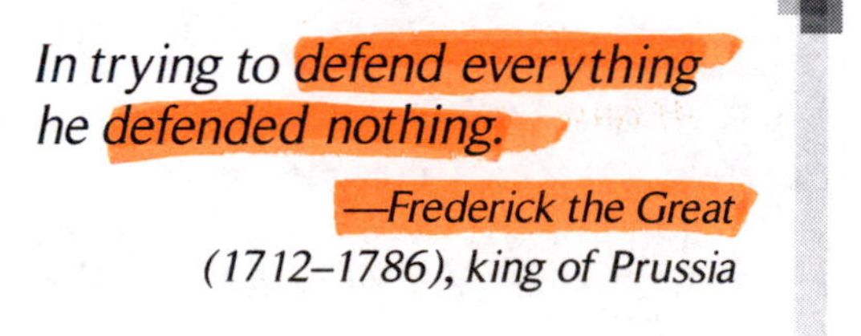

It is not good enough to treat others well who share our values, our focus on work or study, our need for achievement, or our desire for ever increasing levels of power. Every human being deserves to be treated with respect. Much of our intelligence, talent, and energy are a combination of the genes

Focus totally on the business at hand commanding your body to do exactly what you want it to do.

—Arnold Palmer (1929–), American golf champion

we inherit from our parents and the gifts we receive from our Creator. We have no control over those genes and gifts, only what we do with them. The wise leader is sensitive to not lording it over others. Such sensitivity breeds loyalty and support and results in more power being accorded to such leaders.

The best leaders develop a keen sense of who others in the organization are, their position on the issues, and how best to communicate with and influence them without hurting their feelings. They become students of body language, voice tone, and other subtle nuances of human behavior. They quickly pick up on shifts of attitude. They are quick to sense when they are offending others and move to apologize, make amends, and regain full cooperation and support.

Maintaining Power by Being Flexible

Large organizations are constantly in a state of change. Even though we say large bureaucracies resist change, people in those bureaucracies are constantly being hired, fired, retired, transferred, or leave for a better position elsewhere. Projects are constantly going through phases, being completed, being dropped, and new projects are constantly coming online. Processes, objectives, and missions change. Values and priorities shift. What worked for a leader yesterday may fail today. Leaders must be sufficiently flexible to adapt to constant change, rather than cling to what is not working.

On the other hand, leaders can be criticized for changing their position. Some may say leaders need to be steadfast. They need to have a position and stick to it. They want leaders to be dependable, not to flip-flop. Politicians are especially criticized for taking a poll before taking a stand. However, knowing when to give in and when to change is as important as knowing when to stand fast. For those who must frequently be reelected to office, standing fast with a position that is no longer popular with the electorate may result in being voted out of office. It is tough to stand up for any position when you are voted out of office. The trick is to pick your battles carefully, whether in an elected office or any kind of office. It's tough to stay in any type of position of leadership if the followers really want you out.

Maintaining Power by Ego Suppression

Where does a healthy sense of self-assurance end and an annoying arrogance begin? We need a certain degree of confidence to tackle difficult assignments. Being shy and unwilling to face confrontation means you are unlikely to effect change. Overcoming resistance often means being willing to fight for what you believe is right. Winning a few such battles often provides the victor with the very poison that will eventually kill him. Success is difficult to handle; sometimes more so than failure.

> *Progress is impossible without change, and those who cannot change their minds cannot change anything.*
>
> *—George Bernard Shaw*

After a few victories, it is easy for successful leaders to start believing their own press releases. Such releases are written to make the leader and the organization look good. Just like advertising copy, they often stretch the truth a little. We are so used to the hyperbole that we have come to expect the smallest coffee cup at Starbucks is called a tall. We get too big for our britches, as our mothers used to warn.

A symptom of an overblown ego is assuming we are always right. Since we are the ones getting all the attention and praise, surely we must be the ones who are right. We might be riding on a hot streak, but even the best teams lose a few games. Even the best hitters occasionally strike out. The brightest scholars miss a few questions. Sometime we even find ourselves in a slump. Nothing seems to be going right. Since we have experienced so much success in the recent past, it must be our followers or our peers who are letting us down. Perhaps it is our superiors who are failing to properly support us. What's wrong with everybody else? Can't they see I'm right and everyone else simply has to get behind me?

With such an attitude, our followers and our peers become resentful. They don't like having their positions ignored or criticized. Eventually they become willing, maybe even eager, to see us fail. They won't bother to let us know we are headed toward a cliff.

A major characteristic of almost any organization is interdependence. We can't do much of anything without the cooperation of others. It is also easy for others, if sufficiently angered, to set us up for certain failure. Leaders need followers just as a blind man needs a guide dog. Treating the guide dog cruelly could, in the long run, be a huge, and possibly fatal, mistake. *Great* managers and *great* leaders know they need the cooperation of others to achieve *great* results.

Losing or Giving Up Power

A teacher was presenting as examples of great leaders Jesus, Gandhi, John F. Kennedy, and Martin Luther King Jr. A student remarked these were also examples of a crucifixion and three assassinations. Leaders are often assassinated, although most "assassinations" are not bloody. They are more subtle and civilized, at least on the surface. However, to the leader who suddenly finds he or she has been overthrown, the effect can be devastating. How can leaders minimize the chances of being overthrown?

Seldom does one rises to a position of power within an organization and stay there until retirement. If nothing else, the aging process stacks the deck against holding on to power for long. The *Life Cycle of Power* has a natural life cycle that includes birth, growth, maturation, and eventually decline and death. Even in the best of circumstances, we eventually tire of the struggle. We come into a position to effect change. We work to overcome the resistance to change, and hopefully win several battles. Eventually

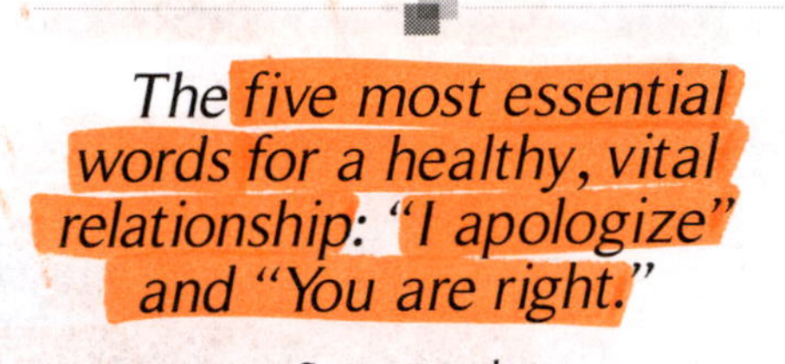

we become the ones who want to maintain what we worked so hard to build—we often become the resisters to change.

Over time we find it harder to maintain our flexibility. Our energy runs low. The energy of those with opposing points of view builds. While it is true that some leaders maintain their power for a long time, in general, it is rare for organizational presidents and others at the top of an organizational chart to maintain that position for over ten years—for many the tenure is much less. The average tenure for college presidents and deans, for example, is under five years.

Perhaps such short tenures are a good thing. Many people feel strongly about imposing term limits on positions of leadership. We only allow the president of the United States to be elected twice, for a total of eight years. Many states, like Ohio, have passed term limits for such elected positions as legislative representatives and senators. Seldom do those term limits extend beyond ten years; many are eight. Even though the voters have the power to end someone's term by electing someone else, there is a strong sentiment among voters that leadership power should have a time limit.

One of the most important acts some leaders do is to gracefully give up their position of leadership. Consider the case of George Washington. While it is proper to honor him for being the general of the Continental Army in the fight for independence and for being the first president of the United States under the new Constitution, Washington's exit from the presidency after serving for two four-year terms represented the first time in recorded history that such a transfer of power was accomplished so peacefully and graciously. Many were eager to have him stay. Some were willing to name him king or emperor for life. Instead, without a single shot being fired, with no attempt to turn over power to a son or daughter, with no mob activity, Washington turned over the presidency to someone with whom he had many differences of opinion. John Adams became the second president of the United States, and after four years turned over the presidency to Thomas Jefferson. It wasn't until Franklin Delano Roosevelt's tenure that this pattern of serving for just one or two terms was broken. Despite Roosevelt's popularity, it wasn't long after Roosevelt's death in office early in his fourth term that Congress passed the Twenty-Second Amendment to the Constitution, which reads: "No person shall be elected to the office of the President more than twice."

For the person who is forcefully tossed out of a position of power, the effect can be painful, even devastating. However, for the organization, such changes are often therapeutic. Someone with new ideas, new skills, new information, new energy, and a new coalition of powerful allies can bring renewal to an organization. Even in the case of Franklin Delano

Any change is resisted because bureaucrats have a vested interest in the chaos in which they exist.

—President Richard M. Nixon

Roosevelt, who deserves tremendous respect for the nation's recovery from the Great Depression and for victory in World War II, his failing health during his last few months in office could have been disastrous for a nation still at war and harshly divided over how to handle all the problems of recovery from war and depression. In retrospect, we now can see Roosevelt should have stepped aside earlier. Clearly, the mood of the country was to limit the presidency to two terms. Despite the fact that passage of an amendment to the U.S. Constitution requires approval of two thirds of both the House and the Senate and ratification of three fourths of the states, the Twenty-Second Amendment was quickly ratified. People simply do not want someone to stay in power for too long.

If you are so fortunate as to rise to a position of great power, give some thought to a graceful exit from that seat of power. Remember the example of George Washington. When the time is right, go back to the farm. Let someone else have a turn. Do not overstay your welcome.

Your Personal Leadership Development Plan

How does one plan out their personal leadership development strategy?

For some, development as a leader just seems to happen. It is only in looking back that one can see the key steps that were taken along the way. For others, they set out early in life to achieve SMART goals. SMART goals are Specific, Measurable, Attainable, Relevant, and Timely. Saying you want to be successful is not specific enough. Saying you want to be a CEO of a Fortune 500 company such as General Electric by the age of 40 may be more specific than needed. But the person who sets the more specific goals, even if they later have to make mid-course adjustments, is more likely to obtain something close to their target. At least ask yourself whether you want to be in the for-profit or not-for-profit sector. Do you want to work for a large corporation or a small firm? Is there a specific product or service that most interests you? Be as specific as possible about your daily activities. Will you be working out of your home or in an office? What will be the major steps along the way? Are there key turning points? What choices will be critical? What education, training, and experience will be needed?

Goals need to be as measurable as possible and the measurement should be multidimensional. Imagine you are already at your goal. What will it look like? Try to draw a three-dimensional picture, filling in as much color, shape, and texture as possible. What will it taste like? What will it smell like? What sounds will you hear? Will you be inside or outside? Will there be sun and wind on your skin? Will there be people talking, music playing, birds chirping, or silence? Involve as many senses as possible. Turn your goal into a clear mental image that is vivid and alive.

What is attainable for you? If your full adult height is less than six feet, then a successful career in the National Basketball Association is probably not attainable. If your political affiliation is the Libertarian party, then becoming president of the United States is probably not attainable. The challenge is to make your goal attainable without selling yourself short. Most of us need some help from people who are willing to be objective and truthful with us. Seek advice, but not from those who stand to gain from your success or failure. Most people find there are only a few people throughout their entire lifetime who can really be trusted to provide sound advice on what is attainable for you. It might be a professional counselor such as a psychologist or job coach. For others, it may be a minister, teacher, or trusted relative.

Closely related is the issue of being relevant. A relevant goal is one that fits the situation. For many students taking this course, an immediate relevant goal is to earn an "A". A more far reaching goal, yet relevant, goal is to eventually obtain a managerial position in your field of accounting marketing, etc.

We all need to put a time frame on our goals. What do you want to be doing at ages 30, 40, 50, 60, and 70? If you have a goal of earning a master's or doctoral degree, aim for a specific graduation date. Consider a deadline your friend. Most of us are natural procrastinators. Do not consider yourself a failure if your PhD is completed at age 41 rather than 40. However, if you did not set the target at 40, or some specific date, then it is unlikely you will get there at all.

I have learned that success is to be measured not so much by the position that one has reached in life as by the obstacles which he has overcome while trying to succeed.

—*Booker T. Washington (1856–1915), author of* Up From Slavery

Many people finally get specific about a date to retire. Financial planners typically ask their clients when they hope to retire and what sort of a lifestyle they hope to maintain with their retirement funds. Why do we get so specific about a date to retire and fail to set target dates for so many other important milestones? We are not really a failure when we miss the target date. Life requires more flexibility than that. We need to set the date so we have a clearer target. If we have to move the target from time to time, so what? At least we have a target. We aren't aimless.

What Matters in the End?

What do you want others to say about you when your career is over? Assume you have reached the end of your career. Looking back over your career, what do you hope you will see? How will you measure it? What achievements will make your feel proud?

Summary

To make a difference as a manager and leader you need to know how to obtain and use power ethically. Large organizations resist change, so power is needed to overcome that resistance to change. There are several forms of power, but most people gain power through long hours, hard work, and gaining results. Do not shy away from power. Instead learn how to use it to produce positive change for yourself and others.

All men seek one goal: success or happiness.
The only way to achieve true success is to express yourself completely in service to society.
First, have a definite, clear, practical ideal—a goal, an objective.
Second, have the necessary means to achieve your ends—wisdom, money, materials and methods.
Third, adjust all your means to that end.

—*Aristotle, Greek philosopher and student of Plato*

Questions for Discussion

1. What is your attitude toward power? Do you shy away from it, or grab for it? What do you want to do with power once you have it?
2. What abuses of power have you experienced at work or school? What steps might you take to make sure your ambition for power doesn't turn into arrogance and abuse of power?
3. As you consider your personal development goals, what roles will there be for earning, using, maintaining, and giving up of power? What steps will you take to increase your chances of obtaining the power you will need?

Chapter 14

Small Business Management

Have you ever thought about starting your own business? Do you wonder how others have done so? What does it take to become a successful small business owner? Is managing a small business different from managing a huge one? This chapter addresses these issues.

What Is a Small Business?

A *small business* is typically defined as one with fewer than 100 employees and independently owned and operated. An *entrepreneurial venture* is defined as a new business having rapid growth and high profitability as its primary objectives. Not all small business owners are focused on growth and high profitability, but instead seek a comfortable niche that provides adequate financial support for their family but exists "under the radar" so as not to attract harsh competition from large companies. An *entrepreneur* is a person who pursues lucrative new business opportunities. An *intrepreneur* is someone who works to create new business ventures while working inside an existing large company. A *big box store* is used to describe huge retail stores such as Walmart that typically have very large but plain looking stores and compete largely by forcing their suppliers to cut their prices and by selling standard products in large volume at low prices. Big box stores make it an especially difficult challenge to manage a small store of the same type in the same neighborhood. To be successful running a small business, it is usually best to focus on some niche offering a unique product or service not offered by the big box store.

Small Business Administration (SBA)

The Small Business Administration of the U.S. government is a great source of helpful information for anyone considering the start of a new business (see http://sba.gov). It provides information on how to find loans and grants, how to register your business, how to obtain licenses and permits, how to find exporting opportunities, plus much more. Free online training is also available on topics such as starting a business, managing a business, financing a business, contracting with the government, and disaster assistance.

Service Corps of Retired Executives (SCORE)

SCORE is partially funded by the SBA as a nonprofit association dedicated to educating entrepreneurs and helping small businesses start, grow, and succeed. Volunteers have served as experienced mentors to small business owners for more than 40 years. According to their website (see http://www.score.org), they currently have over 13,000 volunteers in 364 chapters throughout the United States and its territories. SCORE offers free training and workshops on such topics as accounting and budgeting, government contracting, business planning, cash flow management, financing, human resources, international trade, legal issues, management, sales, plus technology and computers. You can sign on to their national website and use it to locate a chapter near you.

Myths about Starting a Business

You have probably heard all sorts of tall tales about how risky it is to start a new business and about how rich some entrepreneurs have become by taking huge gambles based on some new idea or product. In 2010 the Columbia Pictures movie *Social Network* depicts Harvard undergraduate student and computer programming genius Mark Zuckerberg creating Facebook. About six years later, Zuckerberg became the world's youngest billionaire. The movies like to tell an exciting story of a big gamble that pays off in billions, but how common is this?

Most Startups Fail. There are all sorts of reports about the high percentage of new business failures. Figures as high as 2 out of 3 new business ventures failing within 3 years scare many from even seriously considering starting a new business. However, some of those statistics are questionable. For example, if a researcher looks at the Yellow Pages to get company names and then checks those same pages three years later and finds some business names no longer listed, he should not claim each no-longer-listed business as a failure. Some businesses change their name as they grow larger; it is not a failure for a small business to become a big business. Others are purchased by larger firms at a price that makes the person who started the business very rich; hardly a failure from the point of view of the newly rich entrepreneur.

In both cases, the person who started the business may consider his or her efforts a huge success even though, strictly speaking, the original business no longer exists. In other cases, the entrepreneur does fail several times before hitting on a successful combination of factors that produce a profitable business. So, the truth is that many startups do fail, but the percentage that fail are not as high as many reports have stated. Also, many entrepreneurs who failed in their early attempts to grow a successful business eventually did succeed, especially if they were able to learn important lessons from their failures.

Failure is simply the opportunity to begin again, this time more intelligently.

—Henry Ford

Only Rich People Can Start a New Business. Many new businesses are started by people with very little money of their own. Often they start with their own savings and then use their credit cards, family, friends, and a second mortgage on their home to get the business going. An *angel investor* is defined as an investor who provides financial backing for small business startups or entrepreneurs. Angel investors are typically family members or friends who can provide one-time injections of seed money or ongoing support to carry the startup company through difficult times. After some initial success, some get funding from venture capitalists. *Venture capital* is money provided by a group of wealthy investors, investment banks, or other financial institutions representing groups of individual investors who pool their funds and seek to invest those funds into small businesses with perceived long-term growth potential. Venture capitalists differ from angel investors in that the angel invests primarily in the *person* starting the business, whereas the venture capitalist is primarily concerned with owning a part of a company with high growth potential. To the person who started the company, the downside is that venture capitalists typically insist on having a say in company decisions and a portion of the ownership of the company. In contrast, when the small business owner pays back a loan, then he or she is no longer financially beholden to the people who provided the loan. However, whether the initial funds are borrowed or are raised through investors who become part owners, it is often possible for a person who is not rich to start a new business. The key is to be able to convince others that the business has a high potential for growth. Writing a good business plan (to be described later) is key to convincing investors that this startup has great potential. So, do not assume you have to be rich to start a new business and do not assume you are doomed to failure if you are not able to obtain millions from venture capitalists. Many successful businesses were started on a shoestring.

Anyone Can Be Successful with a Small Business. While it is true that almost anyone can start a new business, it is much harder to keep it going and grow it into a truly successful business venture. Running a successful small business involves much more than just having a good idea, a patent for a new product, or a service that customers want or need. Of course, all those things are important, but to go beyond starting a business requires some knowledge of the topics typically included in a college business curriculum, such as accounting, marketing, finance, management, and information systems. There have been cases where people have learned all these topics on their own without going to a business college and there are cases where the business entrepreneur hired experts in each of those fields. However, many successful small business owners took advantage of the knowledge they gained as a business major in college. There is no guarantee, but you can increase your odds of being successful by first learning all you can about such basic business topics as accounting, finance, marketing, management, and information systems.

The customer is not always right; but the customer is always the customer.

—Russ Vernon, successful entrepreneur of West Point Market

Entrepreneurs Are Their Own Boss. Some entrepreneurs began their professional career working within a large corporation, and after a few years, they sought a way to escape from the feeling their boss was too controlling. However, when you are running your own business you will still have to deal with customers, suppliers, investors, and many others who, to some extent, "boss" you around. If your primary goal in starting a new business is to escape from having to get along with lots of other people, then a startup business, especially one that deals with many customers, is not a good option. Instead of thinking of starting a new business in order to escape from being bossed around, it is better to think of it as an exciting challenge. Learn how to get along with people. Your customer can easily take his or her business to your competitor.

Entrepreneurs Are Gamblers. Most successful small business owners are not gamblers—that is, if you define a gambler as someone who takes very high risks against the odds. Instead, small business owners carefully evaluate the risks and the potential rewards and make sensible decisions based on as much information as they can reasonably obtain in the time available. Most are confident of their own abilities, but seldom take unnecessary or foolish risks. Don't be fooled by what you see in the movies or on television; remember that is all about drama. The real life of an entrepreneur is one of calculated risk, not foolhardy gambling.

Success in business requires training and discipline and hard work. But if you're not frightened by these things, the opportunities are just as great today as they ever were.

—David Rockefeller, member of the wealthy and influential Rockefeller family of New York

If You Have Enough Start Up Capital, You Can't Miss. Of course, you will need enough startup capital to get your business through the first several months until the business is bringing in enough revenue to at least equal your expenses, the so-called break-even point. However, having too much capital at the start may cause you to be somewhat reckless. Instead you need to control the money, especially cash, as though it were as precious as diamonds or gold, because it is. In the long run, the true source of money for any business is not from startup investors, bankers, friends, or anyone other than the customer. Every dollar a business has, started out in the hands of a customer.

If you are starting up a new business and you have not been thoroughly trained in accounting, one of the first people you employ must be an accountant or the services of an accounting firm. Understanding the flow of money through a business is as necessary to a responsible business manager as understanding the flow of blood through the human body is to a responsible medical doctor.

Entrepreneurs Must Have a Genius IQ. It does help to have a strong mind, but being smart in school and being smart in business are not exactly the same thing. Successful entrepreneurs seem to have a good sense about what it takes to make a business a success. Studies do not show successful entrepreneurs to be much different in IQ than the rest of the population; their IQ follows the bell-shaped normal curve with most entrepreneurs having an IQ rather close to the average of the population in general. Many are very good, however, at understanding what customers want and need and at dealing with people successfully. In a few cases, the entrepreneur needs to have a particular talent, such as Mark Zuckerberg's talent for computer programming. But in most cases, the entrepreneur is not a genius. As their business is just starting up, many spend extremely long hours at work, but as the business grows and the founder is able to hire sufficient help, studies do not show that successful entrepreneurs work longer hours or endure more stress than others. So, you don't have to be a genius to be a successful entrepreneur, but it helps to have the courage to strike out on your own.

Marks of the Successful Entrepreneur

We have examined several myths about entrepreneurs, but what are some characteristics common to successful entrepreneurs? Research shows what stands out the most is the strong desire to have their own business. This desire is even stronger than their interest in the particular product or service their current business offers. A dedicated entrepreneur, if he or she fails with one product or service, will simply try another. It is not the product or service that is most important; it is the business. The entrepreneur strives to get and keep customers. In the long run, business is about trust and relationships, so the successful entrepreneur, over the long run, will focus on being trustworthy and upon building lasting relationships, especially with customers.

Studies of successful entrepreneurs indicate they enjoy the challenge. Some have wanted to be a successful business owner from a very young age, but most have first worked for someone else and that experience caused them to want to be more than an employee. They want a piece of the action. They want their success to depend on their ability to attract and keep customers and to run the business profitably. They are often motivated by the hope for, in the long term, a large profit, but some actually prefer to make less money and enjoy

> *It is an ill wind indeed that doesn't blow somebody some good.*
>
> *—Source unknown*

a higher quality of life than what they experienced as an employee within a large corporation. In a large corporation, it is often difficult to see the connection between how hard you work and what talents you bring to the workplace and the resulting success or failure of the business. The owner of a small business can see that relationship much more clearly and can take pride in guiding the startup business into a long-term successful business enterprise.

Successful entrepreneurs are constantly looking for opportunities that could be turned into successful business ventures. When they see a new breakthrough in technology, they see a new business opportunity. When they see changes in the demographic makeup of a community, they see opportunities to offer new products or services to those coming into the community. When they see calamities caused by economic failures, extreme weather, or even natural disasters such as fires or earthquakes, they see business opportunities. That does not mean they are unfeeling for those hurt by disasters; instead, they look beyond the sadness and see opportunities. These opportunities may, in the long run, be more helpful for the victims of a disaster than the sympathy and charity of others.

Consider Franchising

A *franchise* is defined as a legal contract between a successful business and an individual business manager seeking to start the same type of business in a new location. To the new business owner/operator, a franchise offers the business expertise and brand recognition of the well-established business. For example, if you become a franchisee of a McDonald's restaurant, your local restaurant gains from the millions McDonald's spends each year advertising. Also, McDonald's provides training and support and a set of business plans and procedures that have proven highly successful.

McDonald's currently has over 2,400 franchisees in the United States owning and operating over 13,000 restaurants. According to the McDonald's website at http://www.mcdonaldsfranchise.org, a prospective owner of a McDonald's franchise must first be able to raise a minimum of $750,000 from cash in hand, securities and debentures, or real estate, as long as the funds have not been obtained with a personal residence as collateral. McDonald's wants to make sure their new owner/operator has enough startup money to get the new restaurant going. They also expect the franchise candidate to have prior experience operating a restaurant. Of course there are many other franchise opportunities that are not as costly and restrictive as McDonald's, but it is a good idea to learn as much as you can from one of the most successful franchise systems on the planet.

> *McDonald's doesn't confer success on anyone. It takes guts and staying power to make it with one of our restaurants. A total commitment of personal time and energy is the most important thing. You must be willing to work hard and concentrate exclusively on the challenge of operating that restaurant.*
>
> *—Ray Kroc, founder of McDonald's*

Consider Internet Opportunities

Too many people only consider the technical issues of setting up a snazzy website on the Internet and fail to think through exactly how they are going to make money using the Internet. Amazon.com is a great example of a company that uses the Internet to sell books. Recently, it has branched out to sell many more items and get those items to customers quickly. Google.com provides a search service, but makes its money by selling ads that pop up in front of the person's search. The ads that appear are based on the item the person is searching for. eBay used the Internet as an intermediary putting buyers and sellers "together" electronically and charging the seller a commission. eBay does not take ownership of the items that are for sale; they are only an electronic auction house. Amazon.com, Google.com, and eBay.com are examples of spectacular success at using the Internet to implement a highly profitable business plan. Several major newspapers have not been as successful at attempting to charge users for the items they put on their websites. The culture of the Internet is that news items should be immediate and free. People hate to pay for something they have previously been getting for free. Remember, the challenge of using the Internet as a key element of your business plan is not so much the technical issues, which may be considerable, but rather figuring out how to make a buck. That takes business know-how, not just computer know-how.

Causes of Entrepreneurial Failure

There are many reasons for business failures, but the following is a brief discussion of some of the most common.

Selecting a Business with a High Rate of Failure. Have you noticed how often new restaurants open and then close within a year or so? Many people with no business education and no actual experience running a restaurant seem to think they can run a restaurant simply because they frequently eat at a restaurant. It really is a difficult and risky business. Studies regarding the failure rate of restaurants vary from 90% failure rate within the first year to 27%. However, even some of the more conservative estimates suggest approximately 70% of restaurants that opened for business a decade ago failed within that ten-year period. Among the reasons suggested are: the location wasn't right, the menu didn't work, costs were out of control, or the expected volume of customers just never developed. According to a recent study of Small Business Administration loan failure rates by industry code, some of the industries with the highest rate of failure (loan default rates above 30%) are family clothing stores, gambling, doll and stuffed toy manufacturing, passenger car leasing, mortgage and nonmortgage loan brokers, photographic equipment and supplies wholesalers, and the champion with a SBA loan default rate of 74.9% was shellfish fishing (see http://opendata.socrata.com/Business/SBA-Loan-Failure-Rate-by-NAICS-Industry-Code/hc6g-7b34). A word to the wise: Do not even think about going into the shellfish fishing business, especially if there are any BP or Exxon deep sea oil drilling rigs nearby.

Starting in Bad Economic Times. The recent years have been exceptionally difficult in terms of obtaining loans to start or expand a small business. Many banks and other financial organizations have had to recover from the high rate of defaults on home mortgages, and several are only beginning to recover to the point where they can loan out money. The optimism of the 1990s and early 2000s has given way to a much more cautious attitude. However, on the positive side, the costs of buying a building are now at a bargain-basement level, and interest rates are at or near all-time lows. Certain businesses, such as new home construction, have been especially hard hit and will take several years to recover. So, be aware of economic conditions and weigh all the pros and cons. Do not think that it is impossible to start a new business during a recession. There are many businesses in this country that trace their birth to the days of the Great Depression of the 1930s.

> *A wise person should have money in their head, but not in their heart.*
>
> *—Jonathan Swift, 18th-century satirist*

Poor Controls, Especially the Misuse of Funds. It is sometimes difficult for the owner/manager/founder of a business to separate his or her personal funds from that of the business. For many well-established family-owned businesses, it is common to see several family members driving cars owned by the family business, vacation homes owned by the family business, and trips that are part vacation and part business, paid for with business monies. For the startup, it is best to keep a strict accounting of the funds that are directly linked to the business operations. When business is good and hope is running high, it is easy for some family member to get carried away with expenditures for cars, boats, planes, and multiple houses. Most businesses experience swings similar to the ups and downs of the economy in general, and a good small business manager watches over the business funds carefully and makes certain there are sufficient funds saved and set aside to cover upcoming loan repayments, continued costs of expansion, or drops in revenue caused by any downswing in sales.

The other problem that often arises regarding money is the thought that nothing else matters. Money should be thought of as a tool, rather than an end in itself. In business, the accounting system does keep track of money and provides a type of scorecard showing how successful or unsuccessful the organization is with regard to net profit. However, someone who can think of nothing else other than maximizing profit often gets into trouble in areas of ethics or in personal relationships that suffer, because the person has forgotten the importance of family and friends and the critical need for the businessperson to have a reputation of trustworthiness.

You Find You Do Not Enjoy It. Working for yourself, being your own boss, and getting a piece of the action may have all been thoughts that seemed highly important as you entered the world of entrepreneurship. However, some fledgling entrepreneurs find that after a few years, they simply do not enjoy it. They find they are working at the business almost all the time and have little time left for family, friends, exercise, and leisure. They become consumed by the business, and while it may have been stimulating at first, it gradually becomes nothing but a heavy burden. Instead of feeling secure financially, the business owner may feel the constant pressure of needing enough cash to meet the weekly payroll, pay suppliers, and pay all the city, county, state, and federal taxes. While it may have been difficult dealing with a boss at the large corporation, it can also be difficult to deal with demanding customers, employees who do not seem to care about providing great customer service, suppliers who demand their money quickly and threaten to stop deliveries when they payments are late, investors who expect a high return on their investment and a say in the major decisions, and in the case of a family business, other family members who can prove difficult even without the added complications of a family business.

The Business Plan

Most college courses on small business management devote a major part of the curriculum to the writing of a comprehensive business plan. The business plan should tell a compelling story about your business. It should spell out who will be doing what, when, where, how, and why. Most of the people you will want to read your business plan will be busy people, so your plan needs to be focused and clear. It is not about the number of pages, the fancy cover, or fancy PowerPoint slides. Instead, it should be specific about your business objectives and goals and the general parameters that will guide your organization. It should answer the question of how this business will be different from other businesses in the same industry. While many people write such a plan with the objective of raising money to get the business started, many say the most important thing it accomplished was to force them to be logical and disciplined in their approach to starting a business. Finally, a good business plan should be a living document. It should not just sit on a shelf but instead be updated at least once a year. Major corporations that have been in business for over a hundred years use a strategic business plan to help guide the corporation. A business plan is not just for the startup period, but for the entire life of the business.

> *It's good to have money and the things that money can buy, but it's good too to check up once in a while and make sure that you haven't lost the things that money can't buy.*
>
> *—George Horace Lorimer, American journalist and author*

According to the Small Business Administration, a business plan should have, as a minimum, the following major sections:

1. Executive Summary.
2. Business Description and Vision.
3. Definition of the Market.
4. Description of the Products and Services.
5. Organization and Management.
6. Marketing and Sales Strategy.
7. Financial Management.

Greatness is not achieved by never failing but by rising each time we fall.

—Confucius

For additional details and a step-by-step walk-through for writing a business plan, see http://web.sba.gov/busplantemplate/BizPlanStart.cfm#. You can even register for a free online course called "How to Prepare a Business Plan."

Intrapreneurship—Fostering Entrepreneurship within a Large Business

Some large business organizations have successfully created an entrepreneurial spirit within their large business organizational structure. For many business students, this may be a good way to go. The large business provides the financial support and business know-how along with the freedom and encouragement to pursue new business ventures in a way that will make both the large business and the individual a reasonable profit if the venture proves successful. Usually, the employee who came up with the new idea for the business gets to share in the earnings. He or she does not get 100% of those earnings, but they also do not have to shoulder all of the risk. Corporations such as 3M, Google, Apple, and many others have a reputation for supporting a creative environment where innovation is recognized, nurtured, and rewarded. In addition to rewarding good ideas, such companies understand that innovation is self-rewarding. Being perceived as an expert by peers and management is a powerful intrinsic reward. Being allowed to fail is also important. Driving out fear in the workplace can produce an atmosphere where people are free to think creatively and run with innovative ideas. Of course, all business organizations impose some limits on such activities, but those that see the importance of building a culture conducive to innovation and new business development within an existing and supportive business framework often provide both the benefits of the big, well-established business organization and the benefits of the small, startup business, striving to become big and profitable.

Summary

This chapter defined a small business as one with less than 100 employees that is independently owned and operated. An entrepreneurial venture is a new business having growth and high profitability as primary objectives. An entrepreneur is a person who pursues lucrative new business opportunities. An intrepreneur creates new business ventures while working inside an existing large business. Small business managers must compete against big box stores by finding a niche, such as offering unique products or special services not available in big box stores. The Small Business Administration is a branch of the U.S. federal government. The SBA exists to help citizens start and grow their small businesses. SCORE is the Service Corps of Retired Executives, providing free advice from seasoned business owners and managers. There are several myths about small businesses that anyone considering starting a business should recognize. It is not true that most startups fail, that only rich people can start new businesses, that anyone can be successful, that entrepreneurs are their own boss and do not have to take orders from anyone, that entrepreneurs are wild gamblers, if you have enough startup capital you can't fail, and it takes a genius to be a successful entrepreneur. A good business plan can be a big help in laying out exactly what your startup is all about and why anyone should want to invest in your new venture.

Questions for Discussion

1. Have you already started a small business or are seriously considering doing so? If so, what are your biggest challenges? How do you plan to address those challenges?
2. Describe the differences between an entrepreneur and an intrepreneur. What advantages might there be to being one or the other?
3. Why do some small business owners prefer to borrow money rather than take money from venture capitalists?

Chapter 15

Global Business Management

It has been said that arguing against globalization is like arguing against the laws of gravity.

—Kofi Annan (1938–), former secretary-general of the United Nations

Until about 20 years ago, the topic of global business management was not a major concern among American business schools. However, the past 20 years has changed all that. Today, most major businesses are global, and anyone going into the field of business management must be aware of how business is conducted on a worldwide scale. Are you ready to "go global?" What does "going global" mean? Is a global manager any different from an American manager? This chapter looks at some of the basic concepts of global business management.

What Is a Global Business?

There is not total agreement on the definition of several terms related to global business management. In general, *international business* is used to define a business that is primarily located in its home country, such as the United States, but has branch offices, and perhaps factories, in several overseas locations.

A *multinational business* is more heavily involved in business outside its home country with subsidiaries in several countries. A *global business* views the world as one market and itself as a global citizen. It operates all around the world and will make its decisions about hiring, location of plants, and serving customer needs without regard to national borders. Imagine a world without borders and you are beginning to think like a global manager.

The move toward the global business model has profound impact upon the education and experience expected of you if your goal is to become a global business manager. If you were enrolled 20 to 30 years ago in a college program designed to help you with a career in international business, your first decision would have to be which country were you planning to be in. If you planned a career working in Germany, you curriculum would include several courses in the German language, plus courses in German culture, geography, and government. If your choice had been France, then of course you would study French. It was generally accepted that in order to do business in a foreign country, you had to be able to converse in the language of that country. Today, it is still recommended that you learn a foreign language, but a global business manager may be in Germany on Monday, France on Tuesday, Spain on Wednesday, and swing by for meetings in Japan on the way back home to America for the weekend. The next week may include three or four still different countries, and in all cases the language used in the conduct of business would most likely be English. Some business leaders have suggested to today's business schools that if they require any foreign language of business students, it should be Mandarin (Chinese) or Russian instead of the more traditional Spanish, German, French, and Italian.

> *One's destination is never a place, but a new way of seeing things.*
>
> *—Henry Miller (1891–1980), American novelist*

Other business leaders have advised business schools to focus more on teaching students the major global trading associations and the issues businesses face as they strive to obtain sustainable competitive advantage in the complex and ever-changing global marketplace. As one executive put it, "I want the people we hire for our global operations to be able to say something intelligent about how business is done globally in at least one language and it would be okay if that language were English." However, a student with foreign language credit on their college transcript appears to most potential employers to be more interested in global issues than the student who has never taken a foreign language course and has never been outside the U.S. It is not the particular language or the particular foreign country visited in an international exchange program that is so important. Instead, it is important to show that you are sincerely interested in things outside the United States and are willing to leave the comforts of home and spend time in another country.

Why Businesses Go Global

American businesses go global to access new customers. For example, if your business has been operating in the United States for many years and has achieved a market share of 20%, but that market share has been steady or decreasing despite all your efforts to increase marketing, improve your product, and lower your price, then most business leaders will consider expanding into new markets. For many U.S. firms, the likely first step is to export into Canada, because Canada is so close and their language and business practices are so similar. After Canada a logical next choice is Mexico. Many Americans, especially in the Southwest, already speak Spanish and Mexico is close by. Often the next step is into Great Britain and then the rest of Europe.

Over the past two decades, the opportunity to reach customers in Russia and China has excited many American businesses. According to China Daily, the population of China now exceeds 1.341 billion (see http://www.chinadaily.com.cn). Imagine selling just one item to every person in China and you can imagine why so many American business leaders are trying to expand into China. According to the Russian census conducted in 2010, there are approximately 142,905,200 people living in Russia in October 2010. During the decades that both Russia and China were under total Communist control, American businesses were heavily restricted with regard to doing business in either country. Also, during most of the past century, the poverty in both countries was so severe that only a very few Russians or Chinese would have been able to afford American-produced goods and services. Today, some, but not all, restrictions have been lifted and many more Russians and Chinese have sufficient income to purchase items produced anywhere in the world. Other countries that have recently provided new opportunities include India and Brazil; together, these countries are referred to as BRIC (Brazil, Russia, India, and China) or the "Big Four" in terms of newly advanced economic development.

> *Globalization has changed us into a company that searches the world, not just to sell or to source, but to find intellectual capital—the world's best talents and greatest ideas.*
>
> *—Jack Welch (1935–)*

In addition to seeking new customers, American businesses go global to achieve lower costs per unit, either by producing their products with lower-priced raw materials, lower-priced labor, or lower transportation costs. Once a business has learned how to make a particular product and has invested in the equipment to make it, much of the costs are "sunk." A *sunk cost* is money you can't get back. It has already been spent and cannot be recovered. A *fixed cost* is something that costs approximately the same whether you are making just a few units or thousands. *Variable costs*, in contrast, increase per unit produced. Variable costs change as sales change; fixed costs do not. If, for example, you are making a chair out of wood, the raw material of wood will vary depending on the number of chairs you make. However, the investment in the machines used to prepare the wooden parts will have a fixed cost no matter whether you make 100 chairs per month or 1,000. So, if you can expand your market overseas and can therefore make better use of your sunk investment in machinery to manufacture your chairs or whatever product you make, then you are getting better economies of scale. Furthermore, you are capitalizing on your core competencies. Your craftsmen are especially skilled at making wooden chairs and you may as well have them making 1,000 chairs as 100. Also, expanding your business into several different countries spreads your risk. If one country is having bad economic times, perhaps another country will be having good economic times. In general, it is not a good idea to put all your eggs in one basket; spread them out to minimize risk. The same holds true for many businesses. Going global increases your market potential and is often worth the increased complexity.

Steps in Going Global

Most experienced global managers suggest you take it slow. Going global is a complex and risky matter, and going too fast may not allow your business enough time to learn how to deal with each country properly.

Step 1 Exporting. Most American firms begin their ventures into global business by simply starting to sell what they produce in the United States to customers in foreign countries. Exporting allows you to reach a bigger market for the products you are currently producing. You keep control of your company's research and development, design, and production decisions instead of turning them over to someone in a foreign country. You will likely need to make a contractual agreement with a company in the foreign country to distribute and sell your products in that country. It would be too expensive for your company to build or purchase manufacturing and retailing facilities in the overseas country, especially since you are just testing the market for your product in that country.

> *Globalization and free trade do spur economic growth, and they lead to lower prices on many goods.*
>
> *—Robert Reich (1946–), former secretary of labor under President Bill Clinton*

A major consideration for exporting is likely to be tariffs. A *tariff* is a tax or fee a country charges to a business importing products into that country. It is usually done to protect the local businesses that may be producing and selling the same or similar products. Politicians often campaign with the promise they will protect the local citizens (voters) from the nasty foreigners by putting a tariff on all items crossing the border. For example, several U.S. business leaders have charged companies in Japan and elsewhere with exporting Japanese steel into the United States below cost (called "dumping") to hurt the U.S. steel industry. U.S. politicians, anxious to get the votes of steelworkers, pass laws putting tariffs on steel coming into the United States from Japan and on Japanese products made of steel. In return, Japan and other countries impose tariffs on various American products being exported from the United States to Japan. This "war" of tariffs can continue until it is no longer profitable to export. Many of the global trade associations we will discuss later were formed to reduce or eliminate such tariffs and to produce fair trade agreements between countries. See http://www.export.gov for free advice about getting into the export business and information about the various tariffs currently in place.

Step 2 Cooperative Contracts. The next logical step in going global is to contract with a firm in the foreign country to make your product there. There are lots of types of such contracts, but two basic ones are licensing and franchising. When you give a company in a foreign country a *license* to make your product, you let them manufacture your product and sell it and you simply collect a royalty (small fee) on each item they sell. With a *franchise*, in contrast, you make a contract with a foreign company to make your product exactly as you tell them to. You would use the franchise if you want total control over how your product is made. The franchisee in the foreign country assumes almost all of the risk. It would be better to use the licensing approach if you have valuable technical know-how but no international capabilities or resources to enter the foreign market. A licensing agreement has the potential for high income, but you must be able to trust the licensee. The franchising approach is better when you have a service or retailing business, and it is important that you train the franchisee's staff to serve the customers in the way your company has built its reputation for superior customer service. The foreign franchisee bears most of the costs and risks of establishing the foreign location. Examples of worldwide franchise operations include McDonald's, Yum! Brands, and Hilton.

Step 3 Strategic Alliances. The next step would be to put together a strategic alliance, often called a joint venture. A *joint venture* is defined as a legal agreement between two or more companies to form a third company to work together to accomplish some specific goal such as building a particular product. Joint ventures have proven difficult to maintain. Often they are compared to a marriage and we all know that, unfortunately, many marriages today end in divorce. With companies, the arguments that often break up the joint venture center around the differences in corporate culture. For example, one company may have a culture of working directly with potential customers to build a product to the specifications the customer demands, while another may have a culture of building a large inventory of their product and then using mass marketing to sell from inventory. The first company has a culture of production, while the second has a culture of marketing. They both may be making similar products, but the two approaches are very different. The *production-oriented company* will highly value the engineering and manufacturing side of the business, whereas the *marketing-oriented company* will put a higher priority on advertising and sales. Two examples of initially successful joint ventures that are no longer operating as joint ventures are Hero Honda and Sony Ericsson. The Hero company of India joined with Honda of Japan to make motorbikes. Sony of Japan joined with Ericsson of Sweden to make mobile phones. After both joint ventures operated for a few years, both decided to restructure. Joint ventures are challenging at best.

Step 4 Wholly Owned Affiliates. A *wholly owned affiliate* is defined as a contractual agreement between two companies where one company, called the *parent*, wholly owns the other company that is located in another country. For example, Honda Motors of America has an automotive manufacturing

If GE's strategy of investment in China is wrong, it represents a loss of a billion dollars, perhaps a couple of billion dollars. If it is right, it is the future of this company for the next century.

—Jack Welch

plant in Marysville, Ohio, U.S.A., that is 100% owned by Honda Motors of Japan. The people in Ohio appreciate this arrangement because it produces jobs that are much needed for citizens of Ohio. Honda is able to save much of the transportation costs of making cars in Japan and shipping them to the United States. Often, such arrangements also avoid tariffs that would be imposed if the product were made outside the country. Another example is Ford Motor of Germany, which manufactures Ford cars in Germany but is 100% owned by Ford Motor Co. in Detroit, Michigan, U.S.A. Using the wholly owned affiliate approach offers many advantages, but the costs of building manufacturing plants outside a company's home country often are measured in the hundreds of millions of dollars. As a result, this is not a good idea until the market for the product in the foreign country has already been proven by using one or more of the previous steps described above.

Step 5 Global New Ventures. Finally, some companies start out with a global strategy. This requires a huge initial investment, but it allows the company to bring new products to many foreign markets at the same time. Step 1 Exporting could be compared to putting your big toe into the bath to test the water, while Step 5 Global New Ventures is like jumping into deep water from the start. To make this approach work, the founders must develop and communicate a global vision that is especially compelling to investors because the initial investment is so high.

Over the past few decades, several international trade agreements have been formed that students of global business management need to understand. A few of the largest and most significant are described below.

General Agreement on Tariffs and Trade (GATT)

The General Agreement on Tariffs and Trade (commonly called GATT) was formed shortly after World War II ended. Much of Europe was in ruins. Approximately 60 million people (20 million soldiers and 40 million civilians) had been killed and millions more severely wounded. Manufacturing facilities throughout much of Europe and Japan were in ruins. World War I had ended on November 11, 1918. World War II began in 1939, just 21 years after the end of WW I, and lasted through much of 1945. Europe and much of the rest of the world were looking for ways to avoid a World War III. Perhaps the most well-known organization to emerge out of the end of World War II was the United Nations, but other organizations also were formed to address business issues.

Einstein warned, "I know not with what weapons World War III will be fought, but World War IV will be fought with sticks and stones." Einstein's famous quote points out how terribly important it is to prevent World War III from happening in this era of nuclear weapons. History books often describe the reasons for these major wars in terms of political disagreements between countries and attacks of armies and navies. However, a deeper study often reveals economic and business issues also played a role. Tensions between countries build as competing businesses argue over tariffs, who has the right to fish in which waters, which ships can cross which bodies of water or use particular canals or ports, and which countries have access to critical energy sources such as coal and oil. When one nation refused to pay tariffs they feel are unjustified, the other country may use its navy to impose a blockade of ships coming from that nation. If tariffs and blockades fail to work, then sometimes the next action is one of violence. Citizens get involved because businesses are the source of jobs. When a business is perceived to be unfairly blocked from conducting its business and jobs are lost as a result, tensions between the countries become even worse. Jobs are more than just a source of income for people; jobs are also a source of pride and individual dignity.

The *General Agreement on Tariffs and Trade (GATT)* was signed in 1947, just two years after the end of World War II. It was a multilateral agreement regulating tariffs and trade among nearly 150 countries. The countries agreed to hold a series of meetings called rounds to discuss ways to reduce trade barriers and create fair, comprehensive, and enforceable world trade rules. The eighth round of talks produced the World Trade Organization in 1995.

World Trade Organization

The *World Trade Organization (WTO)* is a global international organization dealing with the rules of trade between nations. The goal of the WTO is to help producers of goods and services, exporters, and importers conduct their business. Headquarters for this organization of over 150 nations are in Geneva, Switzerland. Their functions are to administer WTO trade agreements, provide a forum for trade negotiations, handle trade disputes, monitor national trade policies, provide technical assistance and training for developing countries, and cooperate with other international organizations.

Each time there is a meeting of the WTO membership, demonstrators march and protest, accusing the WTO of favoring the rich and powerful nations at the expense of the poorer ones. Some say the actions of the WTO destroy jobs, ignore concerns for workers' health, and overlook the damage being done to the environment by big business. However, the supporters of the WTO argue that the WTO does not dictate policy, but instead provides a place and a procedure for nations to work out their differences in a peaceful manner. Its main function is to ensure that trade flows smoothly, predictably, and freely around the world. For more details see http://wto.org.

European Union

The *European Union (EU)* is an economic and political union of 28 member states located in Europe. After World War II, several attempts were made to form organizations designed to prevent future wars in Europe and to help the devastated nations rebuild their business and political structures. The first such organization was the European Coal and Steel Community, officially launched in 1950. It involved Belgium, France, Italy, Luxembourg, the Netherlands, and West Germany. In 1957 the Treaty of Rome was signed, creating the European Economic Community. One of the primary goals was to eliminate all import and export duties existing between member states. The membership continued to expand, and in 1993 the European Union was formally established. In 2002 the euro replaced the currencies in 12 of the member states, and since then the euro has been accepted as the official currency in 17 countries. It must be miraculous for anyone that had to struggle through World War I and II in Europe to see these 28 European nations today getting along and working out their differences peacefully. Of course, disputes arise every day. But at least to date, none of the disputes has escalated into a war involving armies, navies, or the air forces of any of the EU nations. Recall that 60 million people died in World War II, so any organization that can reduce the chances of having another war of that magnitude is something to respect. For more details, see the official website of the EU at http://europa.eu/index_en.htm .

North American Free Trade Agreement (NAFTA)

The *North American Free Trade Agreement (NAFTA)* was negotiated by President George H. W. Bush and signed by President Bill Clinton on December 8, 1993, and was officially implemented on January 1, 1994. The goal was to eliminate over the next ten years all trade barriers between the United States, Canada, and Mexico. Today, the controversy still rages with Republicans and Democrats blaming each other for various shortcomings of NAFTA. However, U.S. presidents from both parties have been heavily involved with NAFTA and the agreement continues to be amended 20 years after the original agreements were made. The NAFTA agreement states the objectives are to "eliminate barriers to trade in, and facilitate the cross-border movement of goods and services between the territories of the Parties; promote conditions of fair competition in the free trade area; increase substantially investment opportunities in the territories of the Parties; provide adequate and effective protection and enforcement of intellectual property rights in each Party's territory; create effective procedures for the implementation and application of this Agreement, for its joint administration and for the resolution of disputes; and establish a framework for further trilateral, regional and multilateral cooperation to expand and enhance the benefits of this Agreement." See the official website of NAFTA at http://www.nafta-sec-alena.org/en/view.aspx?x=283.

Association of Southeast Asian Nations (ASEAN)

The *Association of Southeast Asian Nations (ASEAN)* was established on August 8, 1967, in Bangkok, Thailand, by the nations of Indonesia, Malaysia, Philippines, Singapore, and Thailand. Brunei Darussalam joined in 1984, Vietnam in 1995, Lao PDR and Myanmar in 1997, and Cambodia in 1999, so today there are ten member states of ASEAN. As with the other international trading organizations already discussed, ASEAN hopes to promote peace by promoting free trade and improving education, research, and transportation among member states. Much like the nations within Europe, these nations have a long history of wars resulting in millions of deaths. Today, ASEAN is dedicated to peace, stability, and prosperity among these nations. For more details, see the official website of ASEAN at http://www.aseansec.org.

Asia-Pacific Economic Cooperation (APEC)

The *Asia-Pacific Economic Cooperation (APEC)* is an organization of 21 Pacific Rim countries seeking to promote free trade and economic cooperation throughout the Asia-Pacific region. It was established in 1989 at least partially in response to the newly formed European Union and the North American Free Trade Area previously discussed. APEC is the premier Asia-Pacific economic forum. Its goal is to "support sustainable economic growth and prosperity in the Asia-Pacific region by championing free and open trade and investment, promoting and accelerating regional economic integration, encouraging economic and technical cooperation, enhancing human security, and facilitating a favorable and sustainable business environment." See APEC's official website at http://www.apec.org/en.

Central America Free Trade Agreement (CAFTA-DR)

On August 5, 2004, the United States signed the *Dominican Republic-Central America-United States Free Trade Agreement (CAFTA-DR)* with five Central American countries (Costa Rica, El Salvador, Guatemala, Honduras, and Nicaragua) and later the Dominican Republic. The goal was to "create new economic opportunities by eliminating tariffs, opening markets, reducing barriers to services, and promoting transparency." For more details. see http://www.ustr.gov/trade-agreements/free-trade-agreements/cafta-dr-dominican-republic-central-america-fta. Since 2004 several amendments have been made. A continuing issue between the United States and each of the countries in these various international trade agreements is the enforcement of fair and humane treatment of workers and the assurance of safety in the workplace. None of these agreements is perfect, and it is likely that amendments will continue to be made to continue to improve the rights of workers and to preserve the environment.

In addition to these major international free trade associations, a student of global business management needs to understand the World Bank and the International Monetary Fund and the role these organizations play in global business.

The World Bank

Since its beginning in 1944, the *World Bank* has expanded from a single institution to a closely associated group of five development institutions with the goal of the elimination of poverty worldwide primarily by providing loans to poor nations. The World Bank was created at the Bretton Woods Conference in 1944 along with the International Monetary Fund (IMF), to be discussed shortly. Both the World Bank and the International Monetary Fund are based in Washington, D.C., U.S.A.; the World Bank is, by custom, headed by an American, while the IMF is led by a European.

While the World Bank first addressed the need to rebuild France and other nations devastated by World War II, the Marshall Plan of 1947 became the prime approach to helping the European countries, and the World Bank turned more toward non-European countries and eventually focused on the poorest developing countries in the world. A major controversy has been the pressure the World Bank has put on these poorest countries to be fiscally responsible and pay back loans. Some have argued that instead of insisting these extremely poor nations pay back their loans to the World Bank, they should instead focus on feeding the starving, providing medicine to the ill, and educating the illiterate. For more details about the World Bank, see http://www.worldbank.org.

The International Monetary Fund

The *International Monetary Fund (IMF)* is an organization of 188 countries working to foster global monetary cooperation, secure financial stability, facilitate international trade, promote high employment and sustainable economic growth, and reduce poverty around the world. Through its economic surveillance, the IMF monitors the economic health of its member nations alerting them to potential risks and providing advice. It also lends money to countries in difficulty and provides technical assistance and training to help countries improve their economic management. The IMF works cooperatively with other international organizations to promote economic growth and reduce poverty. For more information about the IMF, see its official website at http://www.imf.org.

Summary

Today, many business organizations operate on a global basis with a philosophy that they will hire the best people from anywhere in the globe, will seek customers on a worldwide basis, will locate their facilities anywhere in the world, and in general, will operate almost as though there were no national borders drawn on the globe. This has created a climate of global business management that is highly competitive and rapidly changing. To start on the road to becoming a global business, most U.S. companies first try exporting their goods and services made in the United States to other countries. They progress through several stages, usually involving complicated contractual agreements with business organizations outside the United States. At the extreme, these businesses eventually look at the entire globe as their market area. To be competitive in this global marketplace, today's management students need to learn about how business is done on a worldwide basis. As a start, it is good to examine organizations such as the World Trade Organization and the European Union and financial organizations such as the World Bank. Above all, accept the fact that rapid change is inevitable in the dynamic environment of global business management.

Change favors the prepared mind.

—Louis Pasteur, father of microbiology

Questions for Discussion

1. Distinguish among an international business, a multinational business, and a global business. How does the trend toward global business impact your ability to obtain a career in management?
2. Describe the steps a business typically takes to expand globally. Explain what a tariff is, and why tariffs are such an important consideration for global business expansion.
3. Describe how World War II was such an important factor in the formation of numerous multinational trade agreements.

Chapter 16

Emotional Intelligence For Managers and Leaders

Do you know someone who is brilliant, but just can't seem to get along with people? I'll bet most of you have had a teacher who really knew their stuff, but just couldn't teach it. We've all met people who are academically brilliant, but socially and inter-personally inept. Worse yet, have you ever experienced the feeling yourself? Most of us could use a little work on some aspect of our emotional intelligence. It's especially important for managers and leaders.

Cleverness is not wisdom.

—Euripides (480–406 B.C.), Greek writer of tragedy

According to Daniel Goleman, author of several books about the subject, emotional intelligence is being intelligent about our emotions. What does that mean? Goleman believes it is the capacity for recognizing our own feelings and those of others, for motivating ourselves, and for managing emotions in ourselves and in our relationships. Others have defined emotional intelligence as the ability to monitor and regulate one's own feelings, and to gain confidence in using their feelings responsibly to guide their thoughts and actions.

GREAT managers and leaders work through their emotions, both their own and those of their followers. GREAT leaders inspire us, arouse our passions, and make us feel good about ourselves. The beginning of such a process is to be aware of our feelings and learn to control them intelligently. From that base, you can move on to working with others, and there are practical things you can do to sharpen your emotional intelligence.

To be a GREAT leader, it certainly helps to be smart. But, we have all observed, success does not automatically follow intelligence. In fact, for some people, being smart just makes getting along with others more difficult. Because they are so smart, they feel superior to others, and others sense it and resent it. Perhaps you know someone who, just by the way they roll their eyes or blink their eyelids, gives the impression they are superior to everyone else in terms of intelligence. Most people find such body language a big turnoff. As William Feather, publisher and author, said, "Brains aren't everything, but they're important."

Recent research involving business executives has provided overwhelming evidence that being smart isn't what really separates ordinary performers in management from those who become stars. In 2002, Goleman, Boyatzis, and McKee authored a *New York Times* national best-seller, *Primal Leadership: Realizing the Power of Emotional Intelligence*. It was Goleman's third book on the subject. He notes that it takes an IQ of around 120 to gain admission to most graduate programs such as an MBA, a degree that is often a door-opener for future business leaders. Therefore, most people who enter the ranks of middle to upper management have a relatively high IQ, but within those ranks, there is relatively little variation. However, there is little or no selectivity among MBA programs with regard to emotional intelligence (sometimes abbreviated EQ and at other times EI), so there is a much wider range of emotional intelligence than IQ among managers. Unfortunately, there isn't a widely accepted measure of one's Emotional Quotient (EQ). More recently, Goleman has authored *Social Intelligence: The New Science of Human Relations* (2007), and *Focus: The Hidden Driver of Excellence (2013).*

An analysis of the personality traits that accompany high IQ in men who lack these emotional competencies portrays, well, the stereotypical nerd: critical and condescending, inhibited and uncomfortable with sensuality, emotionally bland. By contrast, men with the traits that mark emotional intelligence are poised and outgoing, committed to people and causes, sympathetic and caring, with a rich but appropriate emotional life—they're comfortable with themselves, others, and the social universe they live in.

—Daniel Goleman

The evidence is clear; for success in business and in life, learn how to intelligently handle your emotions and the emotions of others. EQ is what separates the merely smart from the smart and successful.

While Goleman's books are recent, and the coining of the phrase "emotional intelligence" is no more than 20 years old, the concepts are not new. In fact, Rudyard Kipling summed it up very well in his poem, "If," penned in 1895:

> If you can keep your head when all about you
> Are losing theirs and blaming it on you;
> If you can trust yourself when all men doubt you,
> But make allowance for their doubting too:
> If you can wait and not be tired of waiting,
> Or, being lied about, don't deal in lies,
> Or being hated don't give way to hating,
> And yet don't look too good, nor talk too wise;
>
> If you can dream—and not make dreams your master;
> If you can think—and not make thoughts your aim,
> If you can meet with Triumph and Disaster
> And treat those two impostors just the same:
> If you can bear to hear the truth you've spoken
> Twisted by knaves to make a trap for fools,
> Or watch the things you gave your life to, broken,
> And stoop and build 'em up with worn-out tools;
>
> If you can make one heap of all your winnings
> And risk it on one turn of pitch-and-toss,
> And lose, and start again at your beginnings,
> And never breathe a word about your loss:
> If you can force your heart and nerve and sinew
> To serve your turn long after they are gone,
> And so hold on when there is nothing in you
> Except the Will which says to them: "Hold on!"
>
> If you can walk with crowds and keep your virtue,
> Or walk with Kings—nor lose the common touch,
> If neither foes nor loving friends can hurt you,
> If all men count with you, but none too much:

If you can fill the unforgiving minute
With sixty seconds' worth of distance run,
Yours is the Earth and everything that's in it,
And—which is more—you'll be a Man, my son!

—*Rudyard Kipling*

Surely, if Kipling were alive today, he would insist this wisdom applies to women as well as men. A man or woman with a high EQ is able to "keep their head about them when others are losing theirs and blaming it on you." Leaders need a high EQ, but how do you get one?

Emotional Intelligence—The Neglected Subject in School

If you have read to this point in this book, you have already invested heavily in improving your knowledge base. You have already read about the basic principles and concepts of management and leadership, research concerning leadership, and how to write and speak with leadership skill and style. However, this chapter could be the most valuable part of your education. It could unlock the potential that has been held back by an underdeveloped emotional intelligence.

I found that for jobs of all kinds, emotional competencies were twice as prevalent among distinguishing competencies as were technical skills and purely cognitive abilities combined. In general the higher a position in an organization, the more EI mattered. For individuals in leadership positions, 85 percent of their competencies were in the EI domain.

—*Daniel Goleman*

Do not blame yourself for a lack of understanding of emotional intelligence. The whole area is relatively new, at least as it is applied to work. However, now it is all the rage. Goleman wrote his first book, *Emotional Intelligence*, in 1995 to encourage educators to examine this ignored topic. His main theme was that research was providing strong evidence of the importance of emotional intelligence, yet schools were ignoring it completely. That book struck such a responsive chord; he was encouraged to write a follow-up, *Working with Emotional Intelligence*, in 1998 and *Primal Leadership* in 2002. As of this writing, he has authored six books on the subject, so clearly, Goleman hit upon an idea whose time had come.

WHAT IS EMOTIONAL INTELLIGENCE?

According to research conducted at the Center for Creative Leadership, "Nearly 75% of careers are derailed for reasons related to emotional competencies, including inabilities to handle interpersonal problems, unsatisfactory team leadership during times of conflict, or inability to adapt to change or elicit trust." Those who attempt to define emotional intelligence often use words like wisdom or maturity. But that is not saying enough. It is a combination of awareness and skills that allows people to do the right thing in the right way. It recognizes and breaks down the social barriers that prevent people from following a leader. EQ is often what distinguishes who will be the leader among people who are similar as to IQ.

Robert Cooper and Ayman Sawaf, in their bestselling book, *Executive EQ*, define *emotional intelligence* as the ability to sense, understand, and effectively apply the power and acumen of emotions as a source of human energy, information, and influence. Goleman now suggests emotional intelligence is composed of two very broad categories: (1) personal competence; and (2) social competence. *Personal competence* is composed of self- awareness and self-control. *Social competence* is concerned with social awareness and relationship management. All scholars in this new field seem to agree that the first step toward better EQ is self-awareness. Collectively, the components of IQ plus EQ sum to wisdom, and according to the Greek playwright, Sophocles (496–406 B.C.), "Wisdom is the supreme part of happiness."

Self-Awareness

What does it mean to be self-aware? How well do you know yourself? When you are asked to introduce yourself, what do you say? Do you, like most of us, respond with your job title? When you are asked to further elaborate or tell us more about who you really are, how do you respond?

Our market-driven society tries to convince us we are the car we drive, the clothes we wear, and even the beer we drink. For many outside the United States, we Americans appear to be preoccupied with how we look, how expensive a car we drive, how large is our house, where we travel for vacations, and all the trappings of a society obsessed with materialism. When we stop to think about it, we all understand we really are not the total of all our material possessions, but who are we? The key question to begin your journey toward a healthy EQ is, "Who am I?"

Halt! Who Are You? Where Are You Going? Why Are You Going There?

While in Russia, I was told of an old Russian folktale that is set during the time of the Russian Revolution. A Russian Orthodox priest is walking through the woods on his way to church to pray. A revolutionary soldier jumps into his path, points his rifle at the priest, and shouts, "Halt! Who are you? Where are you going? Why are you going there?"

The priest calmly asks the young soldier, "Son, how much are they paying you?" After the startled young soldier replies how many rubles he was being paid, the priest continues, "Son, I will pay you double that if every day you will stop me just as you have done today and ask me those same three questions."

From time to time, we all need to halt what we are doing and ask who we are, where we are going, and why we are going there. Most of us are too busy trying to simply get through our daily routines to sit back and reflect on those important questions. Yet, how can we expect to lead others when we can't answer those simple questions about ourselves? Let's pretend we have been halted at the point of a gun and have been asked those three questions.

Who Are You?

When many of us are asked who we are, we reply with our job title, but healthy self- awareness requires us to drill deeper. We know we are much more than our job title, and we fully realize job titles change. However, many of us know others who died shortly after retiring or losing their job; they seemed to exist as a person only as long as their job. To many people, especially in America, we are our jobs. Get rid of that thought right now. You are much more than your job.

Many of us define success in terms of the rank, power, and income related to our job. It is to be expected that students, especially students majoring in business, should be focused on gaining successful career positions. But it can be overdone.

Our job title, no matter how important, is not all of who we are. Many of us play several important roles. We are also spouses or significant others. We are fathers, mothers, aunts, uncles, brothers, sisters, and other important members of families. We are friends, neighbors, mentors, citizens, and many more roles. However, I want to ask you to think about who you would be if all those roles were gone. Strip all the exterior things away.

Chip Away What Is Not You

The discovery of self involves drilling down deep inside. Just as Michelangelo created the famous statue, David, by chipping away the marble that was not David, we find ourselves by chipping away all the exterior clutter. It involves asking what values we hold most dear. How do we feel about things? When we strip away all the exterior stuff, who are we at our deepest inner self?

Remember, the first thing the Russian soldier shouted at the priest was, "Halt!" Before we can really examine who we are deep inside, we have to halt the constant bombardment of external stimuli entering our brain. How can we do that?

Some find meditation helps. Many people find it useful to find a quiet place where they can safely turn off all their external senses of sight, hearing, smell, taste, and touch. Imagine that somehow you have lost your ability to hear, see, smell, taste, and touch. Mentally turn off your ability to receive all such external stimuli. When we do that, many people say they still hear voices in their mind chattering away and they falsely assume those voices are who they are deep inside. However, you need to go one step deeper and ask, "Who is listening to those voices?"

Deep within each of us, there is an inner self who listens to the voices of your mind and makes choices. Sometimes artists depict the voices as the devil sitting on one shoulder and your guardian angel on the other. Such images may help you "see" your inner self listening to the pros and cons of issues. The real you listens to the debate and ultimately makes a choice. Unless we are seriously mentally ill, we control those choices. It is a mark of mental illness to feel we are being controlled by voices inside our head. You are not your voices and your voices do not control you. You are the human being making choices after listening to your inner voices.

Try it. Find a place where you can safely turn off all your senses and spend a little quiet time with your inner self. Learn who that human being inside you really is. Give this visit with your inner self some time. It is worth it. After all, if you don't know who you are, how do you expect anyone to want to follow you? In the silence, ask the same questions the soldier asked of the priest. Who am I? Where am I going? Why am I going there? Make a promise to yourself to do this on a regular basis. Make a date with your inner self. Hopefully, you will get to know someone you really like—you. If you see some flaws, don't despair. All humans have them. Some of them you can change, others you must learn to accept.

God, grant us grace to accept with serenity the things that cannot be changed, courage to change the things that should be changed, and the wisdom to distinguish one from the other.

—Reinhold Niebuhr (1894–1962), American Christian theological ethicist

One way to look at who we are is to look at the sum total of choices we have made. Who you are is the human being who listens to the voices in your mind and makes choices based on your core values.

How Do We Spend Our Time? What Does That Tell Us About Who We Are?

Another way to discover secrets about our inner self is to look at where we spend our time. Some people may find they are living too much in the past, present, or future. At various times in our lives, we need to invest in securing a greater future for ourselves and our loved ones. At other times, we need to look back and reflect on what we have accomplished in the past. It is good to make a personal assessment of how we do spend our time and ask if we are ignoring the present to rehash the past or to dream about and prepare for the future.

Experts agree we shouldn't postpone all our happiness until some future state when we have finally achieved the college degree we want, the job we desire, and all the material possessions we covet. On the other hand, saving and preparing for the future, within reason, is healthy.

What many of us fail to do is to take the time to look at how we are handling time. If we say, for example, we really value our relationships with our children, but we really don't spend time with them, who are we kidding? One of the most valuable outcomes of the typical time management course is the requirement to record how you spend your time over a period of several days. The key is to make intelligent decisions based on your self-awareness.

What Are Our Feelings?

Finally, with regard to who you are, EQ experts suggest we take an inventory of our feelings. Males are notoriously bad at this. Feelings are expressions of a combination of emotional states and physical sensations. For example, which feelings do you have right now? Are you happy, sad, afraid, annoyed, angry, inspired, calm, embarrassed, sleepy, or tense? Surely you can't be bored reading this exciting stuff.

Many of us have been taught to hide our feelings. While it is often best to keep some feelings to ourselves, sometimes we get so good at hiding our feelings we even hide them from ourselves, and that is not healthy. Emotional self-awareness is about reading one's own emotions, understanding the effect they are having on ourselves, and using these feelings to guide our choices. Some people call this going with our "gut sense."

What Is Our Intuition or Gut Telling Us?

> *The only real valuable thing is intuition.*
>
> *—Albert Einstein (1879–1955), winner of the Nobel Prize in physics*

Chester Barnard, in his classic 1938 book, *Functions of the Executive*, tells of a soldier in World War I who was trained in mountain climbing. The seasoned soldier came upon a situation where he needed to swing by a rope from one cliff to another. In the middle of the swing, he lost his grip on the rope. As he began to fall to certain death, he somehow managed to catch the rope in his teeth. Nowhere in military mountain-climbing training were soldiers ever taught to catch a rope with their teeth. However, there are parts of our brain, according to Barnard, that act on instinct. He advised executives not to ignore such thoughts.

In our quest to be rational and logical, Barnard says we begin to distrust our instincts. Somehow it doesn't sound scientific enough to say we made a business decision on our gut feelings. But Barnard suggests the seasoned executive may, like the mountain-climbing soldier, have unconsciously developed some thoughts that bypass the normal reasoning process.

Daniel Kahneman, winner of the 2002 Nobel Prize in economics and author of *Thinking Fast and Slow*, refers to our ability to think fast as System 1 and our ability to carefully reason through things using facts and logic as System 2. He is a professor of psychology who is now recognized in the field of economics for calling into question the "Economic Man" concept, which says people make decisions based on

It is always with excitement that I wake up in the morning wondering what my intuition will toss up to me, like gifts from the sea. I work with it and rely on it. It's my partner.

—Jonas Salk (1914–1995), developer of the polio vaccine

the facts and what is in their own best interest. That concept, until Kahneman's research, was a fundamental assumption behind the theory of economics. However, Kahneman and his colleague, Amos Tversky, plowed new ground regarding how human beings, even very smart ones, actually make decisions much more frequently using "fast" thinking.

When survival is at stake, our brain may need to think more quickly than normal reasoning requires. The survival instinct takes over. It seems to work better in the seasoned soldier or experienced executive. We can't really explain how instincts work, but we should be aware of them, and as we become more seasoned and experienced, trust them more in guiding our decisions.

Where Are You Going?

Many people will respond to the question, "Where are you going?" with "I don't know." Do you know where you are going with your life? Doesn't it make sense to ask this question, at least once in a while? Consider it right now. Where do you expect to be with your life in ten, 20, or 30 years?

The Russian soldier stopping the priest at gunpoint probably was merely thinking about where the priest was planning to be in the next few minutes. We need to consider a longer horizon. How can you possibly expect others to follow you if you have no idea of where you are going?

If we look at leadership as an opportunity to make a difference, then we need to ask about that difference. How will we recognize success, or even progress? Where are we going with this power? What personal and societal needs are we addressing? If we somehow acquire all the formal and informal power we desire, what are we going to do with it? Where are we going to apply that leadership power?

The struggle of the male to listen to and respect his own intuition's inner prompting is the greatest challenge of all. His conditioning has been so powerful that it has all by destroyed his ability to be self-aware.

—Herb Goldberg (1937–), author, What Men Still Don't Know about Women, Relationships, and Love

Authority without wisdom is like a heavy axe without an edge, fitter to bruise than polish.

—Anne Bradstreet (1612–1672), British poet

What Choices about Where You Are Going Have You Made Already?

While the future is always somewhat uncertain, one clue as to where we are going is to look at where we have been. You have already made several choices along the road. You chose to get a college degree at a particular school. You have already chosen several aspects of your lifestyle. Perhaps you have already chosen a spouse and whether to have children. You may have chosen the line of work you are in right now, but have decided it is not where you want to be in the prime of your career. Perhaps that's why you are now in college. You have already experienced several turning points in your life, and the choices you made at each one tell you something about who you are and where you are going.

While your path ahead may still take many turns, you have started to develop certain patterns. You have many ideas about your strengths and weaknesses. Some weaknesses you may have decided to attack with the goal of overcoming; others you simply accept. Some childhood dreams, such as becoming an astronaut or president of the United States, you may have put aside. Others are still on your list of possibilities.

Most people simply do not give this enough thought. We have neglected the study of where we have been, the choices we have made, and the likely direction we are headed. To build a healthy self-awareness, we need to ask ourselves these questions and take quiet time to reflect on who we are and where we are going.

The last of the human freedoms is to choose one's attitude in any given set of circumstances

—Viktor Frankl (1905–1907), MD, PhD, psychiatrist and Holocaust survivor and author of Man's Search for Meaning

Why Are You Going There?

After we take an inventory of our feelings, our past choices, how we spend our time, and what we hope for our future, we need to ask, "Why?" Why do you want a college degree? Why do you want to be a leader? Whom do you want to lead? Where do you want them to go? Why are we going there?

When people follow us, we have a responsibility to lead them to a better place. We must be worthy of their trust. When we arrive, whose lives will be improved? What will be the cost of the journey? Will there be others who will suffer from our successes along the way? Is it worth it? What is our cause? Why are you doing this? What is your goal? How will you know when you reach it?

It is not enough to know who you are and where you are going. There must be a purpose to it all. We may not always fully understand our purpose in life, but we must keep struggling to find it, especially in those areas where we are leading others.

> *The reason most people never reach their goals is that they don't define them, learn about them, or even seriously consider them as believable or achievable. Winners can tell you where they are going, what they plan to do along the way, and who will be sharing the adventure with them.*
>
> *—Denis Waitley (1933–),*
> *author of* Seeds of Greatness *and* The Psychology of Winning

Adolph Hitler, Joseph Stalin, Osama bin Laden, and Saddam Hussein were all leaders who led their followers into disaster. History is full of examples of leaders who seemed to care only about their personal physical pleasure. I'm not against your personal pleasure, but that purpose is not sufficient.

To find a good reason to lead, begin with the major problems facing the world. If that is too much for you to handle, begin with the major problems facing some fraction of the world. You will have no problem finding worthy causes. Poverty, illness, illiteracy, violence, and injustice are all easy to find. Furthermore, you will have no problem finding organizations poorly led. However, before you can be a great leader of others, you will need to manage yourself.

> *Those who can command themselves command others.*
>
> *—William Hazlitt, English writer*

SELF-MANAGEMENT

In *Primal Leadership*, Goleman defines *self-management* as the combination of self-control, transparency, adaptability, achievement, initiative, and optimism. As Kipling said in "If," you must have the self-control to keep your head, while all those about you are losing theirs and blaming it on you. A hallmark of an emotionally intelligent leader is one who stays calm and clear-headed during a crisis. You have to be the "go-to guy" when the game is on the line.

Cesar Millan, star of the TV show called *The Dog Whisperer*, grew up on a farm in Mexico where his parents kept a pack of dogs. He noticed that a pack of dogs always has a leader, and he suggests people who own dogs must assume the role of pack leader if they desire well-balanced and obedient dogs in their home. Dogs only follow a leader who is calm and assertive. While I do not suggest people are

Nothing great was ever achieved without enthusiasm.

—Ralph Waldo Emerson (1803–1882), American writer

exactly like dogs, there is some advantage to studying animal behavior rather than people behavior. Generally speaking, animals are unable to pretend, whereas people are great at it. With dogs, what you see represents their honest feelings. Humans are much more complex and often go to extremes to cover up how they truly feel. Some basic concepts about leading dogs also apply to leading people, especially the need for the leader to be calm and assertive.

It is not sufficient to be aware of your emotions; you have to keep them under control— which is not to be confused with suppressing them. It involves using your emotions to elevate your performance to a higher level, instead of letting them disable you. Some leaders think all they need to do is to act a certain way. It is about being, not acting. You have probably experienced leaders who act as though they are kind and caring, but everyone knows it is really just an act.

All major religions teach their faithful to avoid merely the appearance of doing kind works so that we may look good to our fellow humans. Instead, good leaders make their intentions transparent. Transparency means people can see through your actions to your motives. That is a good thing because your motives are simply the way you live out your values. We ought to lead our lives out in the open and abhor secrecy. It is not about looking good. It is about being good and doing good things for others.

Adaptability means you can juggle multiple demands without losing focus or energy. You must be comfortable with the inevitable ambiguities of organizational life. Goleman suggests EI leaders are flexible in adapting to new challenges, nimble in adjusting to fluid change, and limber in their thinking in the face of new data or realities. Emotionally intelligent leaders strive for achievement of worthy and challenging goals. They have high personal standards that drive them to seek continuous improvement in themselves and in those they lead. They constantly want to learn more and teach others. Such leaders enthusiastically take the initiative. They seize opportunities, not hesitating to cut through red tape, bend rules for a greater good, and look for ways to create a better future.

No pessimist ever discovered the secrets of the stars, or sailed to an uncharted land, or opened a new doorway for the human spirit.

—Hellen Keller (1880–1968), first deaf and blind person to earn a BA degree; author of five books

Optimism is a hallmark of emotional intelligence. This optimism is especially apparent when setbacks occur. Optimists roll with the punches, see the opportunity in a threat, and find a way to see the positive side of difficulties. They are not naive. However, they learn from their mistakes and keep coming back. I am not advocating a silly version of optimism or the overlooking of serious problems and truly tragic events. Instead, I do suggest you make every effort to look on the positive side of things.

Also, avoid negative people like the plague—negativity is contagious. Be realistic, but not full of doom and gloom. When you catch yourself saying negative things to yourself, learn to put a halt to it. If you keep telling yourself you are going to fail, it will become a self-fulfilling prophecy. Learn to replace negative thoughts with positive ones. People seldom follow a pessimist.

In professional boxing, a champion is someone who gets up one more time than he gets knocked down. If you do not want to get knocked down, do not step into the ring; it simply goes with the territory. Leaders are also targets for getting knocked down. Others may be jealous of your position and power. Perhaps they wanted the position you got. Their value system may be at odds with yours. Expect criticism when you are the one in the driver's seat. Sometimes you will simply have to admit you made a mistake. When you step into a challenging position, you may fail. Some great leaders have failed over and over again. However, most of the great leaders say they learned the most from their failures. As Henry Ford said, "A setback is an opportunity to begin again more intelligently."

Emotional Intelligence Working with Others

What does it mean to have emotional intelligence in working with others? We all want to be competent in social matters, but how is that competence obtained? Goleman defines social competence as social awareness and the management of relations. We must first be aware of how our actions are interpreted by others. Then, we have to apply the best practices of management to personal relationships. We don't think so much about managing a department as managing the people and relationships within that department. Ours is a people business. It all begins with empathy. We must learn how to be more aware of others' feelings, needs, and concerns.

When a good man is hurt all who would be called good must suffer with him.

—Euripides (480–406 B.C.), Greek tragic poet

The person with highly developed empathy can sense others' emotions. They understand and take an active interest in the concerns of others.

Other parts of social awareness involve organizational awareness (reading the currents, decision networks, and politics at the organizational level) and service (recognizing and meeting the needs of others). Leaders with high EI understand the political forces at work in organizations, especially the unspoken rules. They also understand customers and are keenly aware of their needs and willing to do what it takes to ensure customers' needs are met.

The manager relies on control; the leader inspires trust.

—*Warren Bennis (1925–), author of* Managing People is Like Herding Cats

Goleman defines *relationship management* as a combination of inspiration, influence, developing others, change catalyst, conflict management, teamwork, and collaboration. In *Primal Leadership*, he asserts the key concept behind all relationship management is resonance. In the study of sound, resonance means to greatly increase a particular quality of that sound by sympathetic vibration. For example, the wooden base of a guitar greatly increases the sound of the vibrating strings. Leaders must think of resonance as a reservoir of positivity that greatly enhances the best qualities of their followers. The prime, or first, job of leadership is emotional. By increasing the emotional health of followers, leaders increase their effectiveness. It's as though they pluck the guitar string, and beautiful music results. The opposite of resonance is dissonance or negativity. The leader who uses resonance inspires. The leader who uses negativity subtracts from the reservoir of resonance. Great leaders move people to willingly put their energy behind a shared vision of an improved future. They embody what they ask of others.

How to Improve Your Emotional Intelligence

Hendrie Weisinger, in his recent book, *Emotional Intelligence at Work*, advises we can all begin to increase our emotional intelligence by increasing our self-awareness and suggests the following five steps:

1. Examine how you make appraisals.
2. Tune in to your senses.
3. Get in touch with your feelings.
4. Learn what your intentions are.
5. Pay attention to your actions. And I want to add the following:
6. Really know the people around you.
7. Watch how people react to what you do and say.
8. Share your feelings.
9. Love.

You might remember I talked about Shannon & Weaver's Model of Communication in an earlier chapter. There are similarities in emotional intelligence because we are really talking about another form of communication. Instead of words, we are transmitting emotions. A lot of emotional intelligence is expressed in nonverbal ways. But they are powerful messages. It is important for you to take responsibility for the messages you send out and make sure they are communicated completely with those around you. Just like communicating with words, you need to seek feedback regarding what emotional message you sent, how clearly it was received, how it was interpreted, and what action resulted.

Weisinger claims the key is to use your emotions intelligently, which is just what we mean by emotional intelligence. You intentionally make your emotions work for you by using them to help guide your behavior and thinking in ways that enhance your results. Such emotional intelligence can be nurtured, developed, and augmented. Unlike intelligence, it isn't a trait you either have or don't have. Most people increase their emotional intelligence through the years as they get wiser and more mature. You increase your emotional intelligence by learning and practicing the skills and capabilities that comprise emotional intelligence—namely, self-awareness, emotional management, self-motivation, and learning from the experience of your relationships. To a large degree, it is learning from your own mistakes and successes.

1. Examine How You Make Appraisals (Judgments)

Prejudices are what fools use for reason.

—Voltaire (1694–1778), French philosopher and writer.

The first step toward increasing your emotional intelligence is to increase your self- awareness. How do you do that? First, examine how you make appraisals. Appraisals are all the different impressions, interpretations, evaluations, and expectations you have about yourself, about others, and about situations. You judge or put value on or appraise things all the time.

One of your inner voices might be telling you right now that you find this reading boring, interesting, useful, etc. If you are going to be tested on this material and your inner voice is telling you that you find it boring, then one reaction might be to let your eyes pass over the words without really thinking about them, but the more emotionally intelligent thing to do would be to read it more slowly, take notes, or think of ways you could apply this at school, work, or home. After all, there is a test coming. Use your anxiety about that test to put aside your boredom and devote more energy to paying attention to what you are reading.

Your appraisals are influenced by the various factors that shape your personality such as family background, previous experiences, natural abilities, belief systems, and your general state of mental and physical health. Your appraisals generally take the form of inner dialogue. For example, "This presentation is going to be a disaster," or "I'm going to blow this test." "Everyone in my department thinks I'm too inexperienced for this assignment."

Know your prejudices, and explore how they influence your decisions. Move your thoughts from being prejudicial to being well considered, taking into account not only your own feelings, but those of others. Because you are aware of your appraisals and the effect your appraisals have, you can learn to alter them. You can tell yourself things like the following. "I know I tend to discount what Harvey says because I don't respect his opinions, but in this case, he might be right, and I don't want to give the impression that I automatically oppose anything he says." Or you can use it to enhance your own performance. "I've given presentations like this before, and I have usually done very well, so this presentation should be no different, as long as I am prepared." And you can avoid mistakes. "I know that in the past, employees have felt I was 'talking down' to them. I need to do something that shows I respect their opinions."

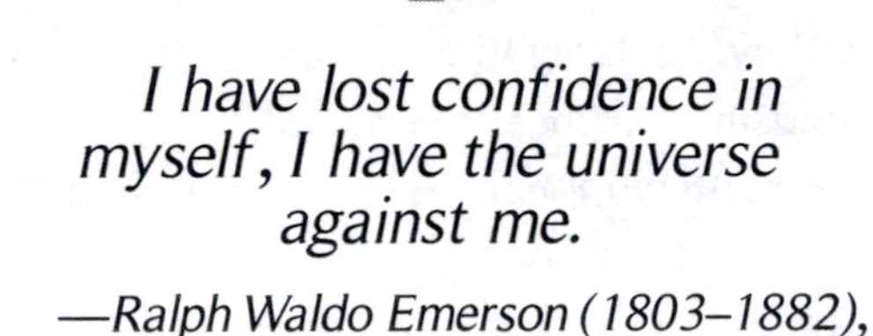

> *I have lost confidence in myself, I have the universe against me.*
>
> *—Ralph Waldo Emerson (1803–1882), American essayist and poet*

Challenges also can be addressed. For example, "Because everyone in the department thinks I am too inexperienced for this assignment, it is important I put in the extra effort to study the background material, understand the facts, and focus so that I can show them I am capable of handling this assignment despite my lack of experience."

By examining how you make appraisals and how such appraisals affect your actions, you can use this knowledge to reassure yourself, relax, and accomplish the task effectively. YOU ARE MAKING YOUR EMOTIONS WORK FOR YOU, NOT AGAINST YOU. As Mark Twain said, "The worst loneliness is not to be comfortable with yourself." This may be a good time to act on your feelings, given that you have already given the matter a great deal of thought. Ask yourself what you think about a situation. Force yourself to have an inner dialogue. Think about the messages you give yourself and how they would be received by others. Practice carrying on a dialogue with yourself when you are calm and relaxed. Learn to speak to yourself in reassuring tones. If you have self-doubts, find a trusted friend or colleague to give you help. How would they appraise the same event?

> *Go confidently in the direction of your dreams.*
>
> *Live the life you have imagined.*
>
> *—Henry David Thoreau (1817–1862), American author, poet, and philosopher*

Build up a solid base of information about your own strengths and weaknesses without dwelling on the weaknesses. Know that everyone has weaknesses. However, if you know what your weaknesses are, you can work on improving those areas or develop coping mechanisms to compensate. It all starts with a better understanding of how you make appraisals or judgments using your inner dialogue.

2. Tune in to Your Senses

The senses of seeing, hearing, smelling, tasting, and touching are the sources of our data about the world. However, this objective data is filtered and transformed by our appraisals. Your hearing may collect the actual words your spouse, boss, or colleague is saying, but your appraisal of that person so filters and transforms those words that what you "hear" is completely different from what is actually said. The old saying, "What you are rings so loudly in my ear, I can't hear what you are saying!" applies here.

A key to tuning into exactly what your senses are providing as information is to practice separating judgments from facts. Instead of saying to yourself, "Joe looks sad," say, "Joe is frowning and his chin is sagging." Instead of feeling sad, Joe may be concentrating.

The next time you are in a meeting, class, or social event, attempt to really "see" what is going on, using as many of your senses as possible. When someone speaks, do the others in the room look directly at that person? Do other voices and sounds stop, or do others keep talking and rustling about in their chairs? Try to develop a list of the most powerful person in the room, the next most powerful, and so on, just by noting how others in the room react when each person speaks. With practice, you should soon be able to accurately determine the "pecking order" and be able to use that information when you need to gain support.

3. Get in Touch with Your Feelings

Tuning in to your emotions is not something that comes easily to most of us. Tuning in to feelings of anger, sadness, and resentment can be painful. However, if you have never felt sad, how can you really tell if you are happy? Nevertheless, many of us ignore our feelings, deny them, or rationalize them.

> *We must interpret a bad temper as a sign of inferiority.*
>
> *—Alfred Adler (1870–1937), Austrian psychoanalyst and pioneer in psychology*

Everybody can remember an experience in which they got angry and later regretted what they said. The emotionally intelligent thing to do would have been to bite your tongue and wait until the feelings were not overwhelming more mature thoughts. Some people suggest taking a deep breath or silently counting to ten before reacting to an emotionally charged situation.

> *"I lose my temper, but it's all over in a minute," said the student.*
>
> *"So is the hydrogen bomb," I replied. "But think of the damage it produces!"*
>
> *—George Sweeting (1924–), former president of the Moody Bible Institute*

Think of the stereotype of the brilliant but moody executive, who offered great ideas but couldn't get along with people because he constantly lost his temper. This is another example of how intelligence alone is not enough.

Knowing your feelings can also have a positive benefit. Some people who appear to be natural leaders are those who are able to gauge the emotion of the situation and use it to advantage. They sense when it is the right time to act, to move forward, and use the enthusiasm of the moment to good purpose.

4. Learn What Your Intentions Are

Some intentions are obvious, while others are subtle. You may not be aware of them or at least never express them. For example, you work for a paycheck, but there might be jobs that you reject, even though you could earn more money. There could be many reasons. Perhaps you don't like the work, the company, the hours, or the commute.

The same could be true for your leadership decisions. Why do you select a particular person for a specific job? You might have reasons that you haven't even thought about. If you didn't really think about them, you may not have been using your emotional intelligence properly.

How can you possibly hope to understand the intentions of others until you understand your own? Learning about your intentions may be painful. Most adults have become quite skilled at hiding their true intentions, even from themselves. Have you ever later felt embarrassed that you really made a selfish choice that hurt others? A simple example would be that you have decided to lower the temperature in your home or office to save heating costs, but later realize you have hurt the health of another whose physical condition requires a warmer environment.

Before entering an important meeting, I often asked my associates what it is we are hoping to accomplish in this meeting. We went over what positions we anticipate others would have. At the start of the project, I like to ask what a totally successful outcome would look like. How would we measure success? How would we know in the end that our fondest intentions have been realized? These questions help us more fully understand what our intentions really are.

Longer-term intentions are even more difficult to ascertain. What do you hope to accomplish this year? Within ten years? During your career and during your lifetime? To young adults, deciding what they hope to accomplish over an entire career or lifetime seems like a daunting challenge. However, failing to ever consider your intentions can result in approaching retirement age with the even more daunting realization that your career has been meaningless.

One suggestion is to notice your own past behavior, and ask why you have done what you have already done and how you feel about key past behaviors. When did you feel happy, satisfied, content, or proud? Such feelings are clues to your intentions. Most people want to revisit such feelings often. Our intentions are a powerful force to harness and apply toward doing good. Understanding the intentions of others, and being able to use that knowledge to motivate others to follow you, is an even more powerful force. Use both very carefully and ethically while being aware of how others are using this force on you. For example, you may be in a job that once was exciting and rewarding, but has become boring and unsatisfying. You might carry on in that job and be miserable for months—or even years—before you realize change would be good.

5. Pay Attention to Your Actions

Because actions are physical, others can observe them and so can we, if we choose to. Often, we choose to ignore them. For example, the next time you notice you are walking slowly to class or to a meeting, ask yourself, "Am I walking slowly because I really don't want to go to this class or this meeting?" Perhaps you are walking slowly because you are deep in thought about what you are going to say when you arrive. Maybe you simply are nursing a knee injury or are wearing uncomfortable shoes. The point is—observe what you and others are doing.

Leonardo da Vinci used to stroll the streets of Florence jotting down his observations in his personal journal, 18 pages of which were purchased in 1994 by Bill Gates for $30.8 million. Many famous leaders have kept a personal journal of their observations.

As a student, are you aware of your actions in the classroom and the communications they are sending to the teacher and your fellow classmates? In most classrooms, the teacher faces the entire class from a position that provides a clear view of each student's face. Do you look the teacher in the eye while listening? Do you nod at some things the teacher says? When others talk, what is your body language saying? When do you choose to speak up? While the teacher or others are talking, do you carry on a hushed conversation with someone sitting close to you? Why did you choose a seat in the front, back, or middle of the room? Why do you listen more intently in some classes than in others? Answers to these questions will provide many clues regarding your interests and intentions.

> *I have always thought it would be a blessing if each person could be blind and deaf for a few days during his early adult life. Darkness would make him appreciate sight; silence would teach him the joys of sound.*
>
> *—Helen Keller (1880–1968), deaf and blind writer*

Similar information is transmitted in meetings in the workplace. Everyone in the meeting is actually communicating to everyone else all the time. It is not just the one speaking at the moment who is delivering information. A person with highly developed emotional intelligence gathers much information about every person at every meeting by paying attention to their own actions and the actions of others. Practice using more of your senses than just your hearing. Above all, be aware of your feelings at the meeting and how not only your voice, but all your actions, transmit information to others about those feelings. Become an observant student of both verbal and nonverbal communication.

6. Really Know the People around You

Managers especially need to have more than a superficial relationship with peers and coworkers. Some managers, in their haste to climb the ladder of success, make the mistake of treating people around them as though they don't matter. Think about those you see every day at work or in class. What do you really know about them? Do you have any idea about their emotions? What makes them happy or sad? Who are they? Where are they going? Why are they going there?

> *The mass of men lead lives of quiet desperation.*
>
> *—Henry David Thoreau (1817–1862), American writer*

People at work generally have deep emotions that are not being expressed. Some work environments are so threatening that everyone walks around on eggshells, afraid to say what is truly on their mind. Heart to Heart Communications in Akron, Ohio, uses a simple technique during seminars to collect unspoken, but heartfelt, emotions. They distribute blank index cards and ask people to anonymously jot down something that needs to be discussed, but is not being discussed at work.

The following examples of quotes from those index cards have been edited to maintain anonymity, but hopefully still capture the depth of emotion:

> I'm scared I might be let go here. I'm also having a rough time at home. What on earth am I going to do if I lose my job and my wife and family at the same time?

> Everyone is walking on eggshells here. We are all afraid this plant is closing and nobody is being honest with us. We need to know what's going to happen. We all have mortgages, kids in school, medical insurance to be concerned about, and bills to pay. Won't anyone be honest with us?

> We all wonder why this manager got sent here. He doesn't know any of us and doesn't seem to be making any effort to get to know us. Who is he, where does he plan to take this place, why is he here, and what does he expect of us?

If you were the manager those people are talking about, wouldn't you want to know about how they feel about these issues before making an important decision? This can be difficult, but necessary.

The news is filled with examples of managers who appear insensitive and cruel because they didn't understand how their message would be received when making difficult announcements like layoffs and plant closings. There are also examples of managers who graciously delivered the bad news in a way that warranted respect from the people most affected by the decision. You cannot lessen the damage, but you can help people make responsible reactions to the news by showing respect for their feelings and an understanding of what they believe to be important.

7. Watch How People React to What You Do and Say

Have you ever had a boss bark out an order and rush out of the room? Such an approach leaves no time to seek clarification, to suggest better ways to accomplish the task, or to learn any of the intentions behind the order. Worse yet, have you ever done it yourself?

> *Poor Ike, he's going to issue orders from the White House and wonder why nothing happens.*
>
> *—Harry Truman, commenting on General Dwight D. Eisenhower's election as president of the United States.*

Begin now to practice "reading" the reaction other people have to what you say and do.

Look for body language clues. A search of Amazon.com for books about body language will turn up a long list of books such as *Getting Anyone to Do Anything*, by David J. Lieberman. Be aware that con artists have made it their business to study nonverbal communication, and some can look you straight in the eye and lie. However, most of us find it difficult to hide the expression of our true feelings through our body language.

Another important area of study for those who aspire to international leadership is the variations in meaning of body language around the globe. Gestures such as a wink can mean something entirely different in Australia. In some countries, it is perfectly acceptable for two adults of the same sex to hold hands while walking together. In Sri Lanka, moving your head from side to side means *yes* and nodding your head up and down means *no*. Someone struggling to learn a new language may say *yes*, when what they really mean is that they understand the words you have said; not that they are saying *yes* to mean they agree.

8. Share Your feelings

Most of us have experienced times when we have shared our feelings and have somehow been embarrassed. Perhaps one of the worst feelings is to tell someone you love them and not get an "I love you, too" in return. We feel as though we have opened up to the other person, and the feelings were not returned. However, this should not be an excuse for hiding all our feelings from everyone.

> *'Tis better to have loved and lost than never to have loved at all.*
>
> *—Tennyson, writing of the death of Arthur Henry Hallam in the poem, "In Memoriam," 1850*

As Tennyson's famous poem says so well, sometimes love hurts. Tennyson's sister was planning to marry Hallam, but he died suddenly at age 22 (and yes, that Hallam is a very distant relative of this author). Handling such a loss is tough, but we all know it is better to share our feelings than to keep them all bottled up inside for fear of being hurt.

Leaders can build trust by appropriate sharing of feelings. Of course, the culture and circumstances have to be considered. People do not want to follow someone who cries and carries on in an immature manner over trivial issues. However, followers do want to follow those who are human and humane. By never revealing how we feel, we may unconsciously portray an image of insensitivity. People begin to wonder if you have any feelings. How can you possibly be sensitive to the feelings of others if you appear to be devoid of feelings yourself?

Watch how individuals react when you share your feelings and listen carefully to what they say. You can gain important information about the validity of your feelings or how you can be misunderstood. Those reactions can be clues to how to better speak to a larger audience in announcing decisions, setting goals, or sharing your vision.

9. Love

Love is seeking to make another person happy.

—Unknown

Leadership is not about you. It is about others and your relationship to them. No one is a leader without followers. Leadership is really about those followers. Having others follow you is a sacred responsibility. We cannot study the topic of leadership as though it were value free. When one person leads many others, there is simultaneously much danger and promise. Leaders can do tremendous harm—or good. What makes the difference is love.

The love described in Corinthians is much more than mere sexual attraction. If you get to know people as people and you take their emotions into consideration, you will eventually learn to care deeply about their needs. Showing you care about people will result in them returning the favors many times over. Following is a more positive quote obtained in a Heart to Heart Communications consulting project:

We'd all follow this guy anywhere. He really seems to care about us.

Don't accept the advice of some cynics, who say you should remain detached from your staff for fear it would prevent you from making the hard, but necessary, decisions. The benefits of caring for people are many times greater.

If I speak in the tongues of men and of angels, but have not love, I am a noisy gong or a clanging cymbal. And if I have prophetic powers, and understand all mysteries and all knowledge, and if I have all faith, so as to remove mountains, but have not love, I am nothing. If I give away all I have, and if I deliver my body to be burned, but have not love, I gain nothing.

Love is patient and kind; love is not jealous or boastful; it is not arrogant or rude. Love does not insist on its own way; it is not irritable or resentful; it does not rejoice at wrong, but rejoices in the right. Love bears all things, believes all things, hopes all things, endures all things.

Love never ends; as for prophecies, they will pass away; as for tongues, they will cease; as for knowledge, it will pass away. For our knowledge is imperfect and our prophecy is imperfect; but when the perfect comes, the imperfect will pass away.

When I was a child I spoke like a child, I reasoned like a child; when I became a man, I gave up childish ways. For now we see in a mirror dimly, but then face to face.

Now I know in part; then I shall understand fully, even as I have been fully understood. So faith, hope, love abide, these three; but the greatest of these is love. Make love your aim.

—I Corinthians 13.1–14.1

This Is Powerful Stuff—Don't Abuse It.

The entire field of emotional intelligence is both powerful and dangerous. Because most people are unable to hide their true emotions, especially in their nonverbal communications, unscrupulous people study this field and put it to unethical use. It is like other powers. It can be used for either good or evil. Used wisely, it can greatly enhance your ability to make a positive difference. Sincerity is important. This is not some little mind game or set of parlor tricks. This is powerful stuff.

Loving people live in a loving world. Hostile people live in a hostile world. It is the same world.

—Wayne Dryer (1940–), American author and motivational speaker

When I was on my game, I could see the entire court from end to end and everyone on it, including myself, and know where the ball and everyone on the court was going.

—Michael Jordan (1963–), former American star basketball player

For Jordan, it was as though he was observing the game from high upon a balcony, yet he was simultaneously in the game on the court. A person with high emotional intelligence can achieve a similar heightened awareness to be applied in classes, at meetings, and one-on-one. Imagine being about to picture not only your next move, but that of everyone in the room. Think of the advantage this will give you. Michael Jordan didn't acquire that ability without a lot of practice, and you won't either.

The next time you are in a classroom or a meeting, start to practice by asking yourself questions such as the following: "What are my feelings right now? Why am I feeling this way? What are my wants right now? Why do I have these wants? What is my body language telling others right now? What observations about others can I detect right now? When each person in the room speaks, how do others react? Who holds the most power in this room? Why is that? What is that person going to do or say next? How will the others react? Where is this meeting headed? Is this the direction I would prefer? Is there a way to change its direction? What are my intentions? Should I apply what I know about emotional intelligence to have others follow me?" With practice, perhaps you, like Michael Jordan, will be able to picture the next move of everyone in the room.

Summary

Once you enter a profession such as business management, almost everyone will be IQ-smart. Research indicates that what separates those who really do well within such a profession from those who only get by is being EQ-smart. Emotional intelligence is an emerging field of study that suggests some people are "smarter" at understanding and controlling their own emotions and the emotions of others. Research also suggests that most people can improve upon their emotional intelligence. However, you have to take it seriously and work at it. This chapter has examined some of the basic tenets of emotional intelligence and has suggested some ways you can work to improve yours.

Questions for Discussion

1. How does IQ differ from EQ?
2. Describe someone you know who has a high level of emotional intelligence. What advantage does this person have over someone with a lower level of emotional intelligence?
3. Imagine you have decided to work on improving your emotional intelligence. What steps will you take?
4. View this YouTube video of Daniel Goleman speaking to employees at Google about emotional intelligence. Discuss why this is such a pertinent topic for these employees. See http://www.youtube.com/watch?v=-hoo_dIOP8k

Chapter 17

Managing Your Career in Business

The best and safest thing is to keep a balance in your life, acknowledge the great powers around us and in us. If you can do that, and live that way, you are really a wise man.

—Euripides (484 BC–406 BC), playwright of ancient Greece

The previous chapters have focused primarily on applying the principles of management and leadership to business organizations. This chapter focuses on *you*. You can apply many of these same principles to the management of your career in business. Students in this course are likely to be facing some of the most difficult personal choices of your entire life. It is important to clearly think through your personal career planning process. All planning is similar in that you need to have a good understanding of your current situation, a clear vision of where you want to be in the future, and a clear process for getting from where you are now to where you want to go. This is true whether you are planning for General Electric or yourself. Also, keep in mind that life is not all about your career.

Applying SWOT to Yourself

As a first step in business planning, you should apply the SWOT analysis. Recall that SWOT stands for Strengths, Weaknesses, Opportunities, and Threats, and that you are to look inside the organization to find the strengths and weaknesses and you are to scan the environment for opportunities and threats. SWOT can work for you as you attempt to clearly describe to yourself your current status.

Strengths. If you are reading this textbook you likely already have many strengths. As a student enrolled in a college program, you have already met the requirement for admission and are well on your way to completing a four-year degree program. You are intelligent, ambitious, goal oriented, competitive, and able to manage the financial and time issues common to today's college students. Many of you are already employed and are gaining valuable work experience, while also gaining academic knowledge and credits toward graduation. Congratulations, you are already a success!

In addition to the strengths common to most students at this stage of their education, what other strengths do you have that will help you stand out among the thousands of others who will be graduating within the next few years? As you complete each of your courses, make a list of the assignments, term papers, and projects you completed, framing them in terms of what skills you have demonstrated by completing these tasks. If you had to make a written report, include that as a demonstration of your written communication skills. If you had to orally present your report in front of the class, include that as evidence of your public speaking expertise. If you had to analyze the financial condition of a business in a case analysis assignment, use that as proof of your mathematical and analytical ability. If you have used specialized software to search databases, compute statistics, or make charts and graphs for presentations, include these computer skills on your resume. If you worked on a team, include that as verification that you can work cooperatively in a team. If you had any leadership role within that team, use that as evidence of your team leadership ability. If you have been working at a job during your college years, use that to show a potential employer that you can balance school and work. If you have children, include that as confirmation that you can handle the competing demands of family, work, and school. While you may have been envious of others whose parents paid for all of their college expenses so they did not have to work, it is time to turn that disadvantage around and use it to demonstrate you have already learned how to manage your time and handle adult responsibilities.

> *We must use time wisely and forever realize that the time is always ripe to do right.*
>
> —Nelson Mandela, *activist and former president of South Africa*

Weaknesses. Nobody is perfect. Now is the time to make an honest assessment of your weaknesses. Some weaknesses can be overcome with additional education, experience, and dedication. Others may simply be things you have to cope with. The key is to be honest and thorough. It is difficult to see ourselves as others see us. If you have a friend or relative who is willing to be totally honest with you, ask that person to observe you doing the types of things you are likely to have to do in your chosen profession.

A common issue for students at this level is deciding just what profession is right for them. An internship is a good way to get to spend some time working in a particular organization observing the various jobs within that organization. Do not be discouraged if you find many of the jobs not to your liking. It is just as important to find out what you do not like as it is to find out what you like. The earlier in life that you do this the better.

Some weaknesses may require professional help to overcome. Shyness is one such weakness. Almost everyone experiences moments of shyness. The key is whether your shyness is so severe that it is keeping

My first language was shy. It's only by having been thrust into the limelight that I have learned to cope with my shyness.

—Al Pacino, actor

you from living your life as you would like to live it. Do not be embarrassed to seek psychological help to overcome such shyness. Do it sooner rather than later. Do not let shyness keep you from putting all your strengths, talents, education, and experience to good use. Think of shyness as like a box that surrounds you. The shyer you become, the smaller that box becomes. Reverse that process and expand your universe.

Opportunities. What is out there for you? In terms of your professional career, learn how to gather information about your career options. Which industries are likely to expand over the next decade? What jobs within those industries are going to be increasing? Which of those industries and jobs are of interest to you? Where will those opportunities be located? Are you willing to move to those locations?

Some of you will have geographical constraints. Now is a good time to look at those geographic limitations objectively. Of course, it would be difficult to move away from your family and current friends, but moving is also an opportunity to make new friends and expand your experiences. There may never be a better time in your life to consider an overseas opportunity or an opportunity in a far distant state.

Many students are highly motivated by starting salaries. Naturally, a high starting salary is desirable. However, it is not the only variable to consider. Recall from the chapter on motivation, intrinsic rewards are powerful motivators. Money has limits in terms of motivation. Another factor to strongly consider is how much you will be learning and growing professionally in the position.

Opportunity is missed by most people because it is dressed in overalls and looks like work.

—Thomas Alva Edison, American inventor

Threats. Be prepared for setbacks. Some have estimated that for those entering the field of business management, the probability of getting fired sometime over the next 20 years is 95%. While some may argue that 95% is high, most will agree that it is a strong possibility, regardless of how good you are at managing. Businesses are typically structured in a pyramid fashion that narrows at the top. The competition for the top management positions is fierce. You may be performing very well, but a new executive may be hired who wants to change the direction of the firm and prefers to bring in his or her own management team. Many American businesses have been seriously downsizing their management positions over the past few year, and sometimes the decision of which managers to terminate is based on criteria other than performance.

A good approach is to keep a savings account with sufficient funds to allow you to survive for several months while you are looking for another job. Of course, this is extremely difficult to do while you are still paying off college loans, starting a family, supporting small children, etc. However, if there is any way possible, having a rainy day fund is one of the best ways of dealing with any possible setback. It is also a way to increase your moral courage. If your boss demands that you do something that is against your values and morals, having that rainy day fund may provide just the strength you need to resist the temptation to violate your personal sense of ethics.

> *If you're willing to accept failure and learn from it, if you're willing to consider failure as a blessing in disguise and bounce back, you've got the potential of harnessing one of the most powerful success forces.*
>
> *—Joseph Sugarman, direct-marketing pioneer*

Setting Specific, Measurable, Attainable, Relevant, and Timely (SMART) Goals for Yourself

One of my students recently said, "I dream of someday working in California." When I asked her to be more specific, she did not seem to understand. Recall that SMART Goals stands for goals that are Specific, Measurable, Attainable, Relevant, and Timely. It is not enough to have a vague dream. Goals must say more precisely what your target is. Just where in California do you want to live and work? What company will be your employer? What will your job title be? What will you be paid? On what date are you moving from Akron, Ohio, to San Diego, California? What education, training, and experience will be expected to get that job? What will you have to do to be successful in that job? What specific steps will you need to take to turn your dream into reality?

> *If you know how to spend less than you get, you have the philosopher's stone.*
>
> *—Benjamin Franklin*

Hal Urban, author of *Life's Greatest Lessons*, also asserts, "Goals are the starting blocks of motivation. They give us a reason to get off our duffs and get going. Set your own goals. Be independent. Instead of just following the crowd or wandering aimlessly in life, choose your own path. Make it the path that leads to the fulfillment of the goals you have set for yourself. Putting a target date on our dreams is the first step in turning them into goals. Goals give us purpose and striving to accomplish them can be fun. You can never be bored for long, if you have exciting things to do."

Decide not to leave this world until you have done something to make it a better place. Goals that are about your job, income, place to live, etc. are important, but you also need to think of a purpose in life that is bigger than yourself. Viktor Frankl, survivor of Auschwitz and author of *Man's Search for Meaning*, was, before being captured by Nazis, a psychologist specializing in treating people who had attempted suicide. During his four years imprisoned at Auschwitz, he observed many suicides. However, he also observed many people who, despite the apparent hopelessness of the situation, maintained hope and even found ways to help others. In his famous book, *Man's Search for Meaning*, written shortly after he was freed, he said the prisoners he observed—including himself—who survived differed from those who did not, primarily based on two factors: love and a purpose greater than self.

> *Goals are dreams with deadlines.*
>
> *—Hal Urban, author of* Life's Greatest Lessons

Success is the progressive accomplishment of worthy goals.

—Hal Urban

Frankl was imprisoned shortly after his marriage to Tilly. During his imprisonment he often carried on, in his mind, conversations with her about what they would do once the war was over and they were able to resume their life together. After he was released he learned the Nazis had killed Tilly on the first day of their imprisonment. However, Frankl eventually came to realize that their love was so strong that it transcended even death. Those "conversations" with Tilly had helped Frankl through some of the toughest times imaginable. Also, Frankl had a passion for helping people so severely depressed that they were suicidal. During his time at Auschwitz he witnessed many suicides and many who resisted suicide even when that seemed the rational choice, given the circumstances. He was eager, once freed, to share his newfound understanding of the psychology of choosing life over death. He lived an active life as a doctor, professor, writer, and public speaker into his 90s. One of his most famous quotations came after being asked by a Harvard student to define the secret to success.

Again and again I therefore admonish my students in Europe and America: Don't aim at success—the more you aim at it and make it a target, the more you are going to miss it. For success, like happiness, cannot be pursued; it must ensue, and it only does so as the unintended side effect of one's personal dedication to a cause greater than oneself or as the by-product of one's surrender to a person other than oneself. Happiness must happen, and the same holds for success: you have to let it happen by not caring about it. I want you to listen to what your conscience commands you to do and go on to carry it out to the best of your knowledge. Then you will live to see that in the long-run—in the long-run, I say!—success will follow you precisely because you had forgotten to think about it.

—Viktor Frankl, author of Man's Search for Meaning

Do not misunderstand Frankl's famous quote. He was not telling students to avoid planning. Instead, he was telling them to "listen to what your conscience commands you to do and go on to carry it out to the best of your knowledge." He wanted his students to avoid going after success just for success. Instead success has to be a by-product of something much more important. Far from being easy, what Frankl told the students to do is look within, find what you conscience is commanding you to do, and then commit your life to doing that to the very best of your ability.

A similar famous quote comes from George Bernard Shaw, Irish playwright and cofounder of the London School of Economics.

This is the true joy in life, the being used for a purpose recognized by yourself as a mighty one; the being worn out before you are thrown on the scrap heap; the being a force of Nature instead of a feverish selfish little clod of ailments and grievances complaining that the world will not devote itself to making you happy.

—George Bernard Shaw

Resolve that before you die, you will do something worthwhile with your education and your life. Follow your calling. A *calling* is defined as where your passion, talent, and cause intersect. It is what Frankl was talking about when he told the students to find what their conscience was commanding them to do. Decide to do something you are passionate about. Your choice of a career should be about much more than just getting a paycheck. Take an objective assessment of your talents and put them to use. Find a cause that is bigger than yourself. A calling is not something reserved for the clergy or the medical profession. Being a good business manager and leader can be a calling.

Building Your Résumé

When a job in business management opens up, it is common for more than 100 résumés to be submitted. How are you going to make your résumé stand out from the other 99? Your résumé is often your first and only chance to make a great impression on your potential employer.

Imagine you are the one charged with the responsibility of reviewing the 100 or more résumés and narrowing the field down to three or four candidates that will be brought in for interviews. How would you proceed? Most will look for any flaw in the résumé as an excuse to discard it. You have to pare down the list of applicants to some small number that others will review more carefully. So, the first rule of writing a résumé is not to give your prospective employer an easy excuse for tossing yours onto the reject pile. Of course, you need to be absolutely sure your résumé is free of all spelling and grammar errors and follows an acceptable format for résumés. The number one purpose for writing a résumé is to get an interview. It is an advertisement for you. Avoid getting tossed out before anyone even talks to you. Get past the first hurdle. A Google search for "résumé examples" will turn up many websites offering free résumé examples for students, professionals, and other categories.

In addition to having a résumé that is perfect with respect to spelling and grammar, your résumé must convince the employer to "buy" you. You must answer the question, "If you hire me what will you get?" What do you bring to the table? In addition to getting you past the initial screening process of having the requisite educational level, number of years' experience, job history, and specific knowledge and skill, your résumé must show how you can be of service to this employer. Why should the employer pick you out of the field of 100 or more applicants? What makes you unique?

Too many job applicants write a résumé that is just a history of your past jobs and degrees. Of course, you must supply that factual information, but write with the intention of creating interest. Your goal is to persuade the employer to call you for an interview. Instead of just stating that you have earned a BS degree in Business Management from State University, provide details of what you have actually done in the process of earning that degree that would be useful to the employer. If you have been a full-time student and have little or no actual work experience, then it is especially important that you use the various classroom assignments to demonstrate your abilities. Now, while you are still taking courses, enter each course with the attitude that "this course is going to provide me with several things I can include on my résumé, such as analytical ability, proficiency in Microsoft Word, Excel, PowerPoint, and using numerous websites on the Internet for research."

Also, consider each of your teachers as potential job references. You want references that will honestly tell your potential employer that you never missed class, got all your assignments done accurately and on time, worked well with others on team projects, wrote a term paper that was free of spelling and grammar errors, clear and concise, well researched, and earned one of the highest scores in the class. You spoke up in class with valuable insights and made oral presentations of a professional quality. Look at each class session as another opportunity to convince the teacher that he or she should recommend you for a good job.

Taking That Internship

Many employers have reduced their reliance on on-campus interviews of prospective employees but have increased their emphasis on selecting future employees from their interns. It is relatively easy for someone to fool an employer during a short interview but difficult to cover up your flaws during a semester-long internship. Many students who are already working part time are hesitant to take an internship that requires them to quit their paying job, pay tuition for the internship course credit, and meet the additional requirements the faculty have established for an official internship that will show up on your transcript. However, most students agree that a good internship is worth it. A good internship gives you the opportunity to actually experience over several weeks what an actual job is like in your chosen field. Some students find they hate it and decide to switch majors. While this can be upsetting, it is much better to find this out while you are still a student and can make changes in your major and your career plans. Far too many people find out too late that the career they thought they wanted really is not what they expected.

Even if your internship does not result in a job offer from that employer, strive to complete your internship in such a manner that you can confidently add your employer to your list of references. When contacted by a potential employer, you want that reference to say you performed your internship in a highly professional manner and they wish they could have offered you a job but there were no job openings available. This can be almost as good as a job offer. It tells other potential employers that another organization would have hired you if they could.

Nailing the Job Interview

You have just landed an interview for the job you have dreamed about. Now what?

Now is the time to apply what you have been taught about analyzing a business. Use the Internet to find out everything you can about the company. Your goal should be to know more about the company than the person interviewing you. That may sound impossible, but it is not. Often the person assigned to interview prospective employees knows a lot about their own job and the department where they work. However, they may not have recently studied all the financial information (income statement, balance sheet, and funds flow statement) instantly available on http://www.google.com/finance.

Go to the organization's website and learn all you can about the history of the company, the goods and services they offer to customers, their main competitors and what makes them different from their chief rivals, how big the firm is in terms of market capitalization (outstanding shares times recent stock price), annual sales, number of stores and/or plants, and number of employees. Does the firm operate around the world, and if so, in which countries? Does the firm have a code of ethics and/or a statement of values and is there evidence they are actually following them? Be well prepared to answer the question, "What do you know about our company?"

The next question to prepare to answer is, "Why do you want to work here?" Here is your opportunity to convince the interviewer that you have really thought through what it would mean to have a job with this company and how your particular skills and talents can be of service to them. Understand that the interviewer's job is to interview lots of prospective employees and eliminate all but a few. Your goal is to convince the interviewer that you should remain in the running for the job. To do that, you need to stand out among the many he or she is interviewing.

Practice with a friend before going to the interview. Among the questions you should practice answering are:

1. Why are you leaving your current job?
2. What were your responsibilities at your previous jobs?
3. What were the major challenges and problems and how did you handle them?
4. What did you like best (and least) about your previous jobs?
5. What is your greatest strength?
6. What is your greatest weakness?
7. How will your strengths help you perform this job?
8. How would you describe yourself?
9. How do you handle stress and pressure?
10. What would your previous supervisor (teacher if you are still in school) say about you?
11. What motivates you?

12. Where do you see yourself in five to ten years? (For more typical interview questions and suggestions for answers, see http://jobsearch.about.com/od/interviewquestionsanswers/a/interviewquest.htm.)

Practice, practice, practice. Record your answers to these questions using a video camera so you can see yourself as others will see you. Work on getting over your nervousness. Everyone gets nervous in a situation as tense as a job interview. That nervousness comes out in different ways. For some, their voice trembles, hands shake, or they perspire excessively. Whatever form your nervousness takes, the best advice is to practice so much that you gain confidence. Practice in a situation that is as realistic as possible. It is not good enough to practice while alone in the shower or in your car. Have someone there to act like the interviewer. Use a video camera. Dress up as you plan to be dressed for the interview so you are used to the necktie or the high heels or whatever you will be wearing that is not normal for you. If excessive sweating is your form of nervous expression, experiment with various brands of antiperspirant until you find one that prevents wetness yet does not irritate your skin. You don't want a new antiperspirant to be causing you to be uncomfortable during your interview. Practice as though you are in a play and this is the dress rehearsal. There are several videos on YouTube that demonstrate good interviewing tips.

Starting Your New Job in Management

For new managers and for those hoping to break into management, one of the big changes relates to time. For the ordinary worker, his or her job begins at a particular time (say, 9 a.m.) and ends at a particular time (say, 5 p.m.). In contrast, managers are expected to come in as early and leave as late as it takes to get the job done. Managers are not supposed to be clock watchers. Getting up to leave exactly at 5 p.m. when you are in the middle of some important managerial job responsibility is just not professional. It will be one of the things your superiors will notice about your initial job behavior. Managers are paid a salary to handle certain responsibilities. They are not paid by the hour. Also, they are not eligible for overtime. In short, stop thinking like an hourly worker and start thinking like a professional. That does not mean that you will be staying at the office far into the night every night. However, there will likely be times when that is exactly what you will be expected to do.

You had to make your résumé stand out from a pile of a hundred or more résumés in order to land the interview. At the interview, you had to stand out among the others being interviewed for the same job. Now that you have landed the job, you still need to find ways to stand out. You are still learning, and the test will not be a multiple choice test but rather a series of day-in-day-out observations your superiors will be making regarding your work habits, your attitude, and your ability to handle stressful situations. It is almost as though the job interview continues. Instead of being overwhelmed by the stress, look at it as an opportunity to demonstrate just how good you can be. Dig into your new job with vigor. Hundreds, perhaps thousands, of others would love to have your opportunity.

Find a mentor. Look for someone who can answer important questions for you. Do not be a pest, but do show respect for the number of years of experience the person has. Learn as much as you can about the corporate culture. Find out how things are *really* done in this organization. A good question to ask to break the ice is, "Tell me about when you felt most proud of your association with this organization." Such a question is much better than asking about problems or about office gossip. It starts on a positive note.

Preparing for Career Setbacks

Some people find losing their job such a devastating blow that they commit suicide while others do not seem to miss a beat in finding a new job and continuing on to a successful career. Those who do research on what separates one from the other have found that some use an emotion-focused approach to coping with job loss while others use a problem-focused approach. The *emotion-focused* individuals are most likely to take trips to "get away," engage in substance abuse, spend excessive time with busywork, avoid discussion of the situation with friends and family, blame others, and seek emotional release in non-productive ways. *Problem-focused* behavior following job loss includes defining the problem, generating alternative solutions, and acting to solve the problem. Problem-focused individuals dealing with job loss are likely to spend more time in job search activity, work more diligently on ways to save money, objectively review their job skills and enroll in educational programs, relocate, and network. Of course, the problem-focused approach is physically and psychologically healthier and more likely to produce successful reemployment.

In addition to being problem focused, those who handle career setbacks more effectively commonly exhibit higher levels of self-efficacy. *Self-efficacy* is defined as believing that you are in control of your life and your own actions and decisions shape that life. A person with high self-efficacy does not attribute their problems to bad luck or to others plotting against them. This does not mean that the person with high self-efficacy beats up on him- or herself when they suffer a job loss. However, it does mean that he or she does not spend much time blaming others, trying to get even, or assuming they are just doomed with bad luck or the victim of some widespread plot to bring them down. Instead they look at the situation more objectively and turn their energy toward solving the problem of finding a new job. Losing their job was still upsetting, but it does no good to wallow in self-pity.

Learning how to manage your own career is key. Be aware of the need to plan ahead. Live beneath your means so you can save enough money to survive while you are looking for your next job. Network with others who will be of help to you in your next job search. Keep abreast of trends in the job market. Know which industries are hiring and which are laying off. Know which parts of the country where the jobs are growing and where jobs are shrinking. Keep your résumé up to date with the courses you continue to take after you complete your degree. Seek certification in new software packages. Do not let a month go by without doing something that will enrich your résumé. Look for opportunities to change jobs every few years so your résumé shows a record of advancement and increasing levels of responsibility and new challenges accepted. Be ready, in case a setback occurs, to jump back into the job market and successfully compete with others for the new job you want.

What is Success?

How would you define success? As Hal Urban says in his bestselling book, *Life's Greatest Lessons*, success is more than making money. Money is not bad. Many religions teach that money is the root of all evil but what they really mean is that the *love* of money is the root of all evil. Money should not be your primary focus. It should be the by-product of all the good work that you do. Honestly earned and properly used, money can be a resource for much good. However, sages throughout the ages have taught that money cannot buy happiness. Money is not all there is to being successful.

Successful people accept life as it really is. They understand that life often is not fair. They fully realize that life is often difficult. However, even with all the difficulties and challenges of life, it is best to accept the responsibility for our own lives instead of blaming others or making excuses. Even in the worst of circumstances, we are still free to choose our attitude. We can look for the good in others rather than dwell on the bad. We can continue throughout our lives to build good relationships with others. We can be respectful of all other human beings, not just those that are like us. The differences we see in others make life more interesting and strengthens our organizations. Successful people have a sense of direction and purpose—they know where they are going. They set goals, meet them, and then set even higher ones. Successful people accept and enjoy challenges.

On Being Happy

What does happiness mean to you? Mihaly Csikszentmihalyi and other psychologists have suggested the study of positive psychology. In the past, much of psychology has focused on those with mental illness and other psychological problems. The field of positive psychology looks at the opposite. What makes for a healthy psychological approach to life?

Our greatest glory is not in never failing, but in rising every time we fail.

—Confucius

Csikszentmihalyi suggests too many of us think of being happy as that state we see in small children playing and eating cake at a birthday party. As adults, that party scene too often changes to one where people are drinking or taking drugs. Such a childlike understanding of what it means to be happy, Csikszentmihalyi asserts, is a major part of the problem. Instead, he suggests adults should consider a state of being he refers to as being "in the flow," "on the ball," "in the moment," "in the groove," or being so totally engrossed in what you are doing that all other thoughts and problems leave your mind. Athletes describe being in such a state of flow when they are so into their game that they can anticipate where the ball and all their teammates are going to be. Some have described it as feeling as though they are on a balcony where they can see both ends of the playing field or court and all the players all at once. It is an elevated state. The fact that the person may have an injury or illness, financial difficulties, relationship problems, or other important matters to handle temporarily fades away, and the person is totally engaged in the task or game at hand. This, Csikszentmihalyi contends, is the picture we should use to replace the childish version of happiness.

Musicians also report they experience such a feeling of flow when they are so into the music they are playing that they no longer think about the notes or the words. Runners also describe a runner's high, where their body is moving in such perfect rhythm that they are no longer conscious of moving their legs and breathing. Writers describe getting so involved in what they are writing that time passes without notice and the words seem to just flow onto the page. Others have described times when they became "lost" searching or chatting on the Web. Csikszentmihalyi has identified the following ten factors as accompanying an experience of flow:

1. Clear, challenging goals.
2. Concentration on a limited field of attention.
3. Loss of feeling of self-consciousness.
4. Distorted sense of time.
5. Direct and immediate feedback.
6. Balance between ability level and challenge—the activity is neither too easy nor too difficult.
7. A sense of personal control over the situation or activity.
8. The activity is intrinsically rewarding so there is an effortlessness of action.
9. A lack of awareness of bodily needs.
10. Absorption into the activity.

The purpose of life is not to be happy—but to matter, to be productive, to be useful, to have it make some difference that you have lived at all.

—Leo Rosten (1908–1997), humorist and author

For a YouTube video of Mihaly Csikszentmihalyi speaking on creativity, fulfillment, and flow and what makes a life worth living, see http://wwwyoutube.com/watch?v=fXIeFJCqsPs.

Making a Difference

Perhaps the greatest thing about being a great manager and leader is that you get to make a difference. If you have had the opportunity to travel to any of the poorest nations, you have noticed that businesses there are not thriving. When businesses are not well managed and do not make a profit, then everyone suffers. Many people who are able and eager to work cannot find a job because the businesses are not growing and there is no reason for them to hire anyone. Governments have nothing to tax because the businesses are not making a profit. Therefore that nation's defenses are weak and they have a history of being taken over by practically any country that wants whatever natural resources are there. The people are largely illiterate because there is no tax revenue to support schools. Diseases that are treated in other countries are left untreated, because there are few, if any, hospitals and the people are too poor to afford medicine and medical treatment that others take for granted. Too many people think that the purpose of a business is simply to make money. Making a profit should be one of the many valuable by-products of managing a business properly. In short, a nation needs a strong and prosperous business sector; it is what makes all else possible.

Act as if what you do makes a difference. It does.

—William James (1842—1910), often referred to as the father of American psychology

Do not wait until you are a top executive to start making a difference. You can make a difference every day by treating others with respect. As someone preparing to become a great manager, get into the habit of treating others with respect. Practice good manners, use language appropriate for an honorable person, have your own heartfelt values and live up to them every day, appreciate the differences in others, and build a solid reputation by behaving in a trustworthy manner every day.

Be ashamed to die until you have won some victory for humanity.

—Horace Mann

Questions for Discussion

1. Remember that a calling includes your passion, your talent, and a cause greater than your self-interest. A calling is not just for people in the ministry. What is yours?
2. Search through your memory to times at work or school where you were so totally engrossed in what you were doing that you were unaware of the time, and all other problems, concerns, and aches and pains temporarily went away. Relate this experience of "being in the flow" to your personal career development plan. What careers might allow you to have such feelings of being in the flow? What preparations of education, training, and experience will it take to enter and succeed in that career?
3. Describe your various school and work projects in terms of the skills and attributes you can bring to a job, and how such things could best be expressed in your résumé.

Part III

READINGS

Power, Politics, and Conflict

By John A. Wagner III and John R. Hollenbeck

Power, politics, and conflict in organizations can increase productivity and efficiency—or reduce them substantially. Political processes can even determine organizational existence and strategic direction. Restructuring, often stimulated as much by internal power struggles as by external market conditions, is prompting managers to search out new strategic directions for their firms. In the process, political considerations are altering the careers of thousands of employees—both managers and nonmanagers. At the same time that these events are creating opportunities for some, they are costing many others their jobs. Understanding power, politics, and conflict is therefore critical to managerial success—and survival—in today's business organizations. To provide this understanding, Chapter 11 begins with a discussion of the nature, sources, and consequence of power. Next, it turns to the closely related topic of organizational politics, the process through which people acquire and use power to get their way. Finally, it examines conflict, describing the origins, results, and resolution of political confrontation in organizations.

Power in Organizations

When asked to define *power*, many people recall master politicians like Great Britain's wartime prime minister Winston Churchill or former U.S. president Bill Clinton describing power as the ability to influence the behaviors of others and persuade them to do things they would not otherwise do. For other people, images of the less powerful come to mind, leading them to define power as the ability to avoid others' attempts to influence their behavior. In truth, both of these views are correct. That is, *power* is the ability both to influence the conduct of others and to resist unwanted influence in return.

According to David McClelland, people are driven to gain and use power by a need for power—which he called *nPow*—that is learned during childhood and adolescence. This need for power can have several different effects on the way people think and behave. Generally speaking, people with high nPow are competitive, aggressive, prestige-conscious, action oriented, and prone to join groups. They are likely to be effective managers if, in addition to pursuing power, they also do the following:

- Use power to accomplish organizational goals instead of using it to satisfy personal interests.
- Coach subordinates and use participatory management techniques rather than autocratic, authoritarian methods.
- Remain aware of the importance of managing interpersonal relations but avoid developing close relationships with subordinates.

McClelland's research has suggested that seeking power and using it to influence others are not activities to be shunned or avoided in and of themselves. In fact, the process of management *requires* that power be used.

Interpersonal Sources of Power

If management requires the use of power, then what is the source of a manager's power? In their pioneering research, John French and Bertram Raven sought to answer this question by identifying the major bases, or sources, of power in organizations. As indicated in Table 1, they discovered five types of power: reward, coercive, legitimate, referent, and expert power.

Reward power is based on the ability to allocate desirable outcomes—either the receipt of positive things or the elimination of negative things. Praise, promotions, raises, desirable job assignments, and time off from work are outcomes that managers often control. If they can make decisions about the distribution of such rewards, managers can use them to acquire and maintain reward power. Similarly, eliminating unwanted outcomes, such as unpleasant working conditions or mandatory overtime, can be used to reward employees. For instance, police officers who receive clerical support to help complete crime reports generally look at this reduction of paperwork as rewarding.

Whereas reward power controls the allocation of desirable outcomes, *coercive power* is based on the distribution of undesirable outcomes—either the receipt of something negative or the removal of something positive. People who control punishing outcomes can get others to conform to their wishes by threatening to penalize them in some way. That is, coercive power exploits fear. To influence subordinates' behaviors, managers may resort to punishments such as public scoldings, assignment of undesirable tasks, loss of pay, or, taken to the extreme, layoffs, demotions, or dismissals.

Type of power	*Source of power*
Reward	Control over rewarding outcomes
Coercive	Control over punishing outcomes
Legitimate	Occupation of legitimate position of authority
Referent	Attractiveness, charisma
Expert	Expertise, knowledge, talent

Table 1 *Five Types of Power and Their Sources*

Legitimate power is based on norms, values, and beliefs that teach that particular people have the legitimate right to govern or influence others. From childhood, people learn to accept the commands of authority figures—first parents, then teachers, and finally bosses. This well-learned lesson gives people with authority the power to influence other people's attitudes and behaviors. In most organizations, authority is distributed in the form of a hierarchy. People who hold positions of hierarchical authority are accorded legitimate power by virtue of the fact that they are office holders. For example, the vice president of marketing at a firm such as Philip Morris issues orders and expects people in subordinate positions to obey them because of the clout that being a vice president affords.

Have you ever admired a teacher, a student leader, or someone else whose personality, way of interacting with other people, values, goals, or other characteristics were exceptionally attractive? If so, you probably wanted to develop and maintain a close, continuing relationship with that person. This desire can provide this individual with *referent power.* Someone you hold in such esteem is likely to influence you through his or her attitudes and behaviors. In time you may come to identify with the admired person to such an extent that you begin to think and act alike. Referent power is also called *charismatic power.*

Famous religious leaders and political figures often develop and use referent power. Mahatma Gandhi, John F. Kennedy, Martin Luther King, Jr., and Nelson Mandela, for example, have all used personal charisma to profoundly influence the thoughts and behaviors of others. Of course, referent power can also be put to more prosaic use. Consider advertising's use of famous athletes and actors to help sell products. Athletic shoe manufacturers such as Nike, Reebok, and Adidas, for example, employ sports celebrities as spokespeople in an effort to influence consumers to buy their products. Similarly, movie producers try to ensure the success of their films by including well-known stars in the cast.

Expert power derives from the possession of expertise, knowledge, and talent. People who are seen as experts in a particular area can influence others in two ways. First, they can provide other people with knowledge that enables or causes those individuals to change their attitudes or behavior. For example, media critics provide reviews that shape people's attitudes about new books, movies, music, and television shows. Second, experts can demand conformity to their wishes as the price for sharing their knowledge. For instance, doctors, lawyers, and accountants provide advice that influences their clients'

Level	*Description*
Compliance	Conformity based on desire to gain rewards or avoid punishment. Continues as long as rewards are received or punishment is withheld.
Identification	Conformity based on attractiveness of the influencer. Continues as long as a relationship with the influencer can be maintained.
Internalization	Conformity based on the intrinsically satisfying nature of adopted attitudes or behaviors. Continues as long as satisfaction continues.

Table 2 *Three Responses to Interpersonal Power*

choices. Auto mechanics, plumbers, and electricians also exert a great deal of influence over customers who are not themselves talented craftspeople.

Conformity Responses to Interpersonal Power

How do employees respond when managers use the different kinds of power identified by French and Raven? According to Herbert Kelman, three distinctly different types of reactions are likely to occur as people respond to attempts to influence their behavior. As indicated in Table 2, they are compliance, identification, and internalization.

Compliance ensues when people conform to the wishes or directives of others so as to acquire favorable outcomes for themselves in return. They adopt new attitudes and behaviors not because these choices are agreeable or personally fulfilling but rather because they lead to specific rewards and approval or head off specific punishments and disapproval. People are likely to continue to display such behaviors only as long as the favorable outcomes remain contingent on conformity.

Of the various types of power identified by French and Raven, reward and coercive power are the most likely to stimulate compliance, because both are based on linking employee performance with the receipt of positive or negative outcomes. Employees who work harder because a supervisor with reward power has promised them incentive payments are displaying compliance behavior. Similarly, employees who work harder to avoid punishments administered by a supervisor with coercive power are likely to continue doing so only while the threat of punishment remains salient.

Identification occurs when people accept the direction or influence of others because they identify with the power holders and seek to maintain relationships with them—not because they value or even agree with what they have been asked to do. French and Raven's concept of referent power is based on the same sort of personal attractiveness as is identification. Consequently, referent power and identification are likely to be closely associated with each other. Charismatic leaders are able to continue influencing other people's behaviors for as long as identification continues.

Finally, through *internalization*, people may adopt others' attitudes and behaviors because this course of action satisfies their personal needs or because they find those attitudes and behaviors to be congruent with their own personal values. In either case, they accept the power holders' influence

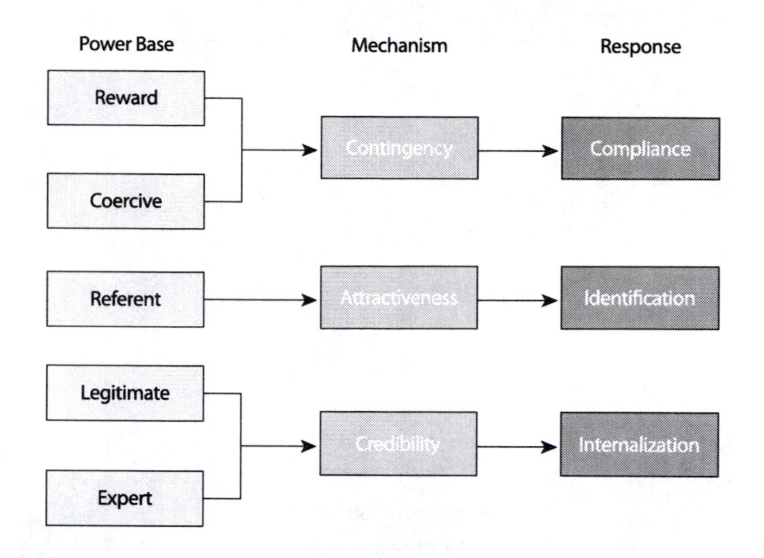

Source: Based on H. C. Kelman, "Compliance, Identification, and Internalization: Three Processes of Attitude Change," *Journal of Conflict Resolution* 2 (1958), 51–60; M. Sussmann and R. P. Vecchio, "A Social Influence Interpretation of Worker Motivation," *Academy of Management Review* 7 (1982), 177–186.

Figure 1 *A Model of Interpersonal Power*

wholeheartedly. Both legitimate and expert power can stimulate internalization, as these forms of power rely on personal credibility—the extent to which a person is perceived as truly possessing authority or expertise. This credibility can be used to convince people of the intrinsic importance of the attitudes and behaviors they are being asked to adopt.

Internalization leads people to find newly adopted attitudes and behaviors personally rewarding and self-reinforcing. A supervisor who can use her expertise to convince colleagues to use consultative leadership can expect the other managers to continue consulting with their subordinates long after she has withdrawn from the situation. Likewise, a manager whose legitimate power lends credibility to the orders he issues can expect his subordinates to follow those orders even in the absence of rewards, punishments, or charismatic attraction.

A Model of Interpersonal Power: Assessment

French and Raven describe the different kinds of interpersonal power used in organizations, and Kelman identifies how people respond to this use. Although valuable as a tool for understanding power and its consequences, the model integrating these ideas, shown in Figure 1, is not entirely without fault. Questions arise as to whether the five bases of power are completely independent, as proposed by French and Raven, or whether they are so closely interrelated as to be virtually indistinguishable from one another. The idea that reward, coercive, and legitimate power often derive from company policies and procedures, for instance, has led some researchers to subsume these three types of power in a

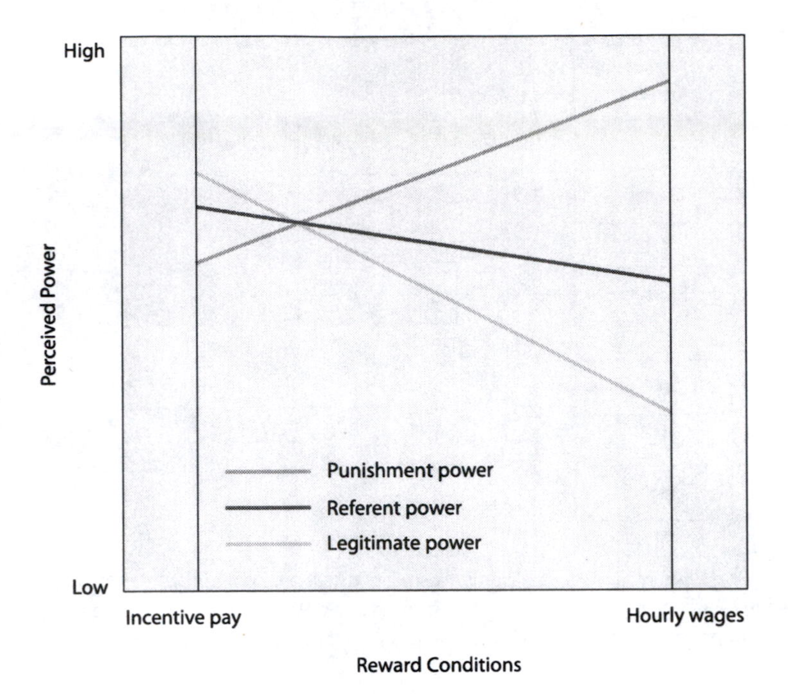

Source: Based on C. N. Greene and P. M. Podsakoff, "Effects of Withdrawal of a Performance-Contingent Reward on Supervisory Influence and Power," *Academy of Management Journal* 24 (1981), 527–542.

Figure 2 *Effects of a Change in Method of Payment on Perceived Bases of Power*

single category labeled *organizational power.* Similarly, because expert and referent power are both based on personal expertise or charisma, they have sometimes been lumped together into the category of *personal power.*

In fact, French and Raven's five bases of power may be even more closely interrelated than this categorization would suggest. In their study of two paper mills, Charles Greene and Philip Podsakoff found that changing just one source of managerial power affected employees' perceptions of three other types of power. Initially, both paper mills used an incentive payment plan in which supervisors' monthly performance appraisals determined the employees' pay. At one mill, the incentive plan was changed to an hourly wage system in which seniority determined an employee's rate of pay. The existing incentive plan was left in place at the other mill. Following this change, the researchers found that employees at the first mill perceived their supervisors as having significantly less reward power—as we might expect. Surprisingly, however, they also saw significant changes in their supervisors' punishment, legitimate, and referent power. As shown in Figure 2, they attributed significantly more punishment power, a little less referent power, and substantially less legitimate power to their supervisors.

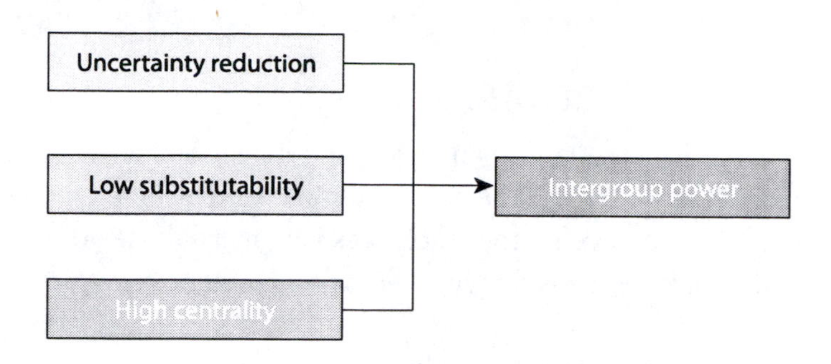

Source: Based on D. J. Hickson, C. R. Hinings, C. A. Lee, R. H. Schneck, and J. M. Pennings, "A Strategic Contingencies Theory of Intraorganizational Power," *Administrative Science Quarterly* 16 (1971), 216–229.

Figure 3 *The Critical Contingencies Model of Power*

In contrast, employees in the second mill, where the incentive plan remained unchanged, reported no significant changes in their perceptions of their supervisors' reward, punishment, legitimate, and referent power. Because all other conditions were held constant in both mills, employees' changed perceptions in the first mill could not be attributed to other unknown factors. Instead, their perceptions of reward, coercive, legitimate, and referent power proved to be closely interrelated. This finding suggests that four of the five types of power identified by French and Raven appear virtually indistinguishable to interested observers.

Despite this limitation, the model created by joining French and Raven's classification scheme with Kelman's theory is useful in analyzing social influence and *interpersonal* power in organizations. Managers can use this model to help predict how subordinates will conform to directives based on a particular type of power. For example, is the use of expertise likely to result in long-term changes in subordinates' behavior? Since the model shown in Figure 1 indicates that internalization is stimulated by the use of expert power, long-term behavioral changes are quite probable. Alternatively, subordinates may find the model useful as a means of understanding—and perhaps influencing—the behaviors of their superiors. For instance, an employee interested in influencing his boss to permanently change her style of management would be well advised to try using personal expertise.

Structural Sources of Power

In addition to the interpersonal sources discussed so far, power also derives from the *structure* of patterned work activities and flows of information found in every organization. ... The discussion here will, therefore, be limited to those characteristics of organizations that shape power relations—uncertainty reduction, substitutability, and centrality. As depicted in Figure 3, these three variables combine to form the critical contingencies model of power.

Uncertainty Reduction

Critical contingencies are the things that an organization and its various parts need to accomplish organizational goals and continue surviving. The raw materials needed by a company to manufacture goods are critical contingencies. So, too, are the employees who make these goods, the customers who buy them, and the banks that provide loans to buy inventory and equipment. Information can also be a critical contingency.

Consider the financial data used by banks to decide whether to grant loans, or the mailing lists employed by catalog merchandisers to locate prospective customers. Uncertainty about the continued availability of such critical contingencies can threaten the organization's wellbeing. If a purchasing manager cannot be certain that she can buy raw materials at reasonable prices, then her organization's ability to start or continue productive work is compromised. Similarly, when a marketing department reports shifting consumer tastes, the firm's ability to sell what it has produced is threatened. Thus, as explained by Gerald Salancik and Jeffrey Pfeffer, the critical contingencies model of power is based on the principle that "those [individuals or groups] most able to cope with [their] organization's critical problems and uncertainties acquire power" by trading *uncertainty reduction* for whatever they want in return.

One way to reduce uncertainty is by gaining *resource control*—that is, by acquiring and maintaining access to those resources that might otherwise be difficult to obtain. A human resources management department may be able to reduce an important source of uncertainty in an organization that has experienced problems in attracting qualified employees if it can hire and retain a productive workforce. Similarly, a purchasing department that can negotiate discounts on raw materials can help reduce uncertainty related to whether the firm can afford to continue to produce its line of goods. Each of these departments, by delivering crucial resources and thereby reducing success-threatening uncertainty, can gain power.

Information control offers another way to reduce uncertainty in organizations. Providing information about critical contingencies is particularly useful when such information can be used to predict or prevent threats to organizational operations. Suppose, for example, that a telecommunication company's legal department learns of impending legislation that will restrict the company's ability to buy additional television stations unless it divests itself of the stations it already owns. By alerting management and recommending ways to form subsidiary companies to allow continued growth, the firm's legal department may eliminate much uncertainty for the firm.

A third way to reduce uncertainty is to acquire *decision-making control*—that is, to have input into the initial decisions about what sorts of resources will be critical contingencies. At any time, events may conspire to give certain groups power over others. This power, in turn, allows its possessors to determine the rules of the game or to decide such basic issues as what the company will produce, to whom it will market the product, and what kinds of materials, skills, and procedures will be needed. In the process, those already in power can make the contingencies they manage even more important to organizational well-being. In this manner, power can be used to acquire power of even greater magnitude—"the rich get richer."

Substitutability

Whether individuals or groups gain power as a result of their success in reducing uncertainty depends partly on their *substitutability.* If others can serve as substitutes and reduce the same sort of uncertainty, then individuals or departments that need help in coping with uncertainty can turn to a variety of sources for aid. Hence no single source is likely to acquire much power under such a scenario. For example, a legal department's ability to interpret laws and regulations is unlikely to yield power for the department if legal specialists working in other departments can fulfill the same function. When substitutes are readily available, other departments can ignore the pressures of any particular group, so each group's ability to amass power is undermined.

If others can get help in coping with uncertainty only from the target person or group, however, this person or group is clearly in a position to barter uncertainty reduction for desired outcomes. For example, a research and development group that serves as a company's sole source of new product ideas can threaten to reduce the flow of innovation if the firm does not provide the desired resources. The less substitutability present in a situation, the more likely that a particular person or group will be able to amass power.

Centrality

The ability of a person or a group to acquire power is also influenced by its *centrality*, or its position within the flow of work in the organization. The ability to reduce uncertainty is unlikely to affect a group's power if no one outside the group knows that it has this ability and no one inside the group recognizes the importance of the ability. Simply because few other people know of its existence, a clerical staff located on the periphery of a company is unlikely to amass much power, even if its typing and filing activities bring it in direct contact with critically important information. When uncertainty emerges that the staff could help resolve, it is likely to be ignored because no one is aware of the knowledge and abilities possessed by the staff members.

The Critical Contingencies Model: Assessment

Despite a few criticisms, research strongly supports the critical contingencies model's suggestion that power is a function of uncertainty reduction, substitutability, and centrality. An analysis of British manufacturing firms in business during the first half of the 20th century confirms this idea. The analysis revealed that accounting departments dominated organizational decision making in the Great Depression era preceding World War II, because they kept costs down at a time when money was scarce.

After the war ended, power shifted to purchasing departments as money became more readily available and strong consumer demand made access to plentiful supplies of raw materials more important. During the 1950s, demand dropped so precipitously that marketing became the most important problem facing British firms. As a result (and as predicted by the model), marketing and sales departments that succeeded in increasing company sales gained power over important decision-making processes.

In another study, researchers examined 29 departments of the University of Illinois, looking at the departments' national reputations, teaching loads, and financial receipts from outside contracts and grants. Their results indicated that each department's ability to influence university decision making was directly related to its reputation, teaching load, and grant contributions.

In addition, the amount of contract and grant money brought in from outside sources had an especially strong effect on departmental power. Contracts and grants provide operating funds critical to the survival of a public institution such as the University of Illinois. Thus, as predicted by the critical contingencies model, the power of each department in the university was directly related to its ability to contribute to the management of critical contingencies.

An even more intriguing piece of evidence supporting the critical contingencies model was discovered by Michel Crozier, a French sociologist who studied a government-owned tobacco company located just outside Paris. As described by Crozier, maintenance mechanics in the tobacco company sought control over their working lives by refusing to share knowledge needed to repair crucial production equipment. The mechanics memorized repair manuals and then threw them away so that no one else could refer to them. In addition, they refused to let production employees or supervisors watch as they repaired the company's machines. They also trained their replacements in a closely guarded apprenticeship process, thereby ensuring that outsiders could not learn what they knew. Some mechanics even altered equipment so completely that the original manufacturer could not figure out how it worked. In this manner, the tobacco company's maintenance mechanics retained absolute control over the information and skill required to repair production equipment. In essence, the maintenance personnel ran the production facility as a result of the information they alone possessed about its equipment.

Crozier's account of the tobacco factory mechanics illustrates the usefulness of the critical contingencies model in explaining why people who have hierarchical authority and formal power sometimes lack the influence needed to manage workplace activities. If subordinates have the knowledge, skills, or abilities required to manage critical contingencies, thereby reducing troublesome uncertainties, they may gain enough power to disobey their hierarchical superiors. In turn, as long as superiors must depend on subordinates to manage such contingencies, it will be the subordinates—not the superiors—who determine which orders will be followed and which will be ignored.

In sum, the critical contingencies model appears to describe the structural bases of power quite accurately. Its utility for contemporary managers lies in the observation that the roots of power lie in the ability to solve crucial organizational problems. Managers must understand and exploit this simple premise, because such knowledge can help them acquire and keep the power needed to do their jobs.

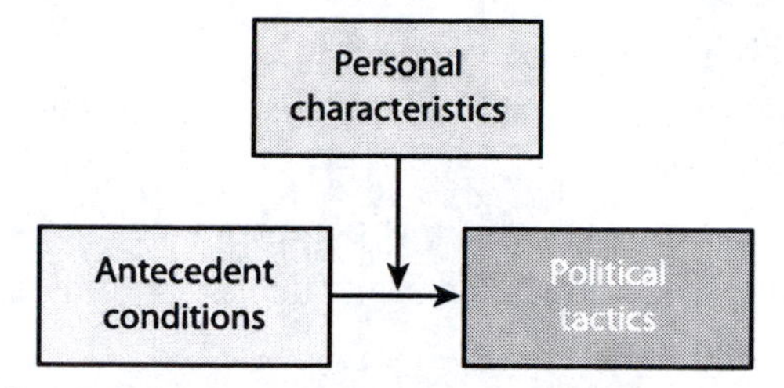

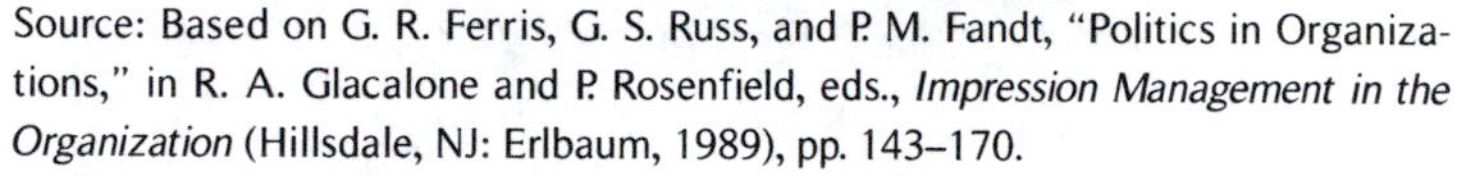
Source: Based on G. R. Ferris, G. S. Russ, and P. M. Fandt, "Politics in Organizations," in R. A. Glacalone and P. Rosenfield, eds., *Impression Management in the Organization* (Hillsdale, NJ: Erlbaum, 1989), pp. 143–170.

Figure 4 *A Model of the Emergence of Politics*

Politics and Political Processes

Politics can be defined as activities in which individuals or groups engage so as to acquire and use power to advance their own interests. In essence, politics is power in action. Although political behavior can be disruptive, it is not necessarily bad. The unsanctioned, unanticipated changes wrought by politics can, in fact, enhance organizational well-being by ridding companies of familiar but dysfunctional ways of doing things. Nonetheless, because politics has a negative connotation, political behavior is seldom discussed openly in organizations. In fact, managers and employees may even deny that politics influences organizational activities. Research indicates, however, that politicking *does* occur and that it has measurable effects on organizational behavior.

Personality and Politics

Why do people engage in politics? As with power in general, certain personal characteristics predispose people to exhibit political behaviors. For example, some people have a need for power (nPow), as identified by McClelland and discussed previously. Just as nPow drives people to seek out influence over others, it also motivates them to use this power for political gain.

Other researchers have suggested that people who exhibit the personality characteristic of *Machiavellianism*—the tendency to seek to control other people through opportunistic, manipulative behaviors—may also be inclined toward politics. In addition, studies have indicated that self-conscious people may be less likely than others to become involved in office politics because they fear being singled out as a focus of public attention and being evaluated negatively for engaging in politics. This fear keeps them from seeking power and using it for personal gain.

Conditions that Stimulate Politics

In addition to personality characteristics such as nPow and Machiavellianism, certain conditions encourage political activity in organizations (see Figure 4). One such condition is *uncertainty* that can be traced

- Interruptions in the availability of critical resources or of information about these resources Ambiguity (no clear meaning) or equivocality (more than one possible meaning) in the information that is available
- Poorly defined goals, objectives, work roles, or performance measures
- Unclear rules for such things as who should make decisions, how decisions should be reached, or when decision making should occur
- Change of any type—for example, reorganization, budgetary reallocations, or procedural modifications
- Dependence on other individuals or groups, especially when that dependence is accompanied by competitiveness or hostility

Source: Based on D. R. Beman and T. W. Sharkey, "The Use and Abuse of Corporate Politics," Business Horizons 30 (1987), 26–30; A. Raia, "Power, Politics, and the Human Resource Professional," Human Resource Planning 8 (1985), 198–209; J. P. Kotter, "Power, Dependence, and Effective Management," Harvard Business Review 53 (1977), 125–136..

Table 3 *Types of Uncertainty that Encourage Politics*

to ambiguity and change (see Table 3). Uncertainty can hide or disguise people's behaviors, enabling them to engage in political activities that would otherwise be detected and prohibited. It can also trigger political behavior, because it gives people a reason to be political—they may resort to politics in efforts to find ways to reduce uncertainty that provide them with added power and other personal benefits.

Besides uncertainty, other conditions that may encourage political behavior include *organizational size*, *hierarchical level*, *membership heterogeneity*, and *decision importance.* Politicking is more prevalent in larger organizations than in smaller ones. The presence of a greater number of people is more likely to hide the behaviors of any one person, enabling him or her to engage in political behaviors with less fear of discovery. Politics is also more common among middle and upper managers, because the power required to engage in politics is usually concentrated among managers at these levels. In heterogeneous organizations, members share few interests and values and therefore see things very differently. Under such circumstances, political processes are likely to emerge as members compete to decide whose interests will be satisfied and whose will not. Finally, important decisions stimulate more politics than unimportant decisions do simply because less important issues attract less interest and attention.

Political Tactics

When personal characteristics and surrounding conditions favor them, a variety of political tactics may surface. Each tactic is intended to increase the power of one person or group relative to others. When power increases, so does the likelihood that the person or group will be able to seek out and acquire self-interested gains.

Acquiring Interpersonal Power: Forming Affiliations

Forming *coalitions* or political affiliations with each other represents an important way for people to increase their power and pursue political gain beyond their individual grasp. By banding together, people can share their collective control over rewards or punishments. They can also combine their expertise, legitimacy, and charisma. For instance, collective bargaining enables union members to obtain wages and conditions far superior to those that they could demand as individuals. Conversely, companies form trade associations so as to exchange information about collective bargaining and union agreements.

As part of the process of forming political affiliations, favors may be used to create a sense of indebtedness. People who pursue this tactic can increase the dependence of others by building up a bank of favors that are owed them. In the U.S. Congress, for instance, representatives from industrial regions will vote for bills providing farm subsidies with the understanding that farm-state representatives will reciprocate by supporting bills that secure industrial assistance grants.

Besides exchanging favors, people engaging in politics sometimes use cooptation to preserve their interests in the face of adversity. In *cooptation*, former rivals become transformed into allies, often by involving them in planning and decision-making processes. Colleges and universities often use this tactic during periods of campus unrest, inviting student protesters to join university representatives on administrative committees. Making opponents part of the team often silences their objections, but carries the risk of making major changes in plans and decisions.

Finally, ingratiation and impression management can be used to build and maintain political relationships. *Ingratiation* is the use of praise and compliments to gain the favor or acceptance of others. Similarly, *impression management* involves behaving in ways intended to build a positive image. Both can increase personal attractiveness, thereby raising the likelihood that others will seek a close relationship.

Acquiring Structural Power: Controlling Critical Resources

As suggested by the critical contingencies model of power, controlling the supply of a critical resource gives people power over those whose success or survival depends on having that resource. A warehouse manager, for example, can decide which orders will be filled immediately and which will be delayed. As a political tool, power of this sort can be used to ensure that personal interests are satisfied. Similarly, controlling access to information sources provides power over those who need that information to reduce uncertainty. Political players often attempt to control access to the people who are sources of important information or expertise. Managers, for instance, may shield the staff specialists who advise them from others in their firm. Engineers who are working on new product development are often sequestered from other employees; cost accountants may be separated from other members of a company's accounting department. Such employees are an important resource because they possess critical information that is unavailable elsewhere.

To succeed as a political tactic, controlling access to important resources, information, or people requires eliminating substitutes for these critical resources and discrediting alternative definitions of what is critical. The presence of substitutes counteracts attempts to gain power by controlling critical resources because it neutralizes political efforts. In addition, successful control of critical resources requires that people have at least the centrality needed to identify which resources are critical and which are not.

Negative Politics

If all else fails, a person may sometimes gain the political upper hand by attacking or blaming others, or making them *scapegoats* for failures. Another tactic is to denigrate or belittle others' accomplishments. Either approach involves a direct attack on the interpersonal sources of power that others might possess in an attempt to weaken their political positions, thereby creating doubt about their ability to control rewards and punishments or reducing their credibility, legitimacy, or attractiveness. Negative politicking can also justify the creation of substitute sources of critical resources or information or reduction of the degree of centrality enjoyed by a person or group. After all, who would want an incompetent individual or group in charge of something that is critically important to organizational survival?

Managing Destructive Politics

You can easily imagine some of the consequences when people band together, hoard resources, or belittle each other for no other reason than to get their own way. Morale may suffer; battle lines between contending individuals or groups may impede important interactions; energy that should go into productive activities may instead be spent on planning attacks and counterattacks if politicking is left uncontrolled. For this reason, controlling political behavior is a major part of every manager's job.

Set an Example

One way to manage destructive politics is to set an example. Managers who do not tolerate deceit and dirty tricks and who refuse to engage in negative politics themselves make it clear that such political tactics are inappropriate. Subordinates are thus discouraged from engaging in destructive political activities. In contrast, managers who engage in negative politics—blaming their mistakes on others, keeping critical information from others—convey the message that politics is acceptable. Little wonder, then, that subordinates in such situations are themselves prone to politicking.

Communicate Openly

Sharing all relevant information with co-workers and colleagues can thwart the effects of destructive politics. Managers who communicate openly with their peers, superiors, and subordinates eliminate the political advantage of withholding information or blocking access to important people. Information that everyone already knows cannot be hoarded or hidden. In addition, open communication ensures that everyone understands and accepts resource allocations. Such understanding eliminates the attractiveness of political maneuvers intended to bias distribution procedures. Shrinking the potential benefits of destructive politicking lessens the incidence of political behaviors.

Reduce Uncertainty

A third way to minimize destructive political behavior is to reduce uncertainty. Clarifying goals, tasks, and responsibilities makes it easier to assess people's behaviors and brings politics out into the open. Expanding decision-making processes by consulting with subordinates or involving them in participatory decision-making processes helps make the resulting decisions understandable and discourages undercover politicking.

Manage Informal Coalitions and Cliques

Managing informal coalitions and cliques can also help reduce destructive politics. Influencing the norms and beliefs that steer group behaviors can ensure that employees continue to serve organizational interests. When cliques resist less severe techniques, job reassignment becomes a viable option. Group politicking is thereby abolished by eliminating the group.

Confront Political Game Players

A fifth approach to managing politics is to confront political game players about their activities. When people engage in politics despite initial attempts to discourage them from this course of action, a private meeting between superior and subordinate may be enough to curb the subordinate's political pursuits. If not, disciplinary measures may become necessary. Punishments such as a public reprimand or a period of layoff without pay ensure that the costs of politicking outweigh its benefits. If this approach does not work, managers who must cope with damaging politics may have no choice except to dismiss political game players.

Anticipate the Emergence of Damaging Politics

In any effort intended to control political behavior, awareness and anticipation are critical. If managers are aware that circumstances are conducive to politicking, they can try to prevent the emergence of politics. Detection of any of the personal characteristics or favorable conditions discussed earlier should be interpreted as a signal indicating the need for management intervention *before* destructive politics crop up.

Conflict in Organizations

Conflict—a process of opposition and confrontation that can occur in organizations between either individuals or groups—occurs when parties exercise power in the pursuit of valued goals or objectives and obstruct the progress of other parties. Key to this definition is the idea that conflict involves the use of power in confrontation, or disputes over clashing interests. Also important is the notion that conflict is a process—something that takes time to unfold, rather than an event that occurs in an instant and then disappears. Finally, to the extent that obstructing progress threatens effectiveness and performance, the definition implies that conflict is a problem that managers must be able to control.

Is Conflict Necessarily Bad?

Conflict might seem inherently undesirable. In fact, many of the models of organization and management discussed in Chapter 2 support this view. Classic theorists often likened organizations to machines and portrayed conflict as symptomatic of breakdown of these machines. Managers in the days of Henri Fayol and Frederick Taylor concerned themselves with discovering ways either to avoid conflict or to suppress it as quickly and forcefully as possible.

In contrast, contemporary theorists argue that conflict is not necessarily bad. To be sure, they say, *dysfunctional* conflict—confrontation that hinders progress toward desired goals—does occur. For example, protracted labor strikes leave both managers and employees with bad feelings, cost companies lost revenues and customers, and cost employees lost wages and benefits. Current research, however, suggests that conflict is often *functional*, having positive effects such as the following:

- Conflict can lessen social tensions, helping to stabilize and integrate relationships. If resolved in a way that allows for the discussion and dissipation of disagreements, it can serve as a safety valve that vents pressures built up over time.
- Conflict lets opposing parties express rival claims and provides the opportunity to readjust the allocation of valued resources. Resource pools may thus be consumed more effectively owing to conflict-induced changes.
- Conflict helps maintain the level of stimulation or activation required to function innovatively. In so doing, it can serve as a source of motivation to seek adaptive change.
- Conflict supplies feedback about the state of interdependencies and power distributions in an organization's structure. The distribution of power required to coordinate work activities then becomes more clearly apparent and readily understood.

- Conflict can help provide a sense of identity and purpose by clarifying differences and boundaries between individuals or groups. Such outcomes are discussed in greater detail later in this chapter.

At the very least, conflict can serve as a red flag signaling the need for change. Believing that conflict can have positive effects, contemporary managers try to manage or resolve disagreements rather than avoid or suppress them.

Conditions That Stimulate Conflict

For conflict to occur, three key conditions must exist: interdependence, political indeterminism, and divergence. *Interdependence* is found where individuals, groups, or organizations depend on each other for assistance, information, feedback, or other coordinative relations. As indicated in Chapter 8, four types of interdependence—pooled, sequential, reciprocal, and comprehensive—can link parties together. Any such linkages can serve as sources of conflict. For example, two groups that share a pool of funds may fight over who will receive money to buy new office equipment. Similarly, employees organized along a sequential assembly process may disagree about the pace of work. In the absence of interdependence, however, parties have nothing to fight about and, in fact, may not even know of each other's existence.

The emergence of conflict also requires *political indeterminism*, which means that the political pecking order among individuals or groups is unclear and subject to question. If power relations are unambiguous and stable, and if they are accepted as valid by all parties, appeals to authority will replace conflict, and differences will be resolved in favor of the most powerful. Only a party whose power is uncertain will gamble on winning through conflict rather than by appealing to power and authority. For this reason, individuals and groups in a newly reorganized company are much more likely to engage in conflict than are parties in an organization with a stable hierarchy of authority.

Finally, for conflict to emerge, there must be *divergence*, or differences or disagreements deemed worth fighting over. For example, differences in the functions they perform may lead individuals or groups to have *varying goals*. Table 11.4 describes some differences in the goal orientations of marketing and manufacturing groups. In this example, each group's approach reflects its particular orientation—marketing's focus on customer service, manufacturing's concern with efficient production runs. In such situations, conflicts may occur over whose goals to pursue and whose to ignore.

Individuals and groups may also have different *time orientations*. For example, tasks like making a sale to a regular customer require only short-term planning and can be initiated or altered quite easily. In contrast, tasks like traditional assembly-line manufacturing operations necessitate a longer time frame, because such activities require extensive preplanning and cannot be changed easily once they have begun. Certain tasks, such as the strategic planning activities that plot an organization's future, may even require time frames of several decades. When parties in a firm have different time orientations, conflicts may develop regarding which orientation should regulate task planning and performance.

Goal focus	Marketing approach	Manufacturing approach
Product variety	Customers demand variety	Variety causes short, often uneconomical production runs
Capacity limits	Manufacturing capacity limits productivity	Inaccurate sales forecasts limit productivity
Product quality	Reasonable quality should be achievable at a cost that is affordable to customers	Offering options that are difficult to manufacture undermines quality
New products	New products are the firm's lifeblood	Unnecessary design changes are costly
Cost control	High cost undermines the firm's competitive position Broad variety, fast delivery, high quality, and rapid responsiveness are not possible at low cost	

Source: Based on information presented in B. S. Shapiro, "Can Marketing and Manufacturing Coexist?" *Harvard Business Review* 55 (September–October 1977), 104–114.

Table 4 *Differences in Goal Orientations: Marketing and Manufacturing*

Often, *resource allocations* among individuals or groups are unequal. Such differences usually stem from the fact that parties must compete with each other to get a share of their organization's resources. When the production department gets new personal computers to help schedule weekly activities, the sales department may find itself forced to do without the new computers it wants for market research. In such instances, someone wins and someone loses, laying the groundwork for additional rounds of conflict.

Another source of conflict may be the practices used to *evaluate* and *reward* groups and their members. Consider, for example, that manufacturing groups are often rewarded for their efficiency, which is achieved by minimizing the quantity of raw materials consumed in production activities. Sales groups, on the other hand, tend to be rewarded for their flexibility, which sometimes sacrifices efficiency. Conflict often arises in such situations as each group tries to meet its own performance criteria or tries to force others to adopt the same criteria.

In addition, status discrepancies invite conflict over stature and position. Although the status of a person or group is generally determined by its position in the organization's hierarchy of authority—with parties higher in the hierarchy having higher status—sometimes other criteria influence status. For instance, a group might argue that its status should depend on the knowledge possessed by its members or that status should be conferred on the basis of such factors as loyalty, seniority, or visibility.

Conflict can emerge in jurisdictional disputes when it is unclear who has responsibility for something. For example, if the personnel and employing departments both interview a prospective employee, the two groups may dispute which has the ultimate right to offer employment and which must take the blame if mistakes are made.

Finally, individuals and groups can differ in the values, assumptions, and general perceptions that guide their performance. Values held by the members of a production group, which stress easy assembly, for instance, may differ from the values held by the research and development staff, which favor complex product designs. These values can clash, leading to conflict, whenever researchers must fight for demanding product specifications that production personnel dismiss as unnecessarily complicated.

Effects of Conflict

Conflict affects relationships among people and groups in many ways. Especially when conflict occurs between groups, several important effects can be predicted to occur within the opposing groups.

First, as noted in Chapter 9, external threats such as intergroup conflict bring about increased group cohesiveness. As a result, groups engaged in conflict become more attractive and important to their own members. Ongoing conflict also stimulates an emphasis on task performance. All efforts within each conflicting group are directed toward meeting the challenge posed by other groups, and concerns about individual members' satisfaction diminish in importance. A sense of urgency surrounds task performance; defeating the enemy becomes uppermost, and much less loafing occurs.

In addition, when a group faces conflict, otherwise reluctant members will often submit to autocratic leadership to manage the crisis, because they perceive participatory decision making as slow and weak. Strong, authoritarian leaders often emerge as a result of this shift. A group in such circumstances is also likely to place much more emphasis on standard procedures and centralized control. As a result, it becomes characterized by structural rigidity. By adhering to established rules and creating and strictly enforcing new ones, the group seeks to eliminate any conflicts that might develop among its members and to ensure that it can succeed repeatedly at its task.

Other changes may occur in the relations between conflicting groups. Hostility often surfaces in the form of hardened "we–they" attitudes. Each group sees itself as virtuous and the other groups as enemies. Intense dislike often accompanies these negative attitudes. As attitudes within each group become more negative, group members may develop distorted perceptions of opposing groups. The resulting negative stereotyping can create even greater differences between groups and further strengthen the cohesiveness within each group.

Eventually, negative attitudes and perceptions of group members may lead to a decrease in communication among conflicting groups. The isolation that results merely adds to the conflict, making resolution even more difficult to achieve. At the same time, conflicting groups often engage in *increased surveillance* intended to provide information about the attitudes, weaknesses, and likely behaviors of other groups.

Negotiation and Restructuring

A variety of conflict-management techniques have been developed to help resolve conflicts and deal with the kinds of negative effects just described. In general, these techniques are of two types: bargaining and negotiation procedures that focus on managing *divergence* among the interests of conflicting parties, and restructuring techniques that focus on managing *interdependence* between conflicting individuals and groups.

Managing Diverging Interests

Bargaining and negotiation are two closely associated processes that are often employed to work out the differences in interests and concerns that generate conflict. *Bargaining* between conflicting parties consists of offers, counteroffers, and concessions exchanged in a search for some mutually acceptable resolution. *Negotiation,* in turn, is the process in which the parties decide what each will give and take in this exchange.

In the business world, relations between management and labor are often the focus of bargaining and negotiation. Both processes also occur elsewhere in organizations, however, as people and groups try to satisfy their own desires and control the extent to which they must sacrifice so as to satisfy others. In tight economies, for example, groups of secretaries who are dependent on the same supply budget may have to bargain with each other to see who will get new office equipment and who will have to make do with existing equipment. A company's sales force may try to negotiate favorable delivery dates for its best clients by offering manufacturing personnel leeway in meeting deadlines for other customers' orders.

In deciding which conflicting interests will be satisfied, parties engaged in bargaining and negotiation can choose the degree to which they will assert themselves and look after their own interests. They can also decide whether they will cooperate with their adversary and put its interests ahead of their own. Five general approaches to managing divergent interests exist that are characterized by different mixes of assertiveness and cooperativeness:

1. *Competition* (assertive, uncooperative) means overpowering other parties in the conflict and promoting one's own concerns at the other parties' expense. One way to accomplish this aim is by resorting to authority to satisfy one's own concerns. Thus the head of a group of account executives may appeal to the director of advertising to protect the group's turf from intrusions by other account execs.
2. *Accommodation* (unassertive, cooperative) allows other parties to satisfy their own concerns at the expense of one's own interests. Differences are smoothed over to maintain superficial harmony. A purchasing department that fails to meet budgetary guidelines because it deliberately overspends on raw materials in an effort to satisfy the demands of production groups is trying to use accommodation to cope with conflict.
3. *Avoidance* (unassertive, uncooperative) requires staying neutral at all costs or refusing to take an active role in conflict resolution procedures. The finance department that "sticks its head in the sand," hoping that dissension about budgetary allocations will simply blow over, is exhibiting avoidance.

Style	*Application*
Competing	When quick, decisive action is required. On important issues where unpopular solutions must be implemented. On issues vital to organizational welfare when your group is certain that its position is correct. Against groups that take advantage of noncompetitive behavior.
Accommodating	When your group is wrong and wants to show reasonableness. When issues are more important to groups other than yours. To bank favors for later issues. To minimize losses when your group is outmatched and losing. When harmony and stability are especially important.
Avoiding	When a conflict is trivial or unimportant. When there is no chance that your group will satisfy its own needs. When the costs of potential disruption outweigh the benefits of resolution. To let groups cool down and gain perspective. When others can resolve the conflict more effectively.
Collaborating	To find an integrative solution when conflicting concerns are too important to be compromised. When the most important objective is to learn. To combine the ideas of people with different perspectives. To gain commitment through the development of consensus. To work through conflicting feelings between groups.
Compromising	When group concerns are important but not worth the disruption associated with more assertive styles. When equally powerful groups are committed to pursuing mutually exclusive concerns. To achieve temporary settlements. To arrive at expedient resolutions under time pressure. As a backup when neither competing nor problem-solving styles are successful.

Table 5 *Application of Different Styles of Managing Divergence*

4. *Collaboration* (assertive, cooperative) attempts to satisfy everyone by working through differences and seeking solutions in which everyone gains. A marketing department and a manufacturing department that meet on a regular basis to plan mutually acceptable production schedules are collaborating.
5. *Compromise* (midrange assertive, cooperative) seeks partial satisfaction of everyone through exchange and sacrifice, settling for acceptable rather than optimal resolution. Contract bargaining between union representatives and management typically involves significant compromise by both sides.

As indicated in Table 5, the appropriateness of each of these approaches depends on the situation and, in many cases, on the time pressure for a negotiated settlement. Beyond these general alternatives, experts on organizational development have devised an assortment of more specific techniques for conflict management that are based on structured sessions of bargaining and negotiation. . . .

Managing Structural Interdependence

In addition to divergence in interests, conflict requires interdependence. It can therefore be managed or resolved by restructuring the connections that tie conflicting parties together.

One way to accomplish this goal is to *develop superordinate goals*, identifying and pursuing a set of performance targets that conflicting parties can achieve only by working together. Sharing a common goal requires the parties to look beyond their differences and learn to cooperate with each other. In the automobile industry, for instance, unions and management, fearing plant closures, have forgone adversarial relations to strengthen the competitiveness of automotive firms. In many companies, teamwork has replaced conflict in the pursuit of the superordinate goal of producing high-quality products for today's world markets.

Expanding the supply of critical resources is another way to restructure. This strategy removes a major source of conflict between individuals and groups that draw from the same supply. Pools of critical resources are not easily enlarged—which is what makes them critical, of course. When this method is successful, it decreases the amount of interdependence between parties, which then compete less for available resources. For example, one way to eliminate interoffice conflicts over the availability of shared computers is to buy a network of personal computers for every department. Some organizations purchase large quantities of used computers at reduced prices instead of a few new ones at full retail price.

A third way to manage conflict by restructuring interdependence is to *clarify existing relationships* and make the political position of each party readily apparent. If it is feasible, this political clarification affects interdependence by strengthening everyone's understanding of how and why they are connected. It also reduces the political indeterminism that must exist for conflict to occur.

A fourth approach is to modify existing structural relationships. This strategy includes a number of mechanisms that either uncouple conflicting parties or modify the structural linkage between them. Two such mechanisms—the *decoupling mechanisms* of slack resources and self-contained tasks—manage conflict by eliminating the interdependence that must exist for conflict to occur.

Slack resources help decouple otherwise interconnected individuals and groups by creating buffers that lessen the ability of one party to affect the activities of another. Suppose one person assembles telephone handsets, and another person connects finished handsets to telephone bodies to form fully assembled units. The two employees are sequentially interdependent, because the second person's ability to perform the work is contingent on the first person's ability to complete the task. The second employee cannot work if the first employee stops producing. If a buffer inventory is created—a supply of finished handsets—on which the second worker can draw when the first worker is not producing anything, we have (at least temporarily) decoupled the two individuals.

In contrast, the creation of *self-contained tasks* involves combining the work of two or more interdependent parties and then assigning this work to several independent parties. If the original parties are groups, then the self-contained groups are usually staffed by employees drawn from each of the interdependent groups. For example, engineering and drafting groups might have problems coordinating engineering specifications and the drawings produced by the drafting group. These two groups might be re-formed into several independent engineering-drafting groups. After this restructuring, the original two groups no longer exist. Key interdependencies that lie outside the original groups are contained within redesigned groups and can be managed without crossing group boundaries or involving outside managers.

Sometimes concerns about minimizing inventory costs rule out the use of slack resources. Among U.S. manufacturers, for instance, the cost of carrying excessive inventory is a major concern and has stimulated increasing interest in just-in-time (JIT) procedures. Using JIT, inventory is acquired only as needed, eliminating the cost of having unused items lying around. In addition, work often cannot be divided into self-contained tasks. For example, the task of producing the parts required to make a car and assembling them into a final product is so immense that many individuals and groups (in fact, many companies) must be involved. In such cases, existing structural relationships may be modified instead by means of various *unit-linking mechanisms*.

Network information systems are one such mechanism. These systems consist of mainframe computers with remote terminals or network servers connected to personal computers that can be used to input and exchange information about organizational performance. If you have taken courses in computer science, you have probably worked with a computer network similar to the *intranets* now used in businesses. Managers use such systems to communicate among themselves and to store information for later review. The networks facilitate the transfer of large amounts of information up and down an organization's hierarchy of authority. In addition, they support lateral exchanges among interdependent individuals and groups. In the process, they facilitate communication that might otherwise develop into misunderstandings and lead to conflict. The fact that many organizations have recently added the corporate position of chief information officer (CIO) reflects the growing use of network information systems to manage interdependent, potentially conflictful relationships.

A second type of unit-linking mechanism consists of several *lateral linkage devices* that managers can use to strengthen communication between interdependent parties. In one of these, an employee may be assigned a liaison position in which he or she is responsible for seeing that communications flow directly and freely between interdependent groups. The *liaison position* represents an alternative to hierarchical communication channels. It reduces both the time needed to communicate between groups and the amount of information distortion likely to occur. The person occupying a liaison position has no authority to issue direct orders, but rather serves as a neutral third party and relies on negotiation, bargaining, and persuasion. This person is called on to mediate between groups if conflict actually emerges, resolving differences and moving the groups toward voluntary intergroup coordination.

The liaison position is the least costly of the lateral linkage devices. Because one person handles the task of coordination, minimal resources are diverted from the primary task of production. In addition, because the position has no formal authority, it is the least disruptive of normal hierarchical relationships. Sometimes, however, a liaison position is not strong enough to manage interdependence relations. Managers then have the option of turning to another type of lateral linkage device, *representative groups*, to coordinate activities among interdependent parties. Representative groups consist of people who represent the interdependent individuals or groups, and who meet to coordinate the interdependent activities.

Two kinds of representative groups exist. One, called a *task force*, is formed to complete a specific task or project and then disbanded. Representatives get together, talk out the differences among the parties they represent, and resolve conflicts before they become manifest. For this reason, companies such as Colgate-Palmolive and Procter & Gamble form product task groups by drawing together members from advertising, marketing, manufacturing, and product research departments. Each product task group identifies consumer needs, designs new products that respond to these needs, and manages their market introduction. Once a new product is successfully launched, the product task group responsible for its introduction is dissolved, and its members return to their former jobs.

The other type of representative group is a more or less permanent structure. Like the members of the task force, the members of this group, called a *standing committee*, represent interdependent parties, but they meet on a regular basis to discuss and resolve ongoing problems. The standing committee is not assigned a specific task, nor is it expected to disband at any particular time. An example of a standing committee is a factory's Monday morning production meeting. At that meeting, representatives from production control, purchasing, quality assurance, shipping, and various assembly groups overview the week's production schedule and try to anticipate problems.

Like task forces, standing committees use face-to-face communication to manage interdependence problems and resolve conflict-related differences. Despite their usefulness in this regard, both of these linkage devices are more costly than the liaison position. Through process loss, their group meetings inevitably consume otherwise productive resources. In addition, because representative groups (especially task forces) are sometimes designed to operate outside customary hierarchical channels, they can prove quite disruptive to normal management procedures.

When neither liaison positions nor representative groups solve intergroup conflict problems, the company may use a third type of lateral linkage device, called an *integrating manager*. Like the liaison position, the integrating manager mediates between interdependent parties. Unlike the liaison position, however, this individual has the formal authority to issue orders and expect obedience. He or she can tell interdependent parties what to do to resolve conflict. Project managers at companies such as Rockwell International and Lockheed fill the role of integrating manager. They oversee the progress of a project by ensuring that the various planning, designing, assembling, and testing groups work together successfully.

Normally, when coordinating the efforts of groups, an integrating manager issues orders only to group supervisors. Giving orders to the people who report to these supervisors might confuse employees, as employees might feel that they were being asked to report to two supervisors. Because an integrating manager disrupts normal hierarchical relationships by short-circuiting the relationships between the group supervisors and their usual superior, this device is used much less often than either the liaison position or representative groups.

Occasionally, even integrating managers cannot provide the guidance needed to manage conflict through structural means. In these rare instances, a fourth type of lateral linkage device, called the *matrix organization structure*, is sometimes employed. Matrix structures are the most complicated of the mechanisms used to coordinate group activities and resolve intergroup conflicts, and they are extremely costly to sustain. The matrix organization structure will be discussed in greater detail in Chapter 12, which covers organization structure, because it is both a conflict resolution device and a specific type of structure. For now, we conclude by suggesting that matrix structures are appropriate only when all other intergroup mechanisms have proved ineffective.

Summary

Power is the ability to influence others and to resist their influence in return. Compliance, identification, and internalization are outcomes that may result from the use of five types of interpersonal power—*reward*, *coercive*, *legitimate*, *referent*, and *expert* power. Power also grows out of uncertainty surrounding the continued availability of *critical contingencies.* It is therefore based on the ability to *reduce this uncertainty* and is enhanced by low *substitutability* and high *centrality.*

Politics is a process through which a person acquires power and uses it to advance the individual's self-interests. It is stimulated by a combination of personal characteristics and antecedent conditions and can involve a variety of tactics, ranging from controlling supplies of critical resources to attacking or blaming others. Several techniques are employed to manage politicking, including setting an example and confronting political game players.

Conflict is a process of opposition and confrontation that requires the presence of interdependence, political indeterminism, and divergence. It can be managed through *bargaining* and *negotiation*, or it can be resolved by restructuring interdependence relations through the use of various *decoupling* or *unit-linking mechanisms*.

Take Charge of Your Career

By Annabelle Reitman

Direct Your Career

One characteristic of successful professionals is the continuous and directed management of their career pathways, which requires assessing current positions and future directions, determining goals, and identifying ways to reach them. Because shifts in personal circumstances, organizational priorities, and the marketplace may call for voluntary or involuntary career moves, or because unexpected opportunities may arise, being prepared to make a change by knowing your capabilities and goals and by understanding how to market yourself is critical. The ability to control your professional progress enhances the effectiveness and efficiency of your career transitions. Directing your career also enhances and expands your employability.

These uncertain and challenging economic times as well as the issues and changes facing training and learning professionals make it more essential than ever to know how and where to position yourself for your next targeted career move. Directing your professional path includes thinking about "what ifs" and ensuring that you have the appropriate job search or marketing tools and resources.

Career moves can take the form of common employment changes such as getting a promotion, moving laterally within an organization, getting a new job in the same field, or changing fields altogether. More specific and limited career moves take the form of professional shifts. In the field of learning and performance, basically four types of professional shifts can take place:

1. A switch in the field of practice, for example, from human resource development to knowledge management, or from training and development to organizational development.
2. A change in the group of clients served, for example, from working with individuals to working with whole organizations or groups and teams.
3. A shift in responsibilities, for example, from delivering stand-up training to developing e-learning programs.
4. A switch in your work setting, for example, from internal consulting to external consulting or teaching.

This *Info-line* is a self-directed refresher course in strategies and practices to promote yourself inside and outside of organizations. This issue will help you to:

- assess your present situation
- determine your priorities
- identify options for next steps
- identify relevant background qualifications for use in your next career move
- create a unique professional niche or package
- understand job search and marketing campaign strategies
- draft a targeted resume
- prepare for job interviews
- survive the job search.

Assess the Situation

Whether you are presently employed and experiencing a plateau or you have lost your job and need to be gainfully employed, first determine what you need from employment to feel satisfied. In preparing to look for new employment, the fundamental question is: What kind of employment will restore your passion for work, serve your present priorities, and allow you to grow and develop as a professional? Consider the questions presented in the sidebar *Assess Your Work Situation* to decide if you want to begin planning a career change.

Determine Your Priorities

An effective and productive job search or marketing campaign begins with a needs assessment to define the role and responsibilities you would like to have in your next employment situation. Before planning your next career move, review how and in what ways your professional interests and priorities have changed. What are your emerging passions with respect to learning and performance? What would you

Assess Your Work Situation

Answer the following list of questions and then review the results. Based on your answers, how satisfied are you with your job or were you with your previous job? If you are currently employed, should you look for a new job? Describe why. If you are unemployed, to what extent are you looking forward to new employment? Why?

- Do you feel that your work is meaningful and rewarding?
- Are your skills, knowledge, and abilities used to the fullest?
- How do you feel about your supervisor? How would you describe your relationship?
- How would you describe your co-workers and your relationship with them?
- How do you feel about the job? Do you feel that you have a match with your organization's culture and mission?
- Does the job provide any opportunities for advancement? Are there positions in the organization that you would like to achieve?
- Is your salary fair in relation to industry standards?
- Is your salary above the national average for your position level and responsibilities?
- Have your professional interests and focus changed? Will your position be able to expand to accommodate those changes?
- Do you have sufficient resources and budget to do your job efficiently and effectively?
- Does your immediate work environment allow for independent actions?
- Do you feel that your efforts and achievements are appreciated or recognized?

like the next challenge to be? The sidebar *What's My Next Move?* at right presents some questions that will help you pinpoint your employment needs.

As you contemplate making a change in your work situation, consider some basic career factors and determine which ones will shape your professional goals and next steps. What are your priorities? Some basic considerations are presented in the sidebar *Set Professional Priorities.*

Identify Career Move Options

Now that you understand your current employment situation and know what you want, what are your career move options? If you are currently employed, you may want to find out if any opportunities exist to make a move within your present organization. Other options to explore are self-employment and seeking a new and better job. The sidebar *Informational Interviewing* describes one method of seeking more information about potential career moves.

Move Within Your Organization

You have three options for making internal changes in your present work situation:

- *Enhance or Enrich Your Present Position*
  Can you modify your responsibilities to use certain skills more effectively or incorporate new challenges? You can achieve this by developing proactive strategies for development of skills and knowledge, for example, through on-the-job training.
- *Make a Lateral Move*
  Can you seek diversity in work assignments by modifying a position within your department? Examples of such modifications include assignments to specific teams or temporary relocations to different sites for cross-training purposes.
- *Seek a Promotion*
  Can you seek a promotion to the position you desire in your current organization? To make this move, you will need to consider your qualifications for the next step, professional development needed to fill any gaps, the competition, and how far up the ladder you can realistically go to achieve your ultimate career goal.

Before initiating any changes within your organization, develop a clear picture of the workplace learning skills, information, or technical expertise needed for the activities you seek to engage in by making a list of these requirements. Which do you already possess? If you possess the requisite skills, you will have to market yourself to your supervisor and others to demonstrate how this change in your position or status benefits not only you but also the department and organization.

Become an External Consultant

Another career option is self-employment. You may want to set up a consulting practice or become a vendor. A few initial steps to plan for when preparing for self-employment are to develop a business plan and a budget and to identify potential clients or customers. In addition, you need to create a business infrastructure, including necessary equipment, a mail service, and additional support. More information about self-employment is available at ASTD's Website.

However, self-employment is for not everyone. Basic characteristics of an entrepreneur include:

- being a self-starter
- having a strong desire to be independent
- being self-disciplined
- being willing to take risks
- being flexible, adaptable, and comfortable with change and the unknown
- having the ability to establish productive business relationships
- having the ability to see the potential of new ideas and to develop them.

What's My Next Move?

Take time to conduct a career needs assessment. Compare your current professional situation with your ideal situation and identify critical gaps. This is the first step toward taking control of your career pathway and mapping out its direction. Some basic questions to consider include:

- Is your present position, or was your last one, fulfilling and challenging work? Why or why not?
- Considering ongoing changes in the learning and performance field, what job possibilities would be of interest to you?
- Have you reached a point in your career when you should consider becoming an entrepreneur?
- Do you have competencies and expertise that you are not currently using, but want to? What type of work opportunities would allow you to use those capabilities?
- Would you want to use your learning and performance savvy in a different type of organization or industry? Why?
- Would you want to change or add to the client base you serve? Why?
- Do you feel that you have balance in your life?
- How does your present position, or did your last one, fall short of your expectations?
- What about the learning and performance field are you passionate about? What do you dislike? How does your position stack up with respect to your likes and dislikes?
- Do you feel that you are contributing to the field and your community?
- How can you best achieve your career mission and ultimate professional goals?

Review your responses. What is your assessment of your career progress and professional situation? Is it great, tolerable, or poor? What are your thoughts regarding specific changes you would seek in your next work situation?

Seek a New Job

Based on your assessment of your current position and your priorities, you may choose to seek a new job altogether. You also may be forced to seek a new position because of a job loss.

When developing an image of your ideal work position, ask yourself the following questions. Retain in your mind the image you develop as you plan to seek a new position.

- What skills and knowledge do you want to use?
- Who are the people you would like to interact with?
- What would you consider the ideal work environment?
- What are the responsibilities and activities you want to engage in?
- What kind of effect do you want your work to have?
- What level of compensation and benefits are you looking for?

SET PROFESSIONAL PRIORITIES

Determine which work characteristics are critical to you as you set your expectations for your next work situation. Refer, if necessary, to your responses in the sidebars *Assess Your Work Situation* and *What's My Next Move?* Next, rank order them. Explain why you have selected these priorities and ranked them in the listed order. How many of these priorities would an internal or external position need to have for you to accept the offer without hesitation? Keep these priorities in mind as you target work opportunities for further exploration.

Work Characteristics	Rank Order
More than adequate wages and benefits	
Independence and autonomy	
Organizational stability	
Time for family	
Time for friends, avocations, volunteerism	
Career advancement or job expansion opportunities	
Comfortable work environment and culture	
Opportunities to use preferred skills and professional savvy	
Challenging and meaningful assignments	
Ideal learning and performance position	
Great working relationships with supervisor and colleagues	
Acceptable commuting distance	
Professional development activities	
Travel opportunities	
Other:	

Informational Interviewing

Informational interviewing is a method of gathering information to decide your next career move. In informational interviewing, you initiate the request, set the agenda, and take the lead. Note that this differs from an employment interview in that it is not a meeting for a specific job opportunity. The goals of informational interviewing are to:

- acquire useful and relevant information and resources
- obtain additional referrals and contact leads
- gain entry to targeted professional or business associations
- gather advice about particular concerns or issues.

As with any other job search activities, there are some do's and don'ts for informational interviewing. Effective practices include:

- ensuring the interviewee understands you don't expect a job
- acknowledging the interviewee's time and requesting a meeting limited to 30 minutes
- being explicit about the intention of the meeting
- preparing an agenda and questions prior to the meeting
- sticking to the agreed-upon length of and reason for the meeting
- taking brief notes during the meeting
- asking questions that build rapport and elicit needed resources
- summarizing briefly one's background and only if asked providing a resume or consulting informational materials
- following up with a thank-you note or email.

Identify Relevant Background

To prepare for the next steps of creating a resume and getting ready to market yourself, pinpoint and assess your specific learning- and performance-related competencies, general skills, and relevant experiences. Job search and marketing documents and presentations are based on this information and data.

Work Content Skills

Work content skills often are called "hard skills." They are usually described as the qualifications for a particular job and are directly related to the knowledge base of a specific profession. They incorporate a special vocabulary and subject matter as requirements for entry and advancement in a particular occupation. They are usually acquired through education or training activities, but can be developed on the job. Examples of skills and knowledge related to learning and performance include:

- instructional design or implementation
- presentation or facilitation skills
- e-learning delivery
- needs assessment
- learning styles
- succession planning
- knowledge management
- human performance improvement fundamentals
- career development process
- organizational development principles.

As you think about your next move as a learning and performance specialist, review your present level of professional expertise. Given the fast pace of changes in the field, do you need to develop or update your work content skills to be more competitive, or can you repurpose some existing skills?

Transferable Skills

Transferable skills also are referred to as "soft skills" and can be used in a broad range of work functions. Generally speaking, the transferable skills that most directly relate to learning and performance involve organizational and interpersonal activities and concerns.

Areas in which you may have transferable skills include:

- business acumen
- oral or written communications
- teaching and counseling
- entrepreneurship and consulting
- research and investigation
- leadership or supervision
- application of computer programs
- problem solving or conflict resolution
- team building
- program design or implementation
- project coordination.

Be aware of your transferable skills and their application in various areas or functions of the learning and performance field. This is particularly important if you are making a career change into the field or are considering a change in your specialization. Demonstrating these skills and your understanding of their application is important for showing that you can make the transition successfully.

Experiences

Experience highlights and achievements are successes you have garnered in present and past jobs and volunteer or community work that you believe will establish your credibility. Select those that will demonstrate the skills and knowledge you would prefer to use. Mapping your accomplishments can be a big confidence booster and helps you tease out specific skills and behaviors to highlight. In assessing your accomplishments and identifying those to incorporate into written and oral presentations, list specific ones that:

- stimulate interest in your candidacy for a job, promotion, or consulting contract
- illustrate how you meet challenges and solve problems above and beyond expectations
- show how you have contributed to the overall organization, department, team, and so forth
- demonstrate your willingness to learn anything it takes to get a job done
- improve your professional image.

Describe each experience in one paragraph. Include the objective or problem and how it was met or resolved and explain why you or someone else considered it an achievement. Explain the results in terms of monies saved, growth or expansion of business, and improvements in processes and procedures.

Create a Professional Niche

A professional niche is a customized bundling of your skills, knowledge, education, and achievements that projects a unique professional image, or "brand identity," to prospective employers and clients. Developing a professional niche may be your most difficult task. However, to stand out from your competition and to reinforce your credibility, you need to establish a unique place for yourself.

To position yourself for a new work experience prepare a summary statement that showcases your qualifications and strengths. The sidebar *Put It All Together* at right describes how to prepare such a statement. Keep in mind that the objective of your written and oral presentations is to get someone's immediate attention focused on you and your qualifications. Because some situations present only a narrow window of opportunity to be noticed and remembered, be prepared to describe your professional niche succinctly.

PUT IT ALL TOGETHER

Putting it all together into a professional niche or package is the final step for getting ready to tell your story to your supervisor or prospective employers or clients. Consider the position or consulting assignment that you want to obtain and match the strongest parts of your background to that position or assignment.

1. To begin, review your work content skills, transferable skills, and experience highlights and successes. Selected information from these areas is the underlying material for creating your professional niche.
2. In priority order, select no more than five work content skills or competencies.
3. In priority order, select no more than five transferable skills or competencies.
4. Select seven to 10 achievements that have taken place within the last five years that support the competencies listed in steps 2 and 3. An achievement can illustrate more than one skill. Describe each achievement in no more than five bulleted sentences.
5. Write a short paragraph summarizing your professional niche. Integrate information you generated in steps 2 through 4. Select the information that most clearly projects your ideal professional image and illustrates your qualifications in relation to your desired position or assignment. Read the paragraph to people who know you. How does it sound? Does it convey your desired professional image? Edit as necessary.

Develop a Resume

A targeted resume is a key marketing tool that highlights your professional expertise and showcases your professional niche. The basics of resumes—purpose, type, content, and format—are presented below.

- *Purpose*

  The purpose of a resume is to get prospective employers interested in you and to call you in for an interview. Your resume is your tool to:
  - grab employers' attention
  - demonstrate that you have what they need
  - show how you can benefit them
  - stand out from your competitors
  - make the first cut.

- *Type*

  Resume types include chronological, functional, and combination. Each type has different roles and uses that depend on the circumstances and your level of experience.
  - Chronological resumes outline your work history starting with your most recent position and ending with the oldest. They show your career progression over time.

Sample Resume: Professional Move

The following resume is an example of a functional resume. Note the emphasis on professional skills and experiences rather than on a chronological listing of positions held.

Jack D. Smith

1234 Main Street
Old Town, VA 22304
(Phone) 703.123.4567
(Email) jds9@aol.com

Profile Summary

Consultant in human performance improvement with an excellent record of guiding individuals and organizations to enhanced productivity and effectiveness. Excels in communication, team building, leadership, and strategic solutions.

Professional Skills and Competencies

- *Coaching:* Clientele includes executives, managers, professionals, administrators, and staff.
- *Training and facilitation:* Topics include leadership, team building, performance management, and train-thetrainer.
- *Consulting:* Concerns include organizational strategies, team building, and strengthening employee performance.
- *Project management:* Types include organizational downsizing, company closings, and workstation improvements.

Professional Experience

- Principal: JDS Associates, Alexandria, VA 1996-Present

A consulting firm specializing in individual and organizational growth and development

- Contract highlights include:
  - *Launched performance management skill development* nationally for 175 partners and senior managers of a major accounting firm that shifted a work culture from individualism to team delivery
  - *Led a highly successful customized performance improvement program* for a federal agency

- *Conducted executive interviews, focus groups, and workshops* with a major high-tech firm, resulting in a culture change from minority harassment tolerance to workplace respect acceptance
- *Facilitated more than 40 in-depth train-the-trainer programs* for about 272 trainers and managers
- *Delivered workshops to more than 2,500 people* from private, public, and nonprofit sectors.

- Vice President: Best Outplacement Firm, Washington, DC 1989-1995

  A leading international outplacement organization specializing in individual and organizational transition

Assignments included:

- *Coached more than 300 executives, managers, and other staff in career and leadership skills* advancing their careers and accounting for more than $300,000 revenue annually
- *Implemented a major downsizing project for a Fortune 500 high-tech, multi-state client* that included training and supervising a team of 18 professionals to deliver workshops for 2,100 employees
- *Delivered leadership core competency assessments to managers* generating roadmaps for performance development linked to goals defined by senior management
- *Conducted 15+ career transition workshops for more than 150 administrative and frontline personne*l empowering them to successfully manage their job search campaigns.

- President: JDS Associates, Inc., Bethesda, MD 1982-1989

  A consulting firm specializing in management and human factors training

Contracts included:

- *Managed a three-year implementation project involving computer workstation setups* for a major accounting firm for their offices in the United States and three other countries
- *Trained more than 600 Fortune 500 companies' PC users* in applied ergonomics increasing productivity by 30 percent.

Other Work Experience

- Department of Human Services, Baltimore, MD

  Major responsibilities included managing four multilingual, cross-functional teams in holistic service delivery; developing and directing a volunteer clearinghouse servicing 75 agencies; and creating a regional roundtable to promote professional development for service providers.

Education and Professional Development

- Master's in Organizational Development from American University, Washington, DC
- Master Trainer Certification, XYZ Consulting Firm, Washington, DC
- MBTI Type Indicator Certification, Type Resources, Inc., Gaithersburg, MD
- Career Architect Certification, Lominger Limited, Inc., Minneapolis, MN
- Organizational Development Concepts & Technologies, NTL, Washington, DC
- MSW (Community Organization), University of Maryland, College Park, MD
- BA (Philosophy), University of Pennsylvania, State College, PA.

Professional Affiliations

- ASTD, Metro DC Chapter, former Secretary
- International Association of Career Management Professionals, DC Chapter, former Treasurer
- Metropolitan Area Career/Life Planning Network

  - Functional resumes present skills and experience and stress accomplishments and strengths rather than a progressive career history. They emphasize selected professional competencies and are especially useful when making a career change. An example of a functional resume is presented in the sidebar *Sample Resume: Professional Move.*
  - Combination or targeted resumes use elements of both chronological and functional resumes and can be tailored to specific work opportunities.

- *Content*

  The content you put into your resume is selected information from your work history that projects the professional image you want to present. The sidebar *Resume Tips* at left provides some field-specific information to include in your resume. Basic data and facts to include are:

  - contact information: name, address, phone number, cell phone number, and email address
  - objective: a precise description of the type of work and responsibilities you are seeking
  - professional summary: learning and performance specialization, breadth of experience, competencies, and competitive edge
  - professional experience: employers, positions, and responsibilities or assignments; if self-employed, services or products provided and client base
  - accomplishments: individual and as team member
  - education: degrees, certifications, additional specialized training, and ongoing professional development
  - professional activities: board or committee activities, volunteer assignments, conference and meeting presentations, and publications
  - awards and certificates.

Resume Tips

Your resume should show that you are up to date with the terminology, issues, methods, and tools of the learning and performance field. A learning-and-performance-focused resume highlights information such as:

- technical competencies, for example, needs assessment, instructional design and delivery, strategic planning, adult learning, and knowledge management
- transferable skills, such as management, communications, problem solving, team or project work, and coaching
- training subject matter expertise, for example, sales, leadership, information technology, supervision, and negotiations
- methods and tools, such as Web-based training, learning styles, focus groups, and benchmarking
- learning related roles, such as performance consulting, analysis, interventions, and evaluation
- current issues, for example learning organizations, corporate universities, retention, organizational performance, and diversity challenges.

In some cases, you may need to provide examples of your expertise and accomplishments. If so, you may want to create a portfolio that contains samples of work that show the variety, quality, and outcomes of your work as well as demonstrate your creativity.

- *Format*

  In preparing your resume, use words, phrases, and a look you are comfortable with. Devote the first third of your resume to describing your professional niche and use the rest of the space to document your credibility and qualifications. Limit headings to topics that are relevant to the position you are seeking. Also, limit the number of pages to two and don't stuff too much information into the two pages; use plenty of white space to make it easy to read. If you use different font sizes and styles, bullet types, and so on to stress certain items, use them sparingly and consistently.

Market Yourself

Consider yourself a "product" that you need to market. Basically, you need to promote yourself as the best candidate for a job, contract, transfer, promotion, and so forth. Strategies for marketing yourself include developing a presentation, networking, and interviewing. Note the importance of having a clear understanding of the requirements of the professional opportunity you are seeking. People frequently are not hired because they fail to illustrate how they can fulfill the potential employer's needs.

Develop a Presentation

Develop a presentation—either oral or written—to communicate deliberately and succinctly how your unique background and experience can solve a potential employer's problem. Consider the specific opportunity and employer and ensure that you answer the following questions in your presentation:

- How does your professional expertise answer the needs of the potential employer? Organize your answer starting with the most relevant experiences.
- In relation to the requirements of the job, what experience highlights and successes demonstrate your qualifications best?
- What is your professional niche? How are you different from anyone else seeking the position?

Learn to Network

Networking is not just to gain job, contract, or client leads. Networking is important to a successful career for many reasons. This systematic and targeted activity enables you to gather information, resources, or support. Before initiating any networking activities, consider which of the following that you want to accomplish:

- obtain specific data, products, services, or knowledge
- gain visibility and increase your "brand recognition"
- hear about opportunities
- get an introduction or referral
- receive advice or counsel
- make a connection.

Take a long-term perspective on networking and stay in contact with people so they are current about your professional activities and career plans, but be patient while establishing relationships; you need to strike a balance between staying in touch and harassing people. Integrate networking into your life and put yourself "in the right place at the right time." Some effective networking practices include:

- introducing yourself with some highlights of your story to generate interest
- following up on a contact within 48 hours to ensure that you are still fresh in a person's mind
- acknowledging assistance received by informing your contact about outcomes
- making requests in a direct, explicit, targeted, and undemanding way
- reconnecting with someone by reintroducing yourself rather than asking if they remember you
- planning what you want out of a networking event before attending
- handing out marketing documents such as business cards, resumes, and consulting brochures by request only
- asking permission to check in with a contact for future leads.

Interviewer's Questions

The following are some typical questions that the interviewer may ask about your professional competencies and background. Use these questions to help you prepare for an interview.

- Tell me about yourself.
- If presently employed: Why are you looking for a new position?
- If presently unemployed: Under what circumstances did you leave your last position?
- If changing careers to the learning and performance field: What attracted you to this field and what do you think you can contribute?
- If making a professional move: Why are you moving from —— to —— (for example, training to change management)?
- How familiar are you with current training methods and tools such as e-learning, virtual team building, focus groups, and so forth?
- Describe the most challenging learning and performance issues that you have had to resolve.
- What transferable skills and experience can you bring to this position?
- A concern we have is —— (for example, employee commitment), what steps would you take to improve the situation?
- As a learning and performance manager, what would you do to increase departmental productivity?
- What do you consider your professional strengths? Weaknesses?

Prepare for Job Interviews

The purposes of an employment interview are to provide the interviewer with detailed information about your qualifications, experiences, and professional characteristics and to provide you with a better understanding of the job's requirements and the working environment. Expect a minimum of two rounds of interviews before a potential employer makes an offer.

Note that if you are interviewing for a consulting contract, you will have to submit a proposal that details the work requirement, plans for completing the work, and estimated costs before the employer offers a contract. In fact, you may have to submit a proposal as part of the screening process to be invited to an interview.

Preparation is the key to successful interviews. Research the potential employer's organization and industry; write down questions to ask about the position, department, employer, and so forth; familiarize yourself with current learning and performance topics and strategies; and review your own background and experience to answer questions readily. The sidebar *Interviewer's Questions* provides some frequently asked questions to help you prepare for the interview.

For the interview, remember to:

- maintain good eye contact, use appropriate body language, listen actively, and so forth

Balancing the Scales

Think about your priorities in accepting a job offer. Review the following list of factors, compare with your ideal, and check the ones you feel are good or reasonable matches.

Draw up a balance sheet. List checked factors on the positive side and unchecked factors on the negative side. Describe why a factor is positive or negative and weigh the factor's importance to you. To accept a position, you should be able to check at least your top three to five priorities.

Offer Factors	*Compared With*
Salary or compensation	Going market rates, present or last job's wages, required income level
Benefits	Present or last job's benefits, ones you would like to have
Perks	Present or last job's perks, ones you would like to have
Job title	Present or last job's title, level of importance to you
Job description and responsibilities	Skills and knowledge you want to use, expand, or attain
Advancement, learning, other possibilities	Your career plan and goals
Organizational characteristics, structure, and culture	Your values, working and social style, personality
Other considerations, such as commute or time requirements	Your personal needs
Specific skills or knowledge used in position	Skills and knowledge you want to use, expand, or attain

- be prepared to promote yourself and your accomplishments
- bring a copy of your resume and, if necessary, refer to it to refresh the interviewer's memory and fill in the details
- prepare opening and closing statements, which should be strong sales pitches to ensure that the interviewer remembers you
- tailor your approach to each situation to illustrate how you would meet the needs of the organization
- identify people who best know your professional qualifications as references; prepare your references to expect a call and to give them information about the opportunity.

Survive the Search

To survive the search, maintain confidence in your ability to keep trying to reach your goal. The sidebar *Balancing the Scales* provides some guidelines for assessing an eventual job offer that will help ensure that you don't accept a position out of desperation.

But what do you do if you don't get an offer or a contract? Assess what you did and identify what you could do differently next time. Was your resume tailored to the specific position or assignment? How could you be more effective in the interview? Review the experience with a trusted colleague or friend who can review the results objectively and make some suggestions that will improve your chances for success the next time. Be flexible, expand your resources for leads, and be receptive to alternative options, and above all, maintain the motivation to continue your job search or marketing campaign. Follow the tips and tools in this *Info-line,* and you are bound to be successful in your job search or marketing campaign. Good luck!

References & Resources

Articles

Vicino, J. "Annual Pay and Compensation Report." *T&D,* January 2003.

Zahn, D. "Training: A Function, Profession, Calling, What?" *T&D,* April 2001.

Zielinski, D. "Training Careers in the 21st Century." *Training,* January 2000.

Books

Andrusia, D., and R. Haskins. *Brand Yourself: How to Create an Identity for a Brilliant Career.* New York: Ballantine Publishing Group, 2000.

Criscito, P.,*Designing the Perfect Resume.* Hauppauge, NY: Barron's Educational Series, 2000.

Crispin, G., and M. Mehler. *CareerXroads 2002: The Directory to Job, Resume, and Career Management Sites on the Web.* Kendall Park, NJ: MMC Group, 2001.

Dikel, M., and F. Roehm. *Guide to Internet Job Searching.* Chicago: VGM Career Books, 2002.

Eyler, D. *The Ultimate Job Book.* New York: Random House Reference, 2002.

Eyre, V., J. Williams, and D. Osen. *Great Interview!* New York: LearningExpress, 2000.

Gunhus, J. *No Parachute Required.* New York: Hyperion, 2001.

Kaplan, R. *How to Say It in Your Job Search.* Englewood Cliffs, NJ: Prentice Hall, 2002.

Meshriy, N. *Thinking Outside the Cubicle: How to Change the Job You Have into the Job You Want.* Oakland, CA: New Harbinger Publications, 2002.

Michelozzi, B. *Coming Alive from Nine to Five.* Palo Alto, CA: Mayfield Publishing Company, 2000.

Pontow, R. *Proven Resumes.* Berkeley, CA: Ten Speed Press, 1999.

Reitman, A., and C. Williams. *Career Moves: Take Charge of Your Training Career NOW!* Alexandria, VA: ASTD Press, 2001.

Rich, J. *Great Resume: Get Noticed, Get Hired.* New York: LearningExpress, 2000.

Wendleton, K. *Kick Off Your Career.* Franklin Lakes, NJ: Career Press, 2002.

Info-lines

Callahan, M. "From Training to Performance Consulting." No. 9702.
David, Mark. "Guide to Successful Executive Coaching." No. 0204.
Newman, A. "Knowledge Management." No. 9903.

Websites

America's Career Infonet. http://www.acinet.org.
ASTD. "Job bank." http://www.jobs.astd.org.
CareerBuilder.com. http://www.headhunter.net.
Consultant Resource Center. http://www.consultant-center.com.
Elance. http://www.elance.com.
FreeAgent.com. http://www.freeagent.com.
Guru.com. http://www.guru.com.
The Herman Group. http://www.herman.net.
HomeEmployed.com. http://www.homeemployed.com.
HotJobs.com. http://www.hotjobs.com.
HR.com. http://www.hr.com.
HRIM Mall. http://www.hrimmall.com.
HR Job Search. http://www.monsterhr.com.
hrtoday.com. http://www.hr-today.com.
Institute of Management Consultants USA. http://www.imcusa.org.
JobHuntersBible.com. http://www.jobhuntersbible.com.
ProvenResumes.com. http://www.provenresumes.com.
Recruiters Network. http://www.recruitersnetwork.com.
Resumania! http://www.resumania.com.
The Resume Place, Inc. http://www.resume-place.com.
TCM.com, Inc. http://www.tcm.com/hr-careers.
Training Forum. http://www.trainingforum.com.
Training Resource Network, Inc. http://www.trninc.com.
Training Supersite. http://www.trainingsupersite.com.
WetFeet. http://www.wetfeet.com.
Working Solo. http://www.workingsolo.com.
WSJ.com. "Career Journal from the Wall Street Journal." http://www.careers.wsj.com.

Glossary

3 E's
Effective, Efficient, and Ethical are the 3 E's of a good plan.

360-Degree Feedback
An employee job performance appraisal system that takes into account evaluations from those above, below, and at the same level as the employee.

Accountability
The subordinates whom the manager has the right to expect to perform the job delegated to him or her, and that the manager has the right to take corrective action if the subordinate fails to do so.

Acid Test
Another name for the quick ratio.

Acquisition
A common business strategy focusing on growth through the purchase of other businesses. Smuckers is a good example.

Adjourning
After the job is done, the team can dissolve; contrast with department.

Administrative Management
A concept advocated by Henri Fayol (1841–1925), suggesting that there are common principles of management that apply to all types of businesses.

Affirmative Action
Taking positive steps to correct previous injustices and prejudices, especially toward qualified minorities, women, persons with disabilities, and veterans.

Age Discrimination Act of 1967
Makes it illegal to discriminate in employment decisions against persons 40 years of age and above.

Agent
A manager with authority to act for the organization or some part of it.

Americans with Disabilities Act of 1990
Makes it illegal to discriminate in employment decisions against people with physical or mental disabilities.

Analysis Paralysis
When planners do so much analysis that they fail to make a timely decision.

Angel Investor
Typically, a wealthy investor worth over $1 million who is willing to invest money to help a start-up business. Some, such as a family member, may do it for free, but most expect a share of the ownership and eventually a higher rate of return than the stock market provides.

Art of War, The
Book written by Sun Tzu over 2,500 years ago containing words of wisdom about leadership.

Asia-Pacific Economic Cooperation (APEC)
An organization of 21 Pacific Rim countries seeking free trade and economic cooperation.

Association of Southeast Asian Nations (ASEAN)
An agreement among several nations in Southeast Asia aimed at promoting peace and free trade among nations such as Vietnam, Indonesia, Thailand, etc.

Authentic Leadership Theory
Those who lead best derive their power from the consent of their followers.

Authority
A person with authority has the power and right to make decisions, give orders, draw on resources, and do whatever is necessary to fulfill the responsibility of his or her managerial position.

Balance Sheet
A financial report summarizing a company's assets, liabilities, and stockholders' equity at a specific point using the formula: Assets = liabilities + stockholders' equity.

Baxter, Cliff
Former chairman of Enron; he committed suicide in 2002.

Behavioral Appraisal
Job performance appraisal based upon observed behaviors of the employee.

Behavioral Approach to Management
A concept advocated by Elton Mayo (1880–1949) and others, focusing on the psychological and sociological aspects of human behavior with regard to worker productivity and job satisfaction.

Benevolence
Kindness and compassion for others.

Big-Box Store
Describes huge retail stores such as Walmart and Costco that typically have very large, but plain-looking, stores and compete on price.

Boston Consulting Group Matrix
The Boston Consulting Group (BCG) matrix classifies all units of a large business into the categories of cows, dogs, question marks, and stars.

Brazil, Russia, India, and China (BRIC)
The Big Four in terms of newly advanced economic development.

Bureaucracy
A concept advocated by Max Weber (1864–1920), suggesting organizations should be run by formal rules and procedures and that workers should advance based upon their performance instead of family connections.

Bureaucratic Control
The use of rules, regulations, and formal authority to guide the performance of employees.

Bureaucratic Structure
A hierarchical organization delineated by clear lines of authority, written rules, and an administrator who strictly enforces the rules.

Business Ethics
A subset of the field of ethics, focusing on the ethical issues facing business leaders.

Calling
Where your passion, talent, and a cause greater than yourself intersect.

Capital Budget
Planned costs to build or buy large items such as buildings or large equipment that would not be a part of the ordinary costs of doing business.

Cash Flow Statement
Report providing summary of cash flowing in and out of the business during a specific period such as a quarter (three months) or year.

Central America Free Trade Agreement (CAFTA)
An agreement between the United States and several Central American countries to promote free trade.

Centralized Organization
Important decisions are made at the top of the organization with little or no input from below.

Channel
In the Shannon & Weaver Communication Model, the vehicle that carries the message from the transmitter to the receiver.

Charismatic Leadership Theory
Leaders use their charm to lead others.

Clan Control
Control that employees impose on themselves based on agreed-upon norms, values, shared goals, and trust.

Closed Shop
A place of business where only people who are already members of a union could be hired.

Concentrate
A common business strategy that focuses on doing one thing (or few things) exceptionally well. Starbucks is a good example.

Confucius
Chinese philosopher who lived around 550 B.C. and defined moral courage.

Conglomerate Diversification
A common business strategy focusing on the purchase of other unrelated businesses. General Electric is a good example.

Contingency Theory of Leadership
Which leadership approach to use is contingent on elements of the leader's personality, the task, workers, and the level of power of the leader.

Contrarian
A person who typically thinks and acts contrary to popular or accepted opinion.

Control
Any process that directs the activities of individuals toward the achievement of the organization's goals.

Cooperative Contracts
One firm signs a legal contract with a business in another country to make their products there.

Coordination
The procedures that link the various parts of an organization to achieve the organization's overall mission.

Corporate Social Responsibility
The expectation that in return for privileges granted by the state government and laws that encourage business investment, a corporation will exhibit good citizenship and support charities and the arts.

Cash Cow
In business, a cash cow is a business unit with low potential for market growth, but your company maintains a large share of the market for the product.

Current Ratio
Current ratio = current assets divided by current liabilities.

Debt-to-Equity Ratio
Total liabilities divided by shareholders' equity.

Decentralized Organization
Many decisions are made at lower levels; people further down the organizational hierarchy feel empowered.

Delegation
Assignment of responsibilities to a subordinate.

Deming, W. Edwards
American statistician (1906–1993), who helped Japan's industrial efforts to recover from World War II by advocating statistical quality control, a concept later accepted in America.

Destination
In the Shannon & Weaver Communication Model, the person who receives the transmitted message.

Differentiate
A common business strategy focusing on setting your product apart from the competition, typically the basis of quality instead of price. Cadillac is an example.

Differentiation
Where a large organization is composed of many different units that work on different tasks using diverse skills and work methods.

Diversity
The condition of being different, not all alike, and includes differences as to color, religion, age, disability status, military experience, sexual orientation, economic class, educational level, gender, race, ethnicity, and nationality.

Diversity Training
Teaches new employees about the importance of diversity in the workforce and how to communicate with employees who are different from them.

Divine Command
Basing your ethics and choices of behavior on God's commandments.

Divine Right of Kings
Belief that kings and queens derive their right to rule from the will of God.

Division of Labor
The assignment of different tasks to different people or groups.

Divisional Organizational Structure
An organizational structure that organizes such divisions as product type, customer type, or geographic region.

Dog
In business, a dog is a business unit whose product has little or no potential for growth, and your firm maintains a low percentage of the market.

Drucker, Peter
Drucker (1909–2005) wrote the famous textbook, *The Practice of Management* (1954), used by many business colleges for decades, thereby influencing management thought for thousands of future managers. He especially emphasizes the importance of customer satisfaction.

Dumping
Exporting products at a price below cost to establish a market in another country. Dumping is considered illegal in many countries.

Earnings per Share (EPS)
Net income divided by shares outstanding.

Effectiveness Communication Problem
A problem regarding how well your message results in the desired behavior.

Emotional Intelligence
The ability to sense, understand, and effectively apply the power and acumen of emotions as a source of human energy, information, and influence. Composed of personal competence and social competence.

Emotion-Focused Behavior
An inappropriate way of dealing with job loss or disappointments, where the focus is largely on damaging emotional reactions such as excessive drinking, abusing drugs, or other escape mechanisms.

Employ-at-Will Laws
Laws enacted in some states that declare employees can be terminated without cause. However, federal laws regarding discrimination still apply.

Enron
In 2000, the seventh largest corporation in the United States with "reported" earnings of $101 billion and 21,000 employees. Enron was bankrupt by the end of 2001.

Entrepreneur
A person who pursues lucrative new business opportunities.

Entrepreneurial Venture
A new business having rapid growth and high profitability as its primary objective.

Equal Employment Opportunities Commission (EEOC)
Federal government agency with the responsibility to enforce the Equal Pay Act and other similar laws.

Equal Pay Act of 1963
Makes it illegal to pay women less than men for the same job.

Equity Theory
People expect that their rewards for their input and abilities will be equal to the rewards of others with similar input and abilities.

Ethical Boundary
Limiting your behavior to what is ethical, as opposed to doing anything as long as there is no law specifically prohibiting it.

Ethical Leader
Someone who is ethical, teaches followers what is right and wrong in a setting, and rewards ethical behavior and punishes unethical action.

Ethics
A category of wisdom focused on the study of what a society considers right or wrong.

Ethics of Conscience
An approach to ethical decision making that takes into consideration the rights of others as human beings.

Ethics of Duty
Leaders are to make choices in light of their duty to protect and benefit others.

Ethics of Justice
An approach to ethical decision making based upon the concept of fairness, the facts, and equal treatment for all.

Ethics of Respect
An avenue to ethical decision making that acknowledges that all human beings, regardless of their station in life, deserve respect, as we respect ourselves.

Ethics of Virtue
An approach to ethical decision making based on what a good person would do.

Ethnocentric
People who are convinced their native culture is superior to all others.

European Union (EU)
An economic and political union of over two dozen European nations with the goal of preventing future wars among European nations.

Expectancy
The employee's perception of the likelihood that their efforts will result in their goal attainment.

Expectancy Theory
Focuses on the expectations of employees.

Exporting
Selling goods made in the home country in another country.

External Locus of Control
A belief that things external to the individual such as chance, fate, God, or other outside forces determine life's events.

External Recruitment
Seeking to fill a position from outside the organization to infuse it with "new blood."

Extrinsic Rewards
Rewards given by someone else such as a raise or a promotion.

Family and Medical Leave Act of 1993
Allows workers to take up to 12 weeks of unpaid leave to care for a newborn or newly adopted child and certain other family medical emergencies.

Fiedler, Fred
Professor and author of *A Theory of Leadership*, describing the Contingency Theory of Leadership.

Fixed Costs
Costs that remain the same, regardless of how many units are produced this month.

Foreign Corrupt Practices Act of 1977
Makes it illegal for any U.S. citizen anywhere in the world to bribe a foreign official.

Forming
Deciding who is on the team.

Franchise
One company makes a legal agreement with another organization to make and sell the first organization's product or service exactly as the first company demands.

Functional Organizational Structure
An organizational structure arranged around the basic business functions such as manufacturing, marketing, finance, information technology, and human resources.

General Agreement on Tariffs and Trade (GATT)
A multilateral agreement signed by nearly 150 countries following World War II, aimed at reducing disputes that start as business disagreement, but could lead to armed conflicts between nations.

Gilbreth, Lillian
Work by Lillian Gilbreth (1876–1972) extended the scientific method advocated earlier by Frederick W. Taylor. She became famous for raising 12 children while continuing her engineering work, which resulted in a 1950 movie entitled *Cheaper by the Dozen.*

Glass Ceiling
Metaphor for an invisible barrier that makes it difficult for women and minorities to rise above a certain level in many organizations.

Global Business
A business that views the whole world as one market and itself as a global citizen.

Global New Venture
A company that starts out as a global company.

Globalization
A common business strategy that focuses on growth through overseas expansion. Avon is a good example.

Goal-Setting Theory
People have conscious goals that energize them and direct their behavior toward a particular end.

Great Man Theory of Leadership
The theory that leaders are born leaders or sent by God to lead.

Greenleaf, Robert K.
Former AT&T executive and college lecturer who authored the book, *Servant Leadership*; founder of the Servant Leadership movement.

Gross Margin
(Revenue – cost of goods sold)/revenue is the formula for the gross margin, sometimes just called margin.

Hawthorne Effect
A concept stemming from Elton Mayo's experiments at the Hawthorne Electric Company, showing worker productivity went up when management showed more interest in the workers and their working conditions.

Hostile Environment
A workplace where an employee is made to feel threatened or is offended.

House, Robert
Professor, author, and advocate of the Path-Goal Theory of Leadership.

Human Relations Approach to Management
A concept advocated by Mary Parker Follett (1868–1933), stressing the importance of management working with workers in a cooperative mode, rather than ruling over them in a command mode.

Human Resource Management (HRM)
Function within large organizations responsible for planning workforce needs, recruiting, hiring, training, performance assessment, fair compensation, benefits, and when absolutely necessary, firing properly.

Income Statement
Report that measures a company's revenues and expenses over a specific accounting period such as a quarter (three months) or a year.

Informal Organizational Structure
The everyday unwritten relationships among the employees working together within the organization.

Information Source
In the Shannon & Weaver Communication Model, what produces the message.

Inspire
To breathe life into.

Instrumentality
The perceived likelihood that performance will be followed by a particular outcome.

Integration
Putting the differentiated units together so that work is coordinated into an overall product.

Internal Locus of Control
A belief that the individual is in charge of the things that occur in life, or at least one's reaction to them.

Internal Recruitment
Promoting from within the organization.

International Business
A business that is primarily located in its home country such as the United States, but has branch offices, and perhaps factories, in several overseas locations.

International Monetary Fund (IMF)
An organization of 188 nations working to foster global monetary cooperation and stabilization around the world.

Intrepreneur
A person who works to create new business ventures while working inside an existing large company.

Intrinsic Rewards
Rewards derived from the satisfaction of performing the job well.

Job Analysis
A detailed examination of each position within the organization, resulting in a job description and a list of job specifications for each position.

Job Description
Listing of the specific tasks and responsibilities the organization expects the employee in each position to perform.

Job Enlargement
Giving employees extra tasks to do to relieve boredom and encourage employee growth and opportunities for advancement.

Job Enrichment
Changing a job to make it more challenging and therefore more rewarding, satisfying, and motivating.

Job Rotation
Allowing employees to move through a series of jobs so they do not get bored and so they are qualified for more than one job.

Job Specification
What education, skills, talents, etc., the organization needs to look for in applicants for each position.

Job Training
Training to help new employees do their jobs correctly.

Joint Venture
Two or more companies sign a legal agreement to form a third company to work together to make and sell a product or products.

Kohlberg's Levels of Moral Reasoning

A classification of levels of moral reasoning defined by Lawrence Kohlberg (1927–1987), beginning with obedience to avoid punishment, through fitting into the norms of society, and ending with the voluntary following of principles.

Lay, Ken

Former CEO of Enron, who died of an apparent heart attack before going to prison for fraud.

Leader-Member Exchange Theory of Leadership

Leaders lead by drawing key followers into their inner circle.

Leader-Member Relations

In Fiedler's Contingency Theory of Leadership, the degree of confidence, trust, and respect employees have in their leader.

Leadership

The art and science of ethically and effectively guiding others toward a positive goal.

Leadership Trait Theory

The theory that potential leaders can be identified early by certain traits.

Lean Manufacturing

Focus on manufacturing that eliminates waste by making labor-related activities more efficient, repeatable, and impactful.

Least Preferred Coworker

In Fiedler's Contingency Theory of Leadership, an indirect way of determining whether a leader is people oriented by asking him or her to describe the employee they would least prefer to work with.

License

One company signs a legal agreement with another country to manufacture and sell the first company's product, with the first company getting a small fee or royalty per item sold.

Life Cycle of Power

The natural progression of power from its birth or beginning through growth, maturation, and eventually decline and the death or end of a leader's power.

Lilly Ledbetter Act of 2009
Amends Title VII of the Civil Rights Act of 1964 to say that the 180-day limit to file an equal-pay lawsuit resets with each new discriminatory paycheck.

Line
Position where the manager has the direct responsibility for a principal activity of the firm.

Long-Term Focus
Looking far beyond the quarterly (every three months) effects when making decisions.

Low-Cost Provider
A common business strategy focused on reducing costs so the price charged to customers will be lower than competitors' prices. Walmart is an example.

Macro Environment
The factors in the economy, government, and general business climate that could greatly affect the organization's competitive status.

Madoff, Bernie
Financier who swindled his clients out of $65 billion.

Management by Objectives (MBO)
An employee performance appraisal method based upon discussions between the manager and the employee and agreed-upon objectives the employee should achieve.

Market Control
Control based on pricing mechanism; if something gets too costly, then the market will show purchases that the same product or service is available elsewhere at a lower cost.

Maslow's Hierarchy of Needs Theory
Lower-level needs such as the need for food and water must first be satisfied before higher-level needs such as esteem and self-actualization become motivators.

Master Budget
Budget of budgets, where all the other budgets are combined.

Matrix Organizational Structure
A structure that is a combination of functional and divisional, where some employees report to two managers, a functional manager, plus a divisional or project manager.

Mechanistic Organizational Structure
An organizational structure that is rigid and inflexible.

Micro Environment
Major factors within the organization's industry that could greatly affect its competitive status.

Monolithic Organization
An organization that employs few, if any, women, minorities, or other groups that differ from the majority, and thus has a highly homogeneous employee population.

Morality
The performance of good ethics.

Multicultural Organization
A group that highly values cultural diversity and actively seeks to utilize and encourage diversity.

National Labor Relations Act of 1935
Law that makes it illegal to prevent workers from having a union if they vote to have one. Also called the **Wagner Act**.

Need for Achievement, Affiliation, and Power
People have varying levels of need for achievement (advancing in your career), affiliation (having strong friendships), and power (influence).

Network Organizational Structure
A collection of organizations that work together to produce a good or service; it looks more like a web than a pyramid.

Noise
In the Shannon & Weaver Communication Model, any interference resulting in the signal being received incorrectly.

Norm
An agreed-upon behavior within a group.

Norming
Agreeing on shared team goals and processes.

North American Free Trade Agreement (NAFTA)
An agreement between the United States, Canada, and Mexico aimed at eliminating all trade barriers.

Ohio State Leadership Studies
Research conducted over 50 years ago at Ohio State University with mixed results regarding whether concern for people was better than concern for the task.

Operating Budget
The budget that lists the revenues and expenses related to the regular and ongoing operations of the organization.

Opportunity
Something the organization could build or buy that would give it a future competitive advantage.

Organic Organizational Structure
A flexible structure that uses teamwork and believes that managers are more like coaches than bosses.

Orientation Session
Training new employees regarding the history of the organization, plus an overview of the current aspects of the company.

Path-Goal Theory of Leadership
Leaders lead best by helping their followers align their personal goals with the goals of the organization.

Performing
Getting the job done as a team.

Personal Competence
In emotional intelligence, personal competence is defined as composing of self-awareness and self-control.

Philosophy
The love of wisdom. Beliefs and concepts of a group or individual.

Planning
Determining where an organization is now, where it could be within a few years, and what it would take to get there.

Pluralistic Organization
An organization that has a relatively diverse employee population as the result of a proactive effort to involve employees from different gender, racial, and cultural backgrounds.

Position Power
In Fiedler's Contingency Theory of Leadership, the amount of power the leader has over variables such as hiring, firing, discipline, promotions, and salary increases.

Positive Psychology
The study of what makes for a healthy psychological approach to life.

Power
The ability to implement change despite resistance.

Prejudice
Judging someone in advance, before an objective, fact-based review.

Price-Earnings Ratio (P/E Ratio)
Price per share divided by earnings per share.

Prince, The
Book written by Niccolo Machiavelli 500 years ago describing the leader's responsibility to defend his followers.

Problem-Focused Behavior
An appropriate way of dealing with job loss focusing on defining the problem, generating alternative solutions, and acting to solve the problem in a nonemotional manner.

Production Budget
Forecasts units to be produced each month per product.

Profit-and-Loss Statement
Another name for the income statement that lists the revenues and expenses for a specific time period; also called P&L statement.

Psychological Contract
The basis for an understanding between workers and management.

Quantitative Management
Concept advocated by Ford W. Harris and others suggesting how mathematics can improve business decision making.

Question Mark
In business, a question mark is a unit where your company has a low percentage of the market, but the potential for growth is high.

Quick Ratio
(Current assets – inventory) divided by current liabilities.

Quid pro Quo
A situation where one person, typically a manager, offers something to another, typically an employee, in exchange for a sexual favor.

Receiver
In the Shannon & Weaver Communication Model, what decodes the message from the channel.

Relationship Management
Combination of inspiration, influence, developing others, change catalyst, conflict management, teamwork, and collaboration.

Responsibility
A person assigned a task is supposed to carry it out.

Results Appraisals
Job performance appraisal based upon actual results such as number of closed sales deals, number of finished goods completed, etc.

Return on Equity (ROE)
(Net income – preferred dividends) divided by common shareholders' equity.

Right-to-Work Laws
Laws enacted in some states saying it is illegal to force workers to join a union or to pay union dues.

Sales Budget
Contains forecasts of sales by month, sales area, and product.

Scientific Management
Concept advocated by Frederick W. Taylor (1856–1915), involving breaking complex tasks down into a series of small movements and then analyzing each movement for efficiency and speed to save time and money.

Self-Efficacy
Belief that you are in control of your life and that your decisions and actions shape that life.

Self-Management
Combination of self-control, transparency, adaptability, achievement, initiative, and optimism.

Semantic Communication Problem
A problem regarding how accurately the meaning of your message was conveyed.

Separation of Labor
Each worker in a factory stays at his or her work station doing a specialized task while the product being made moves along a belt.

Servant Leadership Theory
The leader considers him- or herself to be a servant to all and leads out of a desire to serve, rather than out of a need for money, power, and prestige.

Service Corps of Retired Executives (SCORE)
An organization of retired executives who volunteer to help others start or grow their small businesses.

Sexual Harassment
Any unwanted and offensive action of a sexual nature.

Sexual Harassment Training
Training designed to prevent sexual harassment in the workplace.

Shannon, Claude, and Weaver, Warren
Authors of a famous model of communication.

Short, Fat Organizational Chart
Few layers of managers between the workers and the CEO, so each manager has a broader span of control with more workers reporting to him or her.

Silo
In management, a silo is when workers in one department work in isolation on their part of the project; contrast with teamwork.

Six Sigma
A concept borrowed from statistics referring to a control standard of less than 3.4 defective parts per million.

Skilling, Jeff
Former CEO of Enron; currently serving a prison term for fraud.

Slippery Slope
Making small infractions to ethics that gradually lead to making larger ones.

Small Business
One with less than 100 employees and independently owned and operated.

Small Business Administration (SBA)
Division of the U.S. government, dedicated to helping anyone start or grow a small business.

SMART Goals
Goals or targets that are **s**pecific, **m**easurable, **a**ttainable, **r**elevant, and **t**imely.

Social Competence
In emotional intelligence, social competence is defined as social awareness and relationship management.

Social Loafer
Team member who fails to do his or her fair share of the work, but expects to reap the team's reward.

Socrates
Greek philosopher who lived around 470 B.C. and defined ethics as how we ought to live.

Span of Control
The number of subordinates who report directly to a manager or supervisor.

Specialization
The process in which different individuals and units perform different tasks and develop high skills.

Staff
Position where the person provides specialized or professional skill and advice in support of the line departments.

Stages in Team Building
Forming, storming, norming, performing, and adjourning.

Standard
An expected performance level.

Star
In business, a star is a business unit whose product has a high potential for market growth, and your company maintains a large share of the market.

State of Flow
A frame of mind where the person is concentrating so completely on what they are doing that other thoughts are temporarily set aside.

Storming
Ironing out differences about team goals and individual roles.

Strategic Alliance
Two companies sign a legal agreement to work together, often in a joint venture, to make and sell a product or products.

Strength
Something the organization does exceptionally well.

Sunk Cost
Money a business has already spent and can't get back.

SWOT
A tool of analysis where the organization's **s**trengths, **w**eaknesses, **o**pportunities, and **t**hreats are identified.

Taft-Hartley Act of 1947
An attempt to decrease the power of unions by outlawing the closed shop, where only members of a union could be hired.

Tall Organizational Chart
Many layers of managers between the workers and the chief executive officer.

Tariff
A tax or fees a country charges to a business importing products into that country.

Task Structure
In Fiedler's Contingency Theory of Leadership, the degree to which the job assignments of workers are structured (well defined) or unstructured.

Team
A collection of people carefully chosen for their complementary skills who trust one another and are committed to a common goal, a common approach, and have agreed to hold each other mutually accountable.

Teamwork
A process of cooperative work that most organizations use to increase productivity, reduce costs, improve quality, enhance speed, and capture the creativity and innovation of their employees.

Technical Communication Problem
A problem regarding how accurately your message was conveyed.

Theory of Moral Sentiments, The
Book written by Adam Smith in 1759 admonishing business leaders to operate with high morals and not greed.

Theory X
Managers perceive employees as lazy and unmotivated to do good work.

Theory Y
Managers see employees as naturally motivated to do a good job.

Theory Z

Concept advocated by William Ouchi, suggesting American business leaders should learn from the success of Japanese businesses and build long-lasting relationships with their workers.

Thorndike's Law of Effect

A behavior that is followed by positive consequences (a reward) will likely be repeated.

Threat

Something that could substantially reduce the organization's revenues or increase its expenses.

Three Planning Scenarios

"Optimistic," "pessimistic," and "most likely" are the three planning scenarios most successful planners consider.

Title VII of the Civil Rights Act of 1964

Makes it illegal to discriminate in hiring on the basis of race, color, religion, gender, or national origin.

Training in Management and Leadership

Training to develop the organization's next generation of managers and leaders.

Trait Appraisal

Job performance appraisal based upon traits such as "hard worker," "reliable," and "dependable." Not recommended because it lacks objectivity.

Transactional Theory of Leadership

Leaders use pay and other rewards to trade off with followers to get them to do what the leader wants done.

Transference

A psychological tendency to transfer our feelings for one person onto another.

Transformational Theory of Leadership

Leaders inspire their followers to implement major organization shifts or sea changes.

Transmitter

In the Shannon & Weaver Communication Model, what encodes the message into signals.

Two-Factor Theory
Some factors such as company policies, working conditions, pay, etc., are likely to cause employee dissatisfaction, while other factors such as the nature of the work itself and feelings of achievement are likely to cause satisfaction on the job.

Union Shop
A place of business where the employees are unionized; all employees must pay their fair share of union dues whether or not they are members of that union.

Utilitarianism
A concept of ethics based primarily upon the notion that choices should be made that result in the greatest good for the greatest number of people.

Valence
The value or importance a particular outcome holds for an employee.

Value
Any action or process for which a customer would be willing to pay.

Variable Costs
Costs such as raw materials used, which go up as the level of production goes up.

Venture Capital
Money provided by a group of wealthy investors, investment banks, or other financial institutions representing groups of individual investors, who pool their funds and seek to invest those funds into small businesses with perceived long-term growth potential.

Venture Capitalist
Person or group that invests money in start-up companies in return for a share of the ownership and high returns.

Weakness
Something the organization lacks or does poorly.

Wealth of Nations, The
Book written by Adam Smith in 1776 describing how supply and demand work to establish a fair price.

Wholly Owned Affiliate
A contractual agreement between two companies, where one company, called the parent, wholly owns the other company; for example, Honda Motors of America is owned by Honda Motors of Japan.

Working Capital Ratio
Another name for the current ratio.

World Bank
An organization first formed near the end of World War II to rebuild France and other nations devastated by the war, but more recently to provide loans to poor and developing nations.

World Trade Organization (WTO)
A global international organization formed in 1995 involving over 150 nations to administer trade agreements.